Rethinking the Russian Revolution as Historical Divide

The Russian Revolution of 1917 has often been presented as a complete break with the past, with everything which had gone before swept away, and all aspects of politics, economy, and society reformed and made new. Recently, however, historians have increasingly come to question this view, discovering that Tsarist Russia was much more entangled in the processes of modernisation, and that the new regime contained much more continuity than has previously been acknowledged. This book presents new research findings on a range of different aspects of Russian society, both showing how there was much change before 1917, and much continuity afterwards; and also going beyond this to show that the new Soviet regime established in the 1920s, with its vision of the New Soviet Person, was in fact based on a complicated mixture of new Soviet thinking and ideas developed before 1917 by a variety of non-Bolshevik movements.

Matthias Neumann is a senior lecturer in History at the University of East Anglia, UK.

Andy Willimott is a lecturer in History at the University of Reading, UK.

BASEES/Routledge Series on Russian and East European Studies

This series is published on behalf of BASEES (the British Association for Slavonic and East European Studies). The series comprises original, high-quality, research-level work by both new and established scholars on all aspects of Russian, Soviet, post-Soviet and East European Studies in humanities and social science subjects.

For a full list of available titles please visit: www.routledge.com/BASEES-Routledge-Series-on-Russian-and-East-European-Studies/book-series/BASEES

119. Oil and the Economy of Russia
From the Late-Tsarist to the Post-Soviet Period
Nat Moser

120. The South Caucasus – Security, Energy and Europeanization
Edited by Meliha B. Altunisik and Oktay F. Tanrisever

Rethinking the Russian Revolution as Historical Divide

Edited by
Matthias Neumann and Andy Willimott

Routledge
Taylor & Francis Group
LONDON AND NEW YORK

First published 2018
by Routledge
2 Park Square, Milton Park, Abingdon, Oxon OX14 4RN

and by Routledge
711 Third Avenue, New York, NY 10017

Routledge is an imprint of the Taylor & Francis Group, an informa business

British Library Cataloguing in Publication Data
A catalogue record for this book is available from the British Library

Library of Congress Cataloging in Publication Data
A catalog record for this book has been requested

ISBN: 978-1-138-94562-3 (hbk)
ISBN: 978-1-315-66785-0 (ebk)

Typeset in Times New Roman
by Taylor & Francis Books

MIX
Paper from responsible sources
FSC
www.fsc.org
FSC® C013604

Printed and bound by CPI Group (UK) Ltd, Croydon, CR0 4YY

Contents

Contributors

Matthias Neumann is Senior Lecturer in Modern Russian History at the University of East Anglia, UK. He has published widely on the history of childhood and youth in revolutionary Russia. His book *The Communist Youth League and the Transformation of the Soviet Union, 1917–1932* was published by Routledge in 2011. His new research project examines cultural exchange programmes which enabled American children to visit the Soviet Union during the Cold War.

Andy Willimott is Lecturer in Modern Russian/Soviet History at the University of Reading, UK. He has published on the social and cultural history of revolutionary Russia and the early Soviet state, shedding light on the formation and experience of radical ideology. He is author of *Living the Revolution: Urban Communes & Soviet Socialism, 1917–1932* (2017). His research has been funded by the UK Arts & Humanities Research Council, the Leverhulme Trust, and the British Academy.

J. Arch Getty is Distinguished Research Professor of History at UCLA, USA. He specializes in the Stalin period and the history of the Soviet Communist Party. His seven books and over 50 articles have been published in the US, England, France, Germany, Spain, Hungary, Japan, Turkey, and Russia. Getty was a John Simon Guggenheim Fellow, and has been a Senior Research Fellow at Columbia, Harvard, and the Russian Academy of Sciences in Moscow. He was a Visiting Scholar at the Sorbonne and the École des Hautes Études in Paris, and Visiting Professor at Utrecht University in the Netherlands. His latest book, *Practicing Stalinism: Boyars, Bolsheviks, and the Persistence of Tradition* (2013), investigates the proposition that the Soviet state was a façade hiding a complex of ancient political practices and personalized politics. A Russian translation was published this year in Moscow.

Yulia Gradskova is Associate Professor in History, the Institute of Contemporary History, Södertörn University, Sweden. She has PhD in History (Stockholm University, 2007). Together to Sara Sanders she recently edited a volume *Institutionalizing Gender Equality. Historical and Global*

Perspective (2015). Topics of her research interests include Soviet politics of women's emancipation in the imperial/colonial context and global politics of solidarity, gender equality, and anti-racism.

Susan Grant is Senior Lecturer in Modern European History at Liverpool John Moores University, UK. Her first monograph *Sport and Physical Culture in Soviet Society: Propaganda, Acculturation, and Transformation in the 1920s and 1930s* was published with Routledge in 2012. She is the author of the edited volume, *Russian and Soviet Health Care from an International Perspective: Comparing Professions, Practice and Gender, 1880–1960* (2017) and is preparing a monograph on the history of Soviet nursing. Her latest project is on Soviet gerontology and the history of aging under socialism.

Vera Kaplan is a Senior Lecturer in the Department of History and Director of the Cummings Center for Russian and East European Studies, Tel Aviv University, Israel. Her research interests lie in the areas of cultural and social history and the history of education in Russia, focusing especially on the voluntary associations and history as a profession. Her book *Historians and Historical Societies in the Public Life of Imperial Russia* was published by Indiana University Press in 2017. Her current research project, entitled 'Weathering the Revolution', explores how historians responded to and lived through the great event of their time.

Miriam Neirick is Associate Professor of History at California State University Northridge, USA, where she teaches courses on the history of Russia and women, historical methods and college writing. She is the author of *When Pigs Could Fly and Bears Could Dance: A History of the Soviet Circus* (2012).

Matthew D. Pauly is an Associate Professor of History at Michigan State University, USA. He has received numerous external fellowships and grants, including a 2016–17 US Scholar Fulbright grant for research on a book project entitled, 'City of Children: Juvenile Poverty, Crime, and Salvation in Odessa'. He is the author of *Breaking the Tongue: Language, Education, and Power in Soviet Ukraine, 1923–34* (2014) as well as articles and essays on early Soviet nationalities policy and the intersection between national identity, education, and childhood in late imperial Russia and the Soviet Union.

Matthew Rendle is Senior Lecturer in History at the University of Exeter, UK. He has published articles on landowners, nobles, officers, localities, revolutionary tribunals, and law and justice during the revolutionary period in Russian history. He is the author of *Defenders of the Motherland: The Tsarist Elite in Revolutionary Russia* (2010) and is currently working on a project tentatively entitled 'The State versus the People: Revolutionary Justice in Russia's Civil War'.

Peter Waldron is Professor of Modern History at the University of East Anglia, UK. His books include *Governing Tsarist Russia* (2007) and is co-editor of three volumes on *Russia's Home Front in War and Revolution, 1914–22* (2016 and 2017). His current work deals with Russian politics during the First World War and the 1917 revolutions.

Jonathan Waterlow is the Co-Founder of *Voices in the Dark*, a podcast dedicated to 'Learning How to Human', exploring psychology, philosophy, social dynamics, mental health, psychedelics, and more (www.voicesinthedark.world). He is currently a Research Associate at the University of Bristol, UK, and was previously a British Academy Postdoctoral Fellow at St Antony's College, Oxford. He has worked on political humour and everyday life under Stalin in the 1930s; war crimes trials and investigations from multiple disciplinary perspectives; and most recently on drugs and subcultures in the late Soviet period.

Crossing the divide

Tradition, rupture, and modernity in revolutionary Russia

Andy Willimott and Matthias Neumann

'Revolution' – it has been all but forgotten – was originally an astronomical term, denoting the revolving motion of the planets. This was a process with no beginning and no end, distinctly characterized by the absence of a telos. The word was not understood in the modern sense, as a sudden or fundamental turnover in the politics of state or the overthrow of an established government and social order. Indeed, when the term was first introduced to the sphere of politics in the seventeenth century, it could still have a very opposite meaning to the one it has today. The 'Glorious Revolution of 1688–89' – the usurping of a Catholic monarch and the return of a Protestant to the English throne – was so called because it marked an attempt to return to an old system, a cyclical journey back to a preordained order. It was essentially restoration. In turn, it has been explained, what some have labelled the English Revolution – the overthrow of monarchy in 1640s – was, at the time, actually referred to as 'the Great Rebellion'.[1] But, as historians of this period have recently shown, the definition of 'revolution' was not fixed. In truth, the word 'revolution' was already developing multiple and conflicting meanings from the sixteenth century onward, making room for new interpretations and sowing the seeds for our current understanding of the word.[2]

The fundamental semantic shift between pre-modern and modern conceptions of 'revolution' was very much linked to the experience of the French and American Revolution. During these two monumental events, the revolutionary actors of the time initially sought to 'restore the old order of things that had been disturbed and violated by the despotism of absolute monarchy

1 Tim Harris, 'Did the English Have a Script for Revolution in the Seventeenth Century?', in *Scripting Revolution: A Historical Approach to the Comparative Study of Revolutions,* edited by Keith Michael Baker and Dan Edelstein (Stanford, CA: Stanford University Press, 2015), 25–40.

2 See Baker and Edelstein (eds), *Scripting Revolution*, Chs 1–3. NB. This volume also contains a chapter by Ian D. Thatcher, 'Scripting the Russian Revolution' (213–227), highlighting the range of 'scripts' from which 1917 was born. This can be seen to extend on some of the same intellectual concerns discussed in the present book, as it assesses 1917 as far more than the actions of a revolutionary leadership bound by the ideas of Marx.

or the abuses of colonial power'.[3] However, soon they had to realise that restoration was impossible and began to advocate completely new ideas and programmes. Our modern concept of revolution was born in this way and, as Hannah Arendt remarked, was 'inextricably bound up with the notion that the course of history suddenly begins anew, that an entirely new story, a story never known or told before, is about to unfold (...).'[4] This notion remains essential to the popular understanding of revolution and it is at the very heart of modern revolutionary discourse. However, the actuality of revolutionary upheavals in modern times tells us a very different story. Time and again, successful revolutionaries found themselves unable to totally destroy and overcome the cultural conceptions, traditions, and customs that underpinned the previous regime. In a metaphorical sense conceivably suited to sixteenth-century sensibilities, 'Revolution' might thus be better understood as the upturning of the soil during ploughing – a world being turned upside-down, with the 'new' establishing its roots in the decomposing, but still fertilising, 'old'.

This presents us with an apt image when considering developments in the study of the Russian Revolution. Recent studies have encouraged us to view 1917, and the Soviet republic that emerged out of this episode, as germinations from Russia's broader experience of modernity. Scholars of modern Russian and Soviet history do not deny that the events of 1917 conform to our present understanding of a modern revolution. This was, after all, a year that saw the overthrow of monarchy, the implementation of a new type of government, the rejection of an old social order, and, ultimately, the dawning of a socialist republic. What is more, those driving forth change in Russia at this time consciously associated their actions with a modern revolutionary script that had emerged out of the French Revolution in 1789. But, all the same, scholars have increasingly come to question whether we were too quick to swallow the rhetoric of the Bolsheviks, who, upon seizing power, were inclined to view their actions as part of an entirely new epoch – the turning of a new leaf in human history. The suggestion now is that our focus on 1917 as a caesura has served to blind us to the full array of factors that helped make the world's first avowedly socialist state. Put simply, it has been suggested that 1917 is the wrong departure point for a full analysis of the social, cultural, political, and economic development of the Bolshevik project and Soviet socialism.

Leading the charge for something more akin to a *longue durée* approach to the study of the Russian Revolution from the early 2000s was a group of scholars who soon became known collectively as the modernity school. In a series of essays brought together by Yanni Kotsonis and David Hoffmann around this time, *Russian Modernity*, contributors stressed that late Imperial and Soviet Russia were often subject to the same pan-European developments in modern statecraft. Noting that the 'history of modern Russia has been

3 Hannah Arendt, *On Revolution* (London: Penguin Books, 1990), 44.
4 Ibid., 28.

written as a history distinct from that of "the West"', the editors of this volume rejected what they saw as the tendency to treat Russia as an 'other', or, more specifically, the tendency to cast her outside the framework of modern European development.[5] Hoffman, in particular, was keen to place Russia inside an Enlightenment trajectory understood to foster an 'ethos of progressive social intervention and the rise of mass politics'.[6] Others pointed to universal modern developments taking root in Russia, such as the rise of mass politics, public and political movements, expanding scientific discourses, and growing state intervention. These and other features of modernity – including industrialization, literacy campaigns, urbanization, and secularization – were traced across 1917 as a means of presenting late Imperial Russia and the Soviet Union as practising modern entities.

Inspired by Stephen Kotkin's work on Stalinism and popular engagements with a state-idealized national identity, some contributors also sought to show how 'the internalization of authority' – be it late Imperial autocracy or one-party dictatorship – was a further 'hallmark' of the modern experience.[7] Attempts by ordinary individuals to situate themselves within modern political and ideological developments were cited as a 'mode of thinking' that had roots in the Enlightenment, and certainly became more pronounced under the teleological pronouncements of Marxism.[8] Implicit within this pan-European approach was the belief that past interpretations of the Russian Revolution were reductionist and, in some cases, prone to encouraging the fetishization of Russian 'otherness'. The modernity school was challenging historians to broaden their contextual, geographical, and chronological scope when it came to studying the Russian Revolution and the Bolshevik project in general.

In his book, *Making War, Forging Revolution*, Peter Holquist went on to write about the period 1914–1921 as a 'continuum of crisis' in which the mechanisms of a modern state – mass mobilization, state intervention, attempts at social and political engineering, and population surveillance – all came to the fore in Russia. Bolshevik statecraft was thus shown to fit into a pan-European narrative that extended across and evolved through 1917.[9] Likewise, in *Drafting the Russian Nation*, Joshua Sanborn wrote about the modern methods of conscription, mobilization, and mass politics exhibited by both the Russian Imperial and Soviet armies between 1905 and 1925. He

5 Yanni Kotsonis and David L. Hoffmann (eds), *Russian Modernity: Politics, Knowledge, Practices* (New York: Macmillan Press, 1999).
6 Hoffmann, 'European Modernity and Soviet Socialism' in *Russian Modernity*, especially 246–247.
7 See Stephen Kotkin, *Magnetic Mountain: Stalinism as a Civilization* (Berkeley, CA: University of California Press, 1997), especially Ch. 5. NB. Kotsonis refers to such developments as the 'hallmark of modernity' in his introduction to *Russian Modernity* (1–16).
8 See Hoffmann, in *Russian Modernity*, especially 246–250.
9 Peter Holquist, *Making War, Forging Revolution: Russia's Continuum of Crisis, 1914–1921* (Cambridge, MA: Harvard University Press, 2002), 1–6.

showed how each army functioned as agents of social transformation, even if their ideologies spoke to different end goals.[10] Daniel Beer subsequently traced 'the genesis of the Bolshevik understanding of their inheritance' through a study of the human sciences in Russia between 1880 and 1930. In his book, *Renovating Russia*, Beer highlighted the various intellectual discourses and modern principles that were, in one way or another, appropriated or absorbed by the Bolshevik leadership, helping to set the cognitive parameters of the Russian Revolution. He showed that a programme of social engineering first espoused by Russian liberals came to inform the radical agenda of the Bolshevik regime. In particular, Beer argued, the developing disciplines of psychiatry, psychology, criminology, anthropology, jurisprudence, and sociology can be seen to advance the idea that it was possible to rationalize society through the power of science and reason.[11] In this sense, what separated the scientism and progressivism of a liberal regime from that of a totalitarian regime was 'the factor of extent' – the extremes to which one set of leaders were willing to go when employing the logic of modern progression.[12]

This is modernity as a fundamental belief in the perfectibility of humanity and the tools of human management. It is an approach to the study of modern Russian and Soviet history that came of age under the growing intellectual influence of social theorists such as Zygmunt Bauman, who, across the late 1980s and 1990s, had argued that while modern civilization did not make the Holocaust inevitable, it did make the Holocaust possible, with its managerial procedures and perverse eugenic programme.[13] This thinking was buttressed in the late 1990s by works such as Mark Mazower's *Dark Continent*, which showed the underbelly of modernity in Europe, popularizing a vision of European history that refused to portray progressivism or progressive politics in a wholly positive light.[14] This was a time when accepted political and ideological boundaries were challenged in the search for those deeper, more elemental connections affecting the sweep of history. It was a time when scholars focused on the tone of twentieth-century history, not just its policies. And such thinking continues to resonate, with Sanborn calling on historians to view the period of 1914–1922 not as a break with the tsarist past, but as 'the zenith of Russian progressivism' – the moment that bequeathed to the early Soviet regime 'centralized welfare, institutionalized

10 Joshua A. Sanborn, *Drafting the Russian Nation: Military Conscription, Total War, and Mass Politics, 1905–1925* (DeKalb, IL: Northern Illinois University Press, 2003).

11 Daniel Beer, *Renovating Russia: The Human Sciences and the Fate of Liberal Modernity, 1880–1930* (Ithaca, NY: Cornell University Press, 2008), on influencing the Bolsheviks and the Bolshevik programme, see especially Ch. 5.

12 Beer, *Renovating Russia*, 3–4.

13 Zygmunt Bauman, *Modernity and the Holocaust* (Ithaca, NY: Cornell University Press, 1989), 92.

14 Mark Mazower, *Dark Continent: Europe's Twentieth Century* (London: Penguin Books, 1998).

science, and the general belief that scientific attempts to solve social problems were both appropriate and necessary'.[15] In this case, revolutions are also understood to be about tone as well as policy.

There can be little doubt that the modernity school has had a profound impact on the study of Russian and Soviet history. But that is not to say that the ideas and work associated with this school have escaped criticism. Indeed, as we will see, the most convincing criticisms have tended to relate to the modernity school's early neglect of variation and indeterminacy when writing the history of Russia's modern experience. As is the case in many other fields of historical enquiry today, where once historians used to write the history of 'Great Men' – the Russian Revolution told as the story of Lenin's genius, for instance – we have perhaps come too close to privileging the history of 'Great Ideas' over all else.[16] In other words, if we focus on the power of ideas and modern frameworks in isolation we are likely to obscure the full picture. Or, put another way, now that our ears are open to the tones of modernity, we must seek to better account for the manner of their entry into the world.

Historiographical divisions: 'modernity' vs. 'neo-traditionalism'

With many early modernity school scholars coming out of Columbia University in the 1990s, overtly crediting the influence Stephen Kotkin as they did so, the emerging fault lines of Soviet historiography in the West took on an institutional dimension. Some of the first criticisms of the modernity paradigm came out of Chicago, where the close-reading, archive-driven approach instilled in Sheila Fitzpatrick's graduate students made many sensitive to the broader arguments and intellectual influences associated with the Columbia cohort at that time.[17] The 'Chicago approach' was itself a methodological preoccupation that emerged out of the historiographical disputes of the 1960s and 1970s, when Fitzpatrick helped to initiate the revisionist school, which rejected a cold war scholarship that spoke of totalitarianism, Soviet totalitarian systems, and totalitarian 'Great Men' without much recourse to documentation. With the Soviet Union often still existing in the public imagination in evil caricature, it is not hard to see why there remained a desire to 'dig

15 Joshua A. Sanborn, 'The Zenith of Russian Progressivism: The Home Front during World War I and the Revolution', in *Russia's Home Front in War and Revolution, 1914–22. Book 2: The Experience of War and Revolution*, edited by Adele Lindenmeyr, Christopher Read, and Peter Waldron (Bloomington, IN: Slavica, 2016), 497–507. Also note David L. Hoffman, *Cultivating the Masses: Modern State Practices and Soviet Socialism, 1914–1939* (Ithaca, NY: Cornell University Press, 2011).

16 Andy Willimott, *Living the Revolution: Urban Communes & Soviet Socialism, 1917–1932* (Oxford: Oxford University Press, 2017) 21.

17 Lewis H. Siegelbaum, 'Whither Soviet History? Some Reflections on Recent Anglophone Historiography', *Region: Regional Studies of Russia, Eastern Europe, and Central Asia* 1(2) (2012), 213–230.

deeper', to look beyond systems of power and continue to extend on a social history that revelled in revealing nuance.

Where revisionists had advocated the virtues of social history, with its focus on class relations and the social environment, the modernity school, buoyed by a new intellectual climate being driven by the likes of Bauman, were inclined to reject all social heuristic categories in favour of complete reconceptualization. What happened next, as Ronald Grigor Suny observed, was that those inclined to nuance and 'attentive to the insights of Max Weber' started to highlight 'neo-traditionalist aspects of the Soviet experience that denied or contradicted the move to a generalized modernity'.[18] The German sociologist Weber had famously argued that traditional cultural influences continued to shape the modern world through religion, habits, and customs; his *The Protestant Ethic and the Spirit of Capitalism* (1905) making a case for the continued impact of religion on workers and the Western capitalist system, for instance. The historians Matthew Lenoe and Terry Martin were among the first to press the case for the continued relevance of such structuralist readings of Soviet history, highlighting the unreformed social practices and systems of favour underlining human behaviour within new Soviet institutions. Lenoe disputed the importance attributed to transformational projects and enlightenment discourses in his book, *Closer to the Masses*, which offered an investigation into Soviet print media. He argued that as the media moved to help mobilize the population for the First Five-Year Plan, the 'mass enlightenment project' gave way to the promotion of hierarchical structures based around cadre-class status.[19] Likewise, within his carefully researched book on nationalism in the Soviet Union, *The Affirmative Action Empire*, Martin defended Nicholas Timasheff's 'Great Retreat' paradigm. This was a thesis, first proclaimed in 1946, that sharply differentiated Stalinism from early Soviet socialism; an assessment that modernity school scholars had labelled as misbegotten.[20]

The neo-traditionalist approach was itself not without problem. First and foremost, the terms 'tradition' and 'neo-traditional' were applied in an ahistorical manner. Taking their cue from Andrew G Walder's *Communist*

18 Ronald Grigor Suny, 'Reading Russia and the Soviet Union in the Twentieth Century: How the "West" Wrote Its History of the USSR', in *Cambridge History of Russia* vol. 3: *The Twentieth Century*, edited by Ronald Grigor Suny (Cambridge: Cambridge University Press, 2006), 5–66, especially 60.

19 Matthew Lenoe, *Closer to the Masses: Stalinist Culture, Social Revolution, and Soviet Newspapers* (Cambridge, MA: Harvard University Press, 2004), especially Ch. 5.

20 Terry Martin, *The Affirmative Action Empire: Nations and Nationalism in the Soviet Union 1923–1939* (Ithaca, NY: Cornell University Press, 2001), especially 26–27. See Nicholas S. Timasheff, *The Great Retreat: The Growth and Decline of Communism in Russia* (New York: E. P. Dutton & Company, 1946). Cf. David L. Hoffmann, *Stalinist Values: The Cultural Norms of Soviet Modernity, 1917–1941* (Ithaca, NY: Cornell University Press, 2003), especially 1–14; and [historiography special] 'Ex Tempore Stalinism and the "Great Retreat"', *Kritika: Explorations in Russian and Eurasian History* 5, 4 (2004), 651–733.

Neo-traditionalism, Ken Jowett's *New World Disorder*, and the social sciences of the 1980s, Lenoe and Martin used these terms to denote 'dependence, deference, and particularism'. The notion of 'charismatic authority', as espoused by Max Weber – the idea that political authority rested on the perceived legitimacy of the leader – seemed to underlie many of the assumptions within these accounts. But this was also 'dependence, deference, and particularism' understood in an apophatic sense. That is, as *not* 'independence, contract, and universalism' – the usual markers of western liberal modernity. The accent seemingly on the retreat from 'full' modernity, defining something by stating that which it is not. In other words, 'modernity' was being used as a normative category. As such, the emergent neo-traditional school did not chart the development of traditional forces in Russia and the Soviet Union so much as it sought to identify political practices common or specific to the Communist regime. In the grand scheme of things, such an approach clearly has its limitations. But it has encouraged us: 1) to take more heed of the unintended consequences and specific application of modern formulas; 2) to question some of the most sweeping assertions made by modernity school scholars; and, when taken in conjunction with other trends in the field, 3) to again consider further comparison with other Communist countries.

And, as is the nature of scholarly debate, these criticisms and objections have driven further study, investigation, and reassessment. The crux of the matter, it was becoming clear to more and more scholars, was the gap between Soviet intentions and implementation. Suny, for instance, suggested that scholars start to view modernity as 'a context'. That is not to say that it predetermined historical action; rather, that it provided 'an environment in which certain ideas, aspirations, and practices are more likely to find support than others'.[21] The British scholar David Priestland, more removed from the institutional dynamic at play within these historiographical developments, went on to both criticize and combine elements of neo-traditional and modernity school thinking in his book, *Stalinism and the Politics of Mobilization*. As he saw it: both approaches 'capture important aspects of Stalinist thinking, and both are valuable in relating Bolshevik ideas to broader discourses and political cultures. Yet neither convincingly accounts for the Terror'.[22] So Priestland set out to delineate an explanation of Stalinism that included both 'eschatological concern with establishing the perfect society' and 'Romantic interest in the role of non-rational forces'.[23] He saw both what he called an Enlightenment-driven 'technicist' and Romantic 'revivalist'

21 Ronald Grigor Suny, 'On Ideology, Subjectivity, and Modernity: Disparate Thoughts about Doing Soviet History', *Russian History/Histoire Russe* 33, 1–4 (2007), 1–9, quotations 9.

22 David Priestland, *Stalinism and the Politics of Mobilization: Ideas, Power, and Terror in Inter-war Russia* (Oxford: Oxford University Press, 2007), 14.

23 Ibid., 15.

strand to Bolshevik thinking.[24] The two together – and only together – could explain the various twists and turns of Stalinism at any given time.

The seeds of such a reassessment, as Michael David-Fox has pointed out, were present, if at times overshadowed, in the work of scholars who might have been more closely associated with one or other of the neo-traditionalist and modernity schools.[25] Responding to the developing debate about the gap between intention and implementation, Lynne Viola, who was sceptical as to whether scientism or the goal of social engineering could explain Soviet history, nonetheless argued that Bolshevik visions of state intervention developed in line with what James Scott called 'high modernism', and that where hyper-planning and unintended, chaotic enactment met was where the characteristics of Soviet state management were formed.[26] In turn, Holquist highlighted that 'there existed not only a gulf between utopian planning and messy realization, but the two were intrinsically related'.[27] As David-Fox explained, this was a dialectic vision of the Soviet encounter with modernity, whereby a 'hatred of backwardness and unbound faith in the power of the state led to inevitable failure of grandiose plans, which was then blamed not on the approach itself but on recalcitrance and backwardness, thus perpetuating the cycle'.[28] Succinctly summarizing this exchange, David-Fox noted that the 'scholar who so brilliantly analysed the gulf between planning and implementation invoked high modernism; the modernist scholar, in response, pointed to persistent Russian factors'.[29] Lest we forget, schools of thought always exist better in abstraction, and they rarely resort to full-blown entrenchment for long.

In his authoritative surveying of the field, David-Fox has also pointed to the fact that one long-term issue in particular has coloured our perception or approach to recent historiographical debates: the issue of particularism vs. universalism. This old chestnut, it seems, has both consciously and unconsciously occupied the minds of Russian/Soviet historians for a many years.[30] At various stages, scholars have been driven to incorporate Russia within or excise her from the 'normative' path, to standardize or exceptionalize her social and political construction. In many ways, this historiographical tendency extended on Russia's own nineteenth-century political debates, which often divided along 'Westernizer' and 'Slavophile' lines. And because one can

24 Ibid., *Stalinism*, 37.

25 Michael David-Fox, *Crossing Borders: Modernity Ideology, and Culture in Russia and the Soviet Union* (Pittsburgh, PA: University of Pittsburgh Press, 2015), 44–45.

26 Lynne Viola, 'The Aesthetic of Stalinist Planning and the World of the Special Villages', *Kritika: Explorations in Russian and Eurasian History* 4(1) (2003), 101–128. See also James Scott, *Seeing Like a State: How Certain Schemes to Improve the Human Condition Have Failed* (New Haven, NY: Yale University Press, 1998).

27 Peter Holquist, 'New Terrains and New Chronologies: The Interwar Period through the Lens of Population Politics', *Kritika: Explorations in Russian and Eurasian History* 4(1) (2003), 163–175.

28 David-Fox, *Crossing Borders*, 45.

29 Ibid., 45.

30 Ibid., 22.

associate political messages/connotations with these historiographical approaches, to build on the scholarly research or ideas of either has the potential to pique scepticism, even if historians were attempting to move beyond such preoccupations.

Be it particularism vs. universalism, exceptional vs. synchronous, or continuity vs. discontinuity, then, David-Fox is right to argue that binary oppositions have defined the 'terrain in which interpretations of Russian and Soviet history have revolved until the present day'. In response to this observation, David-Fox has proposed a 'third way'. Instead of associating modernity or normative development with the West, he argues, we should look at late Imperial Russia and the Soviet Union through the prism of what S. N. Eisenstadt called 'multiple modernities'.[31] That is, to differentiate between westernization and modernization, to reject the notion that modernity means the 'convergence of industrial societies', and to look at the 'cultural program of modernity' as experienced in different 'civilizational traditions' and contexts.[32] This is an approach that looks to pluralize the concept of modernity, to move beyond Eurocentric accounts, and to allow for different cultural interpretations of modernity. If we approach the study of Russian and Soviet history on these terms, it might encourage us to better account for the manner of Russia's embrace with modernity. It might enable us to better explain the various twists and turns of modern Russia and the Soviet Union. And, much as Priestland attempted with his study of Stalinism, it might bring neo-traditional and modernity school research together to build a more coherent and convincing picture.

Moving in this direction, some might prefer to employ the language of 'entangled modernities', which, in recent years, has been offered as both a complement and corrective to Eisenstadt's reworked conception of modernity.[33] Those employing 'entangled modernities', in place of 'multiple' or 'alternative', have sought to further remove themselves from Eurocentric, singular, or bastardized visions of modernity; instead, stressing the 'imbrications of modernity and tradition' in their various settings: a framework that points to the interweaving of competing narratives, including modernity and anti-modernity, as well as different cultural contextualizations of the past and future.[34] From this perspective, modern ideas can be seen to interact with certain cultural contexts, and – as the recent boom in global history and comparative history has made all the more obvious – these particular interactions could also set their own precedents and serve to influence other nations and their experience of modernity. For example, the specific imperial context and domination out of which the Russian and Chinese revolutions

31 Ibid., 3, 24.

32 See Shmuel Noah Eisenstadt, 'Multiple Modernities', *Daedalus* 129(1) (2000), 1–29, quotations 24.

33 Johann P. Arnason, 'Entangled Communisms: Imperial Revolutions in Russia and China', *European Journal of Social Theory* 6(3) (2003), 307–325, especially 307–308.

34 Göran Therborn, 'Entangled Modernities', *European Journal of Social Theory* 6(3) (2003), 293–305, especially 295–297.

emerged, it has been suggested, further explains some of the modernizing strategies and governmental patterns of twentieth-century Communism.[35]

Crosspollinations: new and old, universal and particular

In the same vein, rather than accepting the binary conception of 'change and continuity' so often at the heart of historical studies, the editors of this volume argue that the old and the new – the residual and the emergent – will often intersect, together forming and effecting the formation of the world around us. As accounts of 1917 continue to be written, it is clear that historians have begun to focus more attention on the nature of the Russian Revolution and what made it the way it was. Boundaries and chronologies continue to be challenged. Indeed, with this in mind, it might be said that we are all modernists now. But studies on the Russian public sphere and civil society (*obshchestvennost'*), in particular, have also moved beyond the narrow focus of modern state practices and new professions, allowing room for added nuance and 'civilizational traditions'. Thus our eyes have been opened to the particular nature of Russian civil developments, with the very word *obshchestvennost'* – often translated as 'civic-mindedness' – also seen to encapsulate or build on a vision of society more in keeping with Russian sensibilities. That is, a collectivist, as opposed to an individualist society, or a society inclined to foster 'an individual's primary loyalty to the larger community'.[36] In this way, modern civic patterns can be seen to develop in culturally specific and idiosyncratic ways. Members of the Imperial *obshchestvennost'* were meant to reject *soslovie* (estate) particularism – the notion that you belong exclusively to the nobility, clergy, townspeople, or the peasantry – by embracing an all-imperial identity. And, crucially, such visions of civic organization have themselves been shown to help set the parameters of Soviet social activism.[37]

Examining themes such as this complicates and problematizes our understanding of Soviet Russia. Late Imperial culture can be seen as having undergone deep transformational changes that saw the emergence of a small, culturally specific, yet thriving civil and civic society, as well as the beginnings of a Russian mass consumer culture. The Great Reforms of Aleksander II, accelerating urbanization and state-sponsored industrialization, as well as an increased interest in Russian national culture, also facilitated a mushrooming of philanthropic, educational, cultural, and recreational organizations across

35 Arnason, 'Entangled Communisms: Imperial Revolutions in Russia and China', 307–325.

36 Catriona Kelly and Vadim Volkov, 'Obshchestvennost', Sobornost': Collective Identities', in *Constructing Russian Culture in the Age of Revolution: 1881–1940*, edited by Catriona Kelly and David Shepherd (Oxford: Oxford University Press, 1998), 26–27.

37 See Adele Lindenmeyr, *Poverty Is Not a Vice: Charity, Society, and the State in Imperial Russia* (Princeton, NJ: Princeton University Press, 1996), especially Chs 6 and 9.

Imperial Russia.[38] And it is in this urban context that the concept of *obshchestvennost'* came to the fore, connecting the past and the present, ensuring that the forces of Russian modernity were enacted through recognizable means. Subsequently, we can now see that certain social activities fell under the banner of Soviet *obshchestvennost'* precisely because of the cultural, social, and intellectual conceptions acquired in the build up to 1917. Soviet *obshchestvennost'* provided an instrument to integrate a very fragmented population into the new state, allowing Soviet citizens to actively participate in the process of state-building.[39]

Consider also, some of the latest studies into the world of Russian/Soviet activists and would-be revolutionaries. Those that formed the first urban communes of the new republic, for instance – the young idealists who requisitioned dormitory rooms and apartments in order to establish living examples of socialist domesticity – who have been shown to enact their modern revolutionary aspirations within a certain 'civilizational tradition'. Banding together as early as 1918, groups averaging between three and six persons formed these expressly collective cohabitative units as a means of introducing socialism into everyday life. As they did so, they pooled all their money and resources as a sign of their commitment to equality; they established rotas to ensure domestic chores were shared and gender norms challenged; they introduced Taylorist timetabling and monitored schedules as a means of promoting 'rational' and 'productive' lifestyles; they stridently defined themselves in opposition to the parental home, with its patriarchal tendencies and pointless bric-a-brac; and they mimicked Soviet workers' clubs by creating 'red corners' dedicated to reading, study, and enlightenment activities. Taking their cue, in many cases, from the Soviet youth journals and newspapers, these activists wanted to implement modern socialist visions in the here and now. 'Once the preserve of the inconsequential', they strove to elevate domesticity and the management of everyday life to a 'science'.[40] In this they built on a broader modern trend to 'rationally' reform everyday life – an idea also seen in the West, with the rise of liberal ergonomic designs for the home, Lillian Gilbreth's guide to a productive life and mind, taking Taylorism into the home and psychology, as well as a swathe of radical visions for centralized services.[41] But, at the same time, we can see that these urban activists openly acknowledged a rich

38 Joseph Bradley, 'Voluntary Associations, Civic Culture, and *obshchestvennost'* in Moscow', in *Between Tsar and People: Educated Society and the Quest for Public Identity in Late Imperial Russia*, edited by Edith W. Clowes, Samuel D. Kassow, and James L. West (Princeton, NJ: Princeton University Press, 1991), 139–141.

39 Matthias Neumann, *The Communist Youth League and the Transformation of the Soviet Union, 1917–1932* (Abingdon: Routledge, 2011), 18–19. See also Sandra Dahlke, 'Kampagne für Gottlosigkeit: Zum Zusammenhang zwischen Legitimation, Mobilisierung und Partizipation in der Sowjetunion der zwanziger Jahre', *Jahrbücher für Geschichte Osteuropas* 50 (2002), 172–185.

40 Willimott, *Living the Revolution*, 20.

41 Ibid., 72–73.

heritage of Russian collective organization: some commune groups making reference to the example of the pre-revolutionary *arteli* (small labour alliances), radical student *kruzhki* (discussion circles), clandestine political *iacheiki* (cells), and the literary visions of Nikolai Chernyshevsky's *What Is to Be Done?* (1863). All of which drew on a cultural and revolutionary lexicon that privileged the idea of the *kollektiv* (collective) as a small, concentrated unit or brotherhood – a radical vision born of a society inclined to foster 'an individual's primary loyalty to the larger community'.

Some urban communes established rather grand sounding 'committees' to monitor and manage certain everyday tasks, including 'housekeeping' and 'hygiene committees'. Communes were also keen to compare themselves to others, keeping note of the various lifestyle studies printed in the press, and the statistics that accompanied them. As with the formation of commune 'committees', to measure life through 'statistics', and on occasion to produce your own 'data' and 'tables', was to speak the language of modern socialism.[42] But, it has also been argued, 'people do not just conceive ideas through external frameworks, they transfer onto them their own idiosyncrasies and that with which they feel familiar'.[43] Collective association in the form of the Soviet urban commune gained traction with individual activists, in part, because it resonated with something that they felt was culturally familiar. Some commune members, for instance, had direct experience of peasant community life and the *mir* (peasant commune), which had long been associated with egalitarianism and communal habits. And whether or not the Russian countryside really lived up to this acclaim, and the importance bestowed upon it by the Russian intelligentsia of the nineteenth century in particular, it certainly did help to foster a cultural legacy that put the accent on community, equality, sharing, and brotherhood.[44] As such, Russia's collectivist and cultural antecedents can be seen to help effect the manner by which modern socialist ambitions came into being, giving added traction to certain approaches and building on existing cultural conceptions.[45]

In turn, some of the chapters in this volume seek to show how modern forces were enacted through individuals, groups, and institutes still subject to the durable beliefs, practices, and emotions of their forefathers. In all of this, we are beginning to move beyond the binary of 'modernity vs. tradition', and explore how contemporaries encountered revolutionary change within a particular cultural context.

Rethinking the Russian Revolution

As a means of marking the latest historiographical developments within the field on the centenary of the Russian Revolution, this book offers a series of

42 Ibid., 91–93.
43 Ibid., 19.
44 Ibid., 40.
45 See a similar comment on this research in David-Fox, *Crossing Borders*, 116–117.

chapters in which historians seek to show how a non-binary, across-1917 approach can be deployed to offer new insights into a range of topics. The contributors to this book analyse the transformation of Russia, over 1917, as an open-ended process – a history of interactions, entanglements, and vicissitudes across the revolutionary divide. In their own way, they examine how the new and the old, modern aspirations and traditional structures, intersected to make the Soviet world. As historiographical trends continue to lead us to consider and incorporate the *longue durée*, as well as the crosspollination of global and local issues, these chapters offer students and scholars something both modest and important: further, yet much needed, examples of research-led enquiries across 1917. This is important because so much Soviet historiography, and many of the debates surrounding the modernity school paradigm, have fallen on the topic of Stalinism. As the editors of the leading journal *Kritika* noted in 2003, Soviet history in recent years might well have been referred to as '1930s studies'.[46] But by looking at change, continuity, and crosspollination across 1917 more specifically we can gain a fuller understanding of the factors that helped form the Russian Revolution, the Bolshevik project, and the Soviet Union.

What these chapters do not offer is a single, comprehensive account of how to read or rethink the Russian Revolution. Instead, they each come at this task from different angles and with different concerns. Some allocate more time to the shadows of Russia's past than others. Some draw more overtly on certain historiographical examples than others. But, in the end, all come together to question the manner of Russia's march towards modern socialism and the manner by which modern visions were appropriated.

Broadly speaking, we can see three main areas of concern or intellectual influence when it comes to crossing the revolutionary divide of 1917. Firstly, there is the desire, very much leading on from the challenges laid down by the modernity school, to highlight the connection between Russia's late Imperial and Soviet experience of modernity. This continues to extend the lessons of thinkers such as Bauman, but also the greatly influential and frequently referenced Michel Foucault, who also challenged existing preconceptions of the modern world by citing the processes by which individuals are made and identities formed, what he called 'subjectivity', as an important aspect in the formation of modern systems of power and civilizational cohesion.[47] Looking at the means by which identities were fashioned, and how individuals envisioned their own identities, can draw us nearer to both the universal and particular experiences of modernity in Russia. The study of subjectivity in the field of Russian and Soviet history was first broached in earnest in Stephen Kotkin's

46 'From the Editors: "1930s Studies",' *Kritika: Explorations in Russian and Eurasian History* 4(1) (2003), 1–4.

47 See 'The Subject and Power', afterword to Hubert Dreyfus and Paul Rabinow, *Michel Foucault: Beyond Structuralism and Hermeneutics* (Chicago, IL: University of Chicago Press, 1982).

Magnetic Mountain, which noted the work of Foucault and argued that 'Stalinism was not just a political system, let alone the role of an individual. It was a set of values, a social identity, a way of life'.[48] The idea of a Stalinist or Soviet subjectivity was followed up by Jochen Hellbeck and Igal Halfin, who each sought to show how a state-controlled 'official discourse' shaped Soviet citizens and their attempts to self-fashion.[49] But this is also an area that needs further research and a clearer explanation of what parallels or disjuncture could be experienced across 1917 and across Russia's broader experience of modernity. Pointing to the role of Communist state indoctrination programmes with regard to subjectivity, Stephen A. Smith has recently argued that identities can develop along axes other than those determined by the state.[50] If we are to fully understand these not entirely malleable identities, therefore, we need to look at the possible points of connection between axes.

Secondly, it is possible to see the conscious use of history and the past as a means of explaining or framing the pre-revolutionary patterns of the Soviet world. Here we see the influence of Eric Hobsbawm and Terence Ranger's *The Invention of Tradition*, which, setting its sights predominantly on twentieth-century nationalism and nationalists, sought to reveal the creative nature of 'tradition'. Queen Victoria's jubilee of 1887, subsequently repeated due its success, drew on the theme of royal tradition, but was, in fact, a wholly new invention; an invention that would be emulated by the Habsburgs in 1908 and the Romanovs in 1913.[51] Hobsbawm and Ranger wrote about 'tradition' as a conscious 'process of formalization and ritualization, characterized by reference to the past'. They did not fully account for the unconscious use of the past, custom as precedence, or the idea of cultural familiarization; nor was there much room for indeterminacy in their assessment. Nonetheless, extending on this work, David Brandenberger has deployed the concept of the 'usable past' with great effect in his assessment of the Soviet state and Stalinism. He has shown that the Soviet Union was forced to seek out and draw on a 'usable past' precisely because of the weaknesses and indeterminacies within its indoctrination programme. In other words, the Soviet state failed to mobilize society along communist lines, meaning it had to infuse nationalist sentiment

48 Kotkin, *Magnetic Mountain*, 22–23.

49 See Jochen Hellbeck, *Revolution on My Mind: Writing a Diary Under Stalin* (Cambridge, MA: Harvard University Press, 2006); and Igal Halfin, *From Darkness to Light. Class, Consciousness and Salvation in Revolutionary Russia* (Pittsburgh, PA: University of Pittsburgh Press, 2000); Igal Halfin, *Stalinist Confessions. Messianism and Terror at the Leningrad Communist University* (Pittsburgh, PA: University of Pittsburgh Press, 2009); Igal Halfin, *Intimate Enemies. Demonizing the Bolshevik Opposition, 1918–1928* (Pittsburgh, PA: University of Pittsburgh Press, 2007); Igal Halfin, *Terror in my Soul: Communist Autobiographies on Trial* (Cambridge, MA: Harvard University Press, 2003).

50 Stephen A. Smith, *Revolution and the People in Russian and China: A Comparative History* (Cambridge: Cambridge University Press, 2008), 235.

51 Eric Hobsbawm and Terence Ranger (eds), *The Invention of Tradition* (Cambridge: Cambridge University Press, 1983), 7, 281–282.

and Russian tradition into its propaganda message.[52] In this sense, the Soviet Union is presented as a modernist project reinforced by a 'heroic line … drawn from the Russian national past'.[53] More room is given to both the indeterminacy of Soviet propaganda and the restraints of the Bolshevik project. But more work still needs to be done to uncover how the 'usable past' was incorporated in the lives of ordinary Soviets, while avoiding some of more deterministic assertions made by Hobsbawm and Ranger.

Thirdly, there is a case to be made that some of the themes raised in structuralist arguments – if we reject the more restrictive, unambiguous, and overly deterministic explanations associated with this approach – can still yield important insights into modern Russia and the Soviet Union. In short, this might be viewed as the search for contemporary priori. But where structuralist studies into the Soviet past can be criticized for failing to adequately historicize their nominated priori, including Edward Keenan's attempt to explain Soviet history through the loosely defined notion of 'Muscovite tradition' or 'Muscovite political folkways', today's research must try to explain how cultural traditions or contexts persisted and interacted with new developments to form a Soviet experience.[54] This is a vision of structuralism that can be seen to critically extend on Marshall Sahlins' memorable *Islands of History*, which used the example of islander encounters with alien visitors or conquerors to argue that the 'dialogue' between new influences and existing contexts is what shapes the way we interpret the world.[55] So, the 'British were to Hawaiians in general as the Hawaiian chiefs were to their people' because culturally specific perceptions of power persisted, ensuring that 'chief-commoner relations' thereafter developed along both European and Hawaiian lines. As such, Sahlin insisted, 'there is no such thing as immaculate perception'.[56]

More recently, William H. Sewell, a scholar of modern France and social theory, has also made a case for studying the interaction between new 'events' or 'happenings' and the various 'cultural schemas' that might be seen to constitute the established 'structures of social life'.[57] In one aside, Sewell notes that micro-history offers one way to study such interactions.[58] Despite coming under attack from some quarters, then, the growth in micro-history and

52 David Brandenberger, *Propaganda State in Crisis: Soviet Ideology, Indoctrination, and Terror under Stalin, 1927–1941* (New Haven, CT: Yale University Press, 2011).

53 David Brandenberger, '"Simplistic, Pseudo-Socialist Racism": Ideological Debates within Stalin's Creative Intelligentsia, 1936–39', *Kritika: Explorations in Russian and Eurasian History* 13(2) (2012), 365–393, quotation 367.

54 Edward L. Keenan, 'Muscovite Political Folkways', *Russian Review* 45(2) (1986), 115–181.

55 Marshall Sahlins, *Islands of History* (Chicago, IL: University of Chicago Press, 1985), especially 143–145.

56 Sahlins, *Islands of History*, 138–139, 147.

57 William H. Sewell Jr, *Logics of History: Social Theory and Social Transformation* (Chicago, IL: University of Chicago Press), 143.

58 Ibid., 74–75.

thematically focused studies over recent years may well help to facilitate a means of more accurately explaining grand structural influences and historical trajectories.[59]

Sewell argues that where historians have traditionally sought to explain the sequence of events and trends, viewing the passage of time as contingent by nature, the structuralism of the social sciences tended to go in search of the things that determine or pattern time. One has been more concerned with the sequence of events as a means of explaining the world, viewing time as irreversible and embracing circumstance; the other has sought to discover the logic behind social and political developments. But, Sewell suggests, elements of structural thinking, when combined with an historian's 'emphasis on culture, contingency, and agency', can help to explain how certain influences are reproduced, accelerated, reversed, and/or reoriented over time and across events.[60] There has been some movement in this direction in the field of Russian and Soviet history, some studies consciously engaging in theoretical pronouncements; others naturally looking to rectify what they perceive as the weaknesses of recent historiographical interpretations. Daniel T. Orlovsky made some early headway in this regard, insofar as he has long sought to shed light on the 'limits of reform' within certain Russian institutions and institutional life both leading up to and across 1917.[61] J. Arch Getty has sparked some controversy in his book *Practicing Stalinism*, which picks up on some of the ideas presented in Edward Keenan's 'political folkways' article, as arguably he seeks to challenge the field, or remind it, of the need to incorporate structural considerations into explanations of Russian political culture and Russian perceptions of leadership.[62] It remains to be seen how far the field decides to develop the specific arguments of these works in the coming years. But, with studies such as Yanni Kotsonis' *States of Obligation* telling the history of Russian/Soviet taxation as a modern development fundamentally shaped by particular priori and an outlook born of a particular local context, it is also clear that many in the field are seeking to incorporate a reflexivity that accounts for some of the deeper cultural considerations and patterns that have traditionally fuelled structuralist

59 Cf. Jo Guldi and David Armitage, *The History Manifesto* (Cambridge: Cambridge University Press, 2014). This publication has rather misguidedly incorporated micro-history and close studies as the product of an academy that has become overrun by short-termism, neglecting the broader implications and insights offered by such work, while also assuming short- and long-term studies do not speak to one another or work to advance historical scholarship as a whole.

60 Sewell, *Logics of History*, especially 80, 273.

61 See Daniel T. Orlovsky, *The Limits of Reform: The Ministry of Internal Affairs in Imperial Russia, 1802–1881* (Cambridge, MA: Harvard University Press, 1981); and Orlovsky, 'The Hidden Class: White Collar Workers in the Soviet 1920's', in *Making Workers Soviet*, edited by Lewis H. Siegelbaum and Ronald Grigor Suny (Ithaca, NY: Cornell University Press, 1995), 220–252.

62 J. Arch Getty, *Practicing Stalinism: Bolsheviks, Boyars, and the Persistence of Tradition* (New Haven, CT: Yale University Press, 2013).

thinking.[63] Kotsonis seeks to reveal how engrained determinates, in the form of certain cultural perspectives and established sociological and philosophical preoccupations, interacted with and influenced the development of modern taxation policy in Russia and the Soviet Union, as well as the tools of state required to enact this policy.[64]

It might also be said that scholars such as Mark D. Steinberg, Diane P. Koenker, and Boris Kollonitskii have pursued a not dissimilar line of logic, each choosing to study the symbols and schemata through which individuals interpreted the world, lacing detailed personal experience, shared cultural connections, and historical development through their studies. By studying the writings of worker intellectuals at the turn of the twentieth century, Steinberg has revealed the layering of influences that came to make these modern Russian subjects.[65] In the same vein, Koenker has explored the interaction between material reality, established workers' culture, and ideological dreams.[66] While Kollonitskii has pioneered the use of street culture and rumour as a means of tracing popular responses to political crisis, revealing how revolutionary messages and Russian experiences combined to make the social atmosphere that helped drive forward the events of 1917.[67]

One way or another, the latest scholarly trends in the field of Russian and Soviet history are bound by a growing desire to eschew binary conceptions and entrenched interpretive frameworks. Ideas and ideologies do not function in a vacuum, they exist in dialogue with the world around them. Looking at and across the Russian Revolution, this is something that has become increasingly apparent to those writing the history of this event and this period. A cross-pollination of approaches and the pursuit of multicausal explanations have begun to preoccupy the minds of many within the field. The following chapters show how historians are getting to grips with these developments. Exploring various contours of the Russian Revolution in a non-binary, chronologically expansive manner, they seek to further facilitate new insights in the field.

Structure of the book

The chapters of this book have been grouped into two main parts, refelecting the different analytical focus the authors take to the study of the

63 Yanni Kotsonis, *States of Obligation: Taxes and Citizenship in the Russian Empire and Early Soviet Republic* (Toronto: University of Toronto Press, 2014), Ch. 10.

64 Ibid., especially 19–21, 295–296.

65 Mark D. Steinberg, *Moral Communities: The Culture of Class Relations in the Russian Printing Industry, 1867–1907* (Berkeley, CA: University of California Press, 1992); and *Proletarian Imagination: Self, Modernity, and the Sacred in Russia, 1910–1925* (Ithaca, NY: Cornell University Press, 2002).

66 Diane P. Koenker, *Republic of Labor: Russian Printers and Soviet Socialism, 1918–1930* (Ithaca, NY: Cornell University Press, 2005).

67 Boris Kollonitskii, *Simvoly vlasti i bor'ba za vlast': k izucheniju politicheskoj kultury Rossijskoj revoluzii 1917 goda* (St. Petersburg: Dmitry Bulanin, 2001); and *Pogony i bor'ba za vlast v 1917 g.* (St Petersburg: Ostrov, 2001).

revolutionary transformation process. The first part, entitled **'The New State, the Past, and the People'**, will examine how the new rulers of the state, the Bolsheviks, attempted to reconfigure political, social, and cultural practices to make them fit their revolutionary ideals and how they dealt with the rapidly emerging civil society they inherited. The section starts with a contribution by J. Arch Getty, whose chapter examines the problem of persistence, asking the important questions why, in what form, and for how long pre-revolutionary political culture endured across 1917. In the second chapter, Matthew Rendle's contribution poses the question, was the revolutionary justice system introduced by the Bolsheviks in November 1917 really *revolutionary*? He explores the extent to which there was continuity and change in legal culture and practices. The third piece in this section, written by Matthias Neumann, seeks to advance our understanding of the ways the Bolsheviks constructed a Soviet *obshchestvennost'*, a Soviet, state-controlled, civil sphere. Based on a case study of the state-sponsored Communist Youth League (Komsomol), the piece will reveal whether and to what extent Soviet *obshchestvennost'* integrated forms and developments that emerged under the tsarist regime to create a 'managed civil society'. In the final chapter of this part, Miriam Neirick examines the power of pre-revolutionary culture in her study of the development of the Russian circus after 1917. She shows that while the Bolsheviks failed to prevent the restoration of the circus to pre-revolutionary form under NEP, the discourse on the ideological value of circus entertainment was truly revolutionized.

The second part, entitled **'The People, the Past, and the New State'**, shifts the focus more firmly to the people and the way individuals, social groups, and professional groups encountered and engaged with the newly emerging Soviet state. As well as engaging with the modern ideas promoted by the Bolsheviks, in their interaction with the new state these groups and individuals naturally reverted to traditional paradigms and practices, using 'tools' familiar to them from before 1917. In the first chapter of this section Matthew D. Pauly explores how Ukrainian teachers developed a notion of public service that determined their politics in the late Imperial period and how they subsequently adjusted and reconciled their own vision of revolution with that promoted by the Soviet state. This contribution is followed by a chapter on the 'women's question' across the revolutionary divide. Yulia Gradskova examines the ideas and practices of the emancipation of women in the Volga-Ural region, highlighting the independent initiative taken by local intellectuals and women and how this was incorporated into the wider Soviet campaign for the 'solution of the women's question' after 1917. The third contribution, written by Susan Grant, puts the focus on another professional group – nurses. Contrary to teachers, the tsarist-trained nurse lacked the protection of unionism until August 1917. But Grant shows how nurses earned a Soviet identity through professional service and an overwhelming sense of respect for the pre-revolutionary past. The traditions of pre-revolutionary Russian nursing became deeply enmeshed with Soviet medical care values and concepts of professionalism. In the next contribution, Vera Kaplan asks the intriguing question: 'What did historians do at the time of the Great Revolution?' The chapter explores the personal experience of contemporary historians and the life of the historical community during the Revolution, analysing the interactions among the various groups composing this community. Kaplan demonstrates how the establishment of the Soviet archival system led to the steady erosion of the pre-revolutionary historical community's autonomy. Finally, the section is completed by a chapter on pre-revolutionary paradigms in citizen humour of the 1930s. In it Jonathan Waterlow reveals that while ordinary citizens had no choice but to deal directly with the enormous changes of the 1930s, they did so with 'tools' familiar to them from before the Revolution: these included recognizably pre-Soviet concepts, standards of judgement, unofficial forms of language, traditional values, and authority figures. Waterlow challenges the assumption that Soviet citizens were trapped within official Soviet discourses, unable to avoid 'speaking Bolshevik'.

The book closes with an epilogue by Peter Waldron who brings us back to the problem of persistence, reconsidering discourses of tradition and modernity. In a sketch of 200 years of Russian history, Waldron explores the notion of a 'Russian tradition' and emphasizes the importance of taking account of the deep-rooted the socio-economic structures in which modern ideas were adopted and practised. In Russia's case, Waldron contents, policy makers under the tsarist, Soviet and post-Soviet regime persistently failed to modernize an underproductive and uncompetitive economy.

Part I

The new state, the past, and the people

1 The problem of persistence

J. Arch Getty

Historians love watersheds and turning points. They are convenient to explain differences among periods. We put impressive labels on them: retreats are 'Great'; upheavals of various kinds, either in policy or in the streets are 'Revolutions'. We teach watersheds to our undergraduates because they are easy to understand and explain. And we have identified a lot of them just in the first half of the twentieth century: 1905, 1917, 1921, 1929, 1934, 1937, 1941, 1945, and 1953. Moshe Lewin was being conservative when he referred to Soviet history as a series of six different systems, each demarcated by a turning point of some kind.[1]

At any rate, the 1917 Russian Revolution certainly seems to be a major turning point. The economic and political collapses of 1917–1920 are striking. And because both scholars and participants who lived through the period tend to focus (sometimes exclusively) on the complete collapse of state power, the sharp break seems even more compelling. The one thing upon which the Bolsheviks and their enemies ironically agreed was that everything changed; little if anything persisted. Ideology, government, property relations, the ruling elite, established religion, and foreign policy changed suddenly and in obvious ways.

Yet it has been clear for a long time that important elements persisted across the great divide of 1917. Assertions of persistence have generally been global statements about the Soviet period rather than detailed analysis of how or why things persisted. The Soviet period was called the 'revenge of Moscow'. An omnipotent, psychologically challenged Stalin somehow single-handedly shaped the entire Soviet culture along archaic lines. Even Edward Keenan's classic argument for persisting 'deep structures' in Russian history was short on details explaining the workings and survivals of these structures.[2] But we can speak meaningfully of general persistence across big events

1 Moshe Lewin, *The Making of the Soviet System: Essays in the Social History of Interwar Russia* (New York: New Press, 1994).

2 Examples include Boris Souvarine who suggested a flat structural persistence by describing Stalin's rule simply as the 'historical atavism of ancient Muscovy': Boris Souvarine, *Stalin, a Critical Survey of Bolshevism* (New York: Longmans, 1939), 510. Robert C. Tucker took the opposite approach, privileging human

only by looking at the components. William Sewell's studies of the French Revolution emphasized the need to identify 'peculiar ecological situations' and events on a case by case basis. But Sewell also insisted on the need to develop a conceptual apparatus to do this.[3]

This essay seeks to examine political practices that persisted across 1917 in an attempt to get below the surface of persistence using some tools of anthropology. We will reflect on such questions as 'Why did something persist?' 'In what form did it persist?' 'What long- and short-term factors governed its persistence?' and 'Who, if anyone, was aware of a persisting practice?' Aside from such specific questions, we will wonder if different kinds of persistence have anything in common with each other. Is there some thread tying them together, some underlying motor humming along beneath the surface that governs persistence?

The simplest theoretical explanation for persistence is functionalism. First applied to primitive societies, according to functionalist thinking social structure and social relations have a functional utility for the survival of society as a whole. Extending the work of Émile Durkheim and Talcott Parsons, structural functionalists argued that social roles, for example, persist because they are useful to society. There are many examples in the post-1917 period of apparent functionalism, both intentional and unconscious, as we shall see. A secret political police with broad powers, an undemocratic dictatorship, and a venal patronage oligarchy would seem to be functional to both tsars and Bolsheviks, as they would be to any regime facing revolutionary or counter-revolutionary challenges. It is easy to imagine the Bolsheviks selecting elements from the past for their new government to meet immediate utilitarian needs.[4]

But perhaps functionalism is too easy. Attractive as they might be at first glance, functionalist explanations have relatively weak explanatory power. Marshall Sahlins criticized functionalism because it ignores culture. 'Functionalist practice … consists of taking the cultural properties merely as the appearance … cultural content, whose specificity consists in its meaning, is lost altogether in a discourse of "needs"'.[5] 'We speak as if … our culture were constructed out of the "real" activities and experiences of individuals rationally bent upon their practical interests'.[6] Functionalism also cannot easily

agency by seeing Stalin as a kind of omnipotent psychopath in *Stalin in Power: the Revolution from Above, 1928–1941* (New York: Norton, 1990). Edward Keenan, 'Muscovite Political Folkways', *Russian Review* 45(2) (1986).

3 William H. Sewell, Jr, *Logics of History: Social Theory and Social Transformation* (Chicago, IL: University of Chicago Press, 2005), 273, and Ch. 9 in general.

4 Yves Cohen wrote that 'Each practice in its own right was itself partially a political interpretation of tradition in context. People borrowed some aspects of traditional forms while rejecting others, their selection being governed by actual exigencies in the situation at hand'. Yves Cohen, 'The Cult of Number One in an Age of Leaders', *Kritika: Explorations in Russian and Eurasian History* 8(3) (2007), 619.

5 Marshall Sahlins, *Culture and Practical Reason* (Chicago, IL and London: University of Chicago Press, 1967), 76.

6 Ibid., 220.

account for the persistence of practices long after the need for them is gone and when they obviously have become dysfunctional. Sahlins writes of a 'rule of diminishing returns' according to which the more distant a cultural practice is from its purported function, the less that function can describe the phenomenon.[7]

Sahlins' emphasis on structure and culture bring us to historical structuralism, whose contributions may be useful to our analysis of 1917 because they explore the relationship between 'event' (1917, for example) and 'structure' (Russian culture, for example).[8] In its most basic form, a strict structuralism posits that events and other human actions are determined by cultural structures. Events, along with social relations and practices, are merely products of history.

William Sewell finds that such cultural determinism assumes a too rigid causal connection in social life, because while structures define and shape events, events also redefine and reshape structures.[9] As Sahlins had put it, 'civilization … responds transformationally to events, incorporates historical perturbations as structural permutations'.[10] Event and cultural structure influence each other on a two-way street.

There are plenty of 'happenings' but only some rise to the level of turning points that somehow change the structures that govern human conduct. Historical events are happenings that transform structures.[11] Even though events redefine and reshape culture, Sewell also insists on the power of continuity and structure. 'A proper understanding of the role of events in history must be founded on a concept of structure … most social practices … tend to be reproduced with considerable consistency over relatively extended periods of time'.[12]

As a student of the French Revolution, Sewell tries to come to grips with the standard notion of revolutions as 'events' that transform culture and structure. In so doing, he foregrounds *The Event*. For Sewell, a society's cultural structure is a product of the events through which it has passed.[13] But cultural structures can withstand events, fight them off, as it were. His study of the dockworkers of Marseilles shows that structured patterns can often reproduce themselves over long periods of time, even to the point of resisting major revolutionary events.[14] In such cases, dramatic events do not

7 Ibid., 76–78.
8 Discussions of structuralism can be extremely complex and span the fields of linguistics, anthropology, literary criticism, and philosophy. Here we do not champion structuralism, but rather, at the risk of over-simplifications, we will distil elements that would appear to be useful to historians.
9 Sewell, *Logics* makes this point forcefully.
10 Sahlins, *Culture and Practical Reason*, 220.
11 Sewell, *Logics*, 218.
12 Ibid., 226.
13 Ibid., 199–200.
14 See the extended discussion in Sewell, *Logics*, Ch. 9.

dislodge a culture, and it makes sense to speak more of cultural continuity than persistence.

Sewell argues that structure and culture are not flat and unitary.[15] Culture should be plural because 'societies should be conceptualized as the sites of a multitude of overlapping and interlocking cultural structures'. Structures are mutually reinforcing sets of cultural schemas and material resources.[16]

Moreover, embedded in structure is the effect of individual agency. Sewell writes 'What tends to get lost in the language of structure is the efficacy of human action – or "agency" to use the currently favored term.'[17] Sewell believes that historical *agents* can change cultures and influence happenings and events; they do so in revolutions. Moreover, for him agency implies a knowledge of cultural schema and the capacity to reinterpret or mobilize an array of resources of the structure.[18] As we shall also see, however, agency can be 'unconscious' when agents do things for reasons they don't understand. As Pierre Bourdieu put it, there can be 'genesis amnesia' when actors are unaware of the cultural forces influencing them.[19]

For Sahlins, historical events cannot be understood except as references to and reproductions of cultural categories and meanings that comprise the field of possibilities for events. 'The particular culture scheme constitutes the possibilities of worldly reference for the people of a given society.'[20] For him, events indeed consist of references to culture, as *specifications* of culture. Events are not a superstructure sitting on a cultural base, as Marxists would have it.

Cultural categories, when referenced by the event, are modified and transformed; they become 'burdened with the world', in Sahlins' phrase.[21] 'Every actual use of cultural ideas is some reproduction of them, but every such reference is also a difference …'.[22] Every reproduction of culture is therefore an alteration, insofar as in action, the categories by which a present world is orchestrated pick up some novel empirical content.[23]

Sahlins takes the relationships between event and culture and between stability and change even further by abolishing the dichotomies. Because of

15 Here and below, we will use culture and structure interchangeably, borrowing from Sewell's approach. Sewell argues that 'structure is a profoundly cultural phenomenon'. Culture in this sense is the 'whole body of practices, beliefs, institutions, customs, habits, myths, etc. built up by humans and passed on from generation to generation'. Sewell, *Logics*, 157, 161.
16 Ibid., 205.
17 Ibid., 125.
18 Ibid., 143–144.
19 Pierre Bourdieu, *Outline of a Theory of Practice* (Cambridge: Cambridge University Press, 1977), 79, 179.
20 Marshall Sahlins, *Islands of History* (Chicago, IL: University of Chicago Press, 1985), 147.
21 Ibid., 138.
22 Sahlins, *Culture and Practical Reason*, 152–153.
23 Sahlins, *Islands*, 144.

the reciprocal impact of event on culture, 'there is no ground either for the exclusive opposition of stability and change'.[24] Both are going on at the same time; both are part of the same history. As Ferdinand de Saussure put it: 'What predominates in all change is the persistence of the old substance; disregard for the past is only relative. That is why the principle of change is based on the principle of continuity.'[25] Actions in the present are always references to the past. So past and present, system and event, structure and history are in 'indissoluble synthesis' with each other.[26]

Sahlins chides historians who 'notoriously … isolate some changes as strikingly distinctive and call them "events" in opposition to "structure"'. He regards this as a 'pernicious distinction' because an event is not just a happening; it is a '*relation* between a certain happening and a given symbolic system'.[27]

At this point, readers might well take a deep breath, and the historians among them might be shaking their heads. Taken to extreme, the Sahlins version of structuralism erases the differences between event and culture, stability and change, and even past and present. Historians, however, at the risk of being pernicious, will always be attempting to explain events, broadly defined. We will always contrast stability and change, past and present. We have a different metaphor for explaining human action and behaviour, and dissolving everything together isn't particularly helpful.

For purposes of historical analysis, it makes sense to agree with Sewell, who retains a focus on events and defends the difference between stability and change. So where does all this theory get us, aside perhaps from a feeling of gratitude that we are not philosophers or linguists? One does not have to become a full-blown structuralist, neo-structuralist, or post-structuralist to see that there are useful historical tools for us here, and there is no reason that we cannot pick and choose the ones that seem to help. Such propositions, which we will test below, include:

- Events cannot take place or become intelligible to us except in the structural/cultural context that produced them.
- The structure or culture of a society is in fact plural, consisting of multiple overlapping cultures.
- Continuity or persistence takes place at the level of culture.
- Events necessarily influence the cultures that produced them. When the influence is strong, culture changes to the point where we speak of dramatic change.
- When the influence is less strong, we are more likely to speak of persistence because following Sewell, we need to explain 'why some patterns

24 Sahlins, *Culture and Practical Reason*, 153.
25 Ferdinand de Saussure, *Course in General Linguistics* (New York: Philosophical Library), 74.
26 Sahlins, *Islands*, 156.
27 Ibid., 153. Emphasis Sahlins'.

remain constant when much around them is in flux … why transformations fail to occur'.[28]

- Human agency, including random effects of personality, can affect the nature and power of an event. That agency can be conscious and intentional or unintentional.

Below, we will see these elements and tools in action.

In one example, we will focus on an event's cultural references and how the event can change the culture that produced it. The decision to embalm Lenin shows the powerful persistence of the importance of the ruler's body in Russia. Despite our preconceptions and common wisdom, we will suggest that the decision to embalm Lenin in a mausoleum was produced by a particular cultural structure having nothing to do with religious culture, the sacred, or relics and much less with an intention to exploit them. It had to do rather with a profoundy secular culture of the political body and age-old ideas and the body and the state. We will also see the role of human agency: the authors of this event seem to have had little idea of the cultural pressure on them. In a real sense they did not know why they were doing what they did. But time then 'burdened the event', as Sahlins might say, and that event changed the relevant cultural referent. After some years, the cultural specification of the mausoleum-event became culturally spiritual and religious in a way that it had not been before.

In another example, a consideration of social roles, we will see the power of some cultural structures to persist across the watersheds of 1917 and even Stalin's terror. The events of 1917 destroyed one cultural structure: the legitimacy of rule by blooded nobility in tandem with divine right monarchy. But we will also see that a closely related cultural structure – the idea and practice of venal oligarchy based on patronage – persisted. No longer based on familial clan or patrilinear succession, nobility came to have other sources and content under the Bolsheviks, and the persisting power of clan oligarchy continues down to the present day, long past the time when it might have been functional.

Lenin's body

There was no precedent in pre-1917 Russian history for preserving the tsar's body for display in a special building. Russian Orthodox tradition prescribed burial in the earth and Muscovite grand princes were buried beneath the floors of cathedrals. There was also no precedent in Bolshevik thinking. Insofar as there was a party tradition, it was spelled out by Old Bolshevik M. S. Ol'minskii:

> I am a long time supporter of the funeral ritual which the Party advocates. I think that all survivals of religious practice (coffins, funerals, the leave-taking from the corpse or cremation and all that) are nonsense … My body will be used more rationally. It should be sent to a factory

28 Sewell, *Logics*, 273.

> without any ritual, and in the factory the fat should be used for technical purposes and the rest for fertilizer.[29]

Agreeing with Ol'minskii, another comrade actually willed his body to a soap factory.[30]

Thus, insofar as the creation of the Mausoleum is concerned, there would appear to be nothing to persist over the 1917 divide. But if we look beneath the surface of this event, we in fact find structural-cultural continuities, many of which the Bolshevik actors were not themselves aware.

The simplest and most common explanation of the body/mausoleum ensemble is intentional-functional. The idea is that Stalin and his allies gathered in a back room and immediately understood the utility of preserving, displaying, and worshipping his body, thinking and planning that preserving Lenin would play usefully to one cultural structure: a Russian religious tradition of holy, saintly relic providing a substitute worship in order to legitimize the Bolshevik regime. It would enhance the legitimacy of Lenin's successors and of the regime in general by tracing that regime's descent from a founder, a semi-mythical progenitor.

Tempting as this explanation may be, if we look at the evidence on the original decision to preserve and house the body, the opposite was true. We find a different picture, one that does not suggest planning, a cynical use of religion, or conscious planned utility. Among the plural cultural structures and referents (to recall Sewell) we will see that the appropriate cultural schema for the decision was a different one altogether.

In fact, to themselves and in their private counsels the Bolsheviks furiously denied any religious or functional uses of the body, and given the close and secret archival record there is no reason not to believe them. Comparison of the cultural influences on their immediate intentions illustrates the important distinction between long- and short-term persistence, as well as the importance of consciousness and choice.

First of all, we might note that Stalin had little if anything to do with the decision to permanently display Lenin. He was not a member of the Lenin Funeral Commission, chaired by police chief Feliks Dzerzhinskii, where such decisions were made.[31] Stalin was a member of the Politburo, which, as it turned out, rubber-stamped the recommendations of the commission, but he seems to have played no active role in the decision. In fact, Stalin's associate Voroshilov who was a member of the Commission, bitterly opposed the idea of preserving and displaying the body.

29 Cited in Catherine Merridale, *Night of Stone: Death and Memory in Russia* (London: Granta, 2000), 47.

30 Richard Stites, *Revolutionary Dreams: Utopian Vision and Experimental Life in the Russian Revolution* (New York: Oxford University Press, 1989), 114.

31 The commission went through several changes of name and membership over the years. Originally formed as the Lenin Funeral Commission, it later became the Commission for Immortalizing the Memory of V. I. Lenin.

The original idea was to bury Lenin in the ground. On 24 January 1924, the Politburo decided to bury Lenin next to Iakov Sverdlov near the Kremlin wall.[32] On 26 January, Bukharin told the Congress of Soviets that soon Lenin would go 'into the grave'.[33] The next day, the chief orator at Lenin's funeral G. Evdokimov said 'we are burying Lenin' and at the end of the ceremony radio stations across the country reported that 'Ilych is being lowered into his grave.'[34]

The proximate reason for the decision to attempt preservation of the body was not functional utility or legitimacy or pseudo-religion but crowd control. Professor Abrikosov had embalmed the body in customary fashion so it would last the traditional three days until the funeral and burial. Nobody contemplated a longer viewing. But two days later, the crowds obliged the Politburo to move the display from the Hall of Columns to Red Square near the Kremlin wall.[35] Architect A. V. Shchusev was quickly conscripted to design and build a temporary structure there, which was thrown together by 27 January. The crowds kept coming, and soon Shchusev was charged with designing a larger structure, which was completed some weeks later. But it was not made to last because nobody yet contemplated a permanent viewing of the body. This structure was made of wood and called the 'temporary mausoleum'. There would be no permanent stone mausoleum until 1929.

Meanwhile, during the weeks of the extended viewing period, 'time did its work', and Lenin's body began to decay.[36] The Lenin Funeral Commission was faced with making another decision about the body.[37] In February, Commission member and engineer Leonid Krasin claimed that he could preserve the body for a while through freezing, and on the 7th the Commission authorized him to buy expensive German machinery for that purpose.[38] By 14 March, the body continued to deteriorate behind a frosty mist and although Krasin continued to defend the freezing idea, the Commission brought in Professors Zbarskii and Vorob'ev with a new chemical procedure for longer preservation.[39] It was not until 26 July that the Commission made

32 Protocols of the Lenin Funeral Commission, Rossiiskii gosudarstvennyi arkhiv sotsial'no-politicheskoi istorii (hereafter RGASPI), f. 16, op. 2, d. 48, l. 105.

33 Protocols of the Lenin Funeral Commission, RGASPI, f. 16, op. 1, d. 11.

34 Nina Tumarkin, *Lenin Lives! The Lenin Cult in Soviet Russia* (Cambridge, MA: Harvard University Press, 1983). 161–162, 176; Olga Velikanova, *Making of an Idol: on Uses of Lenin* (Gottingen: Muster-Schmidt Verlag, 1996), 54–55.

35 Protocols of the Lenin Funeral Commission, RGASPI, f. 16, op. 2, d. 48, l. 105.

36 Protocols of the Lenin Funeral Commission, RGASPI, f. 16, op. 1, d. 522, l. 48.

37 The documents show that the Politburo entrusted decision making about Lenin's body entirely to the Dzerzhinskii Commission. Dzerzhinskii was the middleman between the two organizations, reporting to the Politburo from the Commission and relaying the Politburo's agreement to the Commission's recommendations. See, for example, Politburo documents in RGASPI f. 17, op. 3, d. 1505, l. 1 and op. 163, d. 396, ll. 55, 57, 59, in which the Politburo receives and approves the Commission reports.

38 Protocols of the Lenin Funeral Commission, now renamed the Commission for Immortalizing the Memory of V. I. Lenin. RGASPI, f. 16, op. 1, d. 51, l. 1.

39 This is the procedure still in use today. Protocols of the Commission for Immortalizing the Memory of V. I. Lenin. RGASPI, f. 16, op. 1, d. 51, l. 1.

the decision to try and embalm and display Lenin 'for a long time', based on Zbarskii and Vorob'ev's procedure.[40]

Already while Lenin had been lying in state, rumours had been circulating that popular pressure favoured preserving the body 'for some time and to build a crypt or vault'.[41] But when the question came up in the Dzerzhinskii Commission, at first in the form of whether or not to have an open casket, there was sharp debate, which Avel Enukidze later euphemistically described as fluster, hesitation, and doubt in the Commission.[42] At its meeting of 23 January, senior Bolsheviks T. Sapronov and K. Voroshilov took sharp issue with N. I. Muralov's suggestion to display the body at all and argued against any quasi-religious overtones. According to Voroshilov, 'We must not resort to canonization. That would be SR-like....[43] We would stop being Marxist-Leninists. If Lenin heard Muralov's speech, he would hardly compliment him. Really, cultured people would cremate the body and put the ashes in an urn.' Otherwise, Voroshilov said, we would be hypocrites and peasants would notice that we were destroying their god and replacing it with our own sacred relics.[44]

Dzerzhinskii dismissed the notion that catering to religion had anything to do with the question: 'this is not a cult of personality, but to a certain extent a cult of Vladimir Il'ich'. Voroshilov feared creating religious relics but Dzerzhinskii replied that Lenin couldn't be a relic because 'relics were about magic and miracles and this was different'.[45]

When Muralov went on to suggest that preserving the body and displaying it could be advantageous [*vygodno*] to the regime, Voroshilov exploded again. Muralov's idea was 'nonsense' [*chepukha*] and 'disgraceful' [*pozor*].[46] Voroshilov had been to London and had seen Marx's grave, which touched him even though 'nobody saw his face which was completely unnecessary'. When someone suggested that such a monument would enhance the memory of Lenin, Avel Enukidze added that,

> It goes without saying that neither we nor our comrades wanted to make a relic of the remains of V. I. Lenin.... We want to preserve the image

40 Protocols of the Commission for Immortalizing the Memory of V. I. Lenin. RGASPI, f. 16, op. 1, d. 492, ll. 1–3.
41 T. Sapronov's report to the Commission for Immortalizing the Memory of V. I. Lenin. RGASPI f. 16, op. 1, d. 109. l. 1.
42 Enukidze speech to the Commission for Immortalizing the Memory of V. I. Lenin. RGASPI f. 16, op. 1, d. 522, l. 53.
43 Reference to the Socialist Revolutionaries, who believed in the importance of individual persons in history and who before the revolution sought to effect change by assassinating key individuals. Lenin, on the other hand, had sharply argued that social forces, not individuals, were decisive.
44 Voroshilov's speech to the Commission. RGASPI f. 16, op. 2, d. 49, ll. 1–5.
45 Dzerzhinskii's speech to the Commission. RGASPI f. 16, op. 2, d. 49, ll. 1–5.
46 This is the only place in the documentation either of the Commission or the Politburo where the question of political utility was mentioned. Voroshilov's speech to the Commission. RGASPI f. 16, op. 2, d. 49, ll. 1–5.

> [*oblik*] of this great leader ... for those hundreds of thousands and maybe millions of people who would be happy to see the face of this person.[47]

Rather than take a principled position on preserving Lenin, Commission members Dzerzhinskii and K. Avanesov took a purely practical approach. As Dzerzhinskii put it, 'to be principled in this question is to be principled in quotation marks'. Would Lenin have approved? Probably not, Dzerzhinskii admitted, because he was a person of exceptional modesty. But he is not here. 'We have only one Lenin, he is not here to judge, and the question is what to do with his body". For Dzerzhinskii, it was simple: everybody loved Lenin; everyone wanted to see him.

> He is so dear to us that if we can preserve the body and see it, then why not do it? ... If science can really preserve the body for a long time, then why not do it? ... If it is impossible, then we won't do it.

For Dzherzhinskii, the question was not 'why' but 'why not?'[48]

First, the discussion was about crowd control, then it was about warming weather, then a temporary building, and finally a permanent stone mausoleum, which they would not build for five years. They seem to have stumbled into the decision; there was no single moment, no single meeting, when a final decision or rationale was put forward. Dzerzhinskii's 'why not?' is the closest we have to a justification for preserving Lenin's body. 'Why not?' seemed instinctively natural and practical at the moment.

But what did that intuitive thing have to do with a body? In remembering his visit to Marx's grave, Voroshilov said that there a body was not necessary to maintain memory. 'It's not about a body.'

But he was wrong. Without recognizing it, Dzerzhinskii and his comrades were unconsciously informed by another Russian tradition, one having nothing to do with what was useful or functional, or with cultural schema about religion. It was about a different, secular cultural referrant: the *body* in Russian political culture. One of the key identifications for both Bolsheviks and peasants was the connection between the person-body and the state. Throughout Russian history the physical body of the ruler not only symbolized the state; in a real sense it was the state.[49]

In his classic analysis of the personal aspects of kingship, Ernst Kantorowicz wrote of the distinction between the 'king's two bodies'. One of these was his corporeal body, the other his body as head and symbol of the state.[50] Upon his

47 Protocol of the Commission. RGASPI f. 16, op. 1, d. 491, l. 12.

48 Dzerzhinskii's speech to the Commission. RGASPI f. 16, op. 2, d. 49, ll. 1–5.

49 Sociologists have noted a universal human tendency to anthropomorphize political power. Edward Shils thought that it 'is rooted in the neural constitution of the human organism' and its intensity from place to place is based on the prevailing culture. Edward Shils, *The Constitution of Society* (Chicago, IL: University of Chicago Press, 1982), 111.

50 Ernst H. Kantorowicz, *The King's Two Bodies: A Study in Medieval Political Theology* (Princeton, NJ: Princeton University Press, 1957).

death, his physical body went into the tomb, while his state body continued, perhaps as a statue. But as Richard Wortman pointed out, in Russia the king did not have two bodies: a physical one and a political one. In Russia they were the same, or at least the identity was so close as to be imperceptible.[51] Even some emblems of the Soviet state carried Lenin's image, and it took a long time to separate them.

For centuries, Russians could not imagine a state not headed by a person. Although they often carried notions of radical reform, social justice, or nostalgia, every revolt and revolution through the centuries from False Dmitri to Pugachev had to be led by a 'true tsar', a pretender who by rights should be the ruler. In the seventeenth century there were 23 'rightful tsar' pretenders; 44 in the eighteenth century, eight of whom claimed to be Peter the Great's son Aleksei and 16 of whom were Peter III, miraculously saved from assassination.[52] Sovereignty, and therefore the rightful power of the 'state' was inseparable from the body.

The Russian word for 'state', *godurdarstvo*, comes from the word *gosudar'* and before it in ancient Slavic, *gospodar'*, both meaning master of a household. 'The concepts of belonging to *gosudar'* and *gosudarstvo* completely overlapped. The state and state interest could only be concretely embodied in the living person of the *gosudar'* and his affairs.'[53] The state could not be an abstraction, a thing in its own right with the tsar as mere custodian.[54] As Michael Cherniavsky put it, the state was not an independent abstraction; it received its legitimacy and reality from the person of the prince.[55]

Even in the revolutionary tumult of 1917 when the tsar had fallen and all kinds of authority were questioned, soldiers refused to swear loyalty to the state (*gosudarstvo*) by saying, '*net gosudaria, net i gosudarstva*', meaning there is no master, so there can be no state.[56] Insults to the ruler in Russia had long

51 Richard Wortman, *Scenarios of Power: Myth and Ceremony in Russian Monarchy from Peter the Great to the Abdication of Nicholas II* (Princeton, NJ: Princeton University Press, 2006), 415.

52 Simon Dixon, *The Modernisation of Russia, 1676–1825* (Cambridge: Cambridge University Press, 1999), 190–191. On pretendership in Russia, see Maureen Perrie's, *The Image of Ivan the Terrible in Russian Folklore* (Cambridge: Cambridge University Press, 1987) and *Pretenders and Popular Monarchism in Early Modern Russia* (Cambridge: Cambridge University Press, 1995). See also Claudio Sergio Ingerflom, 'Les représentations collectives du pouvoir et l'"imposture" en Russie, XVIIIe –XXe siècles', in *La Royauté Sacrée dans le Monde Chrétien*, en collaboration avec A. Boureau (Paris, Editions de l'E.H.E.S.S: 1992), 157–164, and 'Entre le mythe et la parole : l'action. La naissance de la conception politique du pouvoir en Russie', *Annales, Histoire, Sciences Sociales* 4 (1996), 733–757.

53 Oleg Kharkhordin 'What is the State? The Russian Concept of Gosudarstvo in the European Context', *History and Theory* 40 (2001), 214–219.

54 Kharkhordin, 'What is the State? ', 214–219; Dixon, *Modernisation*, 191.

55 Michael Cherniavsky, *Tsar and People: Studies in Russian Myths* (New York: Random House, 1969), 31–33.

56 Claudio Sergio Ingerflom, '"Loyalty to the State" under Peter the Great? Return to the Sources and the Historicity of Concepts', in *Loyalties and Solidarities in Russian Society, History and Culture*, edited by Philip Ross Bullock, Andy Byford, Claudio Nun-Ingerflom, Isabelle Ohayon, Maria Rubins, and Anna

been considered treason to the state, as *lèse majesté*, tantamount to overthrowing the state. When activists invaded Putin's reception office in 2004, they were accused of trying to overthrow the state and received prison terms. In December 2011, penalties for insulting Russian officials were doubled, while those for insulting citizens reduced.[57]

We might well remember the combined chaos and grief surrounding Stalin's death in 1953, when it also seemed that the entire political order of the state might vanish along with the body of the person.[58] As had been the case of the coronation of Nicholas II, people in 1953 were trampled to death in an attempt to be close to the incoming person or the deceased one. In both cases, it was a matter of seeking security and order in the continuation of the state that the body embodied.

The Bolshevik instigators denied any functionalist or quasi-religious overtones even to themselves and in private. That's not what they thought they were doing, and we have the right to consider their intentions. Indeed, as Dzerzhinskii's 'why not' concept suggests, in the short term, they had no clear idea what they were doing and why.

What did inform that decision was another cultural structure: the idea of the body in Russian political thinking. A monument was not enough. There had to be a body. It would be unrealistic to imagine that the early Bolsheviks, for all their materialism and modernity, could simply step out of a thousand years of political culture. They preserved the body as a kind of performance of the state which they could not help but imagine, however unconsciously, as a person. Tradition whispered to them; they heard something but weren't sure what it was. As Pierre Bourdieu put it, 'What is essential goes without saying because it comes without saying: the tradition is silent, not least about itself as tradition.'[59]

In the long run, however, the event of the mausoleum, by referring to a cultural structure about the body, changed that structure. In the longer term it became a space for legitimization of the regime and took on quasi-religious and political functions that were simply not present at the beginning. By the end of the 1930s, there was no more sacred space in the USSR, and it recalled nothing so much as a traditional Orthodox church. In a generally darkened room where you could not see the corners – and therefore the limits – of the sacred space, as in a cathedral, the body was lit by flood lights that correspond to the ancient lighting of candles in a sanctuary directing light to holy icons. The permanent body on display somehow negated time and death and

Winestein (London: School of Slavonic and East European Studies, 2013), 15. See also Claudio Sergio Ingerflom, 'Novoevropeiskaia paradigma "Gosudarstvennost": Teoreticheskie predlosylki i kognitivnye nesootvetstviia', *Rossiia* 21(2) (2011), 110–127.

57 *RIA Novosti*, 10 January 2012.

58 I owe this suggestion to Robert V. Daniels, 'Russian Political Culture and the Post-Revolutionary Impasse', *Russian Review* 46(20 (1987), 169.

59 Bourdieu, *Outline of a Theory of Practice*, 79, 179. Emphasis in original.

spoke to a very un-Bolshevik immortality. Every Soviet schoolchild was taught the slogan, 'Lenin lived, Lenin lives, Lenin will live.' In fact, in the myth of 'Clever Lenin' (based on a similar fable about the deceased Alexander I) Lenin periodically woke up and wandered the Russian land checking on things.[60] The mausoleum now evoked not just ideas about the state, but spiritual notions of immortality.

For decades, until the fall of the Soviet Union, members of the Politburo stood on top of the structure on important occasions, suggesting their legitimate descent and apostolic succession from the holy founder. That need for legitimacy had not been necessary in the early days of the revolution: the 'revolutionary power of the people' had done that. But now, the body became a legitimizing site, and a very important one on the level of national security. The mausoleum, along with the care and chemical preservation of the politically precious body came under the supervision of the secret police, the NKVD. The body was so important that the same 1939 secret Politburo file ordering the NKVD to arrest captured Polish officers (preparatory to their execution) also saw an NKVD order to set up a special laboratory to study the correct 'chemical recipe' and effects of temperature, humidity, and light on Lenin's body. The NKVD also supervised the secret purchase and installation of imported air conditioners for the mausoleum in May 1935, and construction of a new sarcophagus in March 1940.[61] At the time of the German attack in 1941, Lenin's body was among the first objects to be evacuated from Moscow to a safe location far in the rear.[62]

Considerations of consciousness and agency overlay this cultural change. At the creation, culture had been silent. In the longer run, when the body-event referenced and changed culture into something spiritual and immortal (as well as legitimizing), people almost certainly became aware of the connection between the body-event and the new culture that had been changed by it.

What persisted here were the culture(s) of the body in Russian political thinking. In the event of Lenin's body, we have an example of the complexity of persistence(s) and the effects of culture on events. How it started and what it became were two different things. Some cultures from the past (the politics of the state as body) were immediately, if unconsciously, parts of decisions. Other, different strands of culture (the body as transcendent and mystical) only emerged in the longer term under the reciprocal impact of the decision-as-event.

Social roles

Even though they spent their lives fighting and later persecuting Russian aristocrats, the Bolsheviks paradoxically assumed many of the characteristics,

60 Tumarkin, *Lenin Lives!*, 198–199.
61 RGASPI, f. 17, op. 162, d. 26, ll. 148–149; d. 27, l. 51; d. 18, l. 43.
62 RGASPI, f. 17, op. 162, d. 36, l. 40.

prerogatives, and functions of a nobility. The Bolsheviks would surely have denied this strange persistence of social roles connected with the past. As they destroyed the cultural tradition of blooded nobility and divine right monarchy, they referenced and adopted a related one: the structural idea of oligarchy.

Old Bolshevik status recalled the culture of the elite. Like princes, Old Bolshevik status was immutable. It was a quality; eligibility was fixed and there could be no new members. Like boyars, Old Bolsheviks had a special self-image, a vision almost equivalent to a birthright, that gave them the duty to govern. And, for the first 20 years after 1917, as a corporate group they dominated Soviet politics as senior statesmen and powerful regional governors. They were the veterans, known as 'Bolshevik Knights' [*Bol'shevistskie rytsary*] whose brave exploits were legend. They had fought when it was hard, in a revolution no less difficult and were every bit as self-congratulatory as victorious knights conquering a new land.

Some of them even behaved like nobles. When Smolensk first secretary I. P. Rumiantsev came to a district, he brought a supply of kopeks, which coins he tossed to the children from his passing car. Children threw themselves on the money in a free-for-all. When people noted that this was unseemly, Rumiantsev said 'they should know who is driving through'.[63] This was a modern noble riding his latter day carriage through one of his villages, but a noble by Bolshevism rather than birth.

The Old Bolsheviks' sense of themselves as a group apart drew from traditional elite culture and was reflected in their inner society. They lived apart from the general population in guarded and fortified places; their castles included the Kremlin, the House on the Embankment across the river, and a number of reserved buildings, each of which was innocently called a *Dom sovetov* [House of the Soviets]. They socialized exclusively with each other. Their sons and daughters attended the same schools and married the sons and daughters of other Old Bolsheviks with whom they grew up. Old Bolsheviks trusted their children's futures to each other and customarily adopted the orphaned children of their fallen peers. They were a breed apart.

Kinship, a powerful force in Russian culture, even played a role. In medieval Muscovy, marriages had been alliances that affected the political life of the entire clan and heads of kin clans arranged, approved, or disapproved marriages of important clan members. Bolsheviks Trotsky, Zinoviev, Kamenev, Bukharin, Molotov, and Stalin, to name only a few, married other Old Bolsheviks or their offspring, and the first three were directly related to each other by marriage. Bolshevik parents passed judgement on proper marriages for their children, and it was very rare to marry outside the caste. Stalin could have been a medieval boyar clan head when he advised Beria's son Sergo not to marry Gorky's granddaughter, because of the dubious nonparty types surrounding

63 Stenogramma plenuma Zapobkoma VKP(b) ot 26 iiulia 1937g. RGASPI f. 17, op. 21, d. 4093, ll. 10–11.

Gorky's family, 'I see your marriage as a move to establish links' with the oppositionist Russian intelligentsia.[64]

Before the revolution, senior nobles, especially princes and boyars, headed family clans whose fortunes rose and fell with that of the senior member.[65] Access to office and position were competitive and were governed by the *mestnichestvo* ('place order') ranking system, in which one's precedence and therefore power were precisely calculated according to genealogy, one's previous positions, and one's relative standing within one's clan.[66]

The Bolsheviks had their own version of *mestnichestvo* to determine eligibility for officeholding by calculating one's length of service in the party [*partstazh*]. Fine distinctions were made between those who joined the party before 1905, before 1917, and about the precise month in 1917 when one joined. Documents were combed and compared, witnesses polled and their statements taken, calculations made.[67] Beginning in 1923, for the broader party elite, the party established a formal system of *nomenklatura*: a series of lists of positions appointment to which required confirmation by various groups of senior grandees.[68]

64 Sergo Beria, *Beria, My Father: Inside Stalin's Kremlin* (London: Duckworth, 2001), 192.

65 Nancy Shields Kollmann, *By Honor Bound: State and Society in Early Modern Russia* (Ithaca, N.Y., Cornell University Press, 1999); Nancy Shields Kollmann, *Kinship and Politics: the Making of the Muscovite Political System, 1345–1547* (Stanford, CA, Stanford University Press, 1987); Paul Bushkovitch, *Peter the Great: the Struggle for Power, 1671–1725*, (Cambridge: Cambridge University Press, 2001); R. O. Crummey, *Aristocrats and Servitors: the Boyar Elite in Russia, 1613–1689* (Princeton, NJ: Princeton University Press 1983).

66 For an example of *mestnichestvo* in practice, see A. M. Kleimola, 'Boris Godunov and the Politics of Mestnichestvo', *Slavonic and East European Review* 53 (132) (1975), 355–369. In the eighteenth century, Peter I substituted a Table of Ranks for the old *mestnichestno* that emphasized ability and accomplishment, but nevertheless family rank continued to determine access to offices. From the beginning of Peter's reign to the end of the eighteenth century, virtually all significant appointments to high position can be traced to two kinship networks. Dixon, *Modernisation*, 137.

67 Thus in December 1921, a party conference decided to require secretaries of provinces (Gubkom secretaries) to have been party members before February 1917. But a shortage of personnel complicated the idea. By March 1922, only 73% of them had been pre-October members, and at that time there was discussion about softening the requirement from membership before the February 1917 revolution to before October 1917. April 1923 saw another call to enforce the qualification, but by May 1924, the percentage had fallen to 68%. See *Dvenadtsatyi s"ezd RKP(b), 17–25 aprelia 1923 goda. Stenograficheskii otchet (Moscow: Polizdat 1960), 705, 790, 802; Odinnadtsatyi s"ezd RKP(b), mart-aprel' 1922 goda. Stenograficheskii otchet* (Moscow: Polizdat 1961), 49–50, 555, 659; *Trinadtsatyi s"ezd RKP(b), Mai 1924 goda. Stenograficheskii otchet* (Moscow: Polizdat 1963), 118.

68 These practices are discussed in detail in J. Arch Getty, *Practicing Stalinism: Bolsheviks, Boyars, and the Persistence of Tradition* (New Haven, CT: Yale University Press, 2013), Chapters 3 and 4.

Nadezhda Mandelshtam recalls how people came 'to behave like the boyars in medieval Russia who fought each other over their place at the Czar's table, always reserving to itself the final decision as to who should sit at the top.' 'They used the ancient system of *mestnichestvo* and itself named people to first places.'[69] In Soviet documents, regional party committees were often explicitly said to be run on the basis of '*mestnichestvo*', with calculations of precedence becoming part of rivalries between local Bolshevik notables.[70]

In ancient times, honour, as well as the fortunes of one's clan, would not permit accepting a position beneath one's rightful 'place' [*mesto*] and there were disputes about precedence. The same thing was true for Old Bolsheviks. If an Old Bolshevik received a position that his 'quality' did not permit, there were complaints from both his betters and his inferiors on both personal and corporate bases. It was common in the 1920s and even in the 1930s for a Bolshevik to indignantly reject an assignment he considered beneath his status. In 1922 and 1923, Lev Trotsky refused positions as Lenin's deputy at the Council of People's Commissars because he considered a position as 'deputy' to be beneath his station.[71] In a reflection of the power of this cultural tradition (more of which we will see later) Stalin noted that if party grandees declined to accept new positions, there was little the Central Committee could do about it.[72] As late as 1936, Stalin had to write politely to Genrikh Iagoda, recently removed as head of the NKVD police, to 'ask' [*proshu*] that he accept demotion to the post of Commissar of Communications.[73]

Old Bolsheviks were prima donnas, quick to take insult and defend their honour. They had a noble sense of pride that appears anachronistic among those who considered themselves the most modern and democratic. They postured, posed, and wrote florid letters about why their accomplishments and opinions were important, why they should not be subordinated to various persons or committees, or how they had been subjected to unbearable slights and unbearable insults from other comrades.

Mediating slights and insults that might have resulted in duels in an earlier age occupied the time of senior party bodies whose files are filled with accusations of personal insult, pique, complaint, and counter-complaint.[74] Comrade Malyshev made 'rude remarks' about Comrade Avanesov. What about the 'statement of Comrade Kaidanovskii that Comrade Mrachkovskii slandered

69 Nadezhda Mandelshtam, *Hope Against Hope: A Memoir* (New York: Atheneum, 1970), 346, and *Vospominaniia*, (Paris: YMCA Press, 1970), 366.

70 See, for example, a TsK report on the situation in Tula in RGASPI, f. 17, op. 11, d. 548, l. 184. A 1922 internal TsK report also used the word *mestnichestvo* to describe personal conflicts in Riazan, Simbirsk, Saratov, Astrakhan, and elsewhere. Ibid., 24.

71 *Dvenadtsatyi s"ezd*, 198–199.

72 Ibid., 198.

73 Stalin to Yagoda, September 26, 1936. RGASPI, f. 558, op. 11, d. 94, l. 131.

74 See RGASPI f. 613, op. 1, dd. 1–10. TsKK Presidium protocols, RGASPI, f. 613, op. 1, d. 2, ll. 58, 84; d. 14, l. 145; d. 30, l. 92; Izvestiia TsK VKP(b). no 1, January 1923, p. 75.

him?'[75] Comrade Smilga was obliged to take back his accusation against Iaroslavskii's remarks in his speech, while Iaroslavskii had to admit that his remarks about Smilga were 'too sharp'.[76] In 1920, Karl Radek 'exercised a total lack of care in passing around false information and making completely baseless accusations'.[77] In 1921, the Control Commission demanded 'written explanations' from Radek about his possible slander of Zinoviev in criticizing the latter's speech on the German Revolution.[78] Aleksandr Shliapnikov's comparison of the political police (GPU) with the tsarist Okhrana was taken as personal slander against GPU chief Dzherzhinskii and Shliapnikov was forced to apologize.[79]

Did the Bolsheviks realize what they were doing? Did they see the persistence of nobility, that they were taking over the social roles of nobles, complete with all the anachronistic petty concerns about honour and precedence?

Oddly enough, it would seem that they did not. They had simply and naturally stepped into an ancient elite culture. As far as we know from the public and private archival sources, nobody ever said anything like, 'wait a minute, look what we are doing!' Instead, wounded honour was taken seriously and found its way onto Politburo and Orgburo agendas alongside foreign policy, civil war strategy, and key personnel appointments. These high committees spent valuable time sorting out personal disputes. As the very second meeting of the newly formed Orgburo in 1919, in the heat of the civil war, the buro had to referee a 'personal conflict' between comrades Piliaev and Rapoport (neither of whom were particularly high ranking grandees), complete with reports and votes.[80] In 1921, the Orgburo had to 'express confidence' in a group of party workers who felt 'morally insulted' at the indignity of being searched on a train.[81]

To handle the volume of cases of wounded and infringed honour, in 1920 the Central Committee created a separate department, the Conflict Subdepartment of the Organizational Dept to deal with personal accusations. The Conflict Subdepartment was immediately swamped by a heavy workload.[82] One of the official reasons for the creation of the Central Control Commission (TsKK) the following year was 'combatting ... infringement of comradely relations in the party, dissemination of unfounded and unsubstantiated rumours and insinuations which bring disgrace ... to individual members'.[83]

Patronage politics was the métier of elite political life in old Russia. Each noble boyar stood at the apex of a network of clients, relatives, and supporters who protected and promoted each other; loyalty was given to those above and

75 TsKK Presidium protocol, 29 April 1921. RGASPI, f. 613, op. 1, d. 2, ll. 58, 84.
76 TsKK Presidium protocols, RGASPI, f. 613, op. 1, d. 14, l. 145.
77 TsKK Presidium protocol 19 July 1921. RGASPI, f. 613, op. 1, d. 2. l. 137.
78 TsKK Presidium protocol. RGASPI, f. 613, op. 1, d. 13. l. 77.
79 TsKK decision of 31 Oct 1923. RGASPI, f. 613, op. 1, d. 13, l. 16.
80 Orgburo protocol 24 January 1919. RGASPI, f. 17, op. 112, d. 1, l. 5.
81 Orgburo protocol of 15 October 1920. RGASPI, f. 17, op. 112, d. 78, l. 4.
82 RGASPI, f. 17, op. 11, d. 505, l. 31.
83 Graeme Gill, *The Origins of the Stalinist Political System* (Cambridge: Cambridge University Press, 1990), 84.

protection to those below at all levels of the clan. In the times before ideology (and even after), politics largely consisted of competition, intrigue, and manoeuvre with other clans.[84]

Students of medieval and imperial Russia have shown that membership in a client group, whether based on family clan connections or sworn loyalty, was much more important than formal status or function or position.[85]

> Successive outer rings were composed of client groups and/or other constituencies of the members of inner rings. In pre-Petrine times, these groups were primarily clan and family groups; later, they were socio-economic groupings; eventually, in modern times, they were to become bureaucratic and other interest groups.[86]

Later, despite Catherine the Great's love for Enlightenment rational law, 'people continued to organize themselves in patronage groups and to make these groups the prime focus of their activity'.[87] At the beginning of the eighteenth century, Nikita Panin observed, 'government business was determined by the influence of individuals rather than by the power of state institutions'.[88]

Scholars have noticed the continuities in practice from imperial to Soviet times. After 1917,

> clientelism not only continued, but also enjoyed a very significant renaissance that had enormous political implications … The office of governor represents an early analogue of the later Soviet regional party secretaries who, in fact, more completely emulate the old tsarist notion of *khoziain* of the province with their relative independence, control of appointment power and enormous and highly personalized executive authority.[89]

Like nobles everywhere, the Old Bolsheviks after the revolution organized themselves into networks of clients centred around a senior patron.[90] These 'family circles', or 'clans' are prominent in the literature.[91] Both

84 Keenan, 'Muscovite Political Folkways', 156.

85 Kollmann, *By Honor Bound*, xiii, 296; Kollmann, *Kinship and Politics.*

86 Keenan, 'Muscovite Political Folkways', 140.

87 David Ransel, 'Character and Style of Patron-Client Relations in Russia', in *Klientelsysteme im Europa der Fruhen Neuzeit*, edited by Antoni Maczak and Elisabeth Mueller-Luckner (Munich: Oldenbourg, 1988), 216. See also Daniel T. Orlovsky, 'Political Clientelism in Russia: the Historical Perspective', in *Leadership Selection and Patron-Client Relations in the USSR and Yugoslavia*, edited by T. H. Rigby, and Bogdan Harasymiw (London: Allen and Unwin, 1983), 177–179.

88 Ransel, 'Patron-Client', 216, 221.

89 Daniel T. Orlovsky, 'Political Clientelism in Russia: the Historical Perspective', 187, 189.

90 These 'family circles' were first described by Merle Fainsod in his classic *Smolensk Under Soviet Rule* (Cambridge, MA: Harvard University Press, 1958).

91 See Gerald Easter, *Reconstructing the State: Personal Networks and Elite Identity in Soviet Russia* (Cambridge, New York: Cambridge University Press, 2000);

pre-revolutionary noble patron-client and Old Bolshevik clan members protected and promoted each other.[92] They depended on the senior patron for political protection at court and elsewhere, and as a source of office-holding. Clan members protected each other and their chief, while advancing the interests of the group at the expense of other circles. Eventually, Old Bolshevik networks came to control virtually every aspect of life in their provinces: budgets, industry, agriculture, education, police and judiciary, and the press. They were indeed princes of their provinces.

The literature is also full of descriptions of court life under Stalin where senior Old Bolshevik nobles – each of whom stood at the head of a network of 'his people' – jockeyed for position in a constant intrigue that could and did sometimes end in the deaths of those nobles who lost the contest or fell out of favour. They, along with their clients, were exiled or demonstrably killed together as a group, with the winning group taking the spoils. Malenkov and Beria annihilating their rival Zhdanov's clan in the Leningrad Affair of 1948–49 is a good example.[93]

When they moved from province to province, powerful Bolshevik nobles brought their entourages with them. When I. P. Rumiantsev moved from the Vladimir party organization to Smolensk in 1929, he brought with him a 'Vladimir group'. When A. K. Lepa was transferred from Uzbekistan to Tataria in 1933, he brought his 'Tashkent tail'.[94] In 1934, B. P. Sheboldaev brought with him from Saratov to the Azov-Black Sea the 'Saratov Brothers in Law', consisting of two dozen Sheboldaev loyalists, who like all tail members, each imported their own entourages.[95]

J. Arch Getty, *Origins of the Great Purges: the Soviet Communist Party Reconsidered, 1933–1938* (Cambridge, New York: Cambridge University Press, 1985); James R. Harris, *The Great Urals: Regionalism and the Evolution of the Soviet System* (Ithaca, NY, Cornell University Press 1999); Merle Fainsod, *How Russia is Ruled* (Russian Research Center Studies 11) (Cambridge, MA: Harvard University Press, 1967).

92 With full recognition of the narrow specificity of the term to denote kinship, I shall refer to them as 'clans' because as I show elsewhere, they had many of the characteristics of Russian political clans going back centuries: patriarchal systems of authority, personalized rather than institutional politics, collective responsibility and *krugovaia poruka*. On pre-Soviet continuities, see Keenan, 'Muscovite Political Folkways'; Robert V. Daniels, 'Russian Political Culture and the Post-Revolutionary Impasse', *Russian Review* 46(2) (1987), 169; Geoffrey Hosking. 'Patronage and the Russian State', *Slavonic and East European Review* 78(2), 301–320. Kenneth Jowitt, *New World Disorder: the Leninist Extinction* (Berkeley, CA: University of California Press, 1992); Ransel, 'Patron-Client Relations', 211–231. Moreover, the word was used often by contemporaries in the Stalin period and later to describe patron-client political circles. It is especially common today to describe the family circles below Putin.

93 For the Malenkov/Zhdanov rivalry, see Jonathan Harris, *The Split in Stalin's Secretariat, 1939–1948* (New York: Lexington Books, 2008).

94 Protokoly i Stenogramma XVII Tatarskoi oblastnoi konferentsii VKP(b). 10–15 iuniia 1937g. RGASPI f. 17, op. 21, d. 4248, l. 140.

95 RGASPI, f. 17, op. 21, d. 2214, ll. 97ob, 98.

At lower levels, politicians made judgements about each other based on perceptions of whether a person was 'close to' [*blizkii*] or 'connected with' [*sviazan*] a higher-up, and these words appear frequently in official and unofficial documents. When Radzivilovskii arrived in Ivanovo as the new NKVD chief in 1938, his rank as Senior Major of State Security was in itself not enough to establish his authority. Existing staff had to establish that Radzivilovskii was a *blizkii* of Kaganovich, who in turn was close to Stalin; he therefore must be obeyed. Even when a new appointee was manifestly unqualified, proximity to patron gave him power and compelled obedience. In 1937 a physical education instructor was sent to Ivanovo to head the province NKVD Secret Political Department. The fact that he was connected to N. I. Ezhov, who knew him personally, was enough to establish his authority, despite his laughable lack of qualifications.[96]

So why clientelism? It was powerfully Russian and to a great extent – consciously or not – elements of Russian political culture. From an anthropological point of view, it would be surprising if Bolsheviks (and Russians) in 1917 suddenly transformed themselves completely stepping out of their thousand-year-old culture. We should not leap to the conclusion that they could dispense with these practices, or chose to do so, just because of through lack of obvious alternatives. Richard Pipes found it absurd and 'inconceivable that on a single day, October 25, 1917, the course of a thousand-year-old history of a vast and populous country could undergo complete transformation'.[97]

Did the Bolsheviks know what they were doing when they organized themselves into patronage clans; did they recognize what seems to us to be an obvious persistence? Yes and no. At the beginning, almost certainly they did not. As in the case of preserving Lenin's body in a mausoleum, it is a matter of time and consciousness. Short-term recognition would differ from that of the longer term. For the Bolsheviks in the beginning, in the absence of a reliable governing structure, it was about personal trust and proximity to authoritative persons in an almost desperate attempt somehow to govern. The Bolsheviks' external and private internal texts lead one to believe that they would be appalled and insulted at the very idea that they were reconstituting ancient clans.

But in a longer term, there would come a recognition of the persistence of political practices, along with a desire to change them. Stalin led the way here. By the end of the 1920s, he had come to the conclusion that clientelism precluded selecting the right personnel for the right job and had become dysfunctional to an industrializing society. He was explicit about its ancient lineage and bemoaned it as non-party. At the November 1927 Central Committee plenum, he said:

> Both in the center and in the localities, decisions are frequently made in a familial way, as in the home, so to speak … Ivan Ivanovich, a member of

96 Mikhail Shreider, *Zapiski chekista* (Moscow: Vozrashchenie, 1995), 45, 54.
97 Richard Pipes, *Russia under the Bolshevik Regime* (New York: Knopf, 1993), 503.

> the leadership group of such and such an organization has made a terrible mistake and made a mess of things. But Ivan Fedorovich does not want to criticize him, to expose his mistakes ... Decorous and calm. Peace and goodwill.[98]

In October 1931, Stalin told the Orgburo,

> I have the impression that there are no real party organizations in the Transcaucasus. There are chiefs and gangs. [*atamanshchina*] If someone gets promoted to a post, do you think it's because of his qualifications? In most cases, it's not. His only value is whose person is he, who will he support. Is that a party? No, it's a system of chieftains, not a party organization. Whose person is he? Who will he support? Who will he fight? Who will he drink with? Who will he visit as a guest? ... That's a fact ... If you pick people that way, then it will mess you up. It's no good. It's a chieftain system, completely without a Bolshevik approach to picking people ... It's a gang.[99]

In 1934, he referred to provincial Old Bolshevik chiefs as 'feudal princes' who felt that central decisions 'were not written for them, but for fools'. Because of their glorious revolutionary services, 'these conceited bigwigs think that they are irreplaceable, and that they can violate the decisions of the leading bodies with impunity'.[100] He complained that many of them 'had built themselves grandiose dacha-palaces of 15–20 or more rooms, where they luxuriated and frittered away the peoples' money, thus demonstrating their complete dissipation (*razlozhenie*) and degeneration (*pererozhdenie*)'.[101]

There is little doubt that between 1934 and 1939, Stalin waged war on the Old Bolshevik clans.[102] As the pattern of arrests, the texts of interrogations, and explicit statements from Moscow all show, much of the Great Terror of

98 I. V. Stalin, *Sochineniia v. 10*, 329–333. My thanks to James Harris for pointing this out to me. Stalin's reference to 'as in the home' is significant. Boris Mironov wrote that the Stalin regime 'did not frighten the masses, nor did they protest it; rather it suited them because from childhood they had grown accustomed to authoritarian relations and simply knew nothing else'. B. N. Mironov. 'Peasant Popular Culture and the Origins of Soviet Authoritarianism', in *Cultures in Flux: Lower-Class Values, Practices, and Resistance in Late Imperial Russia*, edited by Stephen P. Frank, and Mark D. Steinberg (Princeton, NJ: Princeton University Press 1994), 72.

99 RGASPI, f. 558, op. 11, d. 132, ll. 90–99. Actually, at this time it was a very Bolshevik approach to picking people.

100 Stalin to the 17th Party Congress, XVII s"ezd Vsesoiuznoi Kommunisticheskoi Partii (b), Stenograficheskii otchet (Moscow: Partizdat, 1934), 33, 34–35.

101 'O dachakh otvetstvennykh rabotnikov', Politburo resolution, drafted by Stalin, of 9 February 1938. RGASPI, f. 17, op. 3, d. 995, l. 21. The resolution established a limit of '7–8 average-sized rooms' for personal dachas. Dachas larger than that were to be confiscated.

102 For the details see Getty, *Practicing Stalinism*, Chapters 6–8.

the elite was directed against the clans. Stalin sought to behead, uproot, and destroy them. But whether his intention was to destroy these particular noble clans whose oligarchic outlook blocked his personal power, or to destroy 'clanness' in general in favour of a more modern personnel system, he failed.

It was clear to Stalin, as it is to most students today, that modern technological-industrial societies function best with some kind of meritocracy, some kind of personnel system based on qualifications and expertise. Patronage and clan became distinctly dysfunctional in the Soviet Union. Yet, they persisted, albeit in modified form. When Stalin launched his lethal war against the Old Bolshevik clans, he couldn't destroy clan-as-culture, but his attack did have consequences. After the terror, clans continued to dominate politics but they would never again have the same noble character, and clan leaders would never again have the same prestige and power.

What persisted here was a culture/structure of personal and oligarchic clan politics that trumped meritocracy or bureaucracy and was powerful enough to survive Stalin's terror, industrialization, a world war, and the fall of communism. Event and policy did change patronage culture along the way. The 1917 revolution replaced blood lines with revolutionary service as a marker of power. The 'Stalin Revolution' of the 1930s created a new 'red intelligentsia' of plebeians promoted to leading positions. A new premium was placed on technical competence and qualifications more than loyalty to patron, a new emphasis that would grow in subsequent decades with the expansion of education and of new positions to fill in industry. But even after a terror against clans, a modified culture of patronage endured in politics at the top. Even as Stalin fought against clanness, he used his clan to rule.[103] When he fostered the creation of rational ministries in the 1940s, he was careful to put one of his clients at the helm of each. Later, even with the growth of meritocracy, politics was still a matter for patrons and clients.

Elite clans and patronage politics were and are embedded in Russian political culture. They were part of the 'deep structures' of Russian history described by Edward Keenan, and as Robert Daniels showed in extrapolating from Keenan's theory, they persisted into the Soviet period and, as we now know, beyond.

It was inescapable. In the beginning, neither Stalin, his regional party leaders, nor his successors *chose* patrimonial clan rule. There were no alternative models to contemplate, and no ability to contemplate them. For many centuries, patrimony had been as much a part of Russia as speaking the Russian language. Metaphorically, patrimonialism and patronage were indeed the language of politics, and there was no choice but to speak it. In their political practice, Stalin's successors from Khrushchev to Brezhnev would speak dialects of it, which were intelligible to the elite and the population. When Gorbachev tried to democratize the understanding of the state and the nature of political

103 T. H. Rigby. 'Was Stalin a Disloyal Patron?', *Soviet Studies* 38 (1986), 311–324.

practice, he might as well have been speaking Swahili. Nobody understood him, and the powerful persisting culture defeated him.

Putin returned to the familiar language, and he endures. At this writing, nearly every analysis of Putin's power and government discusses competing clans mediated by a tsar-figure. In Putin's Russia, the leaderships of ministries and committees pass from person to person, from favourite to favourite, and whether it's a bank, a security service, or an oil company, it is entirely possible that the leader has absolutely no specialized qualification for heading a given institution except for loyalty to Putin. They are today's versions of Ezhov's unqualified but connected physical education instructors writ large.

What makes the noble roles example different from the mausoleum example is culture's power to resist change. The body-event of the mausoleum referenced and changed the underlying culture. But in the case of noble social roles, while meritocracy did impact the underlying culture of social roles, that culture turned out to be highly resistant, just like Sewell's dockworkers. Albeit with reduced power and changes in staffing, 'deep structures' resisted Stalin's attempts to destroy or replace them and they persisted for decades.

*****

It seems insufficient to explain persistence with blanket statements about great retreats, the historical revenge of Muscovy, or Stalin's psychology creating an entire culture. It would appear that we could use a conceptual apparatus that approaches the underlying motors of persistence, that reflects the interaction of event, agency, and cultural structure, one that problematizes rather than simplifies. The complicated multivalent and mutually influencing structural relation between event and cultural structure could offer one possibility. Within the supposed watersheds there are multiple happenings and events, often subjectively defined by us as historians. And they relate to multiple, plural cultures in complicated and changing ways. And whether or not we use structuralist event-culture approaches or not, we need to look at each micro-event and its cultural partner-reference because each case is different.

2 How revolutionary was revolutionary justice?

Legal culture in Russia across the revolutionary divide

Matthew Rendle

On 24 November 1917, the Bolsheviks published their vision for a new justice system. Abolishing all existing courts, they established local (later people's) courts for crimes such as murder, theft, and civil disputes, and revolutionary tribunals to combat threatening 'counter-revolutionary' crimes such as plots, revolts, and sabotage. Both courts were instructed to rely on existing laws only insofar as they did not contradict new decrees or party programmes, and to use revolutionary consciousness to reach a verdict.[1] Through this and subsequent decrees, the Bolsheviks intended to create a new legal culture for the revolutionary state.

The concept of legal culture is a contested one among scholars, but it originated from a desire to move the understanding of law away from a narrow focus on 'the set of rules or norms, written or unwritten, about right and wrong behaviour, duties and rights' to a broader 'social study' of law that incorporated the social and legal forces that make law, the structures and rules of law itself, and the impact of law on wider behaviour.[2] This includes 'what people think about law, lawyers and the legal order' and 'ideas, attitudes, opinions and expectations with regard to the legal system'.[3] This broad coverage, as critics have pointed out, undermines legal culture as an analytical and comparative tool, but it retains value as a means of 'assessing important but indeterminate matters', namely, the 'general environment of thought, belief, practices and institutions' within which law existed.[4] By this definition,

1 *Istoriia zakonodatel'stva SSSR i RSFSR po ugolovnom protsessu i organizatsii suda i prokuratury* (Moscow, 1955), 31–32.
2 Lawrence Friedman, *The Legal System: A Social Science Perspective* (New York: Russell Sage Foundation, 1975), 2–3.
3 Lawrence Friedman, 'The Place of Legal Culture in the Sociology of Law', in *Law and Sociology*, edited by M. Freeman (Oxford: Oxford University Press, 2006), 189.
4 Roger Cotterrell, *Law, Culture and Society: Legal Ideas in the Mirror of Social Theory* (Aldershot: Ashgate, 2006), 83, 88. Also David Nelken, 'Defining and Using the Concept of Legal Culture', in *Comparative Law: A Handbook*, edited by E. Örücü and D. Nelken (Oxford: Hart Publishing, 2007), 109–132; and Susan Silbey, 'Legal Cultures and Cultures of Legality', in *Handbook of Cultural Sociology*, edited by J. Hall, L. Grindstaff and M.-C. Lo (Abingdon: Routledge, 2010), 470–479.

changing Russia's legal culture encapsulated Bolshevik ambitions; they did not simply want to alter laws, they wanted to change the relationship between law and the state, and how individuals thought about the legal system and their interactions with it.

Accordingly, Bolshevik legal theorists paid little attention initially to formal laws and punishments. Instead, they focused on repositioning the relationship between law and society. Where the legal system had been an oppressive arm of the exploitative, bourgeois state, it would now support the working classes, protect them from enemies, and form the foundation of a new, proletarian state. It would achieve this through judges who no longer required legal training, being chosen instead by popularly-elected soviets, and through mass involvement in the legal process (ordinary people serving in place of lawyers and the audience having a say in sentencing). Law would no longer serve to repress the people, because the legal system would be inseparable from society. Precise definitions of crimes and punishments were unnecessary since the working classes were fully capable of deciding what was a crime and an appropriate level of punishment. This participation would educate people in the mentality and behaviour expected of a conscientious soviet citizen. The Bolsheviks saw this as 'revolutionary justice'; a radically different legal culture to reflect and serve the Russian Revolution.

But how revolutionary was this new system of revolutionary justice? Bolsheviks painted a picture of polar opposites: legal culture in the oppressive tsarist state versus legal culture in a liberated proletarian state.[5] P. I. Stuchka, legal theorist and Commissar of Justice in 1918, boasted in 1919 that the revolution had cast all 16 volumes of the code of laws of the Russian empire on the bonfire, along with the empire itself. He then argued in 1922 that the 'revolution in law' had been even more 'revolutionary' in deeds than words. He pointed out that both revolutionary courts had been formed and former laws abolished before decrees had officially sanctioned either act.[6] The Bolsheviks' enemies agreed, albeit negatively rather than positively, arguing that elected judges and revolutionary consciousness fostered lawlessness not legal order.[7] This sense of October 1917 as a dividing line was subsequently adopted by many legal historians, whether in Russia or the West.[8]

5 e.g. N. Krylenko, *Sudoustroistvo RSFSR (lektsii po teorii i istorii sudoustroistvo)* (Moscow, 1923); and Ia. Berman, *Ocherki po istorii sudoustroistva RSFSR* (Moscow, 1924).

6 P. Stuchka, 'Proletarian Law (1919)', in *P. I. Stuchka: Selected Writings on Soviet Law and Marxism*, edited by R. Sharlet, P. Maggs, and P. Beirne (Armonk: M. E. Sharpe, 1988), 11; P. Stuchka, 'Five Years of Revolution in Law (1922)', in *Bolshevik Visions*, edited by W. Rosenberg (2nd edition, 2 volumes, Ann Arbor, MI: University of Michigan, 1990), I, 190.

7 See S. V-ii, *Revoliutsionnyi tribunal (Krasnyi sud)* (Rostov na Donu, 1919); and S. Kobiakov, '"Krasnyi sud": Vpechatleniia zashchitnika v revoliutsionnykh tribunalakh', *Arkhiv Russkoi revoliutsii* 7 (1922), 246–275.

8 For e.g., M. Kozhevnikov, *Istoriia sovetskogo suda 1917–1956 gody* (Moscow: Gosudarstvennoe izdatel'stvo iuridicheskoi literatury, 1957); Samuel Kucherov,

Yet at the end of his article in 1922, Stuchka cast doubt on the durability of the revolutionary changes he had earlier described. The New Economic Policy (NEP) in 1921 marked a retreat towards capitalism in many respects, which coincided with and facilitated the growing complexity of legal organs and procedure, culminating in the publication of new law codes in 1922. Stuchka denied this was a return to the pre-1917 system, instead talking of a 'strictly controlled retreat' to preserve the 'victorious' revolution, whilst urging the revolution in law to continue to safeguard against a return to the past. But these new developments had undoubtedly drawn on elements of the past and, as Stuchka himself had admitted in 1919, 'every borrowing leads to conscious or unconscious counter-revolution'.[9]

The idea of a clear break in 1917 has also been questioned subsequently, with some scholars noting similarities between the Soviet legal system and its tsarist predecessor, from the position and politicization of law in an authoritarian state, to statutes, lawyers, and the role of tradition.[10] There are, though, few systematic studies,[11] and none of these were interested in broader legal culture or able to take advantage of recent works that have used archives to explore the everyday activities of courts on either side of 1917.[12] They do, however, also suggest the importance of elements of continuity amid major

The Organs of Soviet Administration of Justice (Leiden: Brill, 1970); John Hazard, *Settling Disputes in Soviet Society* (New York: Columbia University Press, 1960); Richard Pipes, *Legalised Lawlessness: Soviet Revolutionary Justice* (London: Alliance Publishers for the Institute for European Defence & Strategic Studies, 1986); and V. Portnov and M. Slavin, *Stanovlenie pravosudiia Sovetskoi Rossii (1917–1922 gg.)* (Moscow, 1990).

9 Stuchka, 'Five Years', 195; Stuchka, 'Proletarian Law', 15.

10 Harold Berman, *Justice in the USSR* (Cambridge, MA: Harvard University Press, 1963), 226–266; E. Johnson, *An Introduction to the Soviet Legal System* (London: Methuen & Co, 1969), 22–24; V. Bukov, *Ot Rossiiskogo suda prisiazhnykh k proletarskomu pravosudiiu: U istokov totalitarizma* (Moscow, 1997) and William Butler, *Russian Law* (3rd edition, Oxford: Oxford University Press, 2009), 34–35.

11 John Hazard, 'Law and Tradition in the New Russia', *Oxford Slavonic Papers* 4 (1953), 132–150; Nicholas Timasheff, 'The Impact of the Penal Law of Imperial Russia on Soviet Penal Law', *American Slavic and East European Review* 12(4) (1953), 441–462; G. van den Berg, 'Elements of Continuity in Soviet Constitutional Law', in *Russian Law*, edited by William Butler (Leyden: A. W. Sijthoff, 1977), 215–234; and H. Oda, 'The Emergence of *Pravovoe gosudarstvo (Rechtsstaat)* in Russia', *Review of Central and East European Law* 25(3) (1999), 373–434.

12 In English, see Peter Solomon, *Soviet Criminal Justice under Stalin* (Cambridge: Cambridge University Press, 1996); Stephen Frank, *Crime, Cultural Conflict, and Justice in Rural Russia, 1856–1914* (Berkeley, CA: University of California Press, 1999); Jane Burbank, *Russian Peasants Go To Court: Legal Culture in the Countryside, 1905–1917* (Bloomington and Indianapolis, IN: Indiana University Press, 2004); Corinne Gaudin, *Ruling Peasants: Village and State in Late Imperial Russia* (DeKalb, IL: Northern Illinois University Press, 2007); and Tracy McDonald, *Face to the Village: The Riazan Countryside under Soviet Rule, 1921–1930* (Toronto: University of Toronto Press, 2011).

change. Even a recent work championing the 'revolutionary' impact of Soviet law on Western law admitted that for all its innovation, Soviet law remained within the legal tradition inherited by the new government. Indeed, it was this continuity, the author speculated, that may have enabled Soviet law to pose a 'potent' challenge to Western law; it was similar enough to be recognizable and acceptable, yet sufficiently innovative to push Western law in 'uncharted directions'.[13]

Whilst not subscribing to the innovative nature of Soviet law in the same way or examining its impact on the West, this study argues that it was impossible to discard all former laws, institutions, and practices, and that there was not just continuity but that elements of this continuity both influenced and constrained Bolshevik policies. Through an exploration of two key elements of Bolshevik legal culture – the relationship between statutory law and revolutionary consciousness, and society's relationship with the courtroom – it makes two related arguments. On the one hand, the Bolsheviks recognized continuity was as important as change in enabling legal institutions to project state power and engage with the population, and thus consciously incorporated elements of existing legal culture into their new legal system. On the other, the Bolsheviks were unable to implement some changes (and retreated from others) for the same reasons, finding their actions constrained by the persistence of former practices and beliefs. As in other spheres, the Bolsheviks' revolutionary dreams often had to take a back seat to the realities of a fledgling state struggling to survive.

Revolutionary consciousness versus statutory law

Revolutionary justice attempted an uneasy balancing act between the new and the existing from the start with respect to statutory (or written) law. An early draft of the November 1917 decree proposed to abolish the laws of 'overthrown governments',[14] but, as noted, the final version avoided this; instead, courts could use them as long as they did not contradict new decrees, socialist party programmes, or revolutionary consciousness (*soznanie*). The continued use of tsarist-era laws was reaffirmed in the second decree on courts on 7 March 1918 and was not mentioned in the third decree on 20 July. It was not until 30 November 1918 that new regulations on people's courts explicitly prohibited the use of former laws, instructing courts to rely solely on new decrees and 'socialist legal consciousness'.[15]

Apparently, opposition to the idea of 'lawlessness' from within the Bolshevik party and the Central Executive Committee of the Congress of Soviets

13 John Quigley, *Soviet Legal Innovation and the Law of the Western World* (Cambridge: Cambridge University Press, 2007), 57–58.

14 This 'draft' was published without any commentary at the end of the second volume of the Commissariat of Justice's *Materialy Narodnogo Komissariata Iustitsii* [hereafter *Materialy*] 2 (1918), 103–104.

15 *Istoriia zakonodatel'stva*, 32–33, 47, 68.

(VTsIK) forced initial compromises. Opponents wanted new laws in place before old ones were abolished, forcing a 'softening' of the words.[16] But there were practical benefits. The November 1917 decree was only the start of a long process. In Moscow province, for instance, some *uezd* (district) authorities were still discussing the importance of new courts in establishing Bolshevik power and engaging the masses in mid-December, whilst a meeting of *uezd* commissars in early January revealed that a provincial department of justice was still being established, new courts were still needed in towns and *volosti* (parish), and instructions had to be issued. To hasten the process, commissars focused on how existing courts and personnel could be adapted and utilized, yet by April 1918 only half of the province's *uezdy* had a court structure along the lines proposed in November.[17] Other reports and memoirs make it clear that Moscow was far from atypical. Many remote areas took longer, former courts still existed well into 1918, and their administrative structure, cases, and personnel were often adopted by new courts. Against this background, preserving existing laws ensured a degree of legitimacy for new courts and provided guidance for those working in them. Yet justice officials soon became concerned that these courts were insufficiently revolutionary; they were concentrating on the wrong crimes, and dispensing incorrect and lenient sentences given the threats facing the revolution.[18] The state needed to draw a clearer line between revolutionary justice and tsarist-era practices, and emphasizing 'revolutionary' or 'socialist' consciousness over statutory law seemed to offer a quick way to a sharp break.

The Bolsheviks did not define 'revolutionary consciousness', but seem to have meant the experiences, views, and intuition of the ordinary, 'class conscious' workers and peasants who had made the revolution and now supposedly staffed the judicial system; these groups would be aware of their class interests, the interests of the revolution, and thus the interests of the Bolsheviks who saw themselves as the legitimate representatives of the revolution. But, as one scholar noted, these experiences and views, and the understanding of justice emerging from them, could not have come solely from the revolution. People do not entirely reshape their views overnight.[19] Thus, rather than being completely new, revolutionary consciousness was entwined with popular understandings of law and justice that had existed for centuries, or in other words, was a revolutionary version of longstanding elements of customary law (that is, law derived from customs and practices rather than from written statutes).

16 Stuchka, 'Five Years', 192–193. See also O. Maksimova, *Zakonotvorchestvo v sovetskoi Rossii v 1917–1922 godakh* (Moscow, 2011), 75–76.

17 Gosudarstvennyi arkhiv Rossiiskoi Federatsii (GARF), f. R-393, op. 3, d. 217, ll. 168ob–169 (protocol of Kolomenskii soviet, 14 December 1917), 65–65ob (protocol of meeting, 2–3 January 1918); and d. 216, ll. 300–303 (protocol of meeting, 18 January 1918), 333–334 (report, after 2 April 1918).

18 See, e.g. the debates at the 1st All-Russian Congress of Justice Officials in Moscow on 21–25 April 1918, which were published in *Materialy* 1 (1918).

19 Hazard, 'Law', 137.

After all, the tsarist legal system was itself far from objective. A recent study on early modern Russia has emphasized that judges made their decisions partly by following statutory law and official state directives, and partly by being sensitive to local community norms and opinions.[20] After 1864, Russia moved towards a western-style system; a coherent set of laws enforced through a tightly-regulated system of independent public courts staffed by legally-educated and trained professionals alongside a jury, with the judge mediating between the prosecution and the defence.[21] Yet subjective factors – the circumstances of individual cases, the characters and consciousness of those involved in the case, and local customs – continued to play an important role.

Juries were primarily composed of peasants, particularly beyond St Petersburg and Moscow, or the urban working and lower middle classes, and almost half were illiterate. They usually reached verdicts on the basis of accepted 'norms' of behaviour (seemingly influenced more by custom, personal circumstances and experiences, press accounts of crime, and even crime fiction than by official statutes), sympathy for the accused, suspicion of the prosecution, and particular beliefs and expectations in the legal system, not least the misguided belief that the state would impose harsher penalties on the accused than it did. The arguments of lawyers only encouraged this in many trials as lawyers urged jurors to follow their consciences, and often privileged theatricality and style over substance and legal arguments.[22]

Moreover, the reformed tsarist legal system utilized customary law officially in some areas before 1917. On the one hand, courts presided over by justices of the peace existed in urban areas, which dealt quickly and informally with common, petty crimes (such as theft) and civil disputes. Applying the perceived fairness of custom to the authority of statutes, they aimed to make the legal process understandable and desirable.[23] On the other hand, district or *volost'* courts existed in the countryside, which were run by peasants with

20 Nancy Kollmann, *Crime and Punishment in Early Modern Russia* (Cambridge: Cambridge University Press, 2012).

21 See Samuel Kucherov, *Courts, Lawyers and Trials under the Last Three Tsars* (New York: F. A. Praeger, 1953); Richard Wortman, *The Development of a Russian Legal Consciousness* (Chicago, IL: University of Chicago Press, 1976); William Wagner, 'Tsarist Legal Policies at the End of the Nineteenth Century: A Study in Inconsistencies', *Slavonic and East European Review* 54(3) (1976), 371–394; and Jörg Baberowski, 'Law, the Judicial System and the Legal Profession', in *The Cambridge History of Russia. Volume II: Imperial Russia, 1689–1917*, edited by D. Lieven (Cambridge: Cambridge University Press, 2006), 344–368.

22 John Atwell, 'The Russian Jury', *Slavonic and East European Review* 53(130) (1975), 55–57; A. Afanas'ev, 'Jurors and Jury Trials in Imperial Russia, 1866–1885', in *Russia's Great Reforms, 1855–1881*, edited by B. Eklof, J. Bushnell, and L. Zakharova (Bloomington, IN: Indiana University Press, 1994), 214–230; Louise McReynolds, *Murder Most Russian: True Crime and Punishment in Late Imperial Russia* (Ithaca, NY: Cornell University Press, 2013), 13, 37, 45, 92–140, 201–234.

23 Joan Neuberger, 'Popular Legal Cultures: The St Petersburg *Mirovoi sud*', in *Russia's Great Reforms*, 231–246.

verdicts dispensed by three to four elected peasant judges (who did not require previous legal experience). No lawyers or jury were present, but peasants tended to see the panel of local figures who served as judges as a 'jury'. Judges were told to decide cases 'according to conscience, on the basis of evidence contained in the case'; criminal cases tended to pay more attention to written statutes, whereas civil cases relied more on custom. Judges took the character and reputations of those involved seriously, including witnesses, assigning greater weight to those deemed honest, law-abiding, and hard-working, with village observations, opinions, and rumours all playing a role. The sincerity of any repentance on the part of the defendant was also important in influencing the final judgement. All this meant that different outcomes were possible for similar crimes, where factors such as drunkenness could be viewed as a mitigating or an aggravating factor depending on the individual defendant or judge.[24] It also meant that, more broadly, crime was not considered separate from the personality and life of the accused.

It would be surprising if these traditions of assessing cases according to conscience did not inform revolutionary consciousness, particularly given a transition process that saw many *volost'* courts simply renamed as people's courts, and the fact that judges were often far from the class-conscious, Bolshevik-sympathizing figures that the Bolsheviks had intended. There has been no prosopographical analysis of judges after October 1917 beyond general characteristics: most were peasants; the majority only had rudimentary education; very few had any legal education; and whilst judges in provincial courts were usually party members, this number was much lower locally.[25] The most politicized courts were revolutionary tribunals. In late 1920, a report on tribunals across the railway network noted that all tribunal chairmen should have three years experience of party work. Of the 23 tribunals surveyed, only two failed to meet these criteria.[26] Other tribunals, however, did not fare so well; almost all judges were party members, but usually recent recruits, joining after the October Revolution. Most were in their mid-twenties to mid-thirties, from peasant backgrounds and had only basic education. For the vast majority, their only experience of legal work had come since their appointment to the tribunal.[27] Party membership, moreover, was no guarantee

24 Burbank, *Russian Peasants*, 166–179, 188–195, 251–257; Gaudin, *Ruling Peasants*, 93–94, 99–101, 116; Frank, *Crime*, 40–44, 212–213.

25 Kozhevnikov, *Istoriia*, 185–186. A similar picture continued into the 1920s; see, e.g. G. Kamelova and V. Maiorov, *Sovetskaia pravookhranitel'naia sistema Urala v period ee stanovleniia (1921–1929 gg.)* (Cheliabinsk, 2010), 102–141; and McDonald, *Face to the Village*, 89–90.

26 GARF, f. A-353, op. 3, d. 40, l. 130ob (undated report on railway tribunals prior to 1 July 1920).

27 This discussion is based on research in various provincial personnel folders held by the Supreme Tribunal for 1920–1: GARF, f. R-1005, op. 5, dd. 47 (Arkhangel'sk), 50 (Vitebsk), 54 (Viatka), 64 (Moscow), 75 (Petrograd), 79 (Riazan), 81 (Saratov), 89 (Tambov), 93 (Tiumen'), 140 (military tribunals on the western front), 146 (Volga military tribunals), 150 (Moscow military tribunal), 177 (Baltic military tribunals).

of ability or of sufficient class consciousness in any court. Courts faced a constant struggle through the civil war and beyond to find sufficient numbers of efficient and reliable personnel and to retain them as better rewarded, more prestigious posts were available for capable people elsewhere. In the late 1920s, there remained an annual turnover of 24% as the best continued to be poached and the worst had to be removed.[28]

These judges continued to place crimes firmly within a broader social and personal context, even if they utilized new, class-based terminology. Looking at trial transcripts from Moscow's tribunal across 1918–20, for example, it is possible to see certain patterns emerging. Judges were concerned with the defendant's background, from age, education, and family life, to occupation and membership of professional organs. The revolution's influence can be seen in their frequent interest in a defendant's property and capital before and after October as a marker of class and social position. Defendants also often used their final words to stress pertinent aspects of their biography.[29] Transcripts from transport tribunals in Moscow and the Northern regions are briefer, but the judges responded more favourably to younger defendants accused of their first crime who could prove useful to the state if rehabilitated, as well as those from lower social classes, usually described as possessing a 'low cultural level' and deemed to not to realise the consequences of their actions. Others received lighter sentences based on their 'sincere' confession or repentance. Judges were harsher on officials and party members, and those in other positions of authority, as these individuals should have known better.[30] Similarly, 'insincere' explanations were treated harshly. One deserter argued that he was needed back home to work the fields, but the court noted that he deserted in the winter when there was no work to be done![31]

Revolutionary consciousness, therefore, as practised by courts, was deeply rooted in pre-revolutionary consciousness. Bolshevik theorists, of course, did not publicly recognize this link, instead attributing the importance placed on circumstances to new, revolutionary conceptions of crime. Crime itself was seen to have a limited lifespan as the advent of socialism would remove its causes; in the meantime, crime was the manifestation of the remnants of former practices and mentalities, of a primitive consciousness, and of not just a criminal's personality but their socio-economic background. Some theorists did not even use the word 'crime', preferring to talk of a 'socially harmful' act that required a 'penalty' rather than punishment. All criminals, they argued, were capable of reconstruction, but the likelihood of success depended on social background, whilst securing society's defence was more about removing

28 Solomon, *Criminal Justice*, 37.

29 Tsentral'nyi gosudarstvennyi arkhiv Moskovskoi oblasti (TsGAMO), f. 4613, op. 2, d. 12, ll. 12–15ob; d. 56, ll. 59–60; d. 114, ll. 98–100ob (various cases, 1919–21).

30 TsGAMO, f. 4762, op. 2, d. 1, ll. 1–4, 7–9 (Moscow, various cases, 1922–3); GARF, f. R-3042, op. 1, d. 392, ll. 3, 14, 18–18ob (Northern region, various cases, 1920).

31 TsGAMO, f. 4613, op. 2, d. 62, l. 3 (case of Garanov, 18 August 1920).

harmful broader social factors.[32] Yet even these ideas, as revolutionary as they seemed to contemporaries, had their roots in scientific debates on psychopathology, moral contagion, and criminality conducted by liberals prior to 1917.[33]

Nevertheless, revolutionary consciousness, and the need to re-educate and rehabilitate rather than simply punish, was used to justify courts dispensing a wider range of sentences than had been practised before 1917. Most *volost'* courts, for instance, had dispensed either relatively short prison sentences or monetary fines. Other tsarist courts could dispense harsher penalties, including exile and death. Bolshevik courts, though, added forced public labour and public censure to this list, experimented with suspended sentences and substituting property for monetary crimes, and sent people to different types of prisons. In addition, most statistics include a further category for other punishments, most of which remained unspecified but could involve a significant variety of sentences. Even tribunals, after outlining the severity of a defendant's crimes against the state, often reached a verdict of simple public censure, which usually seems to have meant condemnation of the person and their crime, which was then often reported in the local press.[34] Some of this variety was forced upon courts by the problems faced fighting the civil war: suspended sentences alleviated pressures on the prison system; sending deserters to penal battalions maintained the numerical strength of the Red Army; seizing property and land reflected the realities of an economy with massive inflation, limited cash reserves, and unwillingness to pay. Yet there was an increasing tendency by tribunals to sentence people to forced labour without imprisonment, which was seen as a means of rehabilitating people through socially-useful labour.

In practical terms, the importance of subjective factors across 1917 led to wide diversity across Russia that both governments struggled to contain. The tsarist government spent a great deal of time examining *volost'* courts, seeking ways of defining particular local customs and when they should be applied, and frowning upon the frequent emphasis on the reputations and characters of individuals.[35] Similarly, it did not take leading Bolsheviks long to realize that abandoning existing laws exacerbated diversity. New decrees, whilst

32 'Guiding Principles of Law (1919)', in *Bolshevik Visions*, I, 166–167.

33 Daniel Beer, *Renovating Russia: The Human Sciences and the Fate of Liberal Modernity, 1880–1930* (Ithaca, NY: Cornell University Press, 2008), 194–5. Also Sharon Kowalsky, *Deviant Women: Female Crime and Criminality in Revolutionary Russia, 1880–1930* (DeKalb, IL: Northern Illinois University Press, 2009), 9, 60–65.

34 As a typical example, a report on tribunals in the first half of 1919 presented to the 7th All-Russian Congress of Soviets noted that 50% of all sentences involved imprisonment; 17% shooting; 8% fines; 5% public labour without imprisonment; 5% public censure; and 15% something else: GARF, f. A-353, op. 2, d. 23, l. 39g. Over time, shootings fell (not all death sentences were enacted anyway) and public labour increased.

35 Gaudin, *Ruling Peasants*, 116–130.

numerous and wide-ranging, were vague and unsystematic, and rather than leading to a sharper break with the past and more satisfactory verdicts, the result was a period of varying, ineffective punishments for poorly defined and understood crimes. On 12 December 1919, the state published a basic aid, which provided guidance on the nature of criminal law, types of punishments, matters to consider when reaching a verdict, and other advice. Yet there were no definitions of specific crimes and much remained dependent on the interpretations of individual judges.[36]

Diversity became increasingly incompatible with Bolshevik concerns to strengthen central authority, whilst inconsistencies limited the ability of the legal system to project state power and regulate popular actions and beliefs. At a discussion on creating new law codes at the 3rd All-Russian Congress of Justice Officials on 28 June 1920, the representative from the Commissariat of Justice (Narkomiust) was exasperated that harmful crimes, like speculation, were punished by a small fine in one place and a prison sentence in another; 'in the interests of the centralization of power', he went on, 'we must publish law codes'. Some attendees demurred, but as N. V. Krylenko, a prominent jurist and legal theorist, argued, it did not mean resurrecting old laws, but refining socialist legal consciousness, which should 'not only mean the consciousness of one or another judge, but also the cumulative experience' as expressed by particular norms.[37] Lenin also argued in 1922 that law must be uniform and should not pander to 'the long-standing Russian view and semi-barbarous habits that desire to preserve Kaluga law as distinct from Kazan law'. He too did not dismiss revolutionary consciousness, but argued that this consciousness required greater central control and oversight.[38]

This exasperation was exacerbated by changing political and economic conditions. With the political focus shifting from external threats to internal unrest, the NEP in March 1921 reintroduced elements of capitalism into the economy and many felt that the legal system had to change if it was to regulate and support the NEP effectively.[39] At the 4th All-Russian Congress of Justice Officials on 26 January 1922, the Commissar of Justice, D. I. Kurskii, alluded to this and argued that Russia needed revolutionary legality (*zakonnost'*) based on written laws so that law could be understood by a wide mass of workers and peasants.[40] This was not the first time that this term, legality, had been used, but it started to become used more systematically by 1922 as a means of contrasting with the consciousness (*soznanie*) that had dominated legal discourse since the first decree in 1917. Legality stood for order and

36 'Guiding Principles of Law', 165–169.

37 The debate is in *Materialy* XI–XII, 73–81. Quotes from 73–74, 77. On codification debates, see John Hazard, 'Soviet Law: The Bridge Years, 1917–1920', in Butler, *Russian Law*, 235–257.

38 V. Lenin, *Polnoe sobranie sochinenii* (5th edition, 55 volumes, Moscow, 1971–75), XLV, 198–199.

39 N. Chekunov, *Sudebnaia reforma 1922 goda* (St Petersburg, 2004), 6–24.

40 *Materialy* XVI–XVII (1922), 9. The law codes are discussed further on pp. 15–31.

uniformity, and thus an emphasis on statutory law, whilst consciousness reflected arbitrariness. Legality reflected the now stable position of the state, whilst consciousness reflected the improvisation of a state struggling to survive.[41]

A new criminal code was finally published on 1 June (a code covering procedure in criminal cases came into force on 1 July to ensure that these laws were enacted correctly and uniformly), codes on land and labour followed on 30 October, and a civil code on 31 October (with a code of procedure in civil cases on 7 July 1923).[42] These codes were championed as revolutionary, cementing the role of law in a socialist state, but 'significant' similarities in the criminal code to tsarist codes have been noted, especially to those from 1903 and 1845, but even to the 1832 code.[43] Similarly, much of the civil code was taken from a 1913 draft not implemented due to the outbreak of the First World War; even E. B. Pashukanis, a prominent legal theorist, admitted that it amounted to capitalist laws in a socialist state.[44]

Nevertheless, another theorist, whilst acknowledging the debt of the criminal code to previous codes, argued that it still had its source in the revolution.[45] This is most evident in its emphasis on counter-revolutionary crimes. There had been a section dealing with political crimes in the 1903 codes,[46] whilst the concept of justice being used for political objectives was well established before 1917, most obviously in the fight against revolution.[47] The 1922 code, however, turned the precisely-defined crimes of the tsarist era into elastic descriptions that enabled most crimes to be politicized in a way that had not been possible before. People could also be convicted of acts that were not defined as crimes, but were analogous to acts that were, just in case future developments created new crimes. This elasticity was reinforced by lengthy sections on crimes against the order of governance, crimes by officials and economic crimes, whilst the latter (and the terminology used throughout) made the class-based foundations of the new state clear. There remained a place for revolutionary consciousness with judges permitted to sentence within a range

41 See, e.g., Ia. Brandenburgskii, 'Revoliutsionnaia zakonnost', prokuratura i advokatura', *Sovetskoe pravo*, 2 (1922), 3–16; and A. Trainin, 'O revoliutsionnoi zakonnosti', *Pravo i zhizn'*, 1 (1922), 5–8.

42 On their creation, see Maksimova, *Zakonotvorchestvo*, 282–345. Otherwise, see *Ugolovno-protsessual'nyi kodeks RSFSR* (Moscow, 1922) and *Ugolovnyi kodeks RSFSR* (Moscow, 1922), whilst the civil code is reprinted with commentary in T. Novitskaia, *Grazhdanskii kodeks RSFSR 1922 goda* (2nd edition, Moscow, 2012).

43 Timasheff, 'Impact', 441–462.

44 Hazard, 'Law', 41–42. In addition to the codes, other reforms in 1922 (e.g. creating prosecutors and a soviet bar) marked a broader shift back to the complex legal system of pre-1917; Hazard, *Settling Disputes*, 477–491.

45 M. Isaev, 'Ugolovnyi kodeks 1 Iiunia 1922 g.', *Sovetskoe pravo* 2 (1922), 17, 19.

46 Jonathan Daly, 'Political Crime in Late Imperial Russia', *Journal of Modern History* 74(1) (2002), 68–74.

47 This was particularly true from 1906–15 under I. G. Shcheglovitov as Minister of Justice; K. Krakovskii, *'Shcheglovitovskaia iustitsiia' v Rossii* (Moscow, 2014).

of punishments depending on circumstances and even demonstrate greater leniency in 'exceptional circumstances'.[48]

That revolutionary consciousness still informed every verdict may have meant that the revolution had not been abandoned entirely, but it was now only supposed to operate within tightly prescribed boundaries. In practice, a much stronger mix of statutory and customary law continued to inform judicial decisions in the majority of local courts throughout the 1920s, just as it had done prior to 1917 and for much of the civil war. This was particularly true in rural areas where judges sought verdicts and sentences that made sense to them amid numerous laws and directives that they were often slow to hear about, and struggled to understand and remember. As a consequence, by the late 1920s, the Bolsheviks were forced to re-institutionalize the enduring, strong influence of customary law, creating a tiered system of local courts – people's courts relying on written law and lay courts relying on custom – similar to the *volost'* and circuit courts of tsarist Russia.[49] In the end, the uneasy balance between statutory and customary law that had underpinned the tsarist legal system had largely been formally reconstituted by the 1920s, with far fewer revolutionary changes than had been intended. Stuchka had bemoaned in 1922 that law was the 'strongest fortress' and 'best refuge' for any obsolete ideology, but rather than overcoming this fortress, as he claimed, the Bolsheviks might better be seen as adapting it for their own ends.[50]

Becoming citizens: people and the courtroom

Revolutionary justice was not solely about the content and practice of law; equally important was how individuals engaged with and understood the legal system. To change Russia's legal culture, the Bolsheviks intended to ensure that ordinary people were inseparable from the legal process, acting as judges, lawyers, witnesses, and spectators. In reality, as noted, most did not serve as judges, whilst those lawyers who cooperated with the new state steadily regained their pre-revolutionary, professionally-educated status.[51] The scope for participation, then, remained traditional – as defendants, accusers, witnesses, or spectators (either in person or learning about it later). This did not, however, lessen the importance of broader goals; Bolsheviks at all levels hoped that the ideology and practice of revolutionary justice would educate people in the

48 *Ugolovnyi kodeks*, 6 (article 28).

49 See McDonald, *Face to the Village*, 96–98; Daniel Newman, 'Criminal Strategies and Institutional Concerns in the Soviet Legal System: An Analysis of Criminal Appeals in Moscow Province, 1921–28' (unpublished PhD thesis, University of California Los Angeles, 2013); Solomon, *Criminal Justice*, 58–59; and Solomon, 'Criminalization and Decriminalization in Soviet Criminal Policy, 1917–1941', *Law and Society Review* 16(10 (1981–82), 9–44.

50 Stuchka, 'Five Years', 190, 196.

51 See Eugene Huskey, *Russian Lawyers and the Soviet State* (Princeton, NJ: Princeton University Press, 1986).

behaviour, duties, and mentalities expected of a conscientious citizen in the new soviet state.

The desire to educate was central to tribunals, for instance. From the start, officials sought to hold public meetings, attract broad audiences, and publicize sentences in the press. By 1919–20, tribunals were holding travelling sessions that toured villages. A chairman of one tribunal described how the arrival of a session was a major event in remote locations. People arrived with negative preconceptions, initially reluctant to engage with the court as they lacked confidence in it. However, after watching it in action, they became convinced that the tribunal was securing their own interests by removing criminal elements and defending their rights, particularly once it became clear that even local officials were not above the law. People started to speak out and to bring their own cases. Although most were petty cases, in doing so, in the chairman's words, people became citizens and the court became closer to the masses, bringing Bolshevik power and ideology to the localities.[52] Even if one doubts the accuracy of this account, many officials expressed similar ambitions. One talked about the legal process as a 'school', whilst another believed courts enabled peasants to experience justice, not just read about it.[53] This experience, yet another noted, strengthened their 'moral consciousness' and sense of duty to society.[54] Beyond tribunals, the intervention of people's courts into everyday lives – from domestic disputes and divorce to child support and other cases – would help the state to remake society.[55]

These aims were not new. *Volost'* courts before 1917 aimed to provide a forum where peasants administered justice over other peasants, and acquired a link to the state beyond their obligations to pay taxes and provide service; they would act as citizens, participating in official organs and seeing them as a means of defending and enforcing rights.[56] Similarly, the urban peace courts and jury service were to have the same effect.[57] The extent to which this was achieved is questionable.[58] On the one hand, Russians were using courts in

52 Rossiiskii gosudarstvennyi voennyi arkhiv (RGVA), f. 33988, op. 2, d. 245, ll. 4ob–5ob (report, March 1922).

53 GARF, f. R-3042, op. 1, d. 23, l. 37 (anonymous report, early 1921); d. 96, l. 29 (report, 2 March 1922).

54 GARF, f. R-3042, op. 1, d. 95, l. 30 (report of Baltic-Mariinskii tribunal, 20 May 1921).

55 Aaron Retish, 'Controlling Revolution: Understandings of Violence through the Rural Soviet Courts, 1917–1923', *Europe-Asia Studies* 65(9) (2013), 1789–1806.

56 Jane Burbank, 'Legal Culture, Citizenship, and Peasant Jurisprudence: Perspectives from the Early Twentieth Century', in *Reforming Justice in Russia, 1864–1996*, edited by Peter Solomon (Armonk: M. E. Sharpe, 1997), 99.

57 Neuberger, 'Popular Legal Cultures'; McReynolds, *Murder*, 108; Atwell, 'Russian Jury', 46, 60.

58 Historians are divided on this issue. For cautious views, see Gaudin, *Ruling Peasants*, 130–131; Neuberger, 'Popular Legal Cultures', 234–235, 240–242; and V. Bezgin, *Pravovaia kul'tura russkogo sela (vtoraia polovina XIX – nachalo XX veka)* (Tambov, 2012), 71–77. A more positive view is in Burbank, *Russian Peasants*, 268–271, whilst more negative views are in Baberowski, 'Law'; Frank,

increasing numbers in the years before the First World War meaning that they must have seen value in them, and were exposed to the legal process and its values. On the other hand, this did not necessarily make them citizens. Many people probably used courts as a last resort, whilst many peasants, for instance, went to courts to pursue traditional village conflicts or particular crimes, not trusting them to deal effectively with more serious conflicts. Courts also retained a strong element of traditional community justice through their unpredictability, whilst attempts by peace courts to marry statutory law with custom often only emphasized the differences between the two. Nevertheless, elements of law and the legal process were part of more and more people's lives in late Imperial Russia, whether through going to court with cases, serving on juries, or simply reading about cases in newspapers or the 'staggering popularity' of crime fiction with the lower and middle classes.[59] Thus, law had more potential to mould opinions and actions than it had ever enjoyed before in Russia's history.

For revolutionary justice to succeed, it had to engage with people in similar ways, if not more comprehensively, but the turmoil of revolution and civil war made this difficult. It was not that people did not want to use courts (on the contrary, the revolution created new types of disputes), but that the collapse of state authority in 1917 rendered courts powerless and largely pointless, and the numbers using them fluctuated. As the Bolsheviks reconstituted state authority, however, statistics indicate an increasing caseload in courts, and the numbers of cases brought to people's courts by the early 1920s had resumed the steady increase seen in comparable *volost'* courts before 1917. In Moscow, for example, 104,428 cases were brought to people's courts in 1918, of which 73% were criminal cases and 27% were civil cases.[60] This number dropped to 93,035 in 1921 before rising steadily to 131,852 in 1924. By then, only 40% of cases were criminal cases, whereas 60% were civil cases. These trends – rising numbers of civil cases, falling numbers of criminal cases, but a steady growth in cases overall – were replicated across Moscow province, even if the balance remained in favour of criminal cases. In 1921, there had been 74,217 cases of which 76.5% were criminal. This fell slightly for two years before rising to 79,848 in 1924 but now only 65% were criminal.[61] In the Ural region, civil cases were only 31% of the caseload in 1924 but had risen to 57% by 1927.[62]

Crime, 95–103, 113–114, 297–312; and T. Shatkovskaia, *Pravovaia mental'nost' Rossiiskikh krest'ian vtoroi poloviny XIX veka* (Rostov-na-Donu, 2000), 119–120, 207–208.

59 For the prominent position of law and crime in popular culture, see Boris Dralyuk, *Western Crime Fiction Goes East: The Russian Pinkerton Craze, 1907–1934* (Leiden: Brill, 2012); McReynolds, *Murder*, and Jeffrey Brooks, *When Russia Learned to Read: Literacy and Popular Literature, 1861–1917* (Princeton, NJ: Princeton University Press, 1985), 200–208.

60 *Materialy* VI, 9 (report on the activities of Narkomiust, 1919).

61 *Otchet plenumu Moskovskogo soveta R. K. i K. D. o rabote Moskovskogo gubernskogo suda za 1924 god* (Moscow, 1925), 10–11.

62 Kamelova and Maiorov, *Sovetskaia pravookhranitel'naia sistema Urala*, 334.

The statistics on civil cases suggest that people were willingly using the legal system in increasing numbers by the 1920s, but the statistics on criminal cases mask many instances where people were compelled to engage with courts. People's courts and tribunals expended vast amounts of time pursuing activities such as desertion, speculation and banditry (usually resisting food requisitioning) that people saw as integral to survival during the civil war rather than as crimes. The legal system could still mould the actions and opinions of those compelled to go to court, but in a different way than those willingly involved.

Overall, it is as difficult to judge the impact of courts on people after 1917 as it was before. It has been noted, for example, that people respected the judgements of *volost'* courts in the vast majority of cases prior to 1917 even if they lost, paying their fines and serving prison sentences.[63] This respect broke down across the revolution as courts struggled to enforce their rulings; the authorities were particularly concerned with people's courts dispensing fines as the majority of their sentences, which they believed were often not paid or could not be paid, and with people not fulfilling forced terms of community work.[64]

Otherwise, people's voices tend only to be heard through appeals and complaints after 1917, both of which represent a specific, aggrieved segment of those participating in courts and both of which are phrased in ways that mask the writer's true voice in favour of a voice that they hope the authorities will listen to, possibly by altering content, language, or tone. Thus, even in tribunals, where justice was imposed on people, such sources do not reveal much outright opposition to revolutionary justice. To be sure, one defendant wrote angrily to VTsIK that Tambov's tribunal was not a court but a 'farce of a court, a profanation'. It had sentenced him to ten years forced labour for desertion (which he denied) despite, in his words, the fact that his trial marginalized lawyers and was guided by a hostile crowd of soldiers.[65] Many probably had similar experiences (and not just in tribunals) and felt the same.[66] Most appeals, however, suggest that people accepted the concept of counter-revolutionary crimes and the validity of tribunals to investigate them; they simply did not see *their own* actions as counter-revolutionary or criminal, or pleaded that circumstances had forced them to commit crimes and that the tribunal should be merciful.[67] This in itself, though, suggests that the

63 Burbank, *Russian Peasants*, 64–68, 199–200.

64 See, e.g. the concerns expressed by Narkomiust to all provincial executive committees, justice departments and councils of people's courts on 20 January 1920: GARF, f. R-1005, op. 2, d. 1, ll. 50–50ob.

65 GARF, f. R-1235, op. 94, d. 505, l. 206 (appeal, 4 October 1919).

66 Two studies of Moscow's workers reveal widespread opposition to the trial of the Socialist Revolutionaries in 1922; Kevin Murphy, *Revolution and Counterrevolution: Class Struggle in a Moscow Metal Factory* (Oxford: Berghahn Books, 2005), 161–162; and Simon Pirani, *The Russian Revolution in Retreat, 1920–24: Soviet Workers and the New Communist Elite* (Abingdon: Routledge, 2008), 147–155.

67 The emphasis on circumstances also comes through in the lesser comrade courts created to deal with workers' discipline; Lewis Siegelbaum, 'Defining and

Bolsheviks' core messages about what constituted a crime and counter-revolution had failed to be conveyed successfully.

Many appeals and complaints reveal some knowledge of legal procedure and recent laws. This may well have been obtained from others, but it still contributed to an individual's legal consciousness. It has been suggested that legal knowledge enabled people to enjoy advantages in front of the court prior to 1917,[68] but another study has pointed out that with respect to appeals the Bolsheviks usually ignored any arguments in favour of their own interpretation.[69] This is true, but as there was no automatic right of appeal, procedural error or another violation had to be alleged in order to have the case reviewed, and the ability to articulate such errors did not do appellants any harm. Equally, although it could be argued that the mere fact that people were appealing sentences suggests some degree of confidence in the legal system, it could just as easily reflect desperation and routine.

Ultimately, courts had to dispense 'justice' in the eyes of the people for the latter to engage with and respect them. But what was seen as justice across a large and diverse country? Frierson argued that four criteria were central to how peasants defined crime in late Imperial Russia: personal harm, sin, premeditation, and membership of the offender or victim in the community.[70] All these meant that an action could be a crime under certain circumstances, but not under others, and circumstances must be considered to obtain justice. These criteria did not disappear during the revolution, particularly personal harm and premeditation, even in relation to 'new' crimes. Initially, the state diverged from popular views. Would the state suffer, for instance, if its property was stolen or was it a crime that someone struggling to feed a family had bought and sold goods (speculated) to survive? Most thought not, but the Bolsheviks dispensed harsh sentences to reflect how damaging they felt these activities were during the civil war. Yet the massive scale of these crimes forced the authorities to change tack and urge courts to clarify motives and degrees of participation, and distinguish between crimes committed due to a desperate need to survive and 'malignant' (*zlostnyi*) or 'selfish' (*korystnyi*) crimes committed for personal gain, such as illegal brewing or large-scale speculation.[71] Thus circumstances were restored to pre-eminence and, as noted, retained even after the 1922 criminal law code.

Furthermore, revolutionary justice had to reach as many people as possible to be effective and the Bolsheviks were more proactive than their predecessors

Ignoring Labor Discipline in the Early Soviet Period: The Comrades-Disciplinary Courts, 1918–1922', *Slavic Review* 51(40 (1992), 705–730.

68 This comes through repeatedly in Burbank, *Russian Peasants.*

69 Newman, 'Criminal Strategies', especially 170–192.

70 Cathy Frierson, 'Crime and Punishment in the Russian Village: Rural Concepts of Criminality at the End of the Nineteenth Century', *Slavic Review* 46(1) (1987), 55–69.

71 GARF, f. R-3042, op. 1, d. 2, ll. 10–11 (circular to transport tribunals, November 1920).

in this respect. As one official argued, attendance at trials was a more effective way of expanding the numbers exposed to the legal system than publishing sentences in the press, posting them on public buildings or distributing them to village soviets, although these were also useful.[72] This was particularly important for tribunals; because they dealt with crimes of state importance, the Bolsheviks believed it was crucial that their activities and educational messages were spread as widely as possible. The travelling sessions mentioned above were seen as vital in this respect; not only did they reach remote areas, but people there were more receptive than in the towns served by the main tribunals. Tribunals were a novelty and a spectacle – an object of entertainment or curiosity – in a way that they were not in larger urban areas given pressures on workers' time and alternative sources of entertainment. Lacking a permanent building, sessions used various spaces, sometimes the buildings of local authorities, but more commonly unofficial spaces; holding meetings in the public square or in local theatres or factories, or even railway stations and boats.[73] Trials were therefore taking place where people worked and lived, encouraging attendance, even if only for short periods. Some trials were apparently seen by 5,000 people per day with some coming and going, whilst virtually entire villages turned up in other places.[74]

The trial was central to engagement, whether encouraging attendance or providing material for further dissemination. Judgements were all very well, but it was the drama of the trial that drew people into the court's activities and it was the trial dialogue that offered the best means of educating people. The Bolsheviks were keen from the start to emphasize particular trials as examples of certain crimes that could be publicized widely and these laid the foundation for later infamous trials in the late 1920s and the 1930s. This practice was not new. The tsarist state had experimented with high-profile trials of revolutionaries since the 1860s, although the failure to convict Vera Zasulich in 1878 led to restrictions, leaving newspapers and official reports as the main means of dissemination.[75] Even so, the trial of Mendel Beilis in 1913 was reported on by over 100 newspapers, some of which printed the released transcripts verbatim to satisfy the demand for information.[76]

72 RGVA, f. 33988, op. 2, d. 245, ll. 11ob–12 (report on tribunals on the Western Front in 1921, early 1922).

73 GARF, f. R-1005, op. 1, d. 116, l. 216 (report from Baikal, 12 July 1921); f. R-3042, op. 1, d. 84, ll. 8, 13, 16ob (reports from Perm, November 1920, 2 April 1921, and 13 March 1922), d. 95, l. 17 (report from the Baltic-Mariinskii tribunal, 3 December 1920), d. 96, ll. 59–67 (report from Volga tribunal, 12 September 1922).

74 GARF, f. R-3042, op. 1, d. 73 (report from Bugul'ma, 20 June 1920); d. 23, l. 37 (anon. report, early 1921).

75 For a succinct survey of political trials, see Daly, 'Political Crime', 74–77. On Zasulich's trial, see J. Bergman, *Vera Zasulich* (Stanford: Stanford University Press, 1983), 41–58, and A. Siljak, *Angel of Vengeance* (New York: St Martins Griffin, 2008), 215–247.

76 Robert Weinberg, *Blood Libel in Late Imperial Russia: The Ritual Murder Trial of Mendel Beilis* (Bloomington and Indianapolis, IN: Indiana University Press, 2014), 44 (the trial is covered on 44–67).

Similarly, local authorities had also been promoting the pedagogical functions of other prominent trials.[77] Audiences, however, proved to be unpredictable, often sympathetic to Tsarism's enemies even if they had committed crimes.

The Bolsheviks also faltered in their first high-profile trials,[78] but they quickly adopted more effective control over them, utilizing trained lawyers to present their case, manipulating witnesses and evidence, and restricting the scope for the defendants to express their views and the audience to influence proceedings, whilst managing wider publicity. Lenin stressed that such 'model' (*obraztsovyi*) trials, which he defined as enacting fast and forceful repression with a clear explanation to the population of their significance, should be compulsory and tasked Narkomiust to organize them.[79] It was just as important that, as one senior official noted, such trials dealt with everyday crimes of a mass character rather than just high-profile enemies, if not more important.[80] Clearly local officials agreed, holding local 'model' trials, usually involving well-known local officials who had committed common crimes such as taking bribes, seizing property, or exceeding their authority in some way. These trials often lasted for several days and gained extensive local newspaper coverage.[81]

For those not able to attend, the Bolsheviks re-staged trials, further breaking down the boundaries between education and entertainment. There was a history of fictional educational trials before 1917, from church trials of sinners to theatrical productions, and they re-emerged as agitation trials from 1919–1920. These were easy and cheap to organize. Some restaged real trials, others used fictional scenarios. The subjects ranged from obvious political enemies to harmful traits such as illiteracy and drunkenness. There were even trials of the Bolsheviks, proclaiming them innocent of accusations that the October Revolution lacked popular support. Many were improvised, but increasingly booklets were produced containing sample scripts, which could be adapted to reference local places and criminals. Trials encouraged audiences to participate, from shouting comments to voting on a verdict.[82] Their ability to foster

77 See Sandra Dahlke, 'Old Russia in the Dock: The Trial Against Mother Superior Mitrofaniia Before the Moscow District Court (1874)', *Cahiers du Monde Russe* 53(1) (2012), 95–120.

78 See Matthew Rendle, 'Defining the "Political" Crime: Revolutionary Tribunals in Early Soviet Russia', *Europe-Asia Studies* 65(9) (2013), 1771–1788; and Marc Jansen, *A Show Trial under Lenin: The Trial of the Socialist Revolutionaries, Moscow, 1922* (The Hague: Springer, 1982).

79 Lenin, *Polnoe,* XLIV, 396 (Letter to Kurskii, 20 February 1922).

80 GARF, f. A-353, op. 3, d. 40, l. 130ob (report by Iu. Iu. Mezhin on railway tribunals prior to 1 July 1920).

81 See, e.g. trials in Moscow (1–11 October 1919) and Klin (23–26 April 1921) involving a number of local officials, including (in the former) members of local courts, the Cheka and the Red Guard; TsGAMO, f. 4612, op. 1, dd. 96–102 (Moscow); f. 4613, op. 2, d. 114 (Klin).

82 An exhaustive study is Elizabeth Wood, *Performing Justice: Agitation Trials in Early Soviet Russia* (Ithaca, NY: Cornell University Press, 2005). See also Julie

legal consciousness has been questioned since they were ultimately fictional morality tales with few elements of the legal apparatus.[83] But this misses the point: they provided a recognizable image of the court, discussed the same issues and used similar terminology; some audiences became so involved that they expected the sentence to be enacted for real afterwards.

In the 1920s, a new medium became available – film. Whilst newsreels from 1918 onwards had featured footage from trials, these were limited to shots of people and places, with subtitles briefly outlining accusations and verdicts. These increased awareness of trials, but did not really add much else. But by the mid-1920s, films were portraying fictional trials and were capable of much greater realism, including flashbacks to the scene of the crime, which moved the audience's experience beyond anything possible in real or agitational trials. Scripts often covered social crimes, such as drunkenness, slacking, or red tape, where harmful effects were stressed, confessions elicited, and repentance and reintegration achieved.[84]

Alongside this, reading about crimes remained important. The boom in crime fiction prior to 1917 collapsed afterwards; shortages in paper combined with the state monopoly of publishing and the belief that such stories lacked political value, highlighting as they did divisions and social conflict.[85] Despite a mini-revival in the 1920s when some prominent Bolsheviks felt that crime novels could be a means of engaging people with revolutionary adventures and heroes, the general opposition persisted.[86] Similarly, mainstream crimes were rarely reported in the press. 'Political' crime, from political opponents to official corruption, was worth reporting, but whereas coverage had mixed fact, education, and entertainment prior to 1917, the first two now took over. National newspapers such as *Izvestiia* and *Pravda* covered major trials, whilst provincial newspapers printed regular updates. The appearance of travelling sessions of tribunals often prompted a flurry of coverage in district newspapers, further extending their impact. Nevertheless, legal officials complained throughout the civil war that courts never received as much press coverage as they should, urging courts to provide the press with more information and to appoint officials with specific responsibilities in this area.

One solution was for officials to take matters into their own hands. Prior to 1917, a growing number of publications focusing on the law had emerged across Russia, providing a forum to discuss judicial decisions, theoretical issues and professional life, influencing the public self-image of jurists and

Cassiday, *The Enemy on Trial: Early Soviet Courts on Stage and Screen* (DeKalb, IL: Northern Illinois University Press, 2000), 51–80.

83 Wood, *Performing*, 219–220.

84 Cassiday, *Enemy*, 40–41, 81–109, 161–188.

85 Jeffrey Brooks, *Thank You, Comrade Stalin! Soviet Public Culture from Revolution to Cold War* (Princeton, NJ: Princeton University Press, 2000), 6–7.

86 Dralyuk, *Western Crime Fiction*, Ch. 5; Robert Russell, 'Red Pinkertonism: An Aspect of Soviet Literature of the 1920s', *Slavonic and East European Review* 60 (3)(1982), 390–412.

asserting their professional expertise.[87] From 1918 onwards, various organs attempted to revive this discussion. Narkomiust had the resources to lead the way, publishing its *Materialy*, collections of decrees, information, local reports, theoretical articles, and transcripts of legal congresses. It also published *Proletarskaia revoliutsiia i pravo*, also a mix of factual reports and topical discussions, as well as collections of decrees and book reviews. These activities intensified after the civil war as *Materialy* was transformed into a weekly publication, *Ezhenedel'nik sovetskoi iustitsii*, and was joined by others. It was at this time that some provincial judicial organs (for example, Petrograd, Moscow, Tambov, and Saratov) enjoyed sufficient stability and resources to launch their own regular publications.[88] Most of these were aimed primarily at local legal officials as they contain a mix of law, practical advice, theoretical debate, and professional recollections. There was one, however, *Sud idet!*, published in Petrograd from 1924, which was clearly aimed at a broader audience. It cost (by 1927) less than half the price and had over two-and-a-half times the print run than the more formal *Rabochii sud*, which Petrograd's legal authorities also produced. *Sud idet!* mixed dramatic stories of crimes and entertaining memoirs on past cases with articles on decrees, and contemporary and historical political developments. In all, at least 18 publications appeared in the 1920s, some replacing others, some with short, irregular print runs, but all seeking to promote legal culture among the numerous, new justice officials and, hopefully, the wider population. Whether they were successful or not is unknown as print runs do not equate to readership, and most journals, funded by official subsidies, were not subject to market conditions. Nonetheless, they could only have helped to spread wider knowledge of the law and awareness of current legal developments and major cases.

Conclusion

This study has focused on two broad elements of Russia's legal culture over the revolutionary divide, but case studies of other elements would reveal similar findings; if nothing else, the Bolsheviks' ambitions, which developed steadily after October 1917, to rule through the law rather than be subjected to it, and to use law to enhance the authority and efficiency of government, were the same as tsarist intentions. To be sure, the ambitious nature of early Bolshevik attempts to dismantle the tsarist legal system meant that some elements of lasting change were inevitable. It was impossible, however, to build a new legal system with comparable objectives to foster state control, social order, and citizenship without resulting in similarities with the previous system. And, underneath this,

87 William Wagner, *Marriage, Property, and Law in Late Imperial Russia* (Oxford: Clarendon Press, 1994), 33–35.

88 *Rabochii sud* (Petrograd from 1923); *Proletarskii sud* (Moscow from 1922); *Pravo i sud* (Saratov from 1924); *Vestnik proletarskogo prava i iuridicheskikh norm* (Tambov from 1922).

enduring popular conceptions of law and justice were not going to change overnight, despite the revolutionary turmoil. In this sense, revolutionary justice did not succeed in revolutionizing Russia's legal culture. By the end of the civil war, the initial aim to re-forge the relationship between law and the state, and how people understood and interacted with the law, had coalesced into the prosaic ambition to cement central state control over justice so as to use law most effectively in the interests of the state. The mix of old and new laws, the enduring uneasy balance between statutory and customary laws, and the difficulties of engaging people with the legal system in the desired manner and with the intended results, meant that revolutionary justice in its entirety, as envisaged by legal theorists, was never entirely successful. In the end, the Bolsheviks found that a new legal culture could not be easily imposed on to a population.

Elements of continuity were, therefore, forced on the Bolsheviks by the circumstances of civil war, but it was also a conscious choice to accept them, especially with regards to the law codes and the legal apparatus. On the one hand, the legal theorists who led Narkomiust had all been trained as lawyers under Tsarism; it was inevitable that they would search for solutions amid familiar laws, institutions, and practices. On the other hand, local justice officials shared more with the people brought in front of the court, and popular conceptions of law and justice, than they did with Narkomiust, making the continuation of custom inevitable, even if renamed as revolutionary consciousness.

Yet continuities may in fact have been an advantage. It has been suggested that one of the motivations behind reconstituting traditional institutions and practices in 1922 was a desire to foster public respect for the legal system.[89] But the persistence of custom and the emphasis on circumstances may have also gone some way to ensuring that courts continued to reflect popular concerns and beliefs. Ultimately, a truly revolutionary court, one that was entirely new, would not have been able to engage with the population, fulfil its role and exert state authority as effectively as one that retained elements of what was traditional, understood, and largely accepted, despite imperfections. In other words, utilizing elements of the existing legal culture was more effective than trying to build one from scratch. Recent scholarship has highlighted similar continuities across the revolutionary divide in other areas of state activity.[90] As well as providing a more nuanced assessment of how the Bolsheviks secured power, all this work stresses that few revolutions, if any, are entirely revolutionary, and that it is extremely difficult to sustain dramatic revolutionary change over a longer period of time.

89 Solomon, *Criminal Justice*, 40.

90 Beer, *Renovating Russia*; David Hoffmann, *Cultivating the Masses: Modern State Practices and Soviet Socialism, 1914–1939* (Ithaca, NY: Cornell University Press, 2011); Peter Holquist, *Making War, Forging Revolution: Russia's Continuum of Crisis, 1914–1921* (Cambridge, MA: Harvard University Press, 2002); and Joshua Sanborn, *Drafting the Russian Nation: Military Conscription, Total War, and Mass Politics, 1905–1925* (DeKalb, IL: Northern Illinois University Press, 2003).

3 'Taking a leap across the tsarist throne'

Revolutionizing the Russian circus

Miriam Neirick

In 1918, Vitalii Lazarenko, the Soviet Union's 'First Red Popular Jester', compared the Bolshevik revolution to a leap.[1] In the opening monologue of his circus performance, the clown announced:

The dreadful peals of the Russian storms	*Rossiiskikh groz bezumnye raskaty*
trouble the world with their call:	*Trevozhat mir prizyvom:*
forge happiness.	*Schast'e kui.*
'Bolsheviks, oh be they damned!'	*'Bol'sheviki, o bud' oni prokliaty!'*
repeats the nervous bourgeois everywhere.	*Vezde tverdit vzvolnovannyi burzhui.*
Hurry, hurry	*Skorei, skorei*
organize against them	*im propisat' blokadu*
so that our workers cannot hear,	*Chtob slyshat' ikh rabochii nash ni mog*
clasp, or soothe them,	*Prizhat', uniat',*
but we are leaping across their obstacles	*no cherez ikh pregrady*
into the people's minds.	*V umy liudei my delaem pryzhok.*
Let the old world trudge along little by little	*Pust' staryi mir pletetsia ponemnogu*
and glorify the path of hackneyed roads	*I slavit trakt zaezzhennykh dorog.*
Finding our road to freedom, to happiness	*K svobode, k schastiiu naidia svoiu dorogu*
we are taking a leap	*Chrez tsarskii tron*
across the tsarist throne.	*my delaem pryzhok.*[2]

After reciting these verses, Lazarenko literally enacted the revolutionary leap by vaulting across a series of obstacles that had been placed before him in the ring.[3]

1 In 1924, the Moscow Administration of Circuses awarded Lazarenko the title, 'First Red Popular Jester'. G. D. Endzinoi, 'Narodnyi shut (Al'bom Vitaliia Lazarenko)', *Vstrechi s proshlym: sbornik materialov TsGALI, vypusk 1* (Moscow: Sovetskaia Rossiia, 1983), 174.

2 Dmitriev, Iu., *Sovetskii tsirk, ocherk istorii, 1917–1941* (Moscow: Iskusstvo, 1963), 64–65.

3 Ibid., 65.

Lazarenko's leap goes a long way toward explaining why the circus – a Western European import that was peddled by bourgeois entrepreneurs and patronized by the Imperial autocracy – was incorporated into the Soviet cultural administration the following year. On 26 August 1919, Vladimir Il'ich Lenin signed a 'Decree on the Unification of the Theatrical Concern' that, among other things, mandated the state appropriation of private circuses.[4] The old Salomonskii Circus on Tsvetnoi Boulevard in Moscow soon became the First State Circus, and Moscow's Nikitin Circus became the Second State Circus, both to be administered by the newly established Circus Section of the People's Commissariat of Enlightenment's Theatre Department. Within two months, the second State Circus made its debut to a full house, and on 1 September 1920, the first State Circus staged its inaugural performance.[5] In January 1921, the Circus Section supervised the incorporation of all private circuses within the Russian Republic into local departments of public education. Two years later, these circuses came under the centralized control of the Central Management of State Circuses (TsUGTs), which had administered the two Moscow circuses since it was founded in 1922.[6]

Routines like Lazarenko's demonstrated that circus performances could accommodate the revolutionary messages that all forms of art were mandated to propagate at the time. Just like songs, festivals, posters, and plays, post-revolutionary circus performances told the story of the revolution and celebrated its victory.[7] Aristocrats fell from their horses, the autocracy was toppled by a

4 'Dekret ob'edinenii teatral'nogo dela', *Vestnik teatra* 33 (1919), 2; State Archive of the Russian Federation [GARF] f. 2306, op. 24, d. 79. The decree was also signed by Anatoly Lunacharskii, People's Commissar of Enlightenment, Vladimir Bonch-Bruevich, administrative manager of the Council of People's Commissars, and L. Fotieva, Secretary of the Council of People's Commissars.

5 N. Z. M., '2-i Gosudarstvenyi tsirk. Otkrytie sezona', *Vestnik teatra* 36 (1919), 12; 'Otkrytie pervogo Gosudarstvennogo tsirka', *Vestnik teatra* 70 (1920), 14.

6 'Tsirki na mestakh', *Vestnik teatra* 78 (1921); M. E. Shvydkoi (ed.), *Tsirkovoe iskusstvo Rossii, entsiklopediia* (Moscow: Bol'shaia Rossiiskaia entsiklopediia, 2000), 400. The relative efficiency with which the Bolsheviks organized the circuses – they established the state cinemas, by contrast, only in December 1922 – was only the earliest indication of the prominent position the circus would long maintain in the Soviet Union. In 1924, state circuses opened in Kiev, Nizhnii Novgorod, Leningrad, Orel, Tver, Rostov-on-Don, Kazan, Ivanovo-Voznesensk, and Tula. Together with the first Moscow State Circus – the second had since been closed – they attracted 1.5 million viewers in the 1924/25 season. In 1927, Khar'kov also became home to a state circus, and total ticket sales reportedly reached two million. Five years later, the number of circuses had grown to 46. Richard Taylor, 'A "Cinema for the Millions" – Soviet Socialist Realism and the Problem of Film Comedy', *Journal of Contemporary History* 18 (1983), 445; GARF f. 2306 op. 69 d. 504 l. 2; 'Khronologiia gostsirkov', *Tsirk i estrada* 3–4 (1928), 1; M. Khrapchenko, 'Dvadtsat' let sovetskogo tsirka', *Pravda*, 23 November 1939, 4.

7 As Richard Stites explains, at the time of the revolution,

> a whole array of new symbols and rituals were introduced and infused with anti-capitalism, the collective spirit, atheism, and machine worship. Bolshevik artists

clown, and viewers were exhorted to help secure the Bolshevik victory, which was dramatized in pantomimes, *tableaux vivants*, and Lazarenko's stunning jumps. For a time – a very brief time, as it happened – the Soviet circus became an arena for the enactment of the revolutionary leap, and the Bolsheviks' successful transformation of a bourgeois entertainment into a champion of the revolution stood as proof that the leap really had been made.

It should come as no surprise that the circus was another of many popular pre-revolutionary forms of culture that the Bolsheviks appropriated in order to propagate ideological messages. What does come as a surprise is that circus producers began to purge much of the new, explicitly revolutionary content from the circus repertoire in 1920, when some cultural administrators began to worry that the purity of the circus was being corrupted. Aesthetic concerns prompted this policy shift, which was then institutionalized as a result of new economic imperatives that were introduced under the New Economic Policy in 1921 (NEP). In order to stabilize the Soviet economy after the civil war, NEP provided for the partial legalization of private trade, the partial restoration of some property rights, and the partial elimination of subsidies for cultural enterprises like the circus, which now had to compete in a much more saturated cultural marketplace. In order to maintain ticket sales, its producers restored the circus to its recognizably pre-revolutionary form. All of this meant that evidence of the revolutionary leap had become rarer and, therefore, as highly prized as the profits that state circuses were now required to turn, which is why their producers and boosters energetically insisted that the revolution in the circus had not been reversed.

Between 1921 and 1929, the rhetoric surrounding the circus, rather than the show itself, was revolutionized, as official commentators maintained that even entirely conventional, recognizably pre-revolutionary circus programmes provided edifying demonstrations of physical strength, the disciplined will, a conscious attitude toward labour, and atheism. While NEP-era circus performances continued merely to mark time, as critics would complain throughout the decade, it was the set of ideas that circulated about the circus that marked the most meaningful break with the tsarist past.

Because NEP-era productions once again featured sequences of spectacular physical tricks that refused to communicate any single message or tell any seamless story,[8] they readily accommodated the novel meanings ascribed to

> and propagandists went to the people with a culture for the people and in doing so they tried to combine the new with the old, self-consciously infusing circus, fairbooth, *lubok*, folk ditties, songs and dances with revolutionary content.
>
> Richard Stites, Russian Popular Culture, Entertainment and Society Since 1900 (New York: Cambridge University Press, 1992), 39

8 The Soviet circus provides an historical example of Helen Stoddart's theoretical claim that,

> Circus goes further than other forms of live art to mobilize physical energies and sensations which fundamentally resist inscription within film and literary language. Not only has it predominantly side-stepped (if only opportunistically)

them by Soviet commentators. The variety, 'ambivalence', and 'multiple meanings'[9] of the circus – 'a theatre of contradictions'[10] that 'has proved open to widely differing ideological inflections'[11] – historically have accounted for the entertainment's appeal to socio-economically, demographically, and politically diverse viewers, who have recognized in the spectacle different, and even contradictory meanings. The polyvalence of the circus accounted for its broad popularity among audiences, and it also explains the appeal of the circus to NEP-era officials, who put ambiguous circus acts to political use by rhetorically investing them with revolutionary messages. Unlike other obviously bourgeois entertainments that flourished at the time, such as foreign films, shopping arcades, jazz

> linguistic language for mime, music and physical stunts, it has also traditionally avoided arranging its acts in any kind of narrative form and has favoured restless, itinerant and temporary structures.
>
> Helen Stoddart, Rings of Desire, Circus History and Representation (Manchester: Manchester University Press, 2000), 5

9 In her study of an early twentieth-century circus in Dresden, Marline Otte observes: 'Whereas theatrical entertainment increasingly fragmented into a series of class-specific genres, circus audiences came much closer to representing a microcosm of German society at large.' Otte attributes the popularity of circus acts to their 'multiple meanings' and concludes that, 'for decades, circus acts retained their ambivalent essence because doing so allowed them to speak to highly diverse audiences'. Marline Otte, 'Sarrasani's Theatre of the World: Monumental Circus Entertainment in Dresden, from Kaiserreich to Third Reich', *German History* 17(4) (1999), 530, 540, 541. Ernest Albrecht similarly explains that in its golden age at the turn of the twentieth century, the circus in the United States

> was welcomed by every level of society. For the newly arrived the performances of their countrymen gave them a sense of pride. For second-and third-generation Americans … the circus offered nothing more subversive than an irresistible collection of eye-popping oddities. And for fundamentalists who saw entertainment as morally corrupt, the circus's attractions were sold as educational displays.
>
> Ernest Albrecht, The New American Circus (Gainesville, FL: University of Florida Press, 1995), 2

10 Ellen Handy refers to the circus as a 'theatre of contradictions' in her study of the diverse photographic representations of the circus. She attributes 'the disparate visions of its many visual interpreters' to the properties of the circus itself, which is 'a hybrid and episodic entertainment or spectacle'. Ellen Handy, 'Photographing the "splendidest sight that ever was", Cruelty, Alienation, and the Grotesque in the Shadow of the Big Top', in *Images from the World Between: The Circus in Twentieth Century American Art*, edited by Donna Gustafson (New York: The MIT Press and American Federation of Arts, 2001), 92.

11 Stoddart explains that 'in political terms, circus as a dramatic form is neither necessarily radical or reactionary; its language of "show", having absorbed and adapted numerous cultural and historical traditions has proved open to widely differing ideological inflections'. She also observes in the circus 'latent, and usually highly ambiguous, political implications not only at the level of aesthetics … but in their content as well'. Stoddart, *Rings of Desire*, 84–85, 97.

bands, beer gardens, and romance novels, the circus was a popular and arguably revolutionary entertainment. Official commentators who ascribed an ideological meaning to circus performances effectively articulated the myth that even during NEP, the Soviet people and the Bolshevik government together were taking a revolutionary leap across the tsarist throne, rather than a step backward.

This myth was essential to Bolshevik legitimacy, and it relied on another assertion that became central to circus rhetoric at the time, namely that viewers received the revolutionary messages that circus producers claimed to be sending them. Though official commentators offered little evidence to prove this claim, there was hardly any evidence to dispute it, which made circus audiences very easy to idealize. Few viewers left any record of their response to the show, and those reactions that officials did solicit and circulate were used less to document popular reception than to posit an ideal Soviet viewer. As a result, what remains the greatest source of frustration for the historian of the Soviet circus – the total absence of reliable evidence regarding audience reception – was a virtue of the circus for its state producers and official reviewers. Their assertion that Soviet viewers attended the circus to receive the political messages that it purportedly propagated was uncontested by any concrete evidence. The official endorsement of the circus as a revolutionary entertainment, beloved, as such, by whole crowds of Soviet people helped maintain perhaps the most important legitimating myth after the revolution: the myth of popular consensus. Between 1919 and 1929, circus productions, official commentaries, and audience studies claimed to provide real proof that an ideal Soviet public shared the principles and adored the products of a truly revolutionary Soviet state.

The circus was one of many popular entertainments, art forms, and mass media that the Bolsheviks pressed into political service after the revolution. The Bolsheviks relied on easily accessible mass media, such as posters, newspapers, short films, and radio programmes, to propagate political ideas to broad audiences while also entertaining them. They also sponsored the production of novels, fables, plays, festivals, and monumental sculptures that narrated the history of the revolution, depicted its heroes, and mythologized both.[12] James von Geldern explains that the Bolsheviks also subjected more playful forms of popular culture, whose political significance was less certain, to 'structural changes' so that they might more clearly communicate

12 Stites, *Russian Popular Culture*, 1–63; Peter Kenez, *The Birth of the Propaganda State, Soviet Methods of Mass Mobilization, 1917–1929* (Cambridge and New York: Cambridge University Press, 1985), 95–118; James von Geldern, *Bolshevik Festivals, 1917–1920* (Berkeley, CA: University of California Press, 1993); James von Geldern, 'Introduction by James von Geldern', in *Mass Culture in Soviet Russia, Tales, Poems, Songs, Movies, Plays and Folklore, 1917–1953*, edited James von Geldern and Richard Stites (Bloomington, IN: Indiana University Press, 1995), xi–xxvii; Victoria E. Bonnell, *Iconography of Power: Soviet Political Posters under Lenin and Stalin* (Los Angeles: University of California Press, 1997); Katerina Clark, *The Soviet Novel: History as Ritual*, 3rd edition (Bloomington, IN: Indiana University Press, 2000); Richard Taylor, *Film Propaganda, Soviet Russia and Nazi Germany* (New York: Harper & Row Publishers, Inc., 1979), 44–50.

ideological messages and articulate legitimating myths.[13] Marline Otte locates a similar case in the context of interwar Germany, where the 'eagle cowboy' Erich Rudolf Otto Rosenthal, alias Billy Jenkins, made deliberate 'aesthetic choices' that transformed his once polyvalent Wild West circus act into 'a useful tool for Nazi propaganda'.[14] When Jenkins first staged his act after the First World War, he ensured its appeal to diverse audiences by relying on the 'multiple meanings'[15] of the eagle – 'an "empty sign" that could be filled with a wide range of potentially contradictory meanings' by symbolizing, for example, both internationalism and nationalism.[16] Yet when the political situation in Germany began to change during the 1920s, Jenkins altered his acts – he 'even trained his eagles to impersonate the living emblem on military standards, posing over an oversized German flag'[17] – so that their 'ambivalence … receded'.[18] Otte concludes that 'what had once found special appeal on the basis of its multiple meanings came to represent one single meaning, and turned into a powerful endorsement of Nazi ideology.'[19]

What makes the history of the Soviet circus so surprising is that its producers so briefly and only ever incompletely made similar aesthetic choices that altered the structure of circus performances to secure their ideological valence and bring them into line with other newly revolutionized cultural products. Instead, they preserved the circus in its conventional form and left its content ambiguous. Yet by doing so, they did not forfeit the political utility of the entertainment. It was the very ambivalence of the circus with all of its many meanings and potential ideological inflections that made the entertainment such a valuable resource for the Bolsheviks. Official commentators were able to spin such politically productive fictions about the content of the circus because acrobatic flips, fakirs' feats, precocious elephants, conversational clowns, and talking dolls did not communicate any monosemic message that precluded or necessarily refuted the meanings officially ascribed to them. The polyvalence of the show also provided for its popularity among diverse viewers who all appeared to conform to the mythic ideal, even as the circus remained a fun, enchanting, spectacularly amazing entertainment that never lost its appeal to viewers who might have fallen far short of that ideal. The history of the Soviet circus offers unexpected evidence that a popular cultural medium which refused to convey any unambiguous message, narrate any single story, or construct one consistent myth was no less suitable a site for asserting the legitimacy of the Russian revolution than were the didactic, narrative, and monumental forms of culture that are better known by Soviet historians and students of the political uses of popular culture.

13 James von Geldern, *Bolshevik Festivals*, 133.
14 Otte, 'Sarrasani's Theatre of the World', 541.
15 Ibid., 541.
16 Ibid., 539.
17 Ibid., 540.
18 Ibid., 541.
19 Ibid., 541.

Revolutionizing the circus

The circus came to Russia in 1790, when Charles Hughes, the manager of London's Royal Circus, travelled to St Petersburg with a stud of horses and a small troupe of performers, who staged Russia's first circus. Hughes and his partner, Charles Dibdin, had founded the Royal Circus in 1782 to compete with Hughes's former employer, Phillip Astley, who had established Astley's Amphitheatre in London in 1768. Astley is credited with having created the first modern circus, an entertainment that initially consisted only of his performance of tricks on horseback. Astley's equestrian displays made a hit with English men and women of high birth, but few others were so interested in the entertainment value of horses. The showman soon widened his production's appeal by introducing such popular fairground performers as jugglers, acrobats, tightrope walkers, sword-swallowers, strongmen, and clowns into the act. Hughes's Royal Circus did so with similar success and no less so when they travelled to Russia in 1790.[20] Catherine the Great attended a performance and became so taken by the circus and its proprietor – Hughes was himself an accomplished trick rider and became, some speculate, Catherine's lover – that she ordered amphitheatres built for him in St Petersburg and Moscow. Hughes spent three years in Russia, staging circus shows and teaching the equestrian arts. When he left, his horses, his students, and a market for the circus remained.[21]

In Russia, as in Western Europe, the circus held broad popular appeal, and, as a consequence, it attracted entrepreneurs who recognized it as a sensible business venture. In 1827, Nicholas I commissioned Jacques Tournaire, the founder of an itinerant troupe of riders in France, to build the first permanent circus building in St Petersburg. In 1830, M. N. Zagoskin sponsored the

20 The English equestrian performer, J. Bates, was the first to tour Russia in 1764, though he appeared without the other performers featured in Astley's and Hughes's productions. M. Wilson Disher, *Fairs, Circuses and Music Halls* (London: William Collins, 1942); A. H. Saxon, *Enter Foot and Horse, A History of Hippodrama in England and France* (New Haven, CT: Yale University Press, 1968), 10–12; Antony D. Hippisley Coxe, 'Equestrian Drama and the Circus', in *Performance and Politics in Popular Drama, Aspects of Popular Entertainment in Theatre, Film and Television 1800–1976,* edited by David Bradvy, Louis James, and Bernard Sharratt (New York: Cambridge University Press, 1980); George Speaight, *A History of the Circus* (San Diego, CA: A. S. Barnes and Company, 1980), 31–38, 155; Robert Leach, *Revolutionary Theatre* (New York: Routledge, 1994), 4; Stoddart, *Rings of Desire,* 15–16; M. E. Shvydkoi (ed.), *Tsirkovoe iskusstvo Rossii, entsiklopediia* (Moscow: Bol'shaia Rossiiskaia entsiklopediia, 2000), 270; Donna Gustafson, 'Images from the World Between: The Circus in Twentieth Century American Art', in *Images from the World Between: The Circus in Twentieth Century American Art*, (Cambridge, MA and New York: The MIT Press and American Federation of Arts, 2001), 11. Marius Kwint, 'The Circus and Nature in Late Georgian England', in *Histories of Leisure*, edited by Rudy Koshar (New York: Berg, 2002).

21 Speaight, *History of the Circus,* 155; Stoddart, *Rings of Desire*, 15–16.

construction of Moscow's first tent circus in the Neskuchnyi Garden, and in 1853, Guards Colonel Nikolai Novosil'tsev secured the support of Nicholas I for his construction of a winter circus in Moscow. In 1867, Karl Hinne erected a wooden circus in Moscow with the help of Gaetano Chinizelli, who gradually wrested control of the circus away from him. Chinizelli soon found his own rival in the person of Albert Salomonskii, who built Moscow's first stone circus in 1880 on Tsvetnoi Boulevard. Meanwhile, in 1873, three brothers, Dmitri, Petr, and Akim Nikitin, had become the first native Russians to launch a circus enterprise, which enjoyed great success throughout the provinces.[22] Nicholas II confirmed the brothers' reputations as the foremost circus masters in Russia when he commissioned them to raise two circuses on the Khodynka Fields to take part in the public celebrations of his coronation in 1896.[23] In 1911, the brothers opened the last pre-revolutionary circus in Moscow, one of 18 rings they managed at the time.

Though he was obviously no entrepreneur, Vladimir Il'ich Lenin recognized the popular appeal of the circus, and for that reason, it appealed to him too. On 26 August 1919, Lenin signed the 'Decree on the Unification of the Theatrical Concern', and later that year, the newly formed Circus Section undertook the task of 'cleansing' the newly nationalized circuses of 'unhealthy elements' and overseeing their further artistic development, as the decree of 26 August mandated.[24] Prominent members of the Soviet artistic avant-garde, such as Boris Erdman, Il'ia Ehrenburg, the poet Ivan Rukavishnikov, the ballet choreographer Kas'ian Goleizovskii, the painter Pavel Kuznetsov, the sculptor Sergei Konenkov, the theatre director N. M. Foregger and the sole circus 'specialist' M. A. Stanevskii, also known as the clown 'Bom', joined the staff.[25] Since few of them had any training in the circus arts, they were uniquely qualified to carry out their more specific mandate: to reform the circus by replacing its discrete routines with long narrative pantomimes that dramatized revolutionary themes.[26] As a result, the state circuses' first three seasons featured didactic theatrical spectacles that incorporated various circus attractions, as well as more classic circus acts that conveyed new ideological messages.

The first revolutionary pantomime to make its debut was Ivan Rukavishnikov's 'Political Carousel', which was staged at the Second State Circus

22 Russian State Archive of Literature and Art [RGALI] f. 2607 op. 1 d. 103 ll. 65–73; Iu. Dmitriev, *Russkii Tsirk* (Moscow: Iskusstvo, 1953); Iu. A. Dmitriev, *100 let Moskovskomu ordena Lenina gosudarstvennomu tsirku na Tsvetnom Bul'vare*, (Moscow: Vsesoiuznoe biuro propagandy sovetskogo tsirkovogo isksusstva, 1980); Iu. A. Dmitriev, 'Samorodki, k 100 letiiu pervogo Russkogo statsionarnogo tsirka', *Sovetskaia estrada i tsirk* 9 (1973), 18–21.

23 RGALI f. 2607 op. 1 d. 103 l. 68; 'Coronation of the Czar', *The New York Times*, 5 April 1896, 4.

24 'Dekret ob'edinenii teatral'nogo dela', *Vestnik teatra* 33 (1919), 2; GARF f. 2306, op. 24, d. 79.

25 'Tsirk', *Vestnik teatra* 39 (1919), 13.

26 Ibid.

in 1919 under the direction of Foregger on a set designed by Kuznetsov. The performance dramatized the struggle between labour and capital and culminated with the 'joyous celebration of the liberation of labor'.[27] That same season, the first State Circus also staged a pantomime on a less obviously revolutionary theme. Konenkov's 'Samson and Delilah' featured circus wrestlers who created 'living pictures' by assuming various poses to illustrate the events of the story. Konenkov explained that he was inspired by Maksim Gorkii's comparison of the Russian people's fate before the Revolution with the suffering of Samson: 'thrust to the ground by the heavy and rude mechanism of the poorly constructed state machine, the Russian people were constrained and blinded like Samson, who was truly a great sufferer.'[28] Konenkov claimed that viewers responded warmly to the parable of their own recent liberation from oppression.[29] One of the more enthusiastic fans of Konenkov's project was Anatolii Lunacharskii, Commissar of Enlightenment and the circus's most prominent government patron. In an article announcing its debut, he identified the story of Samson and Delilah as one of the 'most ancient stories of the struggle for freedom … of the eternal struggle of light and darkness'.[30] Konenkov's production was, in Lunacharskii's view, a true circus routine – a 'routine of that circus of which we can dream, a circus of exceptionally noble beauty, capable of directly relating the physical perfection of the human being to a deep internal content'.[31]

By the following year, Lunacharskii's dream circus appeared incarnate in the arena of the First State Circus, at least according to Vitalii Lazarenko, who introduced the programme:

Citizens!	*Grazhdane!*
Our circus has set out on a new path!	*Nash tsirk vstupil na novyi put'!*
We will cast vulgarity aside.	*Otbrosim poshlost'.*
We will improve our art	*Podnimem my svoe iskusstvo,*
so that in the circus	*Chtob v tsirke*
you can thoroughly	*vy smogli dushoiu otdokhnut'*
rest, and to bring happiness to the viewer ….	*I radost' prinesti i zriteliu i chuvstvu….*
we will amuse you with	*Vas shutkoi rassmeshim*
smart and lively jokes,	*razumnoi, zhivoi,*
we will show you the beauty, power,	*Pokazhem krasotu i moshch',*
and flexibility of the body!	*i gibkost' tela!*
Eccentrics, jesters, the trapeze flight,	*Ekstsentriki, shuty, s trapetsii polet,*

27 Ibid.; von Geldern, *Bolshevik Festivals*, 118.
28 S. Konenkov, 'V dvadtsatom godu', *Sovetskii tsirk* 2 (1957), 15.
29 Ibid.
30 A. Lunacharskii, 'Na novykh putiakh, Konenkov dlia tsirka', *Vestnik teatra* 44 (1919), 6.
31 Ibid., 7.

the educated, intelligent horse and muscles,	*Uchenyi umnyi kon' I muskuly iz stali*
everything here merges into one maelstrom.	*Vse zdes' slivaetsia v odin vodovorot.*
Bravery and talent, the aerial flip, and	*Otvaga I talent, pryzhok sal'to-mortale,*
the Lights of the Arena	*Ogni Areny vnov'*
will shine anew today	*segodnia zablestiat.*
Artists of the circus, we are setting out on	*Artisty tsirka, my na*
a new path	*novyi put' vstupaem.*
Now the fanfares will announce the opening	*Seichas fanfary vam otkryt'e vozvestiat.*
And so –	*Itak –*
We begin!	*My nachinaem!*[32]

After the cast paraded around the arena, one group of performers entered again, dressed like workers and peasants, carrying saws, axes, blocks, and poles, which they used to assemble several buildings. The performers concluded the pantomime by freezing in their positions to create a *tableau vivant* of 'Workers Creating a City', as the act was entitled.[33] The programme also featured miniature pantomimes that caricatured vulgar, infantile bourgeois women and mocked cowardly members of the Entente and then culminated in the second act with the staging of Rukavishnikov's pantomime, 'Chess', which featured a ring-sized chessboard that served as a field of battle between 'oppressors', in white, and the 'oppressed', in black. The two sides were represented by well-known literary, theatrical, and folkloric figures, including Don Quixote, Carmen, a travelling minstrel, a balalaika player, and Freedom itself pitted against a Sultan, a Yankee, a Toreador, an Iron Knight, and a Friar. The combatants engaged in a lively struggle, using animals, illusion tricks, music, and most other means of waging war in the circus. The side of the oppressed won the day. When the Workers' Leader captured the Sultan, he proclaimed, 'Check', and the other black figures cried 'Mate', prompting the vanquished oppressors to flee from the battlefield in a panic. The victors celebrated with a dance that ended in a still pose featuring Freedom, raised high above the rest, beckoning all the liberated peoples toward him.[34]

Like Konenkov, Rukavishnikov, and their collaborators, Vladimir Maiakovskii and his collaborator, Vitalii Lazarenko, also attempted to convey ideological messages through a conventional and very popular circus genre: the choreographed wrestling bout. Maiakovskii's 'Championship of the Universal Class Struggle',[35] which was staged by the Second State Circus in 1920,

32 Maksimilian Nemchinskii, *Tsirk Rossii naperegonki so vremenem, Modeli tsirkovykh spektaklei 1920–1990 godov* (Moscow: GITIS, 2001), 37.

33 Ibid., 39.

34 Ibid., 40–50.; 'Reorganizatsiia tsirkov', *Vestnik teatra* 63 (1920), 7–8.

35 For the complete text in translation, see Frantisek Deak and Vladimir Mayakovsky, 'The Championship of the Universal Class Struggle', *The Drama Review:*

dramatized the struggle between the Bolshevik revolution and a team of its enemies, who also competed among themselves for the spoils of the 'Imperial War'. The contenders included Lloyd George, Woodrow Wilson, Alexander Mitterrand, the White Army General Baron Petr Wrangel, the Polish nationalist Joseph Pilsudskii, and the 'Almost Champion', a Menshevik. Lazarenko played the roles of Uncle Vania, who officiated the match, and the revolution itself. Appearing as the former, he introduced each competitor with a satirical monologue and then announced that a gold crown inscribed with the phrase, 'Profit of the Imperial War', would be thrown into the ring. The wrestlers battled each other for the prize until Lazarenko reappeared in the role of 'Champion of Revolution'. In a skirmish between 'Revolution' and 'Entente', the clown dexterously flipped his opponent, but failed to pin him. Suddenly transforming himself back into the character of the referee, Lazarenko announced:

Neither side	*Ne mozhet poborot'*
can defeat the other.	*Ni eta storona, ni ta.*
Truce.	*Peremirie.*
Bah!	*T'fu!*
Break for ten minutes.	*Pereryv na desiat' minut.*
All who wish	*Vse kto khochet*
that	*Chtob*
the reds will win in ten minutes,	*Krasnye pobedili cherez desiat' minut,*
should return home	*pust' idut po domam –*
and set off tomorrow to the front as volunteers	*–A zavtra na front dobrovol'tsami–*
to wring Wrangel's neck.	*I Vrangeliu sheiu namnut.*
And I	*A Ia*
already	*Uzhe*
am heading there today	*segodnia tuda zhe*
and, for the sake of haste,	*a dlia skorosti*
in a carriage, no less.	*Vekipazhe dazhe.*[36]

By refusing to enact the red victory, Maiakovskii exhorted viewers to carry the revolution to victory themselves. This device also functioned to introduce some suspense into the event, since a wrestling bout was hardly worth watching if everybody knew which side was going to win.

Some circus performers did go so far as to dramatize the revolution's victory, including Lazarenko himself, who continued to figure the revolution as a stunning leap throughout the civil war. For example, a troupe of equestrian

TDR 17(1) (1973), 53–63. For excerpts of the original and a description of the performance, see Iu. Dmitriev, *Sovetskii tsirk*, 61–62.

36 Dmitriev, *Sovetskii tsirk*, 62.

clowns staged the defeat of the revolution's class enemies at the premier of the Second State Circus. In a classic circus sketch, known as 'The Riding Lesson',[37] or, in this case, as 'Madame Deni's Riding Lesson', the 'Countess Deni', played by a clown, revealed herself to be a miserable student of the equestrian arts – a particularly damning failure given her class position. In the course of her riding lesson, Madame Deni lost her wig, became entangled in her crinoline gown, and drooped from her horse, from which she hung 'suspended in the most surprising and amusing poses'.[38] Monsieur Deni groaned in horror as the Deni's servant futilely attempted to right his mistress. In the climactic sequence, Madame Deni caught her foot in a stirrup and rode through the ring upside down.

Lazarenko was the performer best known for his dramatic enactments of the revolution, which he figured as a stunning leap throughout the civil war. For nearly 20 years Lazarenko would remain a fixture of the Soviet state circuses, where he served as the model Soviet clown, praised in his life, remembered for decades after his death, and given much of the credit for revolutionizing the circus.[39] When Lazarenko launched his career as a clown in 1906, he adopted the *ryzhii*, or red-headed clown persona – a common, buffoon-like figure typically paired with a white-faced clown, known in Russia as the *belyi*, or white clown. The *belyi* clown, often called a *clown debonnaire* in France, was an elegant figure whose subtle make-up and fashionable costumes contrasted sharply with the stiff red hair and outlandish make-up of his mad-cap comrade, the *ryzhii* clown. In the traditional clowning team, order was maintained by the *belyi* clown, who attempted to discipline the disorderly *ryzhii*. For his part, the *ryzhii* flouted the *belyi*'s authority, regularly violating his partner's cherished rules and, more often than not, getting away with it.[40] For example, in 'The American Duel', a classic pre-revolutionary routine,

37 'Riding Lesson' skits were performed in the circus ring at least as early as the 1890s. V. E. Ferroni, *200 let na manezhe* (Moscow: Dizain-studiia, 1997), 63.

38 Dmitriev, *Sovetskii tsirk*, 44.

39 'Gallereia Samorodkov', *Zritel'* 2 (1922), 12–15; *Tridtsatipiatiletnii iubilei Vitaliia Efimovicha Lazarenko* (Moscow: Mosoblit, 1933); Iu. Dmitriev, 'Vitalii Lazarenko, k 40-letiiu artisticheskoi deiatel'nosti', *Sovetskoe iskusstvo*, 16 February 1939, 2; Mikh. Dolgopolov, 'Sorok let na arene tsirka', *Izvestiia*, 15 February 1939, 4; G. V. Aleksandrov, 'Smotr dostizhenii sovetskogo tsirka', *Pravda*, 24 March 1945, 4; A. Argo, 'Zhizn' na arene', *Sovetskii tsirk* 2 (1957), 16–18; RGALI f. 2499, op. 2, d. 297, l. 118; Evgenii Leonov, 'Staryi tsirk spravliaet iubilei', *Literaturnaia gazeta*, 12 November 1980, 8; R. Slavskii, *Vitalii Lazarenko* (Moscow: Iskusstvo, 1980); G. D. Endzinoi, 'Narodnyi shut (Al'bom Vitaliia Lazarenko) in *Vstrechi s proshlym*, Vypusk 1, 1983; S. M. Makarov, *Klounada mirovogo tsirka, Istoriia i repertuar* (Moscow: Rosspen, 2001), 65–75.

40 One of the most influential clowning genres was that of the white-faced clown, whose origins lie in the seventeenth-century *commedia dell'arte*. Following the example of three French farce players who powdered their faces with flour (they are said to have been bakers by trade), actors depicting the *commedia* characters Pedrolino, Gilles, and Pierrot also began to whiten their faces. English pantomime and acrobatic clowns, most famously Joseph Grimaldi, who performed in

the clowning duo, Lepom and Eizhen, challenged each other to a duel, which they executed by placing two scraps of paper, one marked life, the other death, into a hat. The clown who drew death lost the duel and would be shot. Predictably, Eizhen, the ryzhii clown, drew death and, recognizing the horror of his predicament, he bid a dramatic farewell to Lepom and the distraught onlookers. Eizhen stumbled out of the ring and, soon after, a shot resounded in the wings. melodramatically clasping his hands, Lepom moaned, 'Oh, what have I done?' Within seconds, however, Eizhen reappeared, joyously announcing, 'Thank God, a misfire!'[41] Although the disobedient clown obviously would have missed intentionally, he claimed to have obeyed the rules of the duel, attributing his survival to happenstance. In addition to demonstrating the *ryzhii*'s characteristic reliance on chance as a pretext for his own wilful rule-breaking, this routine also exemplified the *ryzhii*'s immunity from the dictates of language – a synecdoche for systems of order and authority more broadly – since the written words 'life' and 'death' failed to dictate the enactment of the experiences they signify.

Although Lazarenko performed without a white-faced partner, in the pre-Revolutionary period he directed his typically red-headed irreverence toward the higher authorities of the Imperial Russian state.[42] In one exemplary sketch, Lazarenko announced that the parliamentary Duma was so named because its only task was to think (*dumat'*) – it was not given anything to do. Lazarenko then read an explicitly anti-tsarist monologue condemning autocratic violence:

Abroad, they study the strength of guns	*Za granitsei silu pushek*
the whole year round	*Izuchaiut Kruglyi god*
and they don't shoot their own.	*I v svoikh tam ne streliaiut,*
And with us, it's the opposite.	*A u nas – naoborot.*[43]

London's variety theatres at the beginning of the nineteenth century, popularized this practice, which eventually became the mark of a discrete clown type. Although Russian clowns almost certainly imported from the West the whiteface persona, which they called simply *belyi* (white), Russia itself may have been the birthplace of the *ryzhii* – a native clown persona whose appearance predated that of the European august. By the 1870s, the evolution of the *ryzhii* had begun to parallel that of the Western buffoon, and the two personas eventually became indistinguishable, especially after the *ryzhii* began to perform as the comic counterpart of the *belyi* in the Russian ring. For a colourful history of the *Commedia dell'arte* including a catalogue of characters and actors who performed them, see Nicoll Allardyce, *Masks, Mimes, and Miracles, Studies in the Popular Theatre* (New York: Cooper Square Publishers, Inc., 1963), 214–379; on the pairing of the whiteface clown and the red-headed august, see John H. Towsen, *Clowns* (New York: Hawthorn Books, 1976), 214–223, 310–311.

41 bid., 159.

42 Vitalii Lazarenko, 'Vitalii Lazarenko, Kloun-prygun', in *Sovetskii tsirk, 1918–1938*, edited by Evgenii Kuznetsov (Moscow, Iskusstvo, 1938), 106.

43 Ibid., 107.

In 1922, Lazarenko wrote that in his performances, he tried to respond critically to the social evils of the day, and his early routines often did address viewers' everyday problems. For example, after the February Revolution, the clown lured the ringmaster – the figure of highest authority within the circus ring – into a satirical dialogue. He asked the ringmaster, 'Tell me, can a dog grow back a tail that's been cut off?' When the ringmaster replied with a resolute 'No', Lazarenko responded that a dog could indeed grow back a tail and guaranteed to prove it. He explained that one must simply hang a sign from the dog announcing that flour is given out here, and the dog will grow five *khvostov* – *khvost* meaning both tail and line.[44]

Whether funny or not, this joke exemplified the satiric humour that, according to Lunacharskii, Soviet performers should wield as an effective weapon in the revolutionary struggle. In a 1920 essay entitled, 'We will laugh', Lunacharskii celebrated the kind of satire that provoked the indignant laughter in which could be heard 'the snap of the whip and at times the peal of the approaching thunder of battle'. For Lunacharskii, laughter was the 'aspen stake that is driven into the recently slaughtered dark wizard, who is prepared to return from his coffin'. It was 'the hammering of sturdy nails into the black grave of the past'. Lunacharskii explained to his readers that they must not consider any victory over a vile enemy to be decisive, especially if the enemy is an entire class or an entire culture. Such an enemy, he wrote, 'entangles you from every side with thousands of poisoned threads, and he has thrust some of these tentacles into your very mind, into your very heart, and, like any hydra, he can be born again from any shoot'. Lunacharskii insisted that laughter could prevent this regeneration: 'There is such a substance, such a disinfectant, that makes everything foul evaporate – that is laughter, a great cleanser!' Lunacharskii concluded that

> in our time, when we have thrown down a gigantic enemy only in Russia, when we are entangled by the miasmas of the old culture that poison all our air, when that enemy still triumphs all around us, waiting for the moment to inflict a new blow, in this time, without dropping our swords from one hand, we take in our other hand a weapon that is already sharp – laughter.[45]

Lazarenko needed both his hands and two strong legs to wield the revolutionary whip-thunderclap-stake-hammer-cleanser-antidote-sword of laughter, and he put them to good use. After the October Revolution, he continued to perform politically tendentious routines, which now, however, were directed not against, but in support of the established authorities. The irreverent *ryzhii* persona hardly suited Lazarenko's new role as the champion of the Bolshevik regime, and he modified his appearance accordingly. Lazarenko abandoned the *ryzhii*'s red wig and exaggerated face paint in favour of a sanitized costume more typical of the *belyi* clown and, therefore, more appropriate to

44 Ibid., 117.
45 A. V. Lunacharskii, 'Budem smeiat'sia', *Vestnik teatra* 58 (1920), 7–8.

the serious work of cleansing the enemy from the hearts and minds of the Soviet people. Fulfilling Lunacharskii's mandate that the Soviet clown dare 'to be a publicist', Lazarenko trumpeted the achievements of the new Soviet state, often casting himself in the role of revolution in his individual monologues, as in his work with Maiakovskii.[46] For example, Lazarenko began one routine he performed in the Second State Circus by reading several couplets about freedom. He then pointed to an inflated bladder, shouted, 'Attention – the old regime', and jumped onto it, causing the bladder to 'burst with a deafening bang'.[47]

The introduction of explicitly ideological routines like these into the Soviet circus repertoire has led several historians of Soviet culture to conclude that the Bolsheviks turned the circus upside down. Richard Stites numbers the circus among the many forms of popular culture that the Bolsheviks 'infused' with 'revolutionary content', with the result that 'this was no longer folk nor popular culture; it was elitist revolutionary enlightenment and pseudo-religious missionary work for moral uplift and political persuasion'.[48] James von Geldern also concludes that a contemporary Soviet critic was correct to accuse the Circus Section of 'destroying the circus' with acts like Rukavishnikov's 'Political Carousel'.[49]

Yet the comic equestrian genre, for one, was hardly destroyed when it was made to ridicule members of the upper classes. Some viewers might not have even noticed that the hapless rider was named 'Countess Deni', just as they might not have known that the story of Samson and Delilah was told as an allegory for the revolution. Similarly, some viewers might have appreciated Lazarenko's performances because they celebrated the Bolshevik victory, while some might have been thrilled by his leaps alone, which were no less stunning because he called them a symbol of the revolution. Others might have admired 'the human body in the circus ... precisely for its independence, resourcefulness and self-reliance', as Helen Stoddart claims all viewers do.[50] Conventional circus acts that were infused with new revolutionary content or integrated into didactic theatrical spectacles still retained much of their appeal as extraordinary and amusing entertainments. The Bolsheviks did not manage to destroy the circus – or, from their point of view, to revolutionize it – by transforming it into an exclusive medium for ideological propaganda immediately after the revolution. While Stites's and von Geldern's conclusion can be more convincingly applied to the few most didactic monologues, pantomimes, and *tableaux vivants* featured in the first several seasons of the state circuses, it still does not account for the fact that in 1920, Soviet cultural administrators began to remove these routines, for fear that they were destroying the circus.

46 A. V. Lunacharskii, 'Zadachi obnovlennogo tsirka', *Vestnik teatra* 3 (1919), 5–6.
47 Vitalii Lazarenko, 'Vitalii Lazarenko, Kloun-prygun', in *Sovetskii tsirk, 1918–1938*, edited by Evgenii Kuznetsov (Moscow, Iskusstvo, 1938), 117.
48 Stites, *Russian Popular Culture*, 39, 51–52.
49 Von Geldern, *Bolshevik Festivals*, 119.
50 Helen Stoddart, *Rings of Desire*, 5.

Rhetorically revolutionizing the circus

In December 1920, the Theatre Department repudiated the Circus Section's attempt to replace varied circus attractions with narrative pantomimes and appointed a new staff of more experienced circus professionals to reverse the reform that had been implemented the previous year.[51] The administration denounced the 'persistent striving to fundamentally "theatricalize" the circus', which had 'radically destroyed the pure forms of circus art and made it impossible to preserve tried and true circus traditions'.[52] This reversal was initiated by Vsevolod Meierhold, who had been appointed to head the Theatre Department in September 1920 and had long deplored efforts to 'theatricalize' the circus, though Maksimilian Nemchinskii convincingly argues that economic imperatives, in addition to purely aesthetic concerns, secured the policy shift. He notes that the Soviet circuses continued to feature large-scale, narrative pantomimes through the 1921 season, well after Meierhold's tenure had ended in February. He also explains that the Circus Section, which was re-named the Central Administration of State Circuses (TsUGTs) in 1922, was reconstituted as a self-financing trust at that time, which meant that 'the administration had to solve the problem of devising programmes according to old methods whose success would be guaranteed'.[53] As a result, between 1920 and 1922, the pure forms of circus art were revived, the tried and true circus traditions were preserved, and the popularity of the circus was restored. Yet what Nemchinskii fails to note is that its producers continued to insist that the revolution in the circus had not been reversed.

After 1922, Soviet circus programmes featured conventional circus attractions that lacked much of the overtly ideological content with which they had been invested during the State Circuses' first three seasons. For example, one typical NEP-era routine was performed in Moscow in 1924 by the German acrobats Peters and Billy. The arena was set with tables, chairs, and barrels to resemble a bar, where the acrobats amused themselves by performing spectacular tricks. Billy climbed onto the shoulders of Peters, who jumped into and out of the barrels and onto the tables. Peters next assembled the furniture into an elaborate pyramid and topped it with a chair. Billy sat on the chair, placed an apple on top of his head, and held a sword above it. Peters then leapt over Billy's head and pressed down on the sword with his leg so that it sliced through the apple. For their act's final trick, Peters jumped over four chairs that were standing in a row.[54]

51 Circus performers including Lazarenko, Leon Tanti, and the clown Serzh were temporarily appointed to the Circus Sections' Artistic Council of the Moscow State Circuses, whose members were removed. 'V tsirkakh', *Vestnik teatra* 76–77 (1920), 23.

52 Ibid.

53 Nemchinskii, *Tsirk v Rossii*, 58.

54 For this and other examples, see, Nemchinskii, *Tsirk v Rossii*, 332–351, 372–383.

This was hardly Lazarenko's revolutionary leap, which was a fact not lost on some NEP-era observers who noted that very little had changed in Soviet circuses since 1917. A delegation from the Voronezh circus reported to have 'found no particular difference between the pre-revolutionary and contemporary circuses' that they attended in Moscow even as early as 1921.[55] According to another review, the debut production of the First State Circus in the 1922 was comprised entirely of 'old acts'.[56] That same season another critic complained that the 'perfidious administration fed' attendants to the Second State Circus 'the worst numbers of past years'.[57] As late as 1929, Sergei Sokolov stated that there was 'still no Soviet circus'.[58] He decried the absence of the 'revolutionary agitator, the proletarian organizer of the masses' from Soviet circus productions, which continued to rely on 'convention, the old traditions left to us from the bourgeois circus'.[59]

Precisely because the Soviet circus was so vulnerable to this criticism throughout the 1920s, its producers and many official observers insisted that the revival of what some considered a typically bourgeois circus actually marked the emergence of an authentically revolutionary entertainment – one that did serve as a political agitator and organizer of the masses. In 1925, Lunacharskii described the circus as being 'close to the masses',[60] which implied not only that the entertainment was popular, but also that it could be used effectively to enlighten, instruct, and influence the Soviet people.[61] He explained that the Bolsheviks appropriated the circuses with the intention of using them as 'one element of the new artistic-educational policies'.[62] As Moris Gorei reported in 1928, it was precisely the edifying function of the Soviet circus that made it authentically revolutionary from its producers' point of view. Gorei quoted two circus officials who explained to him that 'in the Soviet Union, the circus has been made into a "school for the education of the worker and peasant masses"', whereas the circuses of the capitalist West were useful only to the extent that they made a profit.[63] In the Soviet circus, he concluded, the 'the artist is not a phenomenon, but an instructor, who can be successfully imitated'.[64]

55 GARF f. 2312, op. 6, d. 6, l. 2.
56 V. Zh-i., 'Tsirk. Otkrytie pervogo gostsirka', *Zrelishche* 8 (1922), 25.
57 G. Noks, 'Tsirk. Vo vtorom gosudarstvennom', *Zrelishche* 13 (1922), 20.
58 Sergei Sokolov, 'Za sovetizatsiiu tsirka', *Tsirk i estrada* 14 (1929), 8.
59 Ibid.
60 A. Lunacharskii, 'Piat' let Gosudarstvennykh tsirkov', *Tsirk* 3 (1925), 3.
61 In his study of journalism during the 'NEP mass enlightenment project', Matthew Lenoe observes that newspapermen often used the phrase 'closer to the masses' as 'code' for the task of improving the press and using it 'more effectively to influence the masses'. Matthew Lenoe, *Closer to the Masses, Stalinist Culture, Social Revolution, and Soviet Newspapers* (Cambridge, MA: Harvard University Press, 2004), 27.
62 Lunacharskii, 'Piat' let Gosudarstvennykh tsirkov', 3.
63 Moris Gorei, 'Tsirk Frantsuzkii i Russkii', *Tsirk* 8 (1928), 2.
64 Ibid.

In May 1919, the animal trainer Vladimir Leonidovich Durov also assigned a pedagogical role to the 'new healthy art of the circus', which he claimed would contribute to 'the urgent enlightenment of the popular masses'.[65] Durov considered this 'key to the successful building of socialism',[66] and he attempted to contribute to this project himself by literally transforming the circus ring into a 'model school' for his 'four-legged and plumed friends' who 'sat on benches like real school children'.[67] In his memoir, Durov recalled that the public was astonished to see his 'pupils' turn the pages of specially made wooden books with their snouts, beaks, and fins. Even the ass, who sat on the last bench, turned the book's pages with his nose and roared loudly when asked to recite a lesson. All of the animals were diligent students, but Durov's elephant, Baby, was the 'head pupil' and often received a 5+, the highest mark, for his demonstrations of knowledge and skill. When asked to add three plus four, for example, the elephant picked up an enormous piece of chalk with his trunk and drew seven lines on the blackboard. Seeing that the elephant had solved the problem, the pelican hissed in approval, but was immediately silenced by Durov, who shouted, significantly, 'no prompting please! Mine is not an ordinary school, but a model school.' Durov admitted that Baby occasionally drew too few lines, a mistake that would be corrected quickly by his dog Lord, who barked once for each line still needed. Sometimes Baby also drew too many lines, in which case Leo, the sea lion, would erase the extra lines with his fin. 'The public applauded me and my pupils and laughed uproariously', Durov recalled. 'It seemed to them an incredible thing.'[68] Durov's act was meant to serve as an analogy for the custodial relationship that circus viewers and performers and, by extension, Soviet state and society were meant to maintain during this period. Even when they did not perform in actual model schools, trained animals were officially presented as the exemplary pupils of beneficent educators, as Karl Krane explained in 1926, when he stated that in the Soviet Union, 'there are no tamers, only teachers'.[69]

According to the official rhetoric, other Soviet circus performers, whose work was less literally pedagogical than animal trainers', also taught viewers important lessons. In a 1925 essay on 'The Child and the Circus', Lunacharskii claimed that athletic circus performances taught children the value of disciplined work. He described the performer as a 'worker who achieves miracles by means of a persistent desire to attain perfection', and, consequently, provided children with a model of the 'conscious relationship to labour'.[70] According to Lunacharskii, children saw in the circus an example, which they might imitate, of physical strength and agility that had been

65 Vladimir Durov, 'Proekt shkoly tsirka', *Vestnik teatra* 24 (1919), 4.
66 Ibid.
67 V. L. Durov, *My Circus Animals*, trans. John Cournos (New York: Houghton Mifflin Company, 1936), 73–75.
68 Ibid.
69 Karl Krane, 'Sekrety ukrotitelia', *Tsirk* 6 (1926), 11.
70 A. L. 'Rebenok i tsirk', *Tsirk* 3 (1925), 10.

achieved through patient lessons, systematic labour, and courage.[71] Later that year, another reviewer explicitly attributed an edifying function to gymnastic circus performances that, in his view, demonstrated the same rhythm and precision of movement demanded of industrial labourers. These performances acquired an 'educational meaning', he claimed, when they were parodied by clowns, who repeated the actions of jugglers and acrobats more slowly and deliberately in order to demonstrate the potential of the human body to move quickly, intensely, and dynamically.[72] 'In general', he concluded, 'many circus numbers can serve as a good method for the propagandizing of the principles of scientifically organized labour and for convincing the masses of its utility and necessity'.[73] 'Scientifically organized labour' was the Soviet term for Frederick Taylor's methods of scientific management.

One of the more dramatic examples of Soviet rhetorical acrobatics during the NEP period was provided by fakirs and their promoters, who claimed that their performances convinced the Soviet people of the utility and necessity of possessing a strong will. In 1926, the circus director A. M. Dankman heralded the arrival in the Soviet Union of the internationally renowned fakir, To-Ramo, which meant, The Conqueror, in Sanskrit. To-Ramo was famed for the strength of his will, by means of which alone he purportedly subdued wild animals and conquered his own body. In one routine that Dankman described, To-Ramo removed a wild eagle from its cage in the arena, and though the eagle beat its wings malevolently and threatened To-Ramo with its claws, the fakir instantly compelled it to lie lifeless before him. To-Ramo similarly cowed a boa-constrictor with a single glance, forcing it to look indifferently upon a nearby rabbit, just as he had placed an unresisting chicken safely into the mouth of a crocodile.[74] When asked to explain why he chose to perform in the circus, To-Ramo insisted that the promise of fame and fortune hardly enticed him into the ring, and that 'only the conviction that I might show my viewers the strength of will a person can possess and inspire them to follow my example carried me into the arena.'[75]

Although To-Ramo and his admirers encouraged circus viewers to imitate his disciplined will rather than his actual 'experiments', one Soviet promoter of the fakir arts did encourage viewers to try these tricks at home so that they might learn another lesson: that religion is deceitful. In a pamphlet published in 1928, Izmail Urazov heralded such fakir tricks as fire-eating, walking on nails, and live burials as 'miracles of will' that 'debunked divine occurrences' and thereby served as 'anti-religious propaganda'.[76] He explained that circus fakirs modelled their performances on the feats of physical strength and discipline achieved by true Indian fakirs and then described how they trained

71 Ibid.
72 Sotnik, 'Tsirk i trud', *Tsirk* 5 (1925), 10.
73 Ibid.
74 A. M. Dankman, 'To-Ramo', *Tsirk* 1 (1926), 8.
75 To-Ramo in A. M. Dankman, 'To-Ramo', *Tsirk* 1 (1926), 8.
76 Izmail Urazov, *Fakiry* (Moscow: Tea-kino-pechat', 1928), 5.

their bodies to perform some common tricks. For example, to prepare for performances of the 'Human Aquarium', in which the artist first swallowed and then vomited up 30–40 glasses of water along with live fish and frogs, one was to swallow increasingly large amounts of water and, with the last sip, a vomit-inducing emetic. Over time, the dose of emetic was reduced until none was needed to activate the gag reflex after the last gulp of water was consumed. Urazov warned readers that to prevent injury, fish must be swallowed head first, and added that swallowing frogs posed no physical risk, although it might prove unpleasant when a frightened amphibian urinated into one's mouth.[77] Urazov hoped that this and other examples would convince readers of the 'tremendous training, will, and self-control' required of these artists, whose performances revealed all purported 'miracles' to be merely the result of 'training, knowledge, and will'.[78] For Urazov, the circus provided lessons in both self-discipline and atheism.

Another author similarly mouthed the official line on the circus in an article on ventriloquism, a conventional circus genre that he or she claimed propagated anti-religious principles. The author explained that viewers once considered ventriloquism to be a 'mysterious, inexplicable, almost supernatural' phenomenon, but this was before the cheerful, satirical genre of speaking dolls rescued ventriloquism from the 'lot of "miracles"'.[79] Since religious miracles were never presented as amusing or cheerful – 'with the exception of the evangelical legend of Christ's turning water into wine in the Sea of Galilee' – the author doubted whether even the most devout person could discern a 'mystical foundation' in the following trenchant dialogue between a ventriloquist and his doll: 'Karlusha, why is your nose red? Because I'm treating my anemia with vodka.'[80]

Between 1919 and 1929, producers and boosters of the Soviet circus consistently claimed that its performances propagated revolutionary messages to viewers who readily received them. Because the meaning of NEP-era circus acts, just like conventional circus acts performed in most other times and places, remained ambiguous, they readily accommodated the political messages rhetorically ascribed to them by producers, performers, and official commentators. Yet it is hard to imagine that the spectacle of a fakir vomiting frogs and a ventriloquist talking to his doll convinced everyone in the crowd to give up religion. Every child who saw a trapeze act did not necessarily develop a conscious attitude toward labour – though some might have – just as trained animals did not always present themselves to their viewers as products of a successful educational system. One animal trainer reported in 1928 that a group of peasants who had seen his act refused to believe that his performing dogs were trained at all. 'Although they were amazed,' he stated, the peasants

77 Ibid., 8–12.
78 Ibid., 31.
79 'Chrevoveshchateli', *Tsirk* 8 (1927), 11.
80 Ibid.

insisted that his dogs were '"not dogs, but some peculiar type of things" that are born trained'.[81] His viewers had clearly missed the message, though they were still amazed and obviously entertained by the novel spectacle.

Acrobatic displays, animal acts, To-Ramo's feats of will, various ventriloquists, and sundry human aquaria were as entertaining as they had been in the past and still were in the West, which is why they were harnessed to the project of mass enlightenment in the first place. This meant that circus viewers might not have comprehended, concurred with, or been at all concerned with the messages these performances were purported to send, and they still could have enjoyed the show. Lazarenko's routines were perhaps an exception, since he continued to integrate overtly political rhetoric into his amazing displays of physical prowess throughout the 1920s and into the 1930s. Yet given that his routines were exceptional for their political content during the NEP era, just as they were exceptional for their political content before 1917, they hardly provided proof that his revolutionary leaps were anything more than metaphorical. By marking a clear site of continuity between the pre-revolutionary circus and the post-revolutionary circus, his performances seemed to stand as proof that the Soviet circus was 'still just marking time', as A. K. Finikov, a 'working viewer' put it in his 1929 article, 'The Circus is Conservative'. Despite Lazarenko's occasional example and endless official claims to the contrary, Finikov concluded that acrobats, animal trainers, and clowns had yet to be mobilized effectively for the creation of 'our authentic revolutionary circus'.[82]

Reception

The possibility that viewers like Finikov might have missed the messages that circus performances meant to send threatened to dismantle the myth that the Soviet public eagerly attended an authentically revolutionary circus, which is why this possibility was effectively denied by the makers and most official reviewers of the Soviet circus between 1919 and 1929. The question of the audience's response to the circus, and to the theatre, film, and newspapers, was first systematically addressed during the NEP period, when the partial re-introduction of the market allowed for a degree of social differentiation that undermined any assumption of a socio-economically homogenous audience.[83]

81 'Zametki na poliakh', *Tsirk i estrada* 2 (1928), 9.

82 Finikov complained that circus programmes had not changed at all over the past ten to 15 years: 'It is possible that in the course of a season one or two contemporary, tendentious numbers will appear, but as a rule, the circus is still just marking time'. A. K. Finikov, 'Tsirk konservativen (golos Rabochego Zritelia)', *Tsirk i estrada* 20–21 (1929), 5.

83 Lars Kleberg, 'The Nature of the Soviet Audience: Theatrical Ideology and Audience Research in the 1920s', in *Russian Theatre in the Age of Modernism*, edited by Robert Russell and Andrew Barratt (New York: St Martin's Press, 1990); Yuri Tsivian, *Early Cinema in Russia and its Cultural Reception,* edited by Richard Taylor, trans. Alan Bodger (New York: Routledge, 1994); Lenoe, *Closer to the Masses*, 70–100.

Yet while studies of circus viewers recognized the heterogeneity of the audience, acknowledged that the circus appealed to different groups of people for different reasons, and might have represented a sincere attempt to identify viewers' responses, those responses were interpreted in ways that confirmed assertions about circus reception that had been articulated in advance of any study. In the 1920s, audience studies were publicized less to offer any insight into reception than to promote a normative model of proper circus viewing and to provide evidence that Soviet audiences already conformed to it. The official myth regarding reception was an essential element of the revolution in circus rhetoric that was achieved during NEP, when much of the revolutionary content had been removed from circus rings in order to ensure that the show would be well-received.

In 1925, for example, Lunacharskii reported the results of surveys distributed by the editors of the journal *Tsirk* [*Circus*], who received 100 responses from children aged 12–15 years and 50 responses from workers. The survey, which asked respondents to compare the circus, theatre, and film, solicited 'completely unexpected' results from the schoolchildren, according to Lunacharskii.[84] Nearly 90 per cent of young viewers claimed to prefer either theatre or film to the circus, with preferences evenly split between the former two. According to Lunacharskii's summary of the results, the children found nothing interesting, noble, or instructive in the spectacle of people 'spinning around, risking their lives for a piece of bread, cracking dim-witted jokes, and laughing stupidly'.[85] They concluded that the circus is only for NEPmen, who love rude spectacles. This answer was obviously incorrect from Lunacharskii's point of view, and he attributed the children's failure to identify the virtues of the circus to their own incorrect sensibilities. Lunacharskii admitted that he was slightly horrified that these 'already intellectualized young men and women have lost their taste for the delights of physical achievement and concentrate their attention, instead, on the simple and irresponsible delights of the theatre'.[86] He doubted that a single athletic young person would consider the circus a spectacle fit only for NEPmen and to prove this assertion he described the warm reception the circus found among working viewers, who 'love' the circus because they 'have a much more conscious attitude toward the significance of the circus as an educational spectacle'.[87]

Lunacharskii refused to acknowledge that the circus clearly had failed to teach children the benefits of physical development. His argument implied that health, strength, and agility lay in the eyes of the beholder and that those eyes could not be opened by the spectacle of health, strength, and agility alone. This interpretation seemed to contradict his contention that the circus

84 A. L. 'Shkolnaia anketa', *Tsirk* 5 (1925), 5.
85 Ibid.
86 Ibid.
87 Ibid.

was an effective educator, yet Lunacharskii offered it in order to idealize those viewers who preferred the circus precisely because, he claimed, it was an educational spectacle. Lunacharskii insisted that the children surveyed disliked the circus because they failed to recognize its ideological significance, which, according to his reasoning, only proved that viewers who liked the circus did so because they apprehended its educational messages. He presented viewership data less to describe viewers' real responses than to articulate the myth that those who liked the show were already ideal.

In 1927, researchers at the Theatre Research Workshop surveyed viewers at the Moscow state circus and also discovered that, like Lunacharskii's schoolchildren, some viewers 'uniformly disapproved of the circus as a form of art'.[88] They noted, though, that these negative opinions were expressed in 'clumsy, uncouth' phrases by viewers who had arrived in Moscow from elsewhere and were, the authors noted, mainly peasants.[89] Just as Lunacharskii had discounted children's criticisms, the authors of this study simply dismissed those viewers' distaste for the circus, implicitly attributing it to their ignorance and abnormality. Like Lunacharskii's, their evaluation of viewers' responses was meant to idealize those viewers who did like the circus precisely because, the researchers implied, it was a politically educational medium. The study did offer evidence that some of these ideal audience members already existed. Its authors reported that respondents generally approved of demonstrations of 'the agility of the healthy body' and that they disapproved of clown acts that were too often 'boring… [sic] monotonous… [sic] not funny enough… [sic] not satirical… [sic] repellent… [sic] outdated… [sic] pitiful'.[90] The researchers considered this last criticism valid because even though it indicated an absence of agitational content from the circus repertoire, these responses confirmed the official claim that agitational content is what Soviet circus audiences sought.

In 1928, the Theatre Research Workshop provided additional evidence that ideal circus viewers really did exist in the Soviet Union, or at least in Tula, where the study was conducted. Their report included the examples of a Red Army soldier who recognized the edifying function of gymnastic routines and a worker who noted that the 'grand art' of physical performance 'attracts young people to physical culture'.[91] The authors also endorsed viewers' demands for improved clown acts that included 'more satire, more humour'.[92] According to the researchers, viewers responded positively to the routines of Vitalii Lazarenko, who told satiric jokes on the themes of hooliganism, drunkenness, and alimony payments, while also performing more

88 Issledovatel'skaia teatral'naia masterskaia, 'Zritel' tsirka', *Sovetskoe iskusstvo*, August 1927, 58.

89 Ibid.

90 Ibid., 59.

91 Issledovatel'skaia teatral'naia masterskaia, 'Zritel' Tul'skogo tsirka', *Sovetskoe iskusstvo*, February 1928, 54.

92 Ibid.

commonplace clown acts. They noted that 62 per cent of blue collar workers favoured Lazarenko's performance, whereas 62 per cent of white collar workers found it dissatisfying.[93] Although the authors neglected to comment on this discrepancy, their reference to it implied that white collar workers failed to appreciate the agitational content of Lazarenko's act, unlike the implicitly ideal Soviet viewers, who did.

In the 1920s, studies of Soviet audiences concluded that official commentators were correct to claim that viewers liked the circus because it featured edifying displays of physical feats and revolutionary messages. The evidence they offered was highly selective, interpreted subjectively, and therefore unreliable, but nothing more credible existed to contradict it. Any claim that Soviet viewers patronized the circus because it was novel, spectacular, and largely lacking in ideological content must remain merely speculative. The absence of any reliable evidence regarding the reception of the circus is an obvious obstacle for historians, except insofar as it helps explain why Soviet officials privileged its production. For them, the virtue of the circus lay not only in its purported utility as a propagator of public enlightenment and ideological instruction, but in the ease with which its audience could be idealized. Because audiences offered no indication of their responses to the show, other than those that were officially solicited and readily manipulated, Soviet commentators could effectively establish the myth that audiences clapped, laughed, and kept buying tickets to the circus for the same reason that state officials claimed to produce it, namely for purposes of revolutionary enlightenment. The essential fact, for the producers and official observers of Soviet culture, was that so many Soviet people had good reason to like the circus, which they themselves also had good reason to like, regardless of whether, in truth, those reasons were the same. No matter how far the political demands, cultural desires, and basic perceptions of the Soviet people and the Soviet state diverged, the circus appeared to confirm their consistency and congruity. Between 1919 and 1929, the ideological message that the official circus rhetoric conveyed most consistently was the legitimating myth that a homogenous Soviet public unanimously embraced the enlightening product of an authentically revolutionary Soviet state.

Conclusion

Clearly, not everyone was convinced. Spectators complained in surveys and occasionally in the press about the absence of ideological content from performances that, in their view, had hardly been revolutionized. By 1929, circus producers and reviewers had also come to agree that a second revolution in the circus was required, and once again, this revolution would be largely rhetorical. During the period of Stalin's 'Great Break', when Soviet nature, in all of its vegetal, mineral, and human varieties was to be transformed, the

93 Ibid., 55.

circus was said to offer proof that human beings could break the laws of nature by adhering to proper methods of socialist labour. Circus performances during the first Five-Year Plan still remained almost entirely conventional, with the exception that they were less likely to feature the foreign performers who had populated circus rings through the NEP period but were steadily being replaced by young, Soviet trained performers. By the time socialism was declared victorious in the mid-1930s, most observers agreed that these performers – all perfect products of Soviet socialism – had succeeded in transforming crowds of circus viewers into new Soviet men and women, who were inspired by the superhuman feats they saw in the circus to perfect themselves too. According to the official rhetoric, the revolution in the circus had finally been achieved, even though overtly ideological content remained largely absent from its performances. Commentators claimed throughout the late 1930s that young Soviet performers, who physically embodied the future in the present, realistically reflected the optimism of the smiling circus viewers, for whom life had become, very visibly, 'better … more joyous'.[94]

Throughout its history, the Soviet circus remained a productive site for the construction of political myths. Because it was a varied, flexible medium whose content remained ambiguous, the circus could accommodate the multiple, changing, and even contradictory messages that producers, performers, and official reviewers attributed to it rhetorically. This was a key virtue of the entertainment for Soviet state officials, whose political, economic, social, and cultural imperatives were frequently contradictory and underwent periodic revision. Whatever the official fiction – that the Bolshevik revolution had been achieved by 1919, that NEP culture remained revolutionary, that the Soviet people had any reason to smile in 1938 – the circus could both be said and be seen to confirm it consistently, which explains why Soviet cultural administrators chose to produce a mass entertainment that was so different from the didactic media, narrative art forms, and monumental modes of representation that thrived in the post-revolutionary propaganda state.

94 Miriam Neirick, *When Pigs Could Fly and Bears could Dance* (Madison, WI: University of Wisconsin Press, 2012), 77–91. In 1935, Joseph Stalin declared: 'Life has become better, comrades. Life has become more joyous'.

4 The Communist youth league and the construction of Soviet *obshchestvennost'*

Matthias Neumann

Historical paradigms do not die easily. The image of an omnipresent and omnipotent autocratic regime which left no space for civic initiative and social engagement endured for a long time after it had been washed away by the February Revolution of 1917. Indeed, in popular history the paradigm remains prevalent. It is, however, far from the truth as numerous scholars have shown convincingly.[1] Modernity arrived in Russia long before the watershed of 1917. This was reflected in the emergence of a vivid nascent civil society in which social and civic organizations provided autonomous spaces of collective social engagement for the common good.[2] Concepts of a collectivist society enjoyed great currency in late Imperial Russia. *Sobornost* and *obshchestvennost'* were Russian answers to the Western concept of individualism. Numerous philanthropic, educational, cultural, and recreational organizations mushroomed before and after the revolution of 1905, particularly in the growing urban centres. These penetrated not only the middle and upper classes but also the working class. Indeed, as Alice Pate has shown, in the late Imperial period a network of workers, intellectuals, students, professors, and professionals began to form, expressing aspirations and vision for social and political reform.[3] The Great Reforms under Alexander II, accelerating urbanization and state-sponsored industrialization, as well as increased interest in Russian national culture facilitated this development.[4] It was in the urban

1 Adele Lindenmeyr, *Voluntary Associations and the Russian Autocracy: The Case of Private Charity*, The Carl Beck Papers in Russian and East European Studies No 807 (Pittsburgh, PA: University of Pittsburgh Center for Russian and East European Studies, 1990); Edith W. Clowes, Samuel D Kassow and James L. West (eds), *Between Tsar and People: Educated Society and the Quest for Public Identity in Late Imperial Russia*(Princeton, PA: Princeton University Press, 1991); Bradley, *Voluntary Associations in Tsarist Russia: Science, Patriotism and Civil Society* (Cambridge, MA: Harvard University Press, 2009).

2 Catriona Kelly and David Shepherd (eds), *Constructing Russian Culture in the Age of Revolution: 1880–1940* (Oxford: Oxford University Press, 1998).

3 Alice K. Pate, 'Workers and *Obshchestvennost'*: St. Petersburg 1906–1914', *Revolutionary Russia* 15(2) (2002), 53–71.

4 Joseph Bradley, 'Voluntary Associations, Civic Culture, and *obshchestvennost'* in Moscow', in Clowes, Kassow, and West (eds), *Between Tsar and People*, 139–141.

context that the term *obshchestvennost'* came to supply a 'common identity to people of different estates and professions (*and varying political views*) who committed themselves to social duties.'[5]

The old and new *obshchestvennost'*

Obshchestvennost' is a term which is notoriously difficult to define. It carries with it connotation of public sphere, civil society, educated public, and social and political associational engagement.[6] It is possible, albeit problematic, to locate the radical intelligentsia and even revolutionaries, with their visionary service to society, within *obshchestvennost'*, even though they often found themselves at odds with the liberal groups that worked within the existing political system and did not define themselves primarily in opposition to it. The professoriate, for instance, as Samuel Kassow has pointed out, regarded the student movement (*studentchestvo*) as a 'major obstacle in the fight for academic freedom and university autonomy';[7] while the uncensored oppositional press would generally celebrate *studentchestvo*, portraying it as progressive and as part of 'public opinion' in Russia, a marker of an increasingly dynamic Russian society (*obshchestvo*).[8] The blurred and hybrid character of the concept of *obshchestvennost'* was also personified by many revolutionaries. As, for example, in the person of the future Commissar of Health Nikolai A. Semashko. As many young revolutionaries of his generation, he showed a genuine interest in social services and public health while working as a political activist during his student days in the 1890s.[9]

Obshchestvennost', then, provided a conceptual framework that allowed enough diversity to unite people with opposing ideological perspectives. Whereas some wanted to challenge and overthrow the existing order, others supported it and were prepared to work with it; others, in turn, oscillated between these two extreme poles. They all, however, coalesced in their commitment to social engagement and activism, which in itself marked a challenge to an authority of centralized powers and entrenched officialdom. What is apparent from our brief discussion of this concept is that, in theory and practice, the relationship of the imperial Russian state to *obshchestvennost'* can hardly be seen as a clear dichotomy. Indeed, this observation applies even

5 Catriona Kelly and Vadim Volkov, '*Obshchestvennost', Sobornost'*: Collective Identities', in *Constructing Russian Culture in the Age of Revolution: 1880–1940*, edited by Catriona Kelly and David Shepherd (Oxford: Oxford University Press, 1998), 27. Emphasis mine.

6 Michael David-Fox, 'Review of Il'ina, *Obshchestvennye organizatsii Rossii v 1920-e gody*', *Kritika: Explorations in Russian and Eurasian History* 3(1) (2002), 173.

7 Samuel D. Kassow, *Students, Professors, and the State in Tsarist* (Berkeley, CA: University of California Press), 5.

8 Susan Morrissey, *Heralds of Revolution: Russian Students and the Mythologies of Radicalism* (Oxford: Oxford University Press, 1998), 96.

9 A short biography can be found in Anna J. Haines, *Health Work in Soviet Russia* (New York: Vanguard Press, 1928), 35–38.

more so to the relationship between the Soviet state and *obshchestvennost'*. In the 1920s, a huge bureaucratic machine emerged in Soviet Russia, a propaganda and agitation apparatus consisting of a vast number of agencies disseminating the Bolshevik cultural project and monitoring its implementation.[10] This apparatus was, however, not the only agency concerned with the propagation of the Bolsheviks' cultural visions. One of the crucial features of Communist propaganda in the early Soviet period was that it included elements of civil society and thus offered opportunities for collectivist expressions.

Despite its attempt to break completely with the tsarist past, the Bolsheviks inherited the cultural currents of the pre-revolutionary era. Seeking to create an egalitarian society in which the individualistic 'I' would be replaced by the collective 'us', the regime enunciated the formation of a Soviet *obshchestvennost'* (*sovetskaia obshchestvennost'*) through various social and cultural organizations. These new mass organizations were intended to act as transmission belts between the state and society.[11] They severed multiple functions in this context. In becoming pillars of the new Soviet *obshechestvennost'* these organizations were supposed to help integrating a very fragmented population into a structured Soviet society, they were meant to represent and gain mass support for the Bolshevik transformation project, providing it with much needed legitimacy.[12] Stalin later called them 'the root of the socialist organization of the public'.[13] As Sandra Dahlke has asserted, this Soviet civic or public sphere (*Öffentlichkeit* in German) has to be understood as a complex communication network which was created in negotiation between diverse interest groups as well as between society and political authority. The dialogue between these groups, organizations and political actors, was led in the public sphere (*öffentlichen Raum*), making all participants part of it.[14]

The 1920s witnessed an impressive growth in a wide variety of social organizations, from state-sponsored mass organizations such as the Komsomol, or the paramilitary league *OSOAVIAKhIM* to small cultural-enlightenment societies and sport associations.[15] The regime-sponsored voluntary organizations

10 Vladimir Brovkin, *Russia after Lenin: Politics, Culture and Society, 1921–1929* (London: Routledge, 1998), 81.
11 As explained by Lenin with regards to the trade unions: Lenin, 'Speech at a Joint Meeting of Communist Delegates to the Eighth Congress of Soviets, Communist Members of the All-Russia Central Council of Trade Unions and Communist Members of the Moscow City Council of Trade Unions', December 30, 1920, *Collected Works, Vol. 32* (Moscow: Progress Publishers, 1965), 21.
12 Sandra Dahlke, 'Kampagnen für Gottlosigkeit: Zum Zusammenhang zwischen Legitimation, Mobilisierung und Partizipation in der Sowjetunion der zwanziger Jahre'. *Jahrbücher für Geschichte Osteuropas* 50 (2002), 174–175.
13 Karl E. Loewenstein 'Re-Emergence of Public Opinion in the Soviet Union: Khrushchev and Responses to the Secret Speech',*Europe-Asia Studies* 58(8), (December 2006), 1331.
14 Dahlke, 'Kampagnen für Gottlosigkeit', 174.
15 Probably the most complete list of these organizations can be found in Irina N. Il'ina, *Obshchestvennye organizatsii Rossii v 1920- e gody* (Moscow: Institut

(*dobrovol'noe obshchestvo*) and social organizations (*obshchestvennye organisatsii*), in particular, became a focal object and agent in this process of constructing the Soviet public (*sovetskaia obshchestvennost'*). At the same time, we should not forget that many pre-revolutionary associations, cultural clubs, societies and theatre groups continued to function under their existing charters until the late 1920s.[16] The continuing existence of these organizations and societies, and even more so the notable growth in social organizations, constitute a development that, as Irina Il'ina has argued, gives good reason to speak of a 'golden age of Soviet *obshchestvennost'* during the 1920s.[17]

The significant growth in civil and civic activity did not emerge out of a vacuum. It can only be understood in the context of the emergence of a nascent civil society during the last decades of imperial Russia. Without the existence of the latter, it would be difficult to explain the extent to which political and social engagement erupted so abruptly after the collapse of autocracy. As the central power crumbled people established new and autonomous centres of power almost overnight. Indeed, between February and October 1917, in the absence of strong government and political institutions, the outburst of civil and civic activity amongst all classes served to increase the social fragmentation and polarization in the country. In those months, the country entered a period of 'diffused power' rather than 'dual power'.[18] For aspiring rulers of all political convictions the increase in social activity, combined with social polarization and growth of mass politics, had the potential to undermine any post-February regime. The flourishing civil activism had to be channelled in order to legitimize the post-tsarist order, something the Provisional Government failed to recognize and was incapable of addressing in its short reign. The Bolsheviks inherited this challenge and acted immediately. Once in power, they began to pursue the construction of a Soviet *obshchestvennost'* as a means of nurturing and channelling social activism, mobilizing the new Soviet people – allowing them to participate in the endeavour of state building in a controlled environment.

Youth and *obshchestvennost'*

The year 1917 was of course a watershed in Russian history, but this should not permit us to overlook the fact that many pre-revolutionary associations and societies continued their work under the new regime. What is more, new organizations found many of their most active members amongst people who had engaged in civil and civic activity before the revolution. We should bear

rossiiskoi istorii RAN, 2000), 174–214. For a comprehensive review of Il'ina's study see David-Fox, 'Review of Il'ina, *Obshchestvennye organizatsii Rossii*'.

16 Brovkin, *Russia after Lenin*, 81; Joseph Bradley, 'Dobrovol'nye obshchestva v Sovetskoi Rossii, 1917–1932gg.', *Vestnik Moskovskogo Universiteta, Seriia 8, Istoriia* 4 (1994), 34–44.

17 Il'ina, *Obshchestvennye organizatsii Rossii*, 4.

18 Sarah Badcock, 'The Russian Revolution: Broadening Understandings of 1917', *History Compass* 5 (2007), 5–9.

this in mind when studying the social organization that emerged after the Revolution. The fact the Bolshevik regime would attempt to create a new *obshchestvennost'* by creating new mass organizations should not prevent us from properly tracing the origins of these organizations. For many of them, their personal, institutional and cultural links lay in the pre-revolutionary period and in the turmoil of 1917 itself.

The history of the Komsomol, established in October 1918, is no exception. Its origins go back to a number of grassroots organizations, which emerged in and before 1917, and are strongly linked to the evolution of an autonomous youth movement in Petrograd. Better-educated people, i.e. young self-styled 'conscious' workers and students, played a crucial role in the formation of the youth movement, which emerged as part of a wider working-class movement in 1917. In the years after the 1905 revolution, the popularity of educational and cultural activities in working-class clubs, factory evening schools, and reading circles had grown rapidly. In urban centres like Moscow and Petrograd youth circles were established in people's houses and factories. Evening courses brought together young people from different districts and factories and generated new social networks. Reading and drama circles, in particular, proved to be popular among youth aged 15 to 20 years.[19]

Similarly, the student movement, albeit in crisis in 1914, had not disappeared. The disastrous performance of the regime in the war only encouraged the politicization of the students. When the February Revolution erupted, students formally declared their support for the workers' movement and many took part in the street disorders in February.[20] Of course, even before the war, there had been youth student circles and worker circles, and both kept their distinctive characters. However, it is important to note that even then the two clearly interacted.[21] Indeed, young students were often directly involved in organizing workers' circles. For example, Mariia V. Miliukova was a student at the Bestuzhev Courses in St Petersburg at the turn of the century. She was involved in student circles as well as in work with political prisoners for the underground Red Cross. In her unpublished memoir from 1931, she recalled how her circle of university students helped to set up workers' circles, stressing the 'friendly relations' between young workers and students. While the genre of the Soviet *Bildungsroman* requires us to take these descriptions with some caution, there is little doubt that socially and politically conscious students were keen to engage with the worker youth. Miliukova stressed the importance

19 Diane P. Koenker, 'Urban Families, Working-Class Youth Groups, and the 1917 Revolution in Moscow', in *The Family in Imperial Russia*, edited by David L. Ransel (Urbana, IL: University of Illinois Press, 1978), 289, 294; see also 'Workers and *Obshchestvennost'*'.

20 Susan Morrissey, 'From Radicalism to Patriotism? Petersburg Students between Two Revolutions, 1905 and 1917', *Revolutionary Russia* 13(2) (2000), 38–39.

21 Michael C. Hickey, '"People with Pure Souls": Jewish Youth Radicalism in Smolensk, 1900–1914', *Revolutionary Russia* 20(1) (2007), 62–63; see also Morrissey, 'From Radicalism to Patriotism?', 20–21.

of these circles, which were rapidly emerging in the urban environment, as an outlet of civil society (*obshchestvennost'*) in her path to enlightenment:

> the principles of a revolutionary world view gradually formed in us, in the youth, who had gathered here from the far corners of the provinces, where life was then so difficult, where civil society (*obshchestvennost'*) was mostly lacking [and] crushed, and where living even temporarily was somehow suffocation.[22]

Young people who were involved in student and workers' circles before 1917 embodied a link to the existence and ideas of the old *obshchestvennost'* in the youth movement that emerged after the February Revolution. Youth groups, as Diane Koenker has highlighted, were created in various ways in 1917. Some had clear links to existing circles, others would be formed by 'energetic individuals, some representing party organizations and some only the idea of organization'.[23] The agency of young people in this process is clearly evident.

The youth movement that emerged in Russia was, indeed, part of the wider workers' movement. However, even in Petrograd, where young workers showed an astonishing ability to organize themselves, one should not understate the contributions of pupils and students. Some of the – admittedly smaller – district organizations had significant numbers of non-proletarians in their ranks or were even dominated by them in 1917.[24] Neither the student nor the workers' movement was fully homogeneous. Some students aligned themselves with the socialist parties and the workers' movement; others associated themselves with democracy and citizenship.[25] A brief look at the biographies of some of the future first secretaries of the Komsomol Central Committee underscores the importance of students in the movement. E. V. Tsetlin, L. A. Shatskin, N. P. Chaplin and A. I. Mil'chakov were all students at the time they began their involvement in the youth movement in places such as Moscow, Smolensk, and Viatka.[26]

The Bolshevik party's commitment to establishing a nationwide youth league, formally declared in August 1917, was itself a response to the emergence of a significant pre-existing youth movement. The role it played in the formation of the organizational bureau in summer 1918, the financial and organizational help it provided, and its representation through leading Bolsheviks at the First Komsomol Congress are clear evidence of the crucial role the party played in the constitution of the Komsomol. However, closer analysis of the development of the youth movement in 1917 and 1918 – its gradual

22 Susan Morrissey, *Heralds of Revolution*, 38
23 Koenker, 'Urban Families', 294.
24 Isabel Tirado, *Young Guard! The Communist Youth League, Petrograd 1917–1920* (Westport, CT: Greenwood Press, 1988), 55.
25 Morrissey, 'From Radicalism to Patriotism?', 39.
26 A. A. Alekseev *et al. Stroka v biografii. Sekretari i chleny Biuro Tsentral'nogo komiteta komsomola, bozhaki pionerii, predsedateli KMO SSSR, pervye sekretari TSK LKSM soiuznykh respublik* (Moscow: Molodaia gvardiia, 2003) 7–14.

evolution, radicalization and bolshevization – also suggests there was a mutual drive for nationwide institutionalization, with much impulse coming from within the youth organizations. It is clear that without the support and goodwill of the party the All-Russian Congress in October 1918 would not have taken place amidst an escalating civil war. However, neither the party as an institution, nor its leaders, could decide the fate of the Congress.[27]

For the party, after it had survived the first critical months in power, national institutionalization offered an opportunity to bring the various, and still programmatically and socially divergent, youth organizations under one roof, to expand their membership and to ensure their programmatic character and role. This, in turn, would make it easier to ensure political supervision of their activities and incorporate them into the emerging fabric of Soviet *obshchestvennost'*. The Bolshevik vision was to build a society permeated with social organizations created from above.[28] However, in the case of the Komsomol, as in case of many mass organizations that were created during the 1920s, the clear involvement of the political centre could not guarantee that the process was entirely controlled from above. The youth league that was born in autumn 1918 was to some extent an expression of the transitionary state of society and state. As an outlet of social and political activism it had links to the tradition of pre-revolutionary *obshchestvennost'*. At the same time, the involvement of the Bolshevik party made it one of the first acts in the process of formulating a conception of a new Soviet public. It highlighted a move towards more 'direct administrative interference in the process of creation of social organizations'.[29] The existence of a strong core of party members in the leadership, whose allegiance lay not necessarily first with the organization, presaged the creation of an '*obshchestvenaia nomenklatura*',[30] as part of the new Soviet public. In autumn 1918, however, this new public (*novaia obshchestvennost'*) was still in an embryonic state.

The Komsomol and the construction of Soviet *obshchestvennost'*

With respect to the complex relationship between the state and these numerous new social and voluntary organizations, which were set up with the help of the regime, the Komsomol represented a peculiar case right from the start. Even more so than other mass organizations, such as the League of Militant Godless and the civil defence league OSOAVIAKhIM, the Komsomol was distinctly characterized as an *obshchestvenno-politicheskaia organizatsia,* or a

27 Matthias Neumann, *The Communist Youth League and the Transformation of the Soviet Union, 1917–1932* (Abingdon: Routledge, 2011), Chapter 1 (The Birth of the Russian Youth Movement).
28 Alfred B. Evans, Jr, 'Civil Society in the Soviet Union?', in *Russian Civil Society: A Critical Assessment*, edited by Alfred B. Evans, Jr, Laura A. Henry, and Lisa McIntosh Sundstrom (Armonk: M. E. Sharpe, 2006), 30.
29 Il'ina, *Obshchestvennye organizatsii Rossii*, 110. See also Evans, 'Civil Society', 32.
30 A term introduced by Il'ina, *Obshchestvennye organizatsii Rossii*, 142.

social *and* political organization. The principal task of the youth league was to bring up future generations with a socialist consciousness, foster support for the regime among children and adolescents, and engage them in active participation in the Bolshevik transformation project. As Hilary Pilkington has shown, when Lenin said '[t]he entire purpose of training, educating and teaching the youth of today should be to imbue them with communist ethics',[31] he did not think that young people could be simply taught to become communists. The social training and moral education (*vospitanie*) was understood to be a two-way process, allowing constant interaction between the youth and the social system.[32] For Lenin, then, 'the *process* of the construction of the new society' was to take a central place in the formation of the new person.[33] This complex process of fashioning the Soviet person has been described in the works of Jochen Hellbeck. He asserted that 'the Bolshevik regime was pursuing a quintessentially modern agenda of *subjectivization*, of fostering conscious citizen who would become engaged in the program of building socialism of their own will.'[34] The ultimate aim was to achieve a merger of the 'consciousness of the individual and the revolutionary goals of the state' – in the process of which the individual would refashion themself i.e. revolutionizing their mind and soul.[35] That is how it worked so far as the theory was concerned. The problem was, however, that after the end of the Civil War the very concept of constructing socialism was undermined by the introduction of the New Economic Policy. The latter was understood by many youngsters who sympathized with the Bolsheviks as a halt of the construction of the promised new world, a retreat, a betrayal of the ideas 1917. In the contradictory world of NEP it was difficult for young communists to practise the new set of norms and values they associated with socialism.

At the heart of this ambitious programme for refashioning the mind and soul stood the Komsomol's work in schools, as well as in clubs. Here, the organization acted as a means to fulfil the new understanding of collectivism that combined the classic notion of a devotion to the common interest with the fulfilment of newly established procedures and rituals within the league.[36] This included meetings, study circles, and *subbotniki* (voluntary work on weekends) as well as certain behaviour codes which were fiercely debated in the discourse on new communist ethics. Komsomol mass campaigns became the dominant

31 Hilary Pilkington, *Russia's Youth and Its Culture: A Nation's Constructors and Constructed* (London: Routledge, 1994), 46; Lenin, 'On the Task of the Youth Leagues', *Collected Works, Vol. 31*, 291.

32 Pilkington, *Russia's Youth*, 51.

33 Ibid., 52.

34 Jochen Hellbeck, 'Working, Struggling, Becoming: Stalin-Era Autobiographical Texts'. *Russian Review* 60(3) (2001), 342. Emphasis in original.

35 Ibid.

36 For a brief discussion of the understanding of collectivism among students see: Michael David-Fox, *Revolution of the Mind: Higher Learning among the Bolsheviks, 1918–1929* (Ithaca, NY and London: Cornell University Press, 1997), 107–108.

method by which the Bolsheviks sought to implement their cultural concepts and inculcate the new norms and values. The campaigns for *novyi byt* (the new way of life) 'aimed not only to modernize and improve the material conditions of everyday life but to give it transcendent communal or public value'.[37] A resolution at the Seventh Party Congress, in April 1923, defined mass campaigns as an essential instrument of the Komsomol's educational policy: '(…) mass campaigns with a distinctive revolutionary character, which count on the active participation of the youth, must supplement the educational work of the league.'[38] In fact, campaigns did not become a mere supplement, but moved to the very heart of propaganda work during the 1920s. This strong mobilization and participation in the Bolshevik cultural project was one central side to the Komsomol's tasks. Throughout the decade, one campaign followed another, their direction and goals varying widely from the promotion of an increase in productivity to campaigns to fight drunkenness and prostitution. A broad distinction can be drawn between campaigns in the Komsomol that were directed outwards – pursuing the sovietization of the not yet 'conscious masses' of youth, for example, campaigns against illiteracy, religion, and also recruitment campaigns, and inward-directed campaigns – seeking the fashioning of the *komsomol'tsy* (Komsomol members) themselves. Examples of the latter were the countless campaigns for the enforcement of communist ethics and *novyi byt* among the future cadres.[39]

Social work, directed inwards and outwards became a key attribute of this new conception of *obshchestvennost'* for all social organizations. Obviously, 'campaignism' itself always implies a two-sided process, since both the campaigner and the initial recipient are participants in this political instrument that seeks rapid change. Primarily, the initiative came from 'above', but

37 Cited from Kiaer and Naiman's introduction to the collection of essays on everyday life in early Soviet Russia. Christina Kiaer and Eric Naiman, 'Introduction', in *Everyday Life in Early Soviet Russia: Taking the Revolution Inside*, edited by Christina Kiaer and Eric Naiman (Bloomington, IN: Indiana University Press, 2006), 10.

38 *KPSS o komsomole i molodezhi: sbornik rezoliutsii i reshenii sedov. konferentsii i postanovlenii TsK 1917–1956* (Moscow: Molodaia gvardiia, 1957), 71.

39 The concepts and debates on *novyi byt* and the campaigns have been subject to a number of studies: Anne E. Gorsuch, *Youth in Revolutionary Russia: Enthusiasts, Bohemians, Delinquents* (Bloomington, IN: Indiana University Press, 2000), Chapter 3; Corinna Kuhr-Korolev, *Gezähmte Helden. Die Formierung der Sowjetjugend 1917–1932* (Essen: Klartext Verlag, 2005), especially 123–173; idem., 'Die Sowjetische Jugend im Sexual- und Moraldiskurs'. In *Sowjetjugend 1917–1941: Generation zwischen Revolution und Resignation*, edited by Corinna Kuhr-Korolev *et al.* (Essen: Klartext Verlag, 2001), 263–286. Stefan Plaggenborg, *Revolutionskultur: Menschenbilder und kulturelle Praxis in Sowjetrussland zwischen Oktoberrevolution und Stalinismus* (Köln: Böhlau Verlag, 1996); N. B. Lebina, *Povsednevnaia zhizn' sovetskogo goroda: normy i anomalii 1920/1930 gody* (St Petersburg: Zhurnal 'Neva', Letnii sad, 1999); Peter Gooderham, 'The Komsomol and the Worker Youth: The Inculcation of "Communist Values" in Leningrad during NEP'. *Soviet Studies* 34(4) (1982), 506–528.

the execution and implementation was in the hands of those 'below' and often proved beyond the control of the regime. In this respect 'campaigns' became one of the most important means of communication between the new rulers and their devoted followers in Komsomol. It was a dialogue, as Anne Gorsuch has shown, in which the actions and beliefs of young people influenced the regime's response to them considerably, and, vice versa, young people constantly reacted and responded to the official constructions of their generation. Furthermore, this was a two-sided process, because '[y]oung people were also themselves involved in the disciplining process; by telling others how to behave, they helped define themselves.'[40] Beyond 'campaignism', the *kampaneishchina*, which assumed an increasingly negative connotation in the Bolshevik discourse in the 1920 – mainly because the short-term propaganda outbursts were not seen to leave a lasting impact on the mind and souls of Soviet citizens[41] – there were others characteristics that came to define Soviet *obshchestvennost'*. First and foremost was an acceptance of party leadership. But the pursuit of an ideologically acceptable class composition within all social organizations was also an important marker.[42] It is no coincidence that the conception of the new *obshchestvennost'* echoed the key ingredients of what was to become a school of socialist realism: *partiinost'*, *klassovost', narodnost', idenost'. Partiinost'*, a party consciousness of the members implied the latter's leadership and guidance; *klassovost'*, a class content was supposed to be guaranteed through a proactive regulation of the class composition; *narodnost'*, the orientation towards the people through the support of civilizing-enlightening missions; and *ideinost'*, through the political message that permeated the work of these organizations.

Beyond the important social function, which the Komsomol shared with all other mass organizations, it had an attribute that distinguished it from all other bodies. The league was explicitly assigned a role as reserve of the party. It was set out to be a cadre school, an organization from which among its ranks the future leaders would emerge, and indeed did. In doing so the Komsomol did not only become an object, a pillar in Bolshevik conception of a new *obshchestvennost'*, but also an active agent in its construction. Soon after the ratification of its constitution, the Orgburo of the Central Committee of the Party confirmed the monopoly of the Komsomol to organize youth: 'All work, no matter whether carried out amongst the worker and peasant youth or the learning and studying youth, must be united in the hands of the RKSM.'[43] Consequently, the regime sought to liquidate other youth organizations such as the Boy Scouts, but also student organizations. Members of the latter organizations were accepted on an individual basis. Each of them

40 Gorsuch, *Youth in Revolutionary Russia*, 185.
41 Dahlke, 'Kampagnen für Gottlosigkeit', 182.
42 Il'ina, *Obshchestvennye organizatsii Rossii*, 110–111, 120.
43 'Guideline for the Work of the RKSM among Students', confirmed by the Orgburo of the CC of the Bolshevik party, 11 May 1919, in *KPSS o komsomole*, 34–35.

was vetted by a 'liquidation commission', consisting of one member of the Bolshevik party, as well as one of the Komsomol and one of the student organizations, before being allowed to join.[44]

After the Eighth Congress of the Bolshevik party, the Komsomol Central Committee held an enlarged meeting with provincial representatives, from 26–28 April 1919, to discuss the Komsomol's relationship with the party. The plenary adopted a resolution that called for subordination of the Komsomol Central Committee to the Central Committee of the Bolshevik party, as well as of local Komsomol committees to local party bodies. In August 1919, the Komsomol Central Committee and the Central Committee of the Party adopted a joint resolution that followed the same line. The resolution stated that the Komsomol recognizes the programme of the Bolshevik party, that its Central Committee is 'directly subordinate to the Central Committee of the RKP', and that its 'local organizations would work under the control of the local party organizations'.[45] On the local level this control would be exercised by mutual representation between the Komsomol and the party. The resolution asked the local party organizations and cells to establish Komsomol organizations in line with the charter of the league and thereby to use all party members up to the age of 20 years, for whom membership in the Komsomol had now become obligatory. Beyond that, the joint resolution recommended establishing factions of the Bolshevik party in local Komsomol organizations in cases where a non-communist policy, i.e. non-Bolshevik policy, was pursued or petty-bourgeois or kulak elements had become too strong.[46]

Months later, in early October 1919, delegates of the Second Komsomol Congress accepted these changes in the charter. There was no real opposition to the support of the joint resolution by the Komsomol leader O. L. Ryvkin. This is remarkable, given that fierce controversies had sprung up on several other issues. Most delegates, it appears, had no strong objection against closer bonds with the party and the subordination of the league's central and local bodies to it. It seems that the congress's delegates found themselves in a position similar to their trade union counterparts in late 1919, when contemplating the implications of the 'statization' of the trade unions.[47] Many of the Komsomol activists did not recognize a conflict between the position of 'full independence', stated in the first charter, and the subordination of their

44 Ibid.

45 'On the Relationship between the Komsomol and the Bolshevik party', Joint Resolution of the CC of the Bolshevik party and the CC of the Komsomol, 8 August 1919, in *KPSS o komsomole*, 35–36.

46 Ibid., In March 1921 at Tenth Party Congress the compulsory Komsomol membership for all party members up to the age of 20 was reinforced in a resolution 'On Questions of the Party Structure'. Furthermore, young party members were now demanded to *actively* take part in the league's activities. 'Resolution of the Tenth Party Congress of the Bolshevik party', in *KPSS o komsomole*, 44–45.

47 See Diane Koenker, 'The Trade Unions', in *Critical Companion to the Russian Revolution 1914–1921*, edited by Edward Acton, Vladimir Iu. Cherniaev and William G. Rosenberg (Bloomington, IN: Indiana University Press, 1997), 451.

organization to the party. After all their main goal – to build up communism – was congruent, and they considered the party to have a legitimate right to claim oversight of the whole Communist movement. In fact the voting behaviour of the delegates revealed that the joint resolution, to some extent, only formalized policy procedures that had characterized the league's work, particularly in the larger urban organizations, since spring 1919. Furthermore, closer relations between the party and the Komsomol implied a chance for the latter to secure an important role in the state building process and to perform its role in many areas more efficiently – subordination ensured participation. The central leadership subscribed to an integrative vision of the Komsomol. They did not entertain the possibility that it could set itself apart from the rest of the workers' movement and its rightful leaders, the Bolshevik party.[48] The understanding that the Komsomol could not constitute a sort of political party in its own right, with its own programme and tactics, was communicated to the wider members in a long article in *Iunyi kommunist,* in September, shortly before the second congress adopted the new charter.[49]

However, there was another factor in the process of centralization of the league and its subordination to the party which should not be ignored – namely, the vanguardism among young Communists. The first Komsomol Programme had stated: 'Youth, as the most active and revolutionary part of the working-class, is the vanguard of the proletarian revolution.'[50] The party had encouraged that self-perception by continuously praising the youth as the builders of communism. The official party policy described the Komsomol as the prime youth organization, its members the reserve of the party and consequently its members as the vanguard of the youth. Furthermore, central and regional Komsomol leaders and many of its activists had already become Bolshevik cadres in their own right, which added a new side to their identity as Komsomol members. They had clearly gained a party-political consciousness. This was one of the reasons why no strong opposition against the subordination of the organization arose in 1919. Indeed, we must remember that this was a time when the regime struggled for survival, a time that required unity of those allying themselves with the October Revolution.

Nevertheless, it should also be noted that the rank and file and local Komsomol organs were not really involved in this process. The structural change to the Komsomol was clearly a matter between the central bodies of the party and of the Komsomol, and the consequences did not become visible to the rank and file until 1920. Furthermore, in many places, where the local Komsomol was in the position of being the sole representative of Soviet power, the Komsomol activists were hardly affected by these changes. Indeed, in some places, this remained the case well into the 1920s.

48 Tirado, *Red Guard!*, 176.
49 *Iunyi kommunist*, no 11 (September 1919), 3–5.
50 'Programme and Charter of the Communist Youth League, 1918', in Tirado, *Young Guard!*, 231.

This acceptance of the joint resolution at the Komsomol congress in October 1919 determined the party–Komsomol relationship in a new way. The organization was no longer described as 'fully independent' (*vpolne nezavisimyi*), as it had been in the first charter, but 'autonomous' (*autonomnoi*). Nevertheless, the resolution also repeated the need of the Komsomol to have organizational independence (*samodeiatel'nost'*) in its work and stated that party control should not take the character of being patronizing.[51] Conflicts of interest were intrinsic to this structure of the emerging Soviet *obshechestvennost'*. The new relationship between the Komsomol and the Bolshevik party enabled the latter to exert its influence through three different channels down to the local Komsomol organization: first of all, vertically through the Komsomol pyramid, since the Komsomol Central Committee was directly subordinated to the CC of the Bolshevik party; secondly horizontally, through mutual representation at the local level; and thirdly, by the increase of the party core. In doing so, seeds for the construction of, what Il'ina phrased, the *obshchesvennaia nomenklatura* in social organizations during the 1920s were also laid in the Komsomol. It became an increasingly important instrument to assert control, since the anticipated growth of the Komsomol would bring more and more non-party members into the league.

Obshchestvennaia nomenklatura – theory and practice

The creation of the *obshchevennaia nomenklatura* was at the centre of a mounting web of new social organizations under the guidance of the regime. The regime sought to ensure its influence through party members and to get them elected into leading positions of mass organizations. A resolution of the Eight Party Congress in 1924 called on its members:

> the party should make every effort to aid the proper deployment of work in these organizations. Party members should participate actively in them. Party organizations should assist their correct organizational building, pulling party members as well as non-party members into their work and become their ideological and political leaders. All of this requires further attention of the party for the work of the communist party faction in these organizations.[52]

Furthermore, in the 1920s, the election of leaders in these organizations was increasingly replaced by appointments from above. In practice, this growing interference from the centre meant that, in 1925, for example, the

51 'On the Relationship between the Komsomol and the Bolshevik Party', in *KPSS o komsomole*, 36–37.

52 *KPSS v resoliutsiiakh i resheniiakh s"ezdov, konferentsii i plenumov TsK, Tom 3* (Moscow: Izdatel'stvo politicheskoi literatury, 1970), 49; Il'ina, *Obshchestvennye organizatsii Rossii*, 66.

nomenklatura list nominated 51 party members for the Central Committee of the Komsomol and 100 for other mass organizations.[53]

In its pure conception, the organized *nomenklatura* system was a one-way road for the party to ensure its guidance of other organizations. However, things were different in the case of the Komsomol. Because of its role as the reserve of the party, the league was not only on the receiving end. It was not only an object of the process of the creation of an *obshchestvennaia nomenklatura*, but indeed became a crucial driving force in it. Many of the new mass organizations attracted young members in particular. This meant that *komsomol'tsy* and young Bolsheviks, many of whom were also Komsomol members because of their age, were vigorously encouraged to join other mass organizations. A layer of party members and *komsomol'tsy* was seen as essential to ensure a level of control and influence for the regime. In this way, the *nomenklatura* system went far beyond the actual list of appointments through which the Bolshevik party dominated the top level of each new social organization. Taking the Buriat-Mongol Autonomous Soviet Socialist Republic as an example, Komsomol members outnumbered party members in many of its social and cultural organizations in the 1920s. The civil defence league OSOAVIAKhIM, for example, had 2,651 members in 1928, 18% of whom were party members and 19% of whom were Komsomol members. Smaller organizations and societies also had a party and Komsomol core. In 1927 the republic's Down with Illiteracy Society had 364 members, with 14% party members and 23% Komsomol members. Another small organization, the Society of the Friends of Radio had 435 members in 1928, 12% of whom had a party card and 15% of whom were *komsomol'tsy*.[54]

It is not clear from the statistics how Komsomol members with party membership were recorded, although probably the party membership took priority here and was the decisive attribute for the classification. In any case, these examples underscore how the regime saw the Komsomol as an instrument to enforce control and adherence to the party line in other organizations. This permeation of small and large organizations was replicated throughout the Soviet Union. According to some statistics, 30% of the League of the Godless' members were also Komsomol members in 1930.[55] In the countryside this development was particularly highlighted by the Komsomol's serious involvement in the village soviets and other social-political organizations.

In 1926, the Komsomol member N. Zhukov published a long article in *Iunyi kommunist* entitled 'The Komsomol and Soviet *obshchestvennost'* in the Village', on the successes of the Komsomol in the creation of Soviet *obshchestvennost'*. He praised the league's close work with the village soviets and its crucial role in setting up sections and commissions within them.[56] A large number of local

53 T. P. Korzhikhina, and Iu. Iu. Figatner, 'Sovetskaia nomenklatura: stanovlenie, mekhanizmy deistviia', *Voprosy Istorii* 93(7) (1993), 28; Il'ina, *Obshchestvennye organizatsii Rossii*, 67.

54 Il'ina, *Obshchestvennye organizatsii Rossii*, 117.

55 Dahlke, 'Kampagnen für Gottlosigkeit', 177 (footnote 19).

56 *Iunyi kommunist*, no 5 (March 1926), 34–36.

Komsomol activists, he claimed, were taking part in meetings of the village soviets. Furthermore, the Komsomol was helping other social organizations to aid the mechanization of agricultural production and was a driving force behind the organization of peasant committees and more specifically Peasant Committees for Mutual Aid, one of the main socio-political organizations operating in the countryside. Zhukov reported that peasant committees' membership in the *uezd* had grown significantly with the help of the Komsomol. Of its 2,125 members, up to 25 per cent of were young people. The Komsomol had also set up 22 new committees. Furthermore, he made clear that the ruling organs of these committees at *volost'* and village level were permeated by Komsomol activists.[57]

This article on the achievements of the Komsomol creating a Soviet *obshchestvennost'* clearly does not reflect the overall performance of the organization in this area. However, at the very least it highlights the central role some Komsomol functionaries thought their league should be playing in this process. It is also quite clear from this account that the boundaries between state and society had become completely blurred. The Komsomol did act as a social organization, but as a representative of Soviet power it often assumed party and state functions. In other words, it became a party substitute. Komsomol activists regularly ended up in administrative positions in the party-state apparatus. Having its own candidates for the election of village soviets, indeed often organizing the election itself, together with its work in the Mutual Aid Committees and in the local cooperatives put the organization into the position of a state agency.[58] In 1926 Komsomol activists accounted for 6.2% of the members of the *volost'* soviets.[59] Conflicts of interest were naturally intrinsic to this structure of emerging Soviet *obshchestvennost'*. The subordination of the Komsomol to the party enabled the latter, at least in theory, to exert its influence through different channels down to the local Komsomol organization. The reality in the 1920s, however, often looked very different.

A living organization

During the 1920s the Komsomol continued a rather independent development on the ground, encouraged by the often very weak relations between Komsomol cells and the party organization in rural areas. This was particularly the case in the periphery of the country. For example, a *komsomolets* and party member bitterly complained to the Komsomol Central Committee about the lack of organizational links in rural Kirgizia, asserting that there were no connections between *komsomol'tsy* and party members.[60] This was not peculiar to this region. In many places where Komsomol cells existed there was no party cell; many cells had no party representative, and if someone had been

57 Ibid., 35–36.

58 Tirado, 'The Revolution', 102; Merle Fainsod, *Smolensk under Soviet Rule* (London: Macmillan, 1958), 411.

59 Slavnyi put', 324.

60 RGASPI, f. M1, op. 23, d. 315, l. 16.

assigned the role by the party they were often poorly trained and not interested or motivated to take an active part in the league's life.[61] Komsomol officials estimated that in some rural regions Komsomol cells outnumbered party cells by eight to one.[62] Under these circumstances party guidance was difficult to ensure.

In 1925, the Party Organizational Bureau identified insufficient conformity and an inadequate relationship with the local party cells as one of the main shortcomings of the work of the Komsomol in the countryside.[63] For many village cells, and indeed urban cells, this was clearly an understatement. In a survey of the Smolensk region, it was concluded that party guidance did not exist, either in urban or in rural cells. Of 2,230 *komsomol'tsy* in the *uezd*, only 195 were also party members (including candidates), which amounted to just 8%.[64]

The party, then, faced the problem of having to ensure the Komsomol would not function as a rival political organization in terms of influence and control. It was confronted by a serious dilemma. If it allowed the party core within the league to expand rapidly, the Komsomol might assume the character of a junior party which naturally would demand more political participation; if it kept the party core small, while it would still be able to easily control the upper organs, it would have limited influence over large parts of the organization's body. This was an even bigger problem in the countryside, where the Komsomol deeply permeated local government. It carried the risk of the emergence of rivalry and political deviations.

By the mid-1920s, the party started to take a more proactive approach to address the problem. In 1926 the Central Control Commission advised its local commissions to show more attention to the Komsomol's work. The aim was to ensure party directives were obeyed and proper relationships between the organs of the league and the party were established.[65] However, the party was aware that it had to find the right balance in its pursuit of greater control. Hence, it firmly rejected the suggestion that youth under 16 be excluded from the organization and supported the lower age limit of 14 (which ensured a constant influx of immaturity). It also rejected calls for the upper age limit to be lowered to 18.[66] Furthermore, it only allowed adolescents under 20 years

61 A. A. Slezin, *Molodezh' i vlast. Iz istorii molodeznogo dvizhenia v Tsentral'nom Chernozem'e, 1921–1929* (Tambov: Izdatel'stvo TGGU, 2002) Electronic version accessed and downloaded on 18 January 2011. http://window.edu.ru/window_catalog/files/r21614/slezin.pdf, 35; *KPSS o komsomole*, 147.

62 Isabel Tirado, 'The Komsomol and the Young Peasants: The Dilemma of Rural Expansion 1921–1925', *Slavic Review* 52(3) (1993), 470.

63 *KPSS o komsomole*, 121.

64 *RGASPI*, f. M1, op. 23, d. 822, l. 121ob.

65 *Slavnyi put' leninskogo komsomola, Tom 1* (Moscow: Molodaia gvardiia, 1974) 354.

66 Riazanov had called for the age limit to be lowered to 18 at the Tenth Party Congress. Peter Kenez, *The Birth of the Propaganda State: Soviet Methods of Mass Mobilization, 1917–1929* (Cambridge: Cambridge University Press, 1985), 175.

of age to enter the party through the Komsomol.[67] In doing so it bolstered the institution of dual membership as a means to secure influence. During the NEP period the party core of *komsomol'tsy*, i.e. *komsomol'tsy* with dual party and league membership, increased very slowly. Overall, about one-tenth of its members were also in the party. In rural areas the proportion was significantly lower, whereas in urban regions it could be higher.[68]

This core of activists was supposed to be the elite of *komsomol'tsy* through which the party would ensure its guidance of the Komsomol. Internal reports and surveys, however, made clear that this was not the case everywhere. The simple fact that by the beginning of 1927, 60% of the Komsomol's rural network of cells existed in villages and settlements with no representation of the party organization,[69] raised serious doubts about party guidance. Dual membership did not solve the problem in such places because, apart from the membership card, there were few actual links with the party.

However, once again it is difficult to generalize. The party–Komsomol relationship assumed contradictory forms during the 1920s, as was highlighted in a survey among delegates to the Eighth Congress in 1928. The survey identified as the main deficits in the Komsomol–party relationship both that 'the party organizations don't know the work of the league', and that it suppresses the initiative of the youth and adopts a patronizing attitude.[70] Of course, the two phenomena are not mutually exclusive, but, as already stated above, the former often implied that there were no links with the party whatsoever. One delegate, a secretary of a rural *raikom*, is quoted describing the ambivalent party–Komsomol relationship in a questionnaire as follows: 'If the party isn't interested in our work, then it is better it doesn't lead the Komsomol.'[71] Here an underlying antipathy towards the party had begun to surface.

Clearly, the party's influence over the league varied drastically from organizational echelon to echelon, from region to region, town to town and village to village. This could be seen in the Tambov area. On 19–20 April 1925 the plenum of the Tambov *gubkom* of the party had declared that 'the business of the Komsomol's *gubkom* is the business of the party's *gubkom*'.[72] Such attitudes could lead to patronizing relationship between the party and the Komsomol.

67 Georg Brunner, *Das Parteistatut der KPdSU 1903–1961* (Köln: Verlag Wissenschaft und Politik, 1965), 22–23.
68 Ralph T. Fisher, *Pattern for Soviet Youth: A Study of the Congresses of the Komsomol, 1918–1954* (New York: Columbia University Press, 1959), 123; Kenez, *The Birth of the Propaganda State*, 175; *Slavnyi put'*, 380. *RGASPI*, f. M1, op. 23, d. 817, ll. 11, 17. On 1 January 1928, 10.3% of *komsomol'tsy* were reported to be party members.
69 *Slavnyi put'*, 379. At the time of the Eight Komsomol Congress it there were only 18,000 rural party cells but 49,000 rural Komsomol cells. Fisher, *Pattern for Soviet Youth*, 163.
70 *RGASPI*, f. M1, op. 23, d. 818, l. 20.
71 Ibid.
72 Slezin, *Molodezh' i vlast*, 32 (electronic version).

In Voronezh it was stated in a meeting of the bureau of the Komsomol Central Committee that party guidance had reached a level of interference at which 'not a single circular can be issued without the approval of the *raikom* of the party, not a single transfer of *rabotnikovs*, [i.e. activist], not a single general meeting (*sobranie*) or sitting (*zasedanie*)'.[73] However, on the ground many Komsomol cells frequently defended their independence from interference by the local party organizations. In Voronezh the *gubkom* of the party noted, in January 1926 that in a number of *volosti* relations between *komsomol'tsy* and party members had become hostile. Hence, both organizations considered themselves to be independent and saw each other as political rivals.[74]

Without a doubt the party had close control over the top members of the Komsomol's leadership and considerable influence on the league's agenda, but beyond this, in urban and rural areas alike, close party supervision and control was far from being secured. As a result of this, the party's and the Komsomol's leadership tried to increase party control and influence through a number of changes to the Komsomol Regulations. For instance, the Sixth Komsomol Congress in 1924 resolved that all new admissions of non-working class and non-peasant youth required sponsorship by at least one party member, something that was partially retracted for students of certain social origins two years later. Furthermore, party membership for a certain period of time was made a prerequisite even for persons of worker origin serving as secretaries at *uezd* level.[75]

Certainly, the proportion of party members and candidates in the *piaterok* (the five- person ruling groups) of the *gubkomy, obkomy, kraikomy* and Central Committees of the national republics was very high and tended to increase year on year. From 15 February 1927 to 1 October 1928 it rose from 76.9% to 85.0%, with another 11.1% having candidate status.[76] However, among the total membership of these committees, the proportion of non-party members actually tended to increase.[77] In the *gubkomy* of the industrial regions, for instance, the proportion of non-party members had grown from 7.7% to 15.3% in 1927.[78] In the countryside, the proportion of party members in ruling organs was not surprisingly considerably lower. At the beginning of 1928, the proportion of *komsomol'tsy* without party card or candidate status in the committees of the rural *volkomy* and *raikomy* stood at 65.8%; 87.5% of the members of the bureau of village cells were not in the party, and as many as 81.4% of their secretaries.[79] These figures speak for themselves. Party

73 Ibid.
74 Ibid., 32–33.
75 For the amendments of the Komsomol Regulations see Fisher, *Pattern for Soviet Youth*, 116–117.
76 *RGASPI*, f. M1, op. 23, d. 817, l. 28.
77 Ibid., ll. 13, 24–25.
78 Ibid., l. 24
79 Ibid., ll. 29, 36, 38.

guidance and control had its clear limits, making the Komsomol an autonomous and confident socio-political player in many places.

Growing alienation – 'a transmission belt that snapped'

When considering effectiveness of the instrument of dual membership to ensure party control, it should also be noted, that the higher proportion of party members in the upper echelons of the Komsomol could even have a reverse effect in terms of party influence. The dual membership of Komsomol functionaries, even of those at the lower levels of the Komsomol pyramid, inevitably accelerated rank-and-file feelings of alienation from their leadership. Class and age were not the determining factors in this growing divide, but the perception that Komsomol cadres ruled over the membership.[80] The cadres' power, authority, and position, it was obvious to many rank-and-file, was also grounded in their membership of the party. Hence, dual membership amongst cadres further added to growing isolation of Komsomol functionaries from their members. It created a perception of 'us' and 'them', the rank and file activists and cadres, the ordinary member and career bureaucrats/officials (*chinoviki*).

The bureaucratization of mass organizations like the Komsomol, and the creation of an *obshchestvennia nomenklatura* meant that the Komsomol provided opportunities to start a professional career. Various forms of privileges were intrinsic to the Bolshevik *nomenklatura* system. Many young activists found their first job in the Komsomol. This, in turn, spurred many on to pursue a political career.[81] Idealistic commitment to building socialism, careerism, and opportunism all co-existed in revolutionary Russia. They were not necessarily mutually exclusive: often, indeed, they went hand in hand.[82] However, this net of interdependence with the party-state apparatus raised the question of the loyalties and allegiances of *komsomol'tsy* with dual membership. Where did their allegiances lie, with the Komsomol or the party? The long-standing Komsomol member Grigorii Abramovich, a civil war veteran, complained bitterly in a letter to the Komsomol Central Committee that many cadres had simply taken up Komsomol work to ensure 'climbing into the Party'. In his view, '[t]he Komsomol is broken into two camps: activists and non-activists'.[83] The gap increased further through the way those 'staff activists' often used their position for personal gain and, in the process of doing, repressed

80 Sean Guillory, *Profiles in Exhaustion and Pomposity: The Everyday Life of Komsomol Cadres in the 1920s*, The Carl Beck Papers in Russian and East European Studies No 2303 (Pittsburgh, PA: University of Pittsburgh Center for Russian and East European Studies, 2014), 25.

81 A. A. Slezin, 'Kommunisticheskii soiuz molodezhi kak institut politicheskoi sotsializatsii (1921–1929gg)', in *Gumanitarnye nauki: probemy i resheniia: sbornik nauchnykh statei*, edited by A. A. Slezin (St Petersburg: Nestor, 2003), 244.

82 See also Kenez, *The Birth of the Propaganda State*, 186.

83 Quoted from Guillory, *Profiles in Exhaustion and Pomposity*, 26.

participation of ordinary members. As Sean Guillory has shown, the conditions of everyday life in the 1920s, meant that local Komsomol cadres used 'domination over consent' as the prevailing method to exert their authority.[84] It is clear that the underlying forces working within this complex relationship between the party-state and social organizations like the Komsomol meant that the higher the echelons of power, the less likely they were to disagree with the general party line. The *nomenklatura,* one could conclude, started to pursue its own interests. As Il'ina asserted, they preferred not to be in conflict with the general line, and thus frequently made concessions and compromises which were not in the interest of their own organization.[85]

The growing gulf between the leaders and the rank and file, between the masses who were the fuel for the new Soviet *obshchestvennost'* and those who were set to guide it, became increasingly evident in the 1920s. A letter sent to the Komsomol Central Committee and *Komsomol'skaia Pravda,* in 1928, highlighted this development.[86] The authors, some local Komsomol activists, reflected on the campaigns for self-criticism, and fiercely attacked the state of the league concerning the relationship between Komsomol cadres and rank and file. Describing the conflict between the *raikom* and a local Komsomol organization regarding the removal and appointment of a new secretary, the letter writers call him as a 'toady' (*podkhalim*), a 'functionary' and a 'bureaucrat'. They expressed their strong feelings of hostility towards the functionaries of the *raikom* who, as they saw it, inflicted numerous bad things on the *kollektiv.* Whenever they meet one of the functionaries, they wrote, they think: 'How can SUCH BASTARDS (*svolochi*) continue to be in the leadership of such an important organization?' In their opinion, the *raikom* only selects 'talentless' (*bezdarnye*) and useless (*nikchemnye*) people for the *kollektiv* in order to maintain their leadership position. This all happens, they claimed, because the

> top of our *raikom* is alienated from the mass of *komsomol'tsy.* By walking through the factories and works and speaking with the *komsomol'tsy,* reading the protocols, letters and files of the *raikom,* you will see, they stated in the letter, that a huge gulf lies between the *raikom* and the 25,000 *komsomol'tsy* of the *raion.*

In their words 'the *raikom* fears the masses.'[87]

The seven members of the local Komsomol finished their letter with a bleak assessment of the state of affairs, attacking the autocratic and egomaniacal style of the Komsomol leadership of their *raikom,* which was supported by the local party organization. The letter not only highlights the tensions within the ranks of the Komsomol, but it also reveals that some Komsomol organizations were stiflingly

84 Guillory, *Profiles in Exhaustion and Pomposity,* 1.
85 Il'ina, *Obshchestvennye organizatsii Rossii,* 141–142.
86 RGASPI, f. M1, op. 23, d. 822, ll. 13–18.
87 Ibid., ll. 17–18

overregulated, meaning the regime ended up suppressing independent initiative through its *obshchestvennia nomenklatura*. This, in turn, caused disillusionment and political apathy, something that the regime was seriously concerned about.

The coexistence of over- and under-regulation in the league, depending largely on regional factors, is one of the many paradoxes of the Komsomol's organizational development in the 1920s. Naturally, this had a major impact on the way the league performed its role in the arena of social work. The limits of party control and guidance in many places made the Komsomol an autonomous space, a place where young people could act out their idea of civic engagement. Furthermore, even in places were relations with the party were close, the growing responsibilities of the Komsomol meant that it could become an important player in the emerging web of social organizations and state sponsored institutions. This, in turn, gave its members many opportunities for civic participation that were not necessarily defined by the party. The article by Zhukov mentioned earlier provided several good examples for this. In Zhukov's report the party hardly features, but an image of the Komsomol emerges as a powerful and crucial agent in the construction of the Soviet state and the Soviet *obshchestvennost'*. Not only had the Komsomol been active in setting up other social organizations like the Committees for Mutual Aid, but they had also renovated and organized schools and set up 'red corners' (small exhibits of communist literature) and reading rooms to bring enlightenment and political education to the villages.[88] These latter activities reveal the powerful role the Komsomol assumed in the representation of Soviet power in the countryside, as well as the scope of opportunity for civic engagement that came with this. It was not so much a transmission belt between the party and society, but was regularly able to act as an important player in the state-building process in its own right. In doing so, it could provide an autonomous space for activists to express and enact their own visions of the construction of socialism.

Enacting the revolution – an autonomous space

As I have examined elsewhere in more detail, the cultural-educational work of the Komsomol in the 1920s was frequently characterized by disarray and chaos in the 1920.[89] The picture that emerges from recent studies of Soviet youth is that the regime faced major problems imposing its cultural concepts on its youth including those within in the Komsomol. This in itself indicates that there were clear limits to the regime's control of youth and, furthermore, severe constraints to its drive for the political, social, and cultural indoctrination of its avant-garde in the Komsomol. Juvenile delinquency and deviance were widespread social phenomena amongst the unorganized and organized youth alike during the 1920s. In fact, it seems that the *komsomol'tsy* were particularly prone to engage in behaviour often deemed to be

88 *Iunyi kommunist* no 5 (March 1926), 34–36.
89 Neumann, *The Communist Youth League*, Chapters 5 and 6.

un-Soviet, but often understood themselves to be distinctly communist. The Komsomol's involvement in anti-religious campaigns and enlightening work provide an excellent example for this phenomenon.

With little guidance and no clear directives from central Komsomol and party leadership, the local implementation of anti-religious work had led to frequent excesses in 1922 and 1923. Adolescents frequently ended up ridiculing and mocking religion. It was the confrontational, provocative, revolutionary but also iconoclastic character of these first stormy campaigns for which *komsomol'tsy* demonstrated real enthusiasm. Their initiative in these campaigns exceeded by far the limits the regime had set and sought to enforce. A survey of these events in the winter of 1922/23 concluded that generally the campaigns had been met with great interest by the *komsomol'tsy*. They had filled them with much of their own initiative, because directives by the Komsomol Central Committee had arrived too late or were simply ignored.[90] Although the intensity of the anti-religious campaigns of 1923 was not matched until late in the decade, militant anti-religious propaganda and actions on the ground were far from being over. Neither the party nor the Komsomol authorities were able to prevent further outbursts of disorganized, destructive and often violent anti-religious excesses. *Komsomol'tsy* continued their provocative anti-religious actions. Cases were reported of them walking into churches deliberately leaving their hats on in order to provoke those taking part in the religious service, and of them damaging crosses in a cemetery. The Komsomol cell in the Pavlikhinskaia *volost'*, Tver *guberniia*, for instance, entered a church after a drinking session and forced the priest to sing the 'Internationale'.[91] In Boguchar, Siberia, the actions were even more violent. There *komsomol'tsy* filled the locks of the church with nails to prevent the service from taking place and also attempted to set fire to it. When all *komsomol'tsy* had gone on an excursion, one stayed behind charged with burning the church.[92] Victor Isaeev's study of the militarization and radicalization of youth in Siberia provides further accounts of violent excesses. *Komsomol'tsy* crashed drunkenly into religious services, harassed priests and in some cases held them at gun point. In two cases, in 1925 and 1926, members of the Komsomol detonated bombs during religious services and caused deaths with many injured.[93] Isaev concluded that the infringement of widely accepted moral and legal norms by young communists was more the rule than the exception.[94] Beyond the outbursts of atheistic extremism on the ground, the anti-religious work of the

90 *Russkoe i sovetskoe molodezhnoe dvizhenie v dokumentakh 1905–1937* (Moscow: OMPPress, 2002), Doc. 66, Daniel Peris, *Storming the Heavens. The Soviet League of Militant Godless* (Ithaca, NY: Cornell University Press, 1998), 39.

91 *Russkoe i sovetskoe molodezhnoe dvizhenie*, Doc. 77, 80.

92 Ibid., Doc. 77.

93 Viktor I. Isaev, 'Die Militarisierung der Jugend und jugendlicher Radikalismus in Sibirien', in *Sowjetjugend 1917–1941: Generation zwischen Revolution und Resignation*, edited by Corinna Kuhr-Korolev *et al.* (Essen: Klartext Verlag, 2001), 158.

94 Ibid., 160–161.

Komsomol remained very unsystematic and decentralized. There was nothing close to an organized, let alone a well-orchestrated, campaign. A report on anti-religious work in the central-agrarian *raion* in Siberia made this very clear: 'All this work is conducted without a system, without a plan or enough guidance by Komsomol committees'.[95] It is important to stress that anti-religious work and attitudes diverged widely between regions. In some places, little anti-religious work took place and *komsomol'tsy* frequently took part in religious ceremonies.[96]

Of course, it is hard to generalize at this point. Where do youthful escapades and challenging of authority stop and subconscious or conscious political action start? Blowing up a church, destroying religious shrines and icons could be as much a manifestation of an iconoclasm – an expression of revolutionary anticipation and desire that is a more or less conscious political act – as a challenge to traditional hierarchy and authority. What, however, is unquestionable is that both acts had much to do with living in a society in transition. In this transitional period, anti-religious acts were regarded by many *komsomol'tsy* as part of the cultural transformation of the country, an application of Marxist theory and a step further on the way to the establishment of the promised socialist society. From their perspective this justified their often violent actions. Anti-religious hooliganism or communist hooliganism in general were therefore often understood by young Bolsheviks as the continuation of the Revolution by other means.[97] As such, they were direct expressions of their revolutionary intent.

This interpretation is also supported by other studies on youth culture in the 1920s. However, both Gorsuch and Carleton are right to argue that deviant behaviour was not necessarily a conscious act of protest, a sign of counter-revolutionary intent, and nor was it necessarily meant to challenge the party's hegemonic ambitions.[98] On the contrary, Carleton argued, much of this behaviour was a manifestation of what young people understood and expected to be proper and right.[99] This was certainly true for many *komsomol'tsy* and the anti-religious campaigns are a perfect example of this fact. Although disillusioned and frustrated with the NEP, most had not given up their faith in communism as an ideology. However, surrounded by a confused official discourse on what was 'right' and what was 'wrong', and living in a socio-economic environment characterized by contradictions where new norms could hardly

95 *Russkoe i sovetskoe molodezhnoe dvizhenie*, Doc. 77.

96 *RGASPI*, f. M1, op. 23, d. 822, l. 121. The survey is undated, but filed with other material on juvenile deviance in the second half of the 1920s in the *dela* 822 (July 1928–February 1929).

97 Isaev, 'Die Militarisierung der Jugend', 161.

98 Gregory Carleton, *Sexual Revolution in Bolshevik Russia* (Pittsburgh, PA: University of Pittsburgh Press, 2005), 92; Gorsuch, *Youth in Revolutionary Russia*, 182–183.

99 See also Carleton, *Sexual Revolution*, 92.

be lived, the uncoordinated antireligious campaigns provided the freedom to express their direct radical approach to religion. It was an example of the peculiar appropriation of the revolutionary discourse by *komsomol'tsy* who saw their hooliganish behaviour as proletarian and revolutionary.[100] Moreover, it showed how the Komsomol as a key pillar of Soviet *obshchestvennost'* provided a space of relative autonomy for youngsters, somewhere where they could engage in the Bolshevik project on their own terms.

This became particularly pronounced in the involvement of Komsomol activists in the communal movement of the 1920s. Being members of the Komsomol provided these young activists with political credentials and some authority. It gave them the confidence to express their own revolutionary visions of the new way of live and enact them in concrete and immediate form by setting up urban communes. It is thus no surprise that the domestic communes of the 1920s became a preserve of Komsomol activists. As Andy Willimott has shown in his works on the communal movement, they offered an outlet to bridge the growing gap between promise and reality and display their revolutionary identity by building socialism in one apartment. Youngsters were able to practise new collective visions of domesticity, promote equality and sharing of income and resources. In doing so, however, they also consciously appropriated practices of the pre-revolutionary Russian worker *arteli*, the pre-revolutionary labour associations. By the end of the decade, tens of thousands of Soviet youth were living in these manifestations of youthful revolutionary spirit and intent.[101]

For all the success of the dedicated Komsomol communards to enact revolution on 'both the self and society's norms'[102] within the student dorms, factory barracks, and urban apartments, the Komsomol as an organization failed to comprehensively popularize the Bolshevik worldview amongst the wider Soviet youth.[103] This brief examination of the Komsomol's cultural

100 At worst for the regime, as Carleton concluded concerning the confusion of the 'sexual question', this appropriation of the discourse on culture ended in a backlash when youth 'could reverse tack, identifying intensely private or selfish behaviour as revolutionary'. Ibid., 91–92.

101 Andy Willimott, *Living the Revolution: Urban Communes & Soviet Socialism, 1917–1932* (Oxford: Oxford University Press, 2016); idem, 'Everyday Revolution: The Making of the Soviet Urban Communes Russia's',in*Home Front in War and Revolution, 1914–22, Book 2: The Experience of War and Revolution*, edited by Adele Lindenmeyr, Christopher Read, and Peter Waldron (Bloomington, IN: Slavica Publishers, 2016), 431–454.

102 Willimott, *Living the Revolution*, 157.

103 Matthias Neumann, 'Revolutionizing Mind and Soul? Soviet Youth and Cultural Campaigns during the New Economic Policy (1921–8)', *Social History* 33(3) (August 2008), 243–267. Numerous other works have reached similar conclusions: Gorsuch, *Youth in Revolutionary Russia*; Kuhr-Korolev, *Gezähmte Helden*. See also Carleton, *Sexual Revolution*; Kuhr-Korolev *et al.* (eds), *Sowjetjugend 1917*–1941; Brovkin, *Russia after Lenin,* Chapter 5; Eric Naiman, *Sex in Public: The Incarnation of Early Soviet Ideology* (Princeton, NJ: Princeton University Press, 1997).

work and its organizational development has revealed the extraordinary position the communist youth organization found itself in during the NEP – both socially and politically. It was an organization that oscillated between political, social, and cultural isolation and integration. The radicalism of the anti-religious campaigns clearly tended to isolate it, thereby alienating the Komsomol as an institution and its members from the rest of the population, particularly from the older generations. But at the same time, as the surveys on juvenile delinquency and deviance within the Komsomol showed, *komsomol'tsy* themselves were strongly influenced by wider youth culture and did not grow up in isolation.[104]

During the 1920s the Komsomol grew into a mass organization and struggled to find its identity in an environment that caused tensions between individual social integration and organizational isolation; furthermore, tensions emerged between the different organizational levels and between the rank and file and the functionaries. Lack of communication and control, organizational freedom on the ground, patronizing tendencies and bureaucratization in the upper echelons – all these phenomena could be seen in the Komsomol. They caused various alienation processes – between the urban and the rural Komsomol, between the rank and file and the leadership, between the Komsomol and the party, between *komsomol'tsy* and non-organized youth, and between the Komsomol and the wider population. These processes were interlinked and influenced each other.

By analysing the culture of the league, by looking at how the league worked on the level of a local factory or village cell, we can draw a much richer and more complex picture of the organization and its peculiar position in the emergence of Soviet *obshchestvennost'*. After the Civil War, the Komsomol was still in its infancy, and throughout the decade it remained a *living* organization. It was an organization that had been incorporated as an institution into the emerging Soviet *obshchestvennost'* and the Soviet state. However, the institution-building could not keep pace with the rapid expansion of the network on the ground. This was not at all surprising given that it expanded rapidly during the decade, from about 480,000 members in October 1920 to 1,960,000 in May 1928, before rapidly increasing its membership to more than 5 million during the First Five-Year Plan.[105] As a consequence of this, the Komsomol was clearly over-governed in the centre but under-governed at the periphery.

Conclusions – an (un)managed civil society

The Komsomol was born, as were many more social and cultural organizations, amidst the chaos of civil war in conditions of limited democracy and

104 *RGASPI*, f. M1, op. 23, d. 313, l. 38; *RGASPI*, f. M1, op. 23, d. 315, l. 23; *RGASPI*, f. M1, op. 23, d. 822, ll. 87–88, 121.*Russkoe i sovetskoe molodezhnoe dvizhenie,* Doc. 80.

105 For membership figures see Neumann, *The Communist Youth League*, Appendix 1.

independent social activity.[106] The party's involvement made its creation one of the first acts in the process of formulating a conception of a new Soviet public. This, however, must not overshadow its roots in the autonomous youth movement of 1917, as well as its wider links to the tradition of *obshchestvennost'*. The creation of mass organizations such as the Komsomol has to be seen in the context of the regime's attempts to deal with rapidly growing civil and civic activity and the arrival of mass politics in Russia before and during the revolution. This was pivotal, because in the absence of strong political institutions it had the potential to undermine the new regime. As it has been shown, the construction of Soviet *obshchestvennost'* in the 1920s was far from being a process straightforwardly orchestrated by the Bolshevik regime. The youth of the early Soviet period had agency, frequently challenged adult authority and, indeed, at times, political authority. Vladimir Brovkin has argued that the Komsomol became '[a] transmission belt that snapped'.[107] This is certainly true, but must be qualified. As Sean Guillory has recently demonstrated in his study of local Komsomol cadres, in many places the real issue was that there was never a belt to snap.[108]

In the end, then, one can draw the conclusion that during NEP the Komsomol remained an organization whose development and identity was still considerably shaped and determined by its members in an often dialectical process embedded in the dialogue between the 'above' and the 'below'. The Komsomol underwent an uneven development during the 1920s. Being the only state-sponsored youth organization and a constituent part of the emerging Soviet *obshchestvennost'*, it sought to enforce its monopoly but throughout the decade struggled to do so. Religious youth organizations, such as the Baptist youth or Christian youth, still attracted huge numbers of members by 1928.[109] Others, such as the Boy Scouts, were more successfully suppressed by the Komsomol.

The fact that the Komsomol became a reserve of the party *and* a cadre school, singled it out from the many regime-sponsored mass organizations. It was not only an object in the construction of an *obshchestvennaia nomenklatura*, but became an active agent in this process of asserting state influence over various smaller organizations and institutions. Due to the lack of control, however, this also meant that in some places it assumed a powerful position acting as a substitute of the party. The party was aware of this development and fiercely criticized the perception of some *komsomol'tsy* that

106 Il'ina, *Obshchestvennye organizatsii Rossii*, 97.

107 Brovkin, *Russia after Lenin*, 108.

108 Guillory, *Profiles in Exhaustion and Pomposity*, 6.

109 Fisher, *Pattern for Soviet Youth*, 143. The diversity of youth organization and groups, cultural, political, and religious organizations, is best captured in the two volumes of documents by Tsentr Khraneniia Dokumentov Molodezhnykh Organizatsiia (TsKhDMO), *Molodezhnoe dvizhenie v Rossii (1917–28gg.). Dokumenty i materialy. Chast' I. i II* (Moscow, 1993).

it was equal to the party.[110] The recognition of this problem highlights the peculiar position of the Komsomol in its relation to the party-state apparatus.

Although the political and social work of the Komsomol in the 1920s failed to fundamentally transform the minds and souls of its members, it is nevertheless clear that new social practices were inculcated during campaigns, meetings, and club work. The Komsomol thus undeniably became an 'institute of political socialization'[111], and as such a vehicle for the inner cultural revolution during NEP.[112] This process was complex and not a one-way street. The regime tried to impose in a diverse and often contradictory discourse moderation and self-fashioning, but it clearly lost the struggle with authenticity, self-discovery, and self-identification, whenever its concepts clashed with the youth sub-cultures emerging from below. The NEP, with its mix of 'liberal' and authoritarian currents, provided the scope for this development and made the Komsomol into an autonomous space for those wishing to develop a public sphere in which young people could express themselves and their idiosyncratic understanding of Socialist transformation. Soviet *obshchestvennost'*, like its predecessor, had strong unifying connotations in that it aimed to integrate the fragmented populace into a properly structured society. However, Komsomol activists managed to use their organization to express their particularistic interests vis-à-vis the state. Indeed, it would therefore be a gross simplification to assert that voluntary mass organization, such as the Komsomol, constituted 'a mock civil society at best' in the 1920s.[113] These organizations were clearly created to channel genuine enthusiasm and mobilize the population for the project of building socialism. As we have seen, in the social, cultural, and even political practices of the Komsomol, to take one of the most important Soviet mass organizations, the reality during NEP was that such bodies could still provide a space for genuine *samodeiatelnost*, social and civic activity that was spontaneously initiated and enacted by its engaged members. For all the increasing ritualization, centralization, and pressures for uniformity, the lack of consistent party control meant that initiatives from the centre could be appropriated and shaped by activists on the ground. Indeed, as highlighted by the antireligous campaigns, useful '*samodeiatelnost*'' often turned into what the regime regarded as dangerous '*samotek*' (developing a momentum of its own). As far as the 1920s are concerned, it would therefore be problematic to argue these organizations were simply representing 'counterfeit spontaneity'.[114]

The widespread frustration with NEP, and the growing alienation between the Komsomol officialdom and the rank and file, was a clear side product of the system of *obshchestvennaia nomenklatura*. The regime did not manage to

110 *KPSS o komsomole*, 146–147.

111 Slezin, 'Kommunisticheskii soiuz molodezhi kak institut politicheskoi sotsializatsii', 242–257.

112 This argument is fully developed in my article 'Revolutionising Mind and Soul?'.

113 Peris, Storming the Heavens, 67.

114 Kenez, *The Birth of the Propaganda State*, 153.

square the circle in this respect. The inherent tensions between the league's function to act as a collective school of communism and an elitist training ground for the new cadres could not be successfully diffused. Ironically, however, the growing gulf between the upper cadres and rank and file helped to create cohesion amongst certain groups at the bottom of the organizational pyramid. Growing class consciousness and resentment of bureaucratization formed strong bonds in certain sections of the organization. They created an intra-organizational divisions between 'us' and 'them', and with it a reservoir of pent-up frustration and a desire for change which was utilized by the Stalin group at the end of the 1920s. The successful mobilization of rank and file by the Stalin group for the socialist offensive demonstrated that, in spite of the problems of control and guidance, the Komsomol became an important channel of communication between the regime and the young generations. It was only then, during Stalin's revolution, that in a complex interplay of numerous processes – 'statization', bureaucratization, mass recruitment, adultization, and the enforcement of conformity and ideological purity – the scope for genuine spontaneity and grassroots activity was reduced to such an extent that the Komsomol become a mere agent of the party and state. As independent organizations were closed down across the Soviet Union and the 'golden age of Soviet *obshchestvennost'* came to an end, the Komsomol was tamed and turned into a pseudo voluntary organization. In this way, it became fit for purpose as a central pillar of a closely controlled and managed Stalinist civil society.

Part II

The people, the past, and the new state

5 For the people

The image of Ukrainian teachers as public servants

Matthew D. Pauly

Teachers in revolutionary Ukraine have often been imagined as paradigmatic Ukrainian nationalists. Oleksandr Dovzhenko included a prominent image of teachers loudly cheering for Ukrainian autonomy in his classic film *Arsenal*, depicting the revolution in 1917 Kyiv (Kiev). Mikhail Bulgakov, in his novel *White Guard*, placed teachers first among the ranks of Ukrainian nationalists: 'the schoolteachers, medics, small-holders, Ukrainian seminarians … everyone spoke Ukrainian, everyone was in love with a magical Ukraine they imagined free of Polish lords and Moscow officers'.[1] This image of the nationalist teacher is partly sustained by the 1937 memoir of one of the main participants in the Ukrainian revolution, the educator and former teacher Sofiia Rusova, but the political and professional attitudes of teachers before 1917 and after were decidedly more complex.[2] In her work, Rusova describes the motivations of an attachment of some teachers to Ukrainian nationalism explicitly. However, Rusova's account also underscores that many in Ukraine did not think of themselves in national terms, some were deeply hostile to Ukrainian nationalism, and saw the revolution as the opportunity to fulfil multiple other ambitions: democratic governance within the framework of a Russian state, wide-scale land redistribution, and, of course, workers' power. Teachers shared in these concerns as well.

Ultimately the Bolshevik vision of 1917 won out: the realization of a Soviet republic, established in the name of the labouring populations of Ukraine. Although the nationalist and Bolshevik 1917s were antithetical to one another at the time, the potential for overlap between them is apparent even in the writings of the anti-Bolshevik Rusova. In spite of their final victory in 1921, the Bolsheviks were forced over the course of the civil war to come to terms with the Ukrainian national idea and reconsider the image of the nationalist Ukrainian teacher. At the First All-Ukrainian Teachers' Congress in 1925 after the articulation of the new Soviet nationalities policy of Ukrainization, Ukrainian political leaders and educational officials sought to rationalize the

1 Mikhail Bulgakov, *White Guard*, trans. Marian Schwartz (New Haven, CT: Yale University Press, 2008), 65.
2 S. F. Rusova, *Moï spomyny* (Lviv: Khortytsia, 1937).

teachers' role in 1917 and outline work to meet goals that progressive teachers and Soviet authorities agreed upon: raising the cultural level of Ukrainians, promoting 'modern', engaged schooling, and building a socially just state. Speakers at the congress and a key official publication on the teachers' role in 1917 claimed that the effort to build national culture, within the parameters set by the Communist Party, supported the achievement of Soviet goals that coincided with the essential ambition that educators such as Rusova held well before 1917: to serve and uplift the 'people'. They drew from a pre-revolutionary history of teacher populism which for the most active Ukrainian educators took on a decidedly national cast.

The pre-revolutionary place of teachers

Trying to apply a universal label to teachers in the pre-1917 Russian Empire is difficult. For example, Ben Eklof cautions that we should not look to teachers as automatic agents of cultural change in the countryside. Teachers did not stay long enough to make inroads into peasant communities or they lacked a political consciousness and extensive education of their own: 'although teachers had the necessary skills to teach reading and writing, the quantitative evidence suggests that they remained outsiders, to be exploited and utilized, but not to be trusted'.[3] Alternatively, Scott Seregny, argues they were a small, but significant force that sought alliances with the peasantry to force a democratization of education and an overturn of the rural social order. Peasants had their own interests, of course, but these could and did align with teachers. During the Revolution of 1905, teachers grew bolder. Local authorities in Russia and Ukraine appealed for support against the activities of 'unpatriotic' and 'seditious' teachers. The All-Russian Union of Teachers (VSU – *Vserossiiskii uchitelskii soiuz*), which first met in June to press the professional and political agenda of the most activist and progressive teachers, recommended that teachers respond to peasant concern about the Russo-Japanese War by organizing 'propaganda regarding military defeats' and then moving to 'broader criticisms against the autocracy'. Seregny cites reports of teachers who were already engaged in such evening or Sunday 'courses' in political education in Ukraine.[4] Government concessions, embodied in the October Manifesto, only seemed to embolden coordinated activity between peasants and rural teachers throughout the empire. Delegates to the Second Congress of the VSU, held in December 1905, pointed to peasant protests regarding the dismissal of teachers and the refusal of peasant communes to hand over radical teachers as evidence of peasant trust.[5]

3 Ben Eklof, *Russian Peasant Schools: Officialdom, Village Culture, and Popular Pedagogy, 1861–1917* (Berkeley, CA: University of California Press, 1986), 214.
4 Scott Seregny, *Russian Teachers and Peasant Revolution: The Politics of Education in 1905* (Bloomington, IN: Indiana University Press, 1989), 149, 152.
5 Ibid., 195.

The aftermath of the 1905 Revolution would seem grim for the teachers' union movement. Crippled by waves of arrests, the VSU membership declined in numbers and met for the last time in June 1907. At its high point, VSU embraced no more than 13,400 of the most committed, 'militant' teachers.[6] Although urban teachers sought to assume a position of leadership, rural members outnumbered them and the organization was in turn divided by those who sought professional autonomy and those who pushed for achievement of political goals. During the midst of the revolution, the political campaign won out. In the restrictive climate that followed, associational activity was largely limited to mutual aid. But, Christina Ruane insists, teacher leaders continued to emphasize unity and devotion to public service, eschewing hierarchical distinctions. Teachers 'remained wedded to the image of themselves as servants of the people ... they were not members of a nascent middle class, but participants in a new social group that combined old and new social values, a professional intelligentsia.'[7] Whatever 'the people' may have thought of teachers then, the most active believed the people's cause was their primary vocation.

Teachers in the Ukrainian national movement arguably always thought of their duty in this manner. The Ems Decree issued by Alexander II in 1876 had banned the publication and importation of Ukrainian books and affirmed Russian as the language of school instruction in the Ukrainian provinces of the empire.[8] In so doing, the decree 'rendered meaningless the Ukrainophile concept of apolitical cultural work'.[9] Any advocacy of Ukrainian-language schooling became a subversive act. During the midst of the 1905 Revolution, teachers in rural Ukraine rallied for peasant interests regardless of national affiliation, but the revolution also animated the Ukrainian national movement. Alongside the October Manifesto granting new civil rights, Nicholas II's government removed the ban on Ukrainian publications, stirring hope for the creation of state-supported Ukrainian-language schools. However, the government refused to consider such a measure. Teachers began to use the Ukrainian language in the classroom on their own or introduce it as a subject without official authorization.[10] In its June 1906 founding statute as a regional division of VSU, an All-Ukrainian Teachers' Union advocated for native-language schooling for 'all peoples on the territory of Ukraine', explicitly demanding a network of Ukrainian-language schools. Although the new State Duma considered a proposal for the opening of Ukrainian schools in 1908, the measure

6 Eklof, *Russian Peasant School*, 240–241.

7 Christine Ruane, *Gender, Class, and the Professionalization of Russian City Teachers, 1860–1914* (Pittsburgh, PA: University of Pittsburgh Press, 1994), 182.

8 P. I. Drob'iazko, *Ukraïns'ka natsional'na shkola: vytoky i suchasnist'* (Kyïv: Akademiia, 1997), 53.

9 Serhy Yekelchyk, *Ukraine: Birth of a Modern Nation* (New York: Oxford University Press, 2007), 99.

10 Drob'iazko, *Ukraïns'ka natsional'na shkola: vytoky i suchasnist'*, 79; Seregny, *Russian Teachers and Peasant Revolution*, 188–189.

failed to pass.[11] Teachers in the Ukrainian national movement believed such schooling was urgently needed in order to improve the lives of the majority Ukrainian-speaking population and remedy widespread illiteracy. As one teacher wrote in a 1912 edition of the pedagogical journal *Svitlo* (Light): 'If we truly love the people … then before everything we must employ all measures, all effort to obtain a native, Ukrainian school.'[12]

Whither teachers' loyalties?

A leading advocate of Ukrainian-language instruction was Sofiia Rusova, a prominent educator and campaigner. Prior to the First World War, Rusova had been active in Ukrainian national circles in Kyiv and St Petersburg with her husband, Oleksandr Rusov. She taught in the Ukrainian village of Oleshnia in the Chernihiv region, organized the first children's kindergarten in Kyiv, and while in St Petersburg co-edited *Kobzar* (a book of poems by the Ukrainian national bard, Taras Shevchenko) for publication abroad. She was arrested in 1881 for ties to revolutionary circles and remained under police surveillance for her work in the Ukrainian national movement, specifically her organization of secret Ukrainian schools, leadership of a Ukrainophilic pedagogical society, and joint editorship of *Svitlo* (1910–1914). She was also a member of the VSU Central Bureau and, along with other members from Ukraine, helped found the first iteration of the All-Ukrainian Teachers' Union in 1906.[13] When war broke out, Rusova was employed as a professor of the Froebel Pedagogical Institute in Kyiv and was well known as a strong advocate of the formation of Ukrainian national schools, still forbidden by the tsarist government. Because of its concern for political understandings of the revolutionary years, this essay focuses initially on Rusova's 1937 memoir, *Moï spomyny* (My Memories), but Rusova was also the author of numerous of texts on pedagogical theory published over the course of a writing career that began in 1911 and continued to her death in 1940. At the time of the publication of her memoir, she had retired from her position as a professor of pedagogy at the Drahomanov Ukrainian Pedagogical Institute in Prague.[14] She had assumed this position in 1923 after fleeing Soviet Ukraine two years earlier. In 1917 Rusova was 61 years old.

In her memoir, Rusova's frustration with the caution of Ukrainian activists of the pre-revolutionary period is period is clear.[15] Commenting on the

11 Drob'iazko, *Ukraïns'ka natsional'na shkola: vytoky i suchasnist'*, 80.

12 Ibid., 60.

13 Anatolii Borovyk, *Ukraïnizatsiia zahal'noosvitnikh shkil za chasiv vyboriuvannia derzhavnosti, 1917–1920 rr.* (Chernihiv: KP Vydavnytstvo 'Chernihivs'ki oberehy', 2008), 87.

14 Hryhorii Skorovoda (ed.), *Vydatni ukraïns'ki pedahohy: informatsiinyi dovidnyk* (Ternopil': Mandrivets', 2010), 75–76.

15 For a history of the complexity of approaches to the idea of 'Ukrainian' separatism prior to 1905, see: Faith Hillis, *Children of Rus': Right-Bank Ukraine and the Invention of a Russian Nation* (Ithaca, NY: Cornell University Press, 2013).

outlook of Kyivan Ukrainians in the pre-revolutionary period who were apathetic about any future Ukrainian administrative sovereignty or advocated an ambiguously defined federalism, she argued:

> This was a political type, very widespread in Kyiv before the revolution … [these Ukrainians] they sincerely loved ethnographic Ukraine, its nature, but they did not have a distinct political consciousness and, having been educated in the Russian school, in Russian society, they did not believe in the state authority of the Ukrainian people and they all adhered to Russian perspectives, to the Russian political system, viewing federation and a close agreement with Russia as the greatest good fortune for Ukraine![16]

She expressed exasperation at the difficulty of finding a sense of Ukrainianness, what she labels ethnographic Ukraine, in the urban environment. The Ukrainian intellectual circle in Kyiv in her description is a small, tightly bound community of likeminded individuals who clustered around the editorial board of the journal *Svitlo*. They met in Rusova's apartment and at what was called the Ukrainian Club, an apartment on Volodymyrsky Street in central Kyiv, where members read their own writings on Ukrainian themes, and staged theatrical or musical productions under the watchful eyes of the police. A celebration in honour of Taras Shevchenko saw a series of arrests: 'Cossacks rode up with guns, saw a crowd of youths singing [Shevchenko's poem] *Zapovit* (Testament), and drove them into a police detachment, beating the students with their guns … and for what?'[17]

In Rusova's account, Ukrainians appeared simultaneously to not have known what they wanted politically, but in spite of their own lack of ambition, were nevertheless threatening to the tsarist authorities. Rusova clearly thought that educated Ukrainians, including teachers, should have been bolder. Nevertheless, the sort of incoherence of pre-war national expression she cited would carry through to the revolutionary years of 1917–1921. Ukrainian intellectuals were careful because of the punishment they might face by the government, but they also did not have a singular objective. At issue for many was which cause should take priority: national liberation or social justice. In this context, the revolution to come did not offer a readily determined path, but opened a realm of confusing and sometimes conflicting choices.

Rusova's revolution

The First World War reopened discussion of reform in the Russian Empire. In 1915, a newly appointed Minister of Education, Count Pavel Ignatiev sought to respond to growing pressure from liberal educated society for school reform, 'by providing "rungs" on a ladder integrating primary and secondary

16 Rusova, *Moï spomyny*, 177.
17 Ibid., 192.

education and promoting decentralisation by making school inspectors subject to local control and changing their role from supervisors to "facilitators".[18] However, conservative resistance blocked implementation of his proposal and Ignatiev was hesitant to challenge further. He stepped down after less than two years as minister. Teachers, however, had begun to organize in ever greater numbers to protect their interests and lobby for change. Already by April 1915 some 40,000 teachers had joined mutual aid societies or legal aid funds and the All-Russian Pedagogical Society (VPO – *Vserossiiskoe pedagogicheskoe obshchestvo*) held its founding congress in May to continue the work begun by the defunct VSU.[19] As Ruane argues, the 1905 revolution had helped consolidate a professional ethos and political commitment in spite of the demise of the union: 'In order to teach children to be independent thinkers as their child-centered pedagogy advocated, teachers themselves had to be free to think and act as individuals.'[20] The disruption of war in 1915 emboldened teachers to mobilize anew and demand civil rights that they believed were necessary in order for them to build an imagined progressive, reformed school. The VPO was critical to the creation of teachers' organizations throughout the empire, including key chapters in Ukraine.

Still, any expression of Ukrainian cultural distinctiveness in wartime Kyiv was difficult. Fearing possible espionage and separatist agitation, the police arrested Ukrainians from Austrian Galicia residing in the city and shut down the Ukrainian club where Rusova was active. However, some nationally minded Ukrainians continued to act on their beliefs. Rusova reminisced that illiterate wounded soldiers from Ukrainian detachments were instructed in the basics of Ukrainian grammar during their convalescence at a hospital housed in the former club. She and the faculty of Froebel Pedagogical Institute evacuated to Saratov as the front drew closer to Kyiv. Rusova claimed that here, in an environment where 'the Muscovite language' predominated, the circle of Ukrainians grew closer, students and faculty from multiple Kyiv institutions gathered in apartments, socialized in Ukrainian, and discussed the future of Ukraine. Students also taught reading and writing to peasants evacuated from Right Bank Ukraine, assuming what Rusova labels 'cultural guardianship over their countrymen'.[21] Her account affirms George Liber's estimation of the war. It 'radicalized the masses' and 'encouraged many Ukrainian speakers to imagine themselves as Ukrainians'.[22]

18 Ben Eklof, 'Russia and the Soviet Union: Schooling, Citizenship, and the Reach of the State, 1870–1945', in *Mass Education and the Limits of State Building, c. 1870–1930* (New York: Palgrave Macmillan, 2012), 144.
19 N. N. Smirnov, *Na perelome: rossiiskoe uchitel'stvo nakanune i v dni revoliutsii 1917 goda* (Sankt-Peterburg: Nauka, 1994), 63–67.
20 Ruane, *Gender, Class, and the Professionalization of Russian City Teachers*, 165.
21 Rusova, *Moï spomyny*, 201.
22 George Liber, *Total Wars and the Making of Modern Ukraine, 1914–1954* (Toronto: University of Toronto Press, 2016), 44. Also on the role of the war in Ukrainian national imagining, see the collected essays of Wolfram Dornik (ed.),

Rusova's description, retrospectively written, suggested an anticipation of a political shift to come. Clearly, for Rusova, the potential for realization of national ambitions was critical, but there appeared to be a consensus among her wider circle for an alteration in schooling in Ukraine, fulfilment of what Rusova calls 'our idea of the best education': cultural uplift through native-language instruction. Back in Kyiv, when news came of the February Revolution, Rusova claimed its victory partly for Ukraine, noting the role of troops from Volhynia in the overthrow of tsarist authority in Petrograd. But, she underscored, no one knew how to understand the future: 'Would it find expression in a federation with a renewed Muscovy, would it possibly give us – as the bravest patriots believed – full sovereignty, independence.'[23] Rusova's statement suggested, as well as obfuscated, the confusion of decision-making among political activists in Ukraine in early 1917. Even for longtime participants in the Ukrainian national movement, few thought of independence initially as a real choice. As Serhy Yekelchyk reminds us, independence was not the aim of those who began the 'Ukrainian Revolution' it was an idea formulated during the course of events.[24]

Nevertheless, in her memoirs Rusova's choice seems determinative. She joined the Central Rada, the governing centre set up by nationally inclined political activists to administer the predominantly Ukrainian parts of the former Russian Empire, to the frustration of the Provisional Government in Petrograd. The Central Rada vied for authority with commissioners of the Provisional Government and soviets established by socialists in Ukraine's major cities, although for a time most of these workers' and soldiers' councils recognized the Central Rada's de facto authority. The Central Rada met in the former building of the Kyiv Pedagogical Museum, symbolically signalling the importance of education to its initial aims. For Rusova, an unambiguous task of the new 'revolutionary' Ukrainian parliament was the creation of a network of Ukrainian-language schools.[25] Drawing from progressive pedagogical theory, Rusova emphatically proclaimed in a 1917 essay that only native-language instruction would enable children to reach their full potential in the modern world:

> The new school places one main goal before itself – to build, to give the child the means to discover creative, independent activity ... In Ukraine, the native language is Ukrainian; the pupils' active, creative forces should be led by it.[26]

Although Rusova argued that zemstvo assemblies 'unanimously recognized the necessity of the immediate Ukrainization of the school' and the peasantry generally supported this initiative, especially the organization of Ukrainian

Die Ukraine: zwischen Selbstbestimmung und Fremdherrschaft, 1917–1922 (Graz: Leykam, 2011).

23 Rusova, *Moï spomyny*, 203.

24 Yekelchyk, *Ukraine: Birth of a Modern Nation*, 83.

25 Rusova, *Moï spomyny*, 204.

26 S. F. Rusova and O. V. Proskura, *Vybrani pedahohichni tvory* (Kyiv: Osvita, 1996), 208–209.

gymnasiums in provincial centres, in reality the Central Rada's national cultural initiatives were not a priority for Russophone urban residents or a peasantry interested largely in full-scale redistribution of land. The nationalist view of 1917 suggested work towards an extension of a national state was primary, however much its form was in dispute, and the peasant hope for 1917 was for the reorganization of land tenure and a restriction of the power of the state. The revolutionary years saw the birth of multiple peasant bands, the most famous of which were led by the anarchist Nestor Makhno, which strove to protect newly claimed peasant lands from the intrusion of the multiple governments that sought control of Ukraine: nationalist, Bolshevik, and White.[27]

Even Rusova conceded that older peasants questioned the use of the word 'Ukraine', and that part of the aim of the 'new school' in the village was to convince them of their inclusion in the nation. The Central Rada's secretary of education, Ivan Steshenko, appointed Rusova to head the departments of extracurricular and preschool education under the secretariat. From this vantage point, Rusova observed the numerous challenges that faced the task of the Ukrainization of schools and education generally in 1917. Teachers, she maintained, 'enthusiastically' undertook work on Ukrainization, calling for the convocation of an all-Ukrainian teachers' meeting to discuss its implementation and to support a Main Ukrainian School Council, established to compile, fund, and distribute new Ukrainian textbooks.[28] In her description, teachers are the archetypical carriers of the national revolution of 1917, an image that Soviet government would accept and darken. And yet, in the confusion of that year, they received little support from the government. As Rusova conceded, the matter of Ukrainian-language schools quickly lost momentum because of the government's inattention and indecision. Those equipped to teach in Ukrainian in multiple subjects and at all grade levels in the newly established gymnasiums were still too small in number, even if interest was high.

Furthermore, 1917 meant something decidedly different to a significant portion of the population that cared little about Ukrainian nationalism. The political orientation of these individuals varied considerably, from socialist, to Kadet, to unapologetic monarchist, but it undoubtedly included teachers among their numbers (especially at the secondary level) in spite of the image that Rusova painted and the Bolsheviks would later confirm. Rusova highlighted the resistance of Russian parents in particular, who sent telegrams to the Provisional Government in Petrograd, pleading for the 'rescue' of children from 'forced Ukrainization'. Rusova emphasized the absence of any coercion

27 For more on Makhno and the peasant-led anarchist movement in revolutionary Ukraine, see: Felix Schnell, ''Tear Them Apart … And Be Done With It!' The Ataman Leadership of Nestor Makhno as a Culture of Violence', *Ab Imperio* 3 (2008); Alexandre Skirda, *Nestor Makhno – Anarchy's Cossack: The Struggle for Free Soviets in the Ukraine 1917–1921* (Oakland, CA: AK Press, 2004); John Reshetar, *The Ukrainian Revolution, 1917–1920* (New York: Arno Press, 1972), 249–252.

28 Rusova, *Moï spomyny*, 204.

in school enrolment, but still lauded Secretary of Education Steshenko's battle with those who objected to the idea of Ukrainian schooling:

> He [Steshenko] broke all traditional ties with the Russian school, because as a teacher he knew well its national, demoralizing influence and fought persistently with Russians and those 'Little Russians', who equally could not imagine how our education could get along without Russian tutelage.[29]

By using the term 'Little Russian', Rusova was invoking a deep-seated nationalist rejection of Ukrainians who privileged the superiority of Russian-language culture and loyalty to a Russian state.[30] In doing so, she was side-lining variant interpretations of 1917 for ethnic Ukrainians. To be Ukrainian, meant an acceptance and promotion of the Ukrainian national school and, by extrapolation, the Ukrainian national revolution.

And yet, other visions of 1917 clearly competed. The politicians of the Central Rada knew this and so did Rusova. One of the classical historiographical explanations for the 'failure' of the Central Rada and the state that it constructed, the Ukrainian People's Republic, is that it did not privilege resolution of social and economic questions, particularly the redistribution of land and satisfaction of trade union grievances, and allowed the Bolsheviks to tap into lingering peasant and worker resentment.[31] 1917 could not merely mean the fulfilment of national concerns. Rusova acknowledged this when she expressed frustration with lack of student enrollment in her newly Ukrainized courses at the Froebel Institute: 'Where were our conscious Ukrainian women? Did the party struggle absorb them? But the work of leadership of peasants' and workers' institutions gave broad opportunities for social-political work!'[32] By this lament, she suggested that training for employment in Ukrainian kindergartens, schools, and cultural organizations (that she worked to establish near factories) should have been enough for young Ukrainians interested primarily in social justice. Of course, many may have simply been uninterested in Ukrainian-language course work, but others simply thought class concerns trumped the national.

When the October Revolution pushed this idea to the fore, Central Rada representatives supported the Bolsheviks in the fight against what they viewed as the pro-Russian, reactionary troops of the Kyiv Military District, but soon after proclaimed the autonomy of a state of their construction, the Ukrainian

29 Ibid., 205–206.

30 See Andreas Kappeler, *Great Russians and Little Russians: Russian-Ukrainian Relations and Perceptions in Historical Perpsective* (Seattle, WA: Henry M. Jackson School of International Studies, University of Washington, 2003); Serhii Plokhy, *Ukraine and Russia: Representations of the Past* (Toronto: University of Toronto Press, 2008).

31 Reshetar, *The Ukrainian Revolution*, 140–142.

32 Rusova, *Moï spomyny*, 207.

People's Republic (UNR – *Ukraïnska narodna respublika*). A Bolshevik-sponsored Congress of Soviets in Kharkiv in eastern Ukraine declared the first Soviet Ukrainian Republic and began to wage war on the UNR. Red units, made up of units from Russia as well as Ukraine, began to advance on Kyiv. The Central Rada succeeded in suppressing an uprising by Kyivan Bolsheviks, but the Red Army captured the capital on 29 January 1918, a few short days after Rada declared the UNR's independence. Many of the final defenders of this first UNR government in Kyiv were students of a Ukrainian military school, who were encircled and massacred by Red Army forces near the Kruty railway station, north-east of the capital.[33] The schoolhouse was thus, in a way, the last guardian of the nationalist vision of the year 1917.

Division in the teachers' union movement

Already then by 1917 nationally-minded Ukrainian teachers had claimed a separate agenda from their counterparts in Russia. The fall of tsarist government had brought about immediate change towards pedagogical innovation or the institution of native-language schooling. The 'old intelligentsia and bureaucracy' led and staffed the Ministry of Education under Aleksandr Manuilov in St Petersburg and its education districts in Kyiv and elsewhere in Ukraine. Teachers did not wait, however. In April, members of the VPO reconvened as the All-Russian Teachers' Union (VUS – *Vserossiskii uchitelskii soiuz*), and teachers met throughout the empire to form branches of the union, often without direction from the centre.[34] From 4–6 April some 350 delegates assembled in Kyiv for an All-Ukrainian Congress of Teachers. While the Ukrainian teachers considered a range of pedagogical questions, the chief topic of discussion was the Ukrainization of educational institutions. Smirnov argues that attention to this matter was 'dictated most of all by the numerous requests of provincial teachers, who, undoubtedly, witnessed the awakening of national consciousness under the impact of the February events'.[35] The resolutions of the congress made clear that the delegates intended to Ukrainize schools wherever Ukrainians formed a majority without guidance from the Provisional Government.

Rusova spoke on the need to create a professional union for Ukrainian teachers at the April congress and a May preparatory workshop for teachers' summer courses provided the opportunity to begin work in earnest. On 30 May the workshop participants, supported by representatives from the Kyiv provincial and district zemstvos, announced a resurrected All-Ukrainian Teachers' Union. At the union's first general congress in August the question

33 Yekelchyk, *Ukraine: Birth of a Modern Nation*, 71–72; Iarasolav Havryliuk (ed.), *Kruty: sichen' 1918 roku: dokumenty, materialy, doslidzhennia, kinostsenarii*, Second ed. (Kyïv: Vydavnychnyi tsentr 'Prosvita', 2010).

34 Smirnov, *Na perelome: rossiiskoe uchitel'stvo nakanune i v dni revoliutsii 1917 goda*, 99, 141.

35 Ibid., 144.

of Ukrainization became 'the main reason for the division of the teachers' union movement between those for the All-Ukrainian union and those who supported the All-Russian Teachers' Union [VUS]'.[36] The Ukrainian union promised protection for the rights of national minorities and sought to embrace teachers of all nationalities, but acceptance of the basic requirement for Ukrainization united the union's members. In spite of the decrees of the Central Rada in favour of Ukrainian-language schooling, the transfer of instruction outside Kyiv occurred only through the efforts of local union organizations and individual teachers, who were often uninformed about events in the capital.[37] The union survived successive changes of government in Ukraine until the Red Army's final occupation of Kyiv. In February 1920, after some debate at a rump congress, the union dissolved and its members merged with VUS's replacement, the All-Russian Union of Education Workers (Rabpros – *Soiuz rabotnikov prosveshcheniia*).[38]

In the year 1917, the relationship between the All-Ukrainian and All-Russian teachers' unions was partly a reflection of the unresolved relationship between the Provisional Government and Ukraine. Sentiment among opponents to the All-Ukrainian union varied. To be sure, some teachers in Ukraine refused to believe in the existence of a Ukrainian language separate from Russian and viewed any attempt to constitute a Ukrainian political authority as treasonous. Others viewed Ukrainian language schooling as primarily a concern for the lower-level, village school and resisted against any expansion. In the aftermath of the February Revolution, most political parties in the Russian Empire recognized the necessity of native-language instruction, at least at the primary school level. Under pressure from the Central Rada, in March the Provisional Government's Minister of Education Manuilov sanctioned Ukrainian-language instruction in schools in the Kyiv district.[39] However, the government postponed any comprehensive decree on the extent and manner of native-language schooling until the convening of the Constituent Assembly. Tamara Krasovitskaia views this delay as understandable. The government 'did not want to add to and aggravate controversial decisions in the already difficult

36 Borovyk, *Ukraïnizatsiia zahal'noosvitnikh shkil za chasiv vyboriuvannia derzhavnosti, 1917–1920 rr.*, 186–189.

37 During the revolutionary years, the Ukrainian cultural society, 'Prosvita', also assumed a large role in expanding opportunities for education, especially for adults.V. R. Adams'kyi and B. S. Kryshchuk (eds), *"Prosvity" Podillia v dobu Ukraïns'koï revoliutsiï* (Kamianets'-Podils'kyi: Medobory, 2014).

38 For a discussion of Narkompros's failed attempt to influence VUS and the union's dissolution, see: Sheila Fitzpatrick, *The Commissariat of Englightenment: Soviet Organization of Education and the Arts under Lunacharsky, October 1917–1921* (New York: Cambridge University Press, 1970), 36–41.

39 T. Iu. Krasovitskaia, *Rosiiskoe obrazovanie mezhdu reformatorstvom i revoliutsionarizmom, Fevral' 1917–1920 god* (Moskva: Institut rosiiskoi istorii RAN, 2002), 60–61; Drob'iazko, *Ukraïns'ka natsional'na shkola: vytoky i suchasnist'*, 96; Borovyk, *Ukraïnizatsiia zahal'noosvitnikh shkil za chasiv vyboriuvannia derzhavnosti, 1917–1920 rr.*, 34.

social atmosphere'. The country was, after all, still at war and its government was afraid of unilaterally antagonizing those who preferred Russian instruction.[40] This caution (or outright resistance) was shared by the head of the Kyiv school district as well teachers in many of Ukraine's principal cities and towns.[41] However, local affiliates of the All-Ukrainian union grew exponentially between 1917–1920 at the expense of the VUS. By January 1919 there were 20,515 members of the All-Ukrainian union, 'at the time of recurring changes of power and instability in society' the All-Ukrainian Teachers' Union became the authoritative organization for the 'majority of teachers' in Ukraine.[42]

In Petrograd, the work of progressive educators had continued. The State Committee of Education (GKNO) under the Ministry of Education—a deliberative forum in which representatives from VUS, the Petrograd Soviet, and other unions took part—drafted a series of sweeping education reforms for the entire empire. For example, taking its lead from Ignatiev's proposal, the committee insisted on the creation of a single, integrated primary school. But the committee's initiatives reforms continued to meet opposition, especially from conservative parents and were never realized before the October Revolution. Yevgeny Balashov argues that it did not matter: 'no "bourgeois" reforms could have satisfied the radical demands of the Bolsheviks'.[43] The new Soviet government dissolved the GKNO in November 1917. Yet, Soviet educators and the RSFSR Commissariat of Education (Narkompros – *Narodnyi komissariat prosveschenii*a) drew upon the deliberations of the GKNO and non-Bolshevik progressive educators to design new policy, embodied most pointedly in the October 1918 'Declaration of the United Labour School'. Sheila Fitzpatrick emphasizes the debate that proceeded and followed the formulation of this document, underscoring that Narkompros tried out multiple models during the civil war: 'It was not looking for any single blueprint of the future school. What it valued in its experimental schools was a spirit of freedom, of community activity, and perhaps above all of hope'.[44] These essential principles were consistent with pre-revolutionary progressive theory, even if Narkomporos privileged a Marxist concern for polytechnic labour training in the years to come.

Ukrainization as the basis for accommodation

Rusova did not evacuate with the Central Rada government to Zhytomyr, but remained in the city. Her account of Kyiv under Bolshevik administration is

40 Krasovitskaia, *Rosiiskoe obrazovanie mezhdu reformatorstvom i revoliutsionarizmom, Fevral' 1917–1920 god.*

41 Borovyk, *Ukraïnizatsiia zahal'noosvitnikh shkil za chasiv vyboriuvannia derzhavnosti, 1917–1920 rr.*, 189–190.

42 Ibid., 194, 201, 207.

43 E. M. Balashov, *Shkola v rossiiskom obshchestve 1917–1927 rr.: stanovlenie "novogo cheloveka"* (Sankt-Peterburg: Rossiiskaia akademiia nauk, Sankt-Peterburgskii institut istorii, 2003), 16–19.

44 Fitzpatrick, *The Commissariat of Englightenment*, 50.

bleak, focusing on Bolshevik arrest of and search for members of the Central Rada who remained, the deprivations of daily life, and the drunken rampages of a Red sailors' militia that she claims specifically targeted ethnic Ukrainians. However, her description of a meeting between Volodymyr Zatonsky, the Commissar of Education for the first Soviet Ukrainian Republic, and the teachers of the city of Kyiv is revealing because it serves as reminder of how the Bolshevik 1917 and nationalist 1917 overlapped. According to Rusova, Zatonsky listened to the protests of teachers regarding violence in the city with a sort of condescending humour, but nevertheless promised to protect an official from the Central Rada's Secretariat of Education, Petro Kholodny, who was then in hiding. Zatonsky apparently chose to intervene because he had served as Kholodny's assistant in the physics department of Kyiv Polytechnic Institute in 1913.[45] The conflicting nationalist and Bolshevik visions of 1917 intersect in this personal linkage between Zatonsky and Kholodny but could not reconcile. However, the Bolsheviks repeated difficulty in entirely suppressing the challenge of nationalism in the years of war ultimately forced a Bolshevik adaptation of Kholodny's 1917.

The history of the Ukrainian revolution becomes decidedly complicated after 1917. Representatives of the UNR signed a separate peace treaty with the Central Powers at Brest Litovsk on 9 February 1918. The Central Powers acknowledged the Rada's authority over Ukraine, forced Soviet Russian recognition of the UNR, and compelled the Red Army to give up Kyiv. In a secret clause of the treaty, the Rada agreed to provide the Central Powers with food in exchange for military aid. However, once German military commanders had pushed the Soviet government out of Ukraine, they began to grow frustrated with the Rada's leftist agenda and failure to collect the foodstuffs it had promised. They helped engineer a coup against the Rada with the sanction of large landowners and installed a former tsarist general, Pavlo Skoropadsky, as Hetman (Cossack leader) of the Ukrainian State in late April. Although Skoropadsky attempted to appeal to Ukrainian national sensibilities by expanding the network of Ukrainian schools begun under the Rada, his government was hampered by its acquiescence to German requisitions of peasant grain. Peasant anger turned into armed rebellion.[46] The German army, forced to demobilize after its defeat on the Western Front, quit Ukraine. Skoropadsky fled and a growing insurgent force led by the former Rada Secretary of War, Symon Petliura, took Kyiv and announced the return of the UNR. Once again, the Red Army advanced and seized Kyiv in February 1919. The UNR's

45 Rusova, *Moï spomyny*, 209–210.

46 Skoropadsky's Minister of Education, Mykola Vasylenko, retained many leading UNR educators (including Kholodny and Rusova) and is generally credited with making gains for Ukrainian-language schooling. Fearful of antagonizing speakers, he charted a careful path, choosing to open new Ukrainian secondary schools and post-secondary schools alongside rather than forcibly converting the language of instruction for existing ones. V. A. Smolii (ed.), *Narysy istoriï ukraïns'koï revoliutsiï, 1917–1921 rokiv*, 2 vols, vol. 1 (Kyiv: Naukova dumka, 2011), 304–306.

political executive, the Directory, retreated to the south-west and attempted to stage a new offensive. Incursions with General Anton Denikin's White Army, the breakdown of tentative alliances peasant warlords, and internal political strife undermined the UNR's fortunes. After a brief period of occupation by the troops of the White Army and the Galician (West Ukrainian) Army, Kyiv returned to Soviet hands in December 1919. The Directory, under Petliura's leadership, made one more bid to retake the city, this time with through an alliance with Poland that required UNR assent to Polish rule over the former Habsburg land of Galicia and western Volhynia.[47] The combined Ukrainian-Polish army captured the capital in May 1920, but were soon ejected. After fighting a war for its own survival, Poland signed a peace treaty with the Soviets in March 1921, recognizing the control of a Ukrainian Socialist Soviet Republic (UkrSSR) over much of central and eastern Ukraine.[48] Only when military victory over the UNR seemed likely, 'did the Bolsheviks re-evaluate their nationality policy in Ukraine. Having won on the battlefield, they now reviewed their recent political mistakes.'[49]

During the course of the Bolsheviks' initial two occupations of Kyiv, little was done for education. Although the Bolsheviks formed a series of Soviet governments, real power rested with the Red Army's military commanders. Volodymyr Zatonsky also served as commissar of education in the second Ukrainian Soviet government of early 1919 and advocated for the 'equality of languages', but 'at that time it was impossible to think even of any schools'.[50] The then leader of the Soviet Ukrainian government, Christian Rakovsky, was 'hostile to the Ukrainian national movement, which he considered an invention of the Ukrainian intelligentsia' and educational institutions, if they operated at all, used Russian.[51] Rakovsky believed Ukrainian teachers to be '"nationalists" and pro-UNR' and those from western Ukraine to be especially

47 In so doing, Petliura abandoned any hope of restoring the West Ukrainian People's Republic (ZUNR – *Zakhidnoukraïnska Narodna Respublika*), which had formally entered into union with the UNR in January 1919, but broke with Petliura's Directory over a prospective alliance with Denikin. By 1920 the Polish Army had wrested control of Galicia from the ZUNR.

48 Yekelchyk, *Ukraine: Birth of a Modern Nation*, 73–76, 79–83; Serhii. Plokhy, *The Gates of Europe: A History of Ukraine* (New York: Basic Books, 2015), 208–211, 215–226. Not all in the UNR government were opposed to conciliation with Soviet Russia. Volodymyr Vynnychenko, the leftist chairman of the Directory, failed in his attempts to negotiate a peace deal with the Bolsheviks and resigned after falling out with Petliura.

49 Liber, *Total Wars and the Making of Modern Ukraine*, 75.

50 M. Iu. Vyhovs'kyi, *Nomenklatura systemy osvity v USRR 1920–1930-x rokiv: sotsial'ne pokhodzhennia personal'nyi sklad ta funktsiï* (Kyiv: Heneza, 2006), 195–196; Jurij Borys, *The Sovietization of Ukraine, 1917–1923: The Communist Doctrine and Practice of National Self-Determination* (Edmonton: Canadian Institute of Ukrainian Studies, 1980), 189, 216.

51 Borys, *The Sovietization of Ukraine, 1917–1923*, 215; Yekelchyk, *Ukraine: Birth of a Modern Nation*, 80.

'"infected" with fanaticism'.[52] This does not mean that the Bolsheviks had no support among teachers in Ukraine. The party historically enjoyed the loyalty of some teachers in the industrial districts of Kyiv and Odesa and the leadership of the All-Ukrainian Teachers' Union attempted to cooperate with education administrators during each period of Soviet rule in the capital.[53] But the lack of military control and economic stability hampered any Soviet attempt to build Ukrainian schools on the model of the RSFSR 'Declaration of the United Labour School' and teacher enthusiasm for Bolshevism in Ukraine was low.

In late 1919, the Bolsheviks made an adjustment. Lenin authored a document on Soviet policy for Ukraine which was adopted with some modification by the Central Committee of the All-Russian Community Party (Bolshevik) on 29 November. Lenin urged local Bolsheviks to 'be conciliatory towards "national feelings"' and the final paragraph of the party's resolution acknowledged the equality of languages, clearing the way for wider administrative use of Ukrainian.[54] Soviet Ukraine was to be in close alliance with the RSFSR and, importantly, the Communist Party (Bolshevik) of Ukraine (KP(b)U – *Komunistychna partiia (bilshovykiv) Ukraïny*) was to effectively operate as a branch of the All-Russian party. Stephen Velychenko sees these sorts of 'concessions' as hypocritical measures born of short-term expediency; Borys argues that military victory in fact allowed Lenin to reverse course, demanding the merger of non-Bolshevik, Ukrainian national communists with the KP(b)U, a purge of the KP(b)U, and formal union with Russia.[55] Nevertheless, the importance of taking Ukrainian national culture seriously was not lost on party leaders in Moscow and Ukraine once internal party consolidation had been wrought and political and economic centralization assured. Suspicion of the Ukrainian intelligentsia and peasantry remained, but the reality of governing a majority Ukrainian-speaking population forced most to concede the need for some accommodation.

The 1923 Soviet nationalities policy of Ukrainization was premised on the idea that elements of national culture advocated by the UNR Central Rada

52 Stephen Velychenko, *Painting Imperialism and Nationalism Red: The Ukrainian Marxist Critique of Russian Communist Rule in Ukraine, 1918–1925* (Toronto: University of Toronto Press, 2015), 157.

53 Smirnov, *Na perelome: rossiiskoe uchitel'stvo nakanune i v dni revoliutsii 1917 goda*, 246; Borovyk, *Ukraïnizatsiia zahal'noosvitnikh shkil za chasiv vyboriuvannia derzhavnosti, 1917–1920 rr.*, 195, 204.

54 Borys, *The Sovietization of Ukraine*, 252–253.

55 Velychenko, *Painting Imperialism and Nationalism Red*, 28–29; Borys, *The Sovietization of Ukraine*, 363–364. For more on Ukrainian national communist alternatives to Bolshevism, see Velychenko's comprehensive analysis as well as Iwan Majstrenko, *Borot'bism: A Chapter in the History of Ukrainian Communism* (New York: Research Program on the USSR, 1954); James E. Mace, *Communism and the Dilemmas of National Liberation: National Communism in Soviet Ukraine, 1918–1933* (Cambridge, MA: Harvard Ukrainian Research Institute, 1983), 40–84.

could be co-opted and transformed to serve the new proletarian state. Specifically, the Communist Party needed UkrSSR teachers to use the Ukrainian language to instruct children (and the wider public) in the values of socialism and to prepare them for employment and economic and political leadership.[56] In the 1920s this meant relying on teachers trained in the pre-revolutionary period by figures such as Kholodny and Rusova. Acknowledgment of this Bolshevik adjustment does not mean we should ignore the very real opposition between Bolsheviks like Zatonsky on one hand and national intellectuals like Kholodny and Rusova on the other. Kholodny and Rusova would spend the remainder of the civil war in the service of the resurrected UNR Ministry of Education, continually on the run from Bolshevik forces, fleeing Soviet Ukraine entirely after the civil war's end.[57] Zatonsky would be instrumental to the restoration of Bolshevik power in Ukraine. Although he supported Ukrainization, he also warned of the danger of 'coercive Ukrainization' in the schools and in 1933 as the Commissar of Education helped purge the educational field of 'national-deviationists' whose version of Ukrainization was then deemed counter-revolutionary.[58]

However, in the years following 1923, the Soviet state's demand for Ukrainian-speaking teachers required a re-framing of the Ukrainian teachers' position in 1917. Myroslav Havryliv, a Galician Bolshevik and director of the prestigious Kharkiv Institute of People's Education, authored *The October Revolution and Teachers*, a defining and widely circulated document on the subject in 1924.[59] Havryliv argued that the revolutionary events of 1917 had confused teachers:

> The political whirlpool spun the head of the Ukrainian intellectual and with it the educator of the teacher's union; there was no opportunity to

56 See: Matthew D. Pauly, *Breaking the Tongue: Language, Education, and Power in Soviet Ukraine, 1923–34* (Toronto: University of Toronto Press, 2014); Terry Martin, *The Affirmative Action Empire: Nations and Nationalism in the Soviet Union, 1923–39* (Ithaca, NY: Cornell University Press, 2001), 75–124; George Liber, *Soviet Nationality Policy, Urban Growth, and Identity Change in the Ukrainian SSR, 1923–1934* (New York: Cambridge University Press, 1992), 26–46, 84, 92, 118.

57 Kholodny fled first to Tarnów, Poland with the retreating UNR government in November 1920. Rusova worked briefly under the Soviets in the people's education section of Kamianets-Podilsky, where she had taught as a professor in the UNR State Ukrainian University. She left at the end of 1921, concluding life was no longer tolerable in Soviet Ukraine, a country of 'bondage, grief, falsehood, and ruin'. Rusova, *Moï spomyny*, 254–260.

58 Vyhovs'kyi, *Nomenklatura systemy osvity v USRR 1920–1930-x rokiv: sotsial'ne pokhodzhennia personal'nyi sklad ta funktsiï*, 191–214.

59 Havryliv joined the Bolshevik party in 1919. He committed suicide in 1932 in anticipation of his likely arrest. Vasyl' Marochko and Götz Hillig, *Represovani pedahohy Ukraïny: zhertvy politychnoho teroru* (Kyiv: Naukovyi svit, 2003), 83–84, 164; Oleksandr Rubl'ov, *Zakhidnoukraïns'ka intelihentsiia u zahal'nonatsional'nykh politychnykh ta kul'turnykh protsesakh, 1914–1939* (Kyiv: Instytut istoriï Ukraïny, 2004), 52–53, 108, 526–527.

> make sense of the chaos of the events ... The Ukrainian intelligentsia fell from the heights of their loftiest dreams into an abyss of the deepest disappointment, they entered into a horrible crisis, and became disconcerted.[60]

Teachers opposed the old order, but were constrained by their deference to the leadership of more elite intellectuals. Although they claimed to serve the 'people', their conception of the people was amorphous, as if a 'people's culture' could stand above class. In the pre-revolutionary period, Havryliv maintained, this 'people's culture' is 'what the teacher served, valued, not suspecting even that it was bourgeois in its essence, not serving the people, but the ruling class.' During the civil war, nationally conscious teachers rightly looked at tsarism as 'a national oppressor', but continued to follow the lead of 'democrats' who privileged the national revolution over the social and 'rejected the victory of the working class'.[61]

Havryliv insisted teachers were by nature revolutionary. But, the Communist party's commitment to the national idea was a necessary pre-requisite for a shift in loyalty to Soviet power: 'Until the nationalities policy became more sensitive and more just, when institutions Ukrainized not in words, but in fact, when Russian chauvinism began to be driven from the workplace, until the Ukrainian educational worker felt that the latter disappeared, it could be said [there was] an objective fence between him and the Soviet citizenship.'[62] If their revolutionary aims had been misdirected towards the service of the nation, teachers' essential ambition was to provide a public good and Ukrainization was a critical element for many of them personally and professionally. And this orientation fit with the new rationale of the Soviet nationalities policy. Social improvement among a largely rural population whose cultural development and language had been restricted could come only with education in the national language. Soviet nationalities policy, with its emphasis on national identification and separation of cultural services according to national language, meant that this effort continued to be pursued through a Ukrainian-specific context.

Defining redemption

In January 1925, one year after the publication of Havryliv's piece, Ukrainian government and party leaders, as well as members of the Ukrainian branch of

60 Myroslav Havryliv, *Zhovtneva revoliutsiia i vchytel'stvo* (Kharkiv: Chervonyi shliakh, 1924), 22–23.

61 Ibid., 10.

62 Ibid., 38. Commissar of Education Oleksander Shumsky made a similar argument in a 1924 article which argued that Ukrainian teachers initially viewed the urban Bolsheviks as foreign, teachers' 'political evolution was parallel to that of peasant masses – they followed rich peasants and were susceptible to slogans of freedom, democracy, and national liberation.' O. Shums'kyi, 'Na tret'omu fronti: do uchytel's'koho z"izdu', *Shliakh osvity* 11–12 (1924), viii.

the Union of Education Workers (Robos – *Spilka robitnykiv osvity*), also sought to explain the teachers' initial suspicion of the Bolsheviks and reorientation on the basis of this mission at the First All-Ukrainian Teachers' Congress.[63] In the opening session of the congress, these leaders placed their greatest emphasis on teachers' past mistakes and path to salvation. The congress offered teachers an opportunity to publicly express their loyalty to Soviet power, to applaud Soviet defined nationalities policy and to embrace Soviet-sanctioned pedagogical methods, but also to atone. An acknowledgment of sin allowed Soviet education and the teacher to move forward while still embracing elements of the past. Continuity could be maintained by declarations of rupture, even if forced.

After the raising of the red flag by Red Army soldiers, a clear signal of new time, the teachers' congress began its proceedings on 5 January. Oleksandr Mizernytsky, the head of the Central Bureau of Robos, was the first to speak and he attempted to offer a rationale for the teachers' previous mistaken alignment.[64] Like Havryliv, he conceded: 'The teacher in the school during the time of the existence of the tsarism was a tool for the oppression of the working class.' Although the teacher served the interests of the bourgeoisie, he could not belong to the ruling class and this was the reason for his 'bewilderment' and 'tragedy'. Teachers rebelled occasionally against the tsarist order (and the bourgeoisie that sustained it), but perpetuated lessons defined by it in their daily work. Furthermore, even though the teacher claimed to stand for the people, in rural locations: 'He was close to the petty bourgeois ideology that was sustained in the peasantry; he floundered in the tenets of this petty bourgeois.'[65]

Although Mizernytsky invoked the same language of delusion as Havryliv, his tone was more accusatory and a detailed description of teachers' orientation during the revolutionary years suggested a more obstinate attachment to Ukrainian nationalism during the revolutionary years. In general, his comments suggest a foolish obstinacy to the nationalist cause: 'From the beginning of the Central Rada teachers as a defined public group took part in state construction, especially in the formation of the state apparatus for management

63 The All-Ukrainian Teachers' Union also held a 'first' congress under the auspices of the Central Rada in April 1917. For the Soviet organizers of the 1925 congress this earlier congress was illegitimate and in naming their congress 'first' they turned the teachers to zero time.

64 Mizernytsky was a former member of the Ukrainian national communist party, Ukrainian Communist Party (Borotbists), which merged with the KP(b)U, the Ukrainian branch of the Communist Party, in 1920. In addition to his position in Robos, he was main editor of the pedagogical journal *Radians'ka osvita* and a former deputy head of the primary school section of the Ukrainian People's Commissariat of Education, Narkomos. He was arrested in 1934 for 'bourgeois nationalism' and sent to a labour camp in the Kuznetsk Basin. Marochko and Hillig, *Represovani pedahohy Ukraïny: zhertvy politychnoho teroru*, 64–69.

65 *Pershyi Vseukraïns'skyi uchytel'skyi z'ïzd v Kharkovi vid 5 do 11 sichnia 1925 (zi znimkamy uchasnykiv z'ïzdu)*, (Kharkiv: Derzhavne vydavnytstvo Ukraïny, 1925), 1.

of matters of the people's education.' When the Red Army defeated the nationalist forces for control of Ukraine, the teachers failed to adjust. They had so fervently carried 'flags with the slogan of established [UNR] assemblies' that they could not immediately reject them.[66] From the perspective of the Robos leader then, teachers had been synonymous with the Ukrainian national movement.

To repeat, this characterization likely applied only to the most active, Ukrainophone teacher. Some proportion of teachers, especially in areas where UNR authority was weak or absent, ignored the passing of UNR power, lamented the monarchists' final demise, or sincerely applauded Bolshevism. However, nationally minded teachers such as Rusova viewed Soviet victory as problematic if not tragic. For them, Mizernytsky's principal charge – teachers believed the UNR offered 'harmony' between state and wider 'society' [*suspilstvo*] – was probably true. As opponents of the tsarist order, which they saw as deaf to the interests of all the Ukrainian people, they undoubtedly wanted such a harmony and, as participants in the Ukrainian national movement, the UNR obviously represented an opportunity to merge their beliefs with a state defined as Ukrainian. While Mizernytsky recognized the pre-October Revolution legitimacy of a 'single united front against the Russian bourgeoisie', in the context of the victory of Soviet power this front was no longer needed. Yet, teachers allegedly persisted in their beliefs: 'They did not realize that the tactics changed from this shift in conditions, especially the tactic of a single national front, and that the end of this harmony should have therefore come.'[67]

The term 'society' held multiple meanings for Soviet officials like Mizernytsky. In this context, it suggested an ethnic Ukrainian society that had to now forfeit the idea of a national state. But, as Stuart Finkel has argued, the Bolsheviks also understood society (*obshchestvo*, to use the Russian equivalent), to be an educated public that continued to maintain the illusion of independent action (and thus choice for broad, class harmony).[68] Like intellectuals in Russia at the end of the civil war, teachers in Ukraine could not persist in behaviour that suggested a denial of the premises of Soviet rule. As Mizernytsky claimed:

> They did not understand that the dictatorship of the proletariat represented the organized class of the proletariat, which held power, and that society was opposed to the state; that means they [teachers] opposed the proletariat, and took themselves for some indeterminate, small class group 'in between'.[69]

Society (*suspilstvo/obshchestvo*) remained in opposition if it thought itself above the dictates of political life in Soviet Ukraine.

66 Ibid., 2.
67 Ibid.
68 Stuart Finkel, *On the Ideological Front: The Russian Intelligentsia and the Making of the Soviet Public Sphere* (New Haven, CT: Yale University Press, 2007), 12.
69 *Pershyi Vseukraïns'skyi uchytel'skyi z'ïzd v Kharkovi vid 5 do 11 sichnia 1925 (zi znimkamy uchasnykiv z'ïzdu)*, 2.

Nevertheless, a fundamental belief for teachers in the pre-revolutionary Russian empire was that they occupied a place 'in between', not of the people but for the people, a profession that understood the people's needs and could advocate on their behalf. Sofiia Rusova was prominent expression of this idea. Although an insistence on this position was intolerable for the Bolsheviks, Mizernytsky's positing of this liminality also suggested an out. For Finkel, the Bolsheviks approach to society created the framework for a new relationship with the state; society would be 'purged of the disturbing heterogeneity that characterized the bourgeois public sphere and infused instead with the enforced harmony and unity that was a central element of the Soviet utopian project'.[70] This remained an aspiration rather than a reality and some institutional heterogeneity remained, but Finkel's use of the term 'harmony' suggests a recalibration of its meaning. In Soviet Ukraine, teachers could find their new place because 'the majority of teachers remained an inactive mass'. Although they might have desired a restoration of the UNR, because they did not directly act on this wish, their redemption was possible. In Mizernytsky's speech, time played a part. The UNR existed for a 'short time', teachers 'waited', bourgeois nationalist influences 'weakened', and hope 'disappeared'.[71] But teachers needed also actively to work in 'harmony' with the Soviet state, to teach in the school and engage in public work. Ultimately, of course, Soviet officials like Mizernytsky (and especially Robos) needed to open a window for this redemption if they desired the consolidation of a Soviet education system, but the teachers' congress was nevertheless a critical moment in the teachers' public adjustment.

Other speakers at the conference's opening session similarly underscored the teacher's past deeds, in an arguably more damning way, but still opening a path for a redemption. Emanuel Kviring, the secretary of the KP(b)U Central Committee emphasized the attraction of nationalism to teachers in 1917: 'the great majority of the intelligentsia marched with petty bourgeois slogans, not understanding that only the working class can solve the national concern'.[72] Fyodor Ugarov (Uhariv), the Russian-born head of the All-Ukrainian Council of Professional Trade Unions, while declaring a hesitancy to discuss past disagreements with teachers, nevertheless offered the greatest detail about their past failings. He claimed that teachers had, in the early years of Soviet power, 'asked us to build in Ukraine our professional organizations, [as] independent [*samostiini*] organizations, not uniting them with the Russian professional movement'. In the midst of the civil war, this was an impossibility – whatever the Ukrainian wishes were – unity and organizational centralization were critical; after definitive Soviet victory, some teachers reportedly continued to raise the question of a separate Ukrainian organization. Ugarov viewed the

70 Finkel, *On the Ideological Front*, 12.

71 *Pershyi Vseukraïns'skyi uchytel'skyi z'ïzd v Kharkovi vid 5 do 11 sichnia 1925 (zi znimkamy uchasnykiv z'ïzdu)*, 2.

72 Ibid., 4.

persistence of this sort of attitude with disdain, alluding to the danger of 'assaults by the enemy'.[73]

Ugarov dictated a path for a return that compelled teachers to recognize the danger of nationalism (structured as a sentiment of the past), but also accept an accommodation with Soviet power. In doing so teachers moved from confession to conversion and redemption:

> I remind you my comrades that we need to forget old sins [*hrikhy*] and to now concentrate all our wisdom, all our energy on taking this path together with the working class … [and] exit onto the threshold of socialism.[74]

This 'forgetting' still implied a moment of conscious disavowal that required a rejection of past political loyalties, particularly towards Ukrainian nationalism, but also allowed for pre-revolutionary notions of public service and instruction according to progressive methods embraced by Rusova and others to continue in altered forms.

Transformation was to be secured through civic engagement and participation in these sorts of highly public forums. Thus, although Ugarov's criticism of teachers was unambiguous, so was the importance he placed on the teacher's role:

> In the villages of Ukraine, we have comrades, around 200,000 members of our union [Robos], and this is a great force. And you, comrades, teachers in the village, are the most cultured people amongst this lack of consciousness, this ignorance that is there.[75]

Vlas Chubar, the head of the Ukrainian Council of People's Commissars, also acknowledged the teachers assumed a considerable burden in their efforts given the lack of 'consciousness' of peasants and workers alike.[76] One of the conference's principal objectives was to inspire and embolden these teachers. Oleksandr Shumsky, the Commissar of Education, explained further that teachers not only confronted ignorance, and lack of supplies, but also an unsympathetic population, confused by the teachers' sudden political transformation. Still, Shumsky insisted, the best teachers had embraced a 'new outlook' in good faith and needed to remain steadfast in their commitment; if they did so, they 'can become a conductor of the idea of communism in the village, amongst the workers and peasants'.[77] Indeed, they had no other choice if they sought to rescue their reputation and livelihoods. But teachers, at least those who imagined themselves to be public servants as well as educators, were engaged in the sort of struggle that had preoccupied them before the revolution, even if their tutelage was now directed to a singularly defined political goal.

73 Ibid., 9.
74 Ibid., 10.
75 Ibid., 9.
76 Ibid., 7.
77 Ibid., 11.

Salvation could not be secured without public work, but a reorientation of the school was necessary as well. Speakers at the conference tended to emphasize a methodological break from the old. Yet, here too there were linkages with the past. Shumsky argued that construction of a new educational system could not begin until 1924 in Ukraine, after the tumult of the civil war, when the 'remnants' of the pre-revolutionary school could finally be dismantled: 'And only after having finally won, having abandoned the basic, principal elements of the old school, old methods of the old system, we can proceed with the new construction'.[78] Chubar also conceded shortcomings in the Soviet government's educational initiatives, citing a lack of funds, but insisted the teachers' efforts in the school were critical to the consolidation of Soviet power. He underscored the principal means for the transformation of the school, use of progressive pedagogy, specifically the complex method, a system of instruction that eschewed disciplinary teaching in favour of interdisciplinary, thematic lessons and experiential learning.[79] Citing a recent visit to a rural school, Chubar relayed that teachers at this school complained: 'our complex method was a great obstacle to the carrying out of work in the field of education'.[80] Teachers did not understand the method's dictates and necessity. Chubar argued that recently established teachers' preparatory courses would prepare (and convince) teachers for their new roles in educational reform.[81]

Past challenges remained; schools had not transformed themselves overnight with the advent of Soviet power, but the impulse to change was not exclusively Bolshevik. The teachers' conference with its opening raising of the red flag, singing of the Internationale, and proceedings interrupted by frequent bursts of applause suggested a Bolshevik turn. Teachers were reportedly different, newly aligned with Soviet power, as Shumsky put it, they constituted a 'basic driving force, which shifts the school from its old foundations'.[82] Unlike the pre-revolutionary era, they were joined by new associations, the Young Communist League (the Komosmol) and the Young Pioneers, who aided 'in construction of the new school', but also ensured schools conformed to the ambitions of the socialist regime 'to ensure that there is no hostility between our organization of teachers and our proletarian school'.[83] Exemplary young teachers may also have been members of the Komsomol and leaders of the Young Pioneer detachments

78 Ibid., 10.

79 See: Pauly, *Breaking the Tongue*, 104–130.

80 *Pershyi Vseukraïns'skyi uchytel'skyi z'ïzd v Kharkovi vid 5 do 11 sichnia 1925 (zi znimkamy uchasnykiv z'ïzdu)*, 8.

81 Activist teachers, of course, had already been engaged in retraining since the early days of the UNR. Borovyk, *Ukraïnizatsiia zahal'noosvitnikh shkil za chasiv vyboriuvannia derzhavnosti, 1917–1920 rr.*, 126–171. On pre-revolutionary preparatory courses in Ukraine, see Natalia Andriichuk, *Pidhotovka vchyteliv narodnoï shkoly v uchytel'skykh seminariakh Ukraïny, 1860–1917 rr.* (Zhytomyr: Vyd-vo ZHDU im. I. Franka, 2010).

82 *Pershyi Vseukraïns'skyi uchytel'skyi z'ïzd v Kharkovi vid 5 do 11 sichnia 1925 (zi znimkamy uchasnykiv z'ïzdu)*, 11.

83 Ibid., 12.

for young children tied to a school, but here the conference's speakers suggested not just a supporting role, but a corrective function. And, as one teacher-delegate chosen to respond to these defining speeches confirmed, 'red teachers' needed such guidance if they were to fulfil the revolutionary aspirations of the new school: 'Help us join the ranks of the Communist party (applause), and we will give everything with our strength to forge an unshakeable, stone foundation on which to stand, situated in the path of all sudden attacks by the bourgeoisie.' How was this not a description for a fundamentally different mission? Rusova in a 1923 essay on Soviet education published in the emigré journal, *Nova shkola*, would seem to agree: 'The Bolsheviks have in their educational activities one goal, one task – to create children like themselves "Communists".'[84]

Continuities in spite of revolution

The shift was not as dramatic as presented. Rural teachers resisted change, as Chubar suggested, and could count little on Komsomol and Young Pioneer guidance in a countryside where the party presence was weak. Furthermore, the calls from the teachers' congress were not exclusively Bolshevik. A 1923 essay by Sofiia Rusova, *The United Active [Labour] School*, begun while she taught at the new Ukrainian State University in Kamianets-Podilsky (established by the besieged UNR government), but published while she was in exile in Prague suggested an overlap between her ideas – rooted in a pre-revolutionary intellectual current of progressive pedagogy – and Bolshevik ambitions. Whereas Soviet educators 'opposed instruction in religion, nationalism, and "bourgeois" morality' as a component of progressive education,[85] Rusova advocated precisely such lessons in her plans for a non-Soviet Ukraine. Yet, her designs shared an intellectual kinship with those embodied in the 1918 RSFSR 'Declaration of the United Labour School', as well as GKNO's proposals and Ignatiev's ideas before it.

Rusova believed her ideas would inform an imagined school network for a non-Soviet Ukraine. The premise of her published collection of lectures was that every state needs a school that is 'national' [*natsionalna*] because 'it unites in its walls children of all levels [*verstv*] of people, gives children the same education and calls all in the same manner to work for the benefit of the needed and valued state'.[86] At an obvious level the Bolsheviks would have objected to Rusova's use of the term of 'national' in this context, schools could not be classless or class-blind.[87] Nevertheless, in the mid-1920s, schooling was open to

84 Oksana Dzhus and Zinoviia Nahachevs'ka, eds, *Sofiia Rusova: z malovidomoho i nevidomoho*, 3 vols, vol. 1 (Ivano-Frankivs'k: Hostynets', 2006), 301.

85 Larry E. Holmes, *The Kremlin and the Schoolhouse: Reforming Education in Soviet Russia, 1917–1931* (Bloomington: Indiana University Press, 1991), 3.

86 *Pershyi Vseukraïns'skyi uchytel'skyi z'ïzd v Kharkovi vid 5 do 11 sichnia 1925 (zi znimkamy uchasnykiv z'ïzdu)*, 13.

87 However, the Soviets also attempted to create mono-ethnic schools, believing such an arrangement enabled native-language schooling and the efficient transfer of political instruction.

all children, even if the Soviet state expected education to work to the benefit of children of industrial labourers and the rural poor and to guard against corruption by the bourgeoisie. The Soviet state desired a school, in Rusova's words 'united from top to bottom', that taught the entire children's population of Soviet Ukraine skills it deemed necessary for service to the state.

Like the Soviets, Rusova desired an education that was compulsory and free of dues. She criticized a proposal for a Ukrainian united school passed by the UNR government-in-exile in Tarnów, Poland that failed to specify these two requirements.[88] As much as the Soviet state failed to fund schools adequately, relying on locally generated taxes, it did not require children to pay for tuition and its expectation was that all school-age children would complete primary schools, even if 'full' seven-year primary schools were few in number in the 1920s and complaints about low attendance were common. By Rusova's yardstick, Soviet Ukraine was working towards the very goals that UNR had failed to meet when it was control of Ukraine and the tsarist state had not previously accepted. Although the final achievement of near universal enrolment was revolutionary in the 1930s, the ambition was not. It reflected an enduring goal of educational reformers like Rusova who begin their advocacy under tsarist rule.

The methodology advocated by Rusova was also that embraced by the Soviet Ukrainian educational system. As Rusova insisted, 'the modern, united school must entirely correspond to the new scientific and everyday demands'. She continued that 'instead of the past, entirely passive school' the best path for the achievement of this goal was the creation 'a school of labour or to take the phrase of the best modern pedagogues, the active school'. This methodology was the inspiration for the Soviet Ukrainian educators' embrace of the complex system of the 1920s noted by Chubar at the 1925 Teachers' Congress, that is their rejection of a disciplinary model and emphasis on interactive, applied learning. Like the Ukrainian People's Commissariat of Education (Narkomos – *Narodnii komisariat osvity)*, Rusova advocated the observation of nature through excursions, participation in agricultural work, and the integration of this work into classroom modules. Her model was premised on an example a model from Weimar Germany, the Landerziehungsheime ('New Schools'), but it was a model that Soviets did not reject as foreign to their purposes once they assumed power.[89]

There were still fundamental differences between the approach Rusova proposed and that embraced by the Soviet Ukrainian educational system touted in the 1925 Teachers' Congress. To be sure, both Rusova and Soviet Ukrainian educational officials rejected 'vocationalism' at the primary school level. Rusova wrote, 'teachers need to never forget that the "work" [*pratsia*] is

88 S. F. Rusova, *Iedyna diial'na (trudova) shkola: vstupna lektsiia na katedru pedahohiky* (Leipzig: Ukraïns'ke vyd-vo v Katerynoslavi, 1923), 10.

89 For a recent treatment of literary depictions of this school, see: Richard von Faber, *Totale Institutionen?: Kadettenanstalten, Klosterschulen und Landerziehungsheime in Schöner Literatur* (Würzburg: Königshausen and Neumann, 2013).

not the final goal, but only a method for education and instruction, that best develops all the abilities of the children'.[90] The designers of the Soviet educational system, mindful of narrow apprenticeship training of the tsarist past, similarly rejected this notion and insisted on the students' acquisition of generalized knowledge at the primary level. However, while Rusova focused on the value of work to moral training, Soviet educators expected a wider understanding of kinds of labour and saw schools as preparing students for eventual labour-oriented employment. Two-year secondary 'professional' schools in Soviet Ukraine, as distinct from their Russian counterparts, were oriented towards specific sectors of the economy, even if Ukrainian administrators insisted on their non-vocational nature.[91] Rusova's preference for the term 'active school' is indicative of the separation between her approach and Narkomos, which specifically labelled primary schools in Soviet Ukraine 'labour schools'.

Furthermore, Rusova believed that student involvement in 'work' was more easily accomplished in the village as opposed to the city. This belief was motivated by Rusova's brand of Ukrainian nationalism, which held that Ukrainian national traits were expressed in peasant farming practices and 'our Ukrainian' decorative carpentry. Labour in this sense was a window into national consciousness: 'In this way, contemporary culture of the native country become for them [children] not something cut out of glass, in an unknown form, but something living, organic.'[92] The conviction, coupled with Rusova's emphasis on Ukrainian language instruction as a key component of the 'national school' spoke to a different kind of curricular content, even if the methodology was similar. Narkomos too embraced Ukrainian language instruction and in so doing undermined the claims of nationalist educators like Rusova, as well as offering a means for propagandizing the Soviet message to the Ukrainian-speaking majority of the republic's population. But the Soviet message was pointedly different. Narkomos educators did not valorize the peasant and saw the potential of petty bourgeois contagion in the village school. The Soviet complex method privileged an understanding of labour in the urban setting; Narkomos encouraged schools to place themselves under the patronage of factories and pushed linkages between superior urban schools and their less fortunate rural counterparts.

But in the end, both Rusova and Soviet educators believed that schooling promoted a collective, public good and claimed a role for teachers in public service, even if they imagined teachers to reinforce the aims of dissimilar states. Schooling in the UNR and Soviet Ukraine aimed to produce self-reliant, civically minded pupils who would contribute to the collective good through instruction that was attuned to children's individual psychology. In a

90 Rusova, *Iedyna diial'na (trudova) shkola: vstupna lektsiia na katedru pedahohiky*, 24.
91 See: Pauly, *Breaking the Tongue*, 47–48.
92 Rusova, *Iedyna diial'na (trudova) shkola: vstupna lektsiia na katedru pedahohiky*, 28, 30.

description that reads as if it were lifted from the 1925 Teachers' Congress or a Narkomos circular, Rusova insisted that children needed to assume responsibility for their own curriculum:

> This all [activity designed by children at the teacher's lead] gives school that democratic-social direction, that can lead the most to an education of true citizens. In the active school, an active, collective life forms naturally: every common work leads to collective discipline for its organization.

Like Soviet pupils who raised funds for the building of airplanes, pupils in UNR schools donated their money and time with the help of teachers to hospitals and orphanages in the civil war and 'this lent the work a social, humanitarian significance, offering the pupils a path for their physical efforts'.[93] Rusova concludes, that a united school 'will give Ukraine its active-civic education needed for its new life of new citizens with awakened activeness, enduring will, and well-developed cultural strengths'.[94]

The Soviet school aspired to do the same, although the Ukraine that its teachers served was different. Teaching in the Soviet, Ukrainized national school meant embracing the task of lifting up the 'poorest peasantry' as a whole and connecting their future and that of the village in general to the city. However, its final objective was the realization of a unified Soviet polity that integrated Ukrainian-speaking rural inhabitants into urban centres and tied them to the common task of 'building socialism'. In this context, the multiple 1917s in Ukraine could be reconciled.

Conclusion

Sofiia Rusova published another book while in exile in 1924, *The New School of Social Upbringing*. In it she argued:

> The previous, oppressive, formal, hypocritical school must perish, and on its ruins must be affirmed, born a new school of labour, a school of social upbringing, built on respect towards the individual and an understanding of its public obligations to every child, to every pupil of the new school.[95]

Rusova remained anti-Bolshevik for the remainder of her life, but her statement on its own would not have found great objection in Soviet Ukraine. For Rusova and the Bolsheviks, the overthrow of the pre-revolutionary old and the creation of a 'socially useful' new were key. The revolutions of 1917 suggested multiple ways this could be done and the rivals generally detested each

93 Ibid., 29.
94 Ibid., 31.
95 Sofiia Rusova, *Nova shkola sotsiial'noho vykhovannia* (Leipzig: Ukraïns'ke vyd-vo v Katerynoslavi, 1924), 5.

other's preferred solutions. But in the aftermath of the civil war, the Soviet authorities reworked their perspective on the position of teachers, whom they had previously contended had led the nationalist opposition against them. As Havryliv put it, activist teachers were 'an army, which can realize a cultural October in the village!'[96] The vehicle of the Ukrainian 'school of labour' provided an opportunity for a merger of the nationalist and Bolshevik 1917s, however much it was done on Bolshevik terms. The newly redefined October was a reflection of elements of both.

96 Havryliv, *Zhovtneva revoliutsiia i vchytel'stvo*, 42.

6 'The woman of the Orient is not the voiceless slave anymore'

The non-Russian women of Volga-Ural region and 'women's question'

Yulia Gradskova

This chapter assesses the pursuit of women's emancipation by focusing on the evolution of different projects designed to improve the situation of non-Russian women, both before and after the Bolshevik revolution of 1917. The subordinated economic, social, and juridical situation of women – usually addressed as the 'women's question' – was widely discussed in Russia at the beginning of the twentieth century, when women's organizations of different political persuasions were created throughout the country.[1] New ideas became widespread and an important topic for social and political discussions and activism, not only in the imperial centre, but also among the non-Russian subjects of the Empire. Recent research on national projects of education for women in the Volga-Ural region, in particular in Tatarstan, suggests that intellectual elites believed that providing women with more rights and improving their education and social status was an important step towards modernity and, furthermore, a means to throw off the yoke of Russification and authoritarianism.[2] But, after the Bolsheviks took power in 1917 they decried previous solutions to the 'women's question' and hailed their own programme of female emancipation. This programme stated that both the liberation of 'enslaved' women and the peoples of previously 'enslaved nations' was an important precondition for building the Communist society.

In their campaign for the emancipation of women – in particular, non-Russian women were often addressed as 'women of the Orient' or 'women of

1 Richard Stites, *The Women's Liberation Movement in Russia. Feminism, Nihilism and Bolshevism, 1860–1930* (Princeton, NJ: Princeton University Press, 1978); Irina Iukina, *Russkii feminism kak vyzov sovremennosti* (Sankt Petersburg: Aleteia, 2007); Barbara A. Engel, *Women in Russia, 1700–2000* (Cambridge: Cambridge University Press, 2004).

2 Engel, *Women in Russia*; Alta Makhmutova, '*Pora i nam zazhech zariu svobody*', *Jadidism i zhenskoe dvizhenie* (Kazan: Tatarskoe knizhnoe izdatelstvo, 2006); Dmitrii Iskhakov, 'Jadidism', in *Islam i musulmanskaia kultura v Srednem Povolzhie: istoriia i sovremennost* (Kazan: Masterlain, 2002); Azade-Ayse Rorlich, 'The Challenge of Belonging: The Muslims of Late Imperial Russia and the Contested Terrain of Identity and Gender', in *Democracy and Pluralism in Muslim Eurasia*, edited by Yaacov Ro'I (London and New York: Frank Cass, 2004), 39–52.

national minorities' (*natsionalki*)[3] – the Bolsheviks presented their project of 'bringing culture' and granting rights to previously 'enslaved' women as historically unique, based on the principles of equality and progression. However, the Bolsheviks were unwilling to acknowledge that the results of their campaigns designed at solving the 'women's question' were often contradictory and complicated. Indeed, these policies had dramatic consequences for minority groups, including those living in the Volga-Ural region.[4] Existing scholarship evaluates decolonization, Sovietization, and recolonization[5] in varying ways: Baberowski stresses that the Soviet policy of 'bringing culture' to non-Russian people was mainly a continuation of the civilizing mission undertaken by Russian imperial politicians;[6] whilst Martin draws attention to the modernising and affirmative policies developed during the early Soviet period.[7] And yet, the gender aspect of these policies remains understudied.

This chapter will investigate Soviet solutions to the 'women's question' for women of the 'national minorities' during the 1920s and early 1930s. It does so by exploring the similarities and differences to pre-revolutionary ideas and projects pursued by different actors. Special focus will be given to the period between the liberal-democratic revolution in February of 1917 and the Bolshevik revolution of October: a period when all the local ideas on women's roles in the society could be publicly discussed and, in part, were transformed into laws and programmes. This necessarily raises some significant questions: What were the similarities and differences of the Bolshevik views on improvement of the situation of non-Russian women with earlier projects of civilizing the 'Orient'? How much did organizational structures and forms of work proposed by the Soviet emancipators differ from those that were elaborated by the local communities and women-activists? And which aspects of the Bolshevik policies for emancipation of women provoked most resistance and why?

3 Yulia Gradskova, 'Kuli semii kuli: "zhenshchiny ugnetennykh narodov" i sovetskie kulturnye politiki' in *Tam vnutri. Praktiki vnutrennei kolonizatsii v kulturnoi istorii Rossii,* edited by A. Etkind, D. Uffelman, and I. Kukulin (Moscow: NLO, 2012), 664–683.

4 See Madina Tlostanova, *Gender Epistemologies and Eurasian Borderlands* (Basingstoke: Palgrave Macmillan, 2010); Helen Faller, *Nation, Language, Islam: Tatarstan's Sovereignty Movement* (Budapest: CEU-Press, 2011); Seppo Lallukka, *From Fugitive Peasants to Diaspora: Eastern Mari in Tsarist and Soviet Russia* (Helsinki: Academia Scientiarum Fennica, 2003).

5 See, for example, Jörg Baberowski, 'Stalinismus als imperiales Phänomen: Die islamischen Regionen der Sowjetunion, 1920–1941', in *Stalinismus: neue Forschung und Konzepte*, edited by Stefan Plaggenborg (Berlin: Berlin Verlag A. Spitz, 1998), 113–151; Terry Martin, *The Affirmative Action Empire, Nations and Nationalism in the Soviet Union, 1923–1939* (Ithaca, NY: Cornell University Press, 2001); Francine Hirsch, *Empire of Nations, Ethnographic Knowledge and the Making of the Soviet Union* (Ithaca, NY: Cornell University Press, 2005).

6 See Baberowski, 'Stalinismus als imperiales Phänomen'.

7 See Martin, *The Affirmative Action Empire*; Yuri Slezkine, *Arctic Mirrors: Russia and the Small Peoples of the North* (Ithaca, NY: Cornell University Press, 1994).

The present analysis is based on archival documents preserved in the State Archive of the Russian Federation, particularly all documents of the Commission for the Improvement of Work and Everyday Life of Women,[8] and in the National Archives of the Republic of Tatarstan. Furthermore, this chapter incorporates pre-Soviet documents and materials of periodical publications on culture and education among non-Russian people of the Volga-Ural region, including published documents of the Soviet secret police (OGPU).[9] To reach a specific and detailed analysis, the present study limits its ethno-geographical scope to documents concerning emancipation and *culturalization*[10] policies with respect to only three nationalities living in the multi-ethnic Volga-Ural region: Tatars, Bashkirs, and Mari. All these people are native inhabitants of the region, but differ in their religion, language and relationships with the Russian imperial centre. The documents consulted herein were originally written in Russian or translated into Russian.[11]

The chapter offers a short description of the Volga-Ural region before examining the changing views on women's role in the society that existed in these regions before the Bolshevik revolution. The second part of this chapter then extends its analysis to Soviet ideas, practices, and the institutions created to bring culture and emancipation to non-Russian women of the region.

Volga-Ural region and the 'women's question'

Following the victory of the Russian Army over the Kazan Khanate (1552), the Turkic and Finno-Ugric language groups populating the territories between the Volga and Urals were subjected to Russian colonisation. Prior to the early twentieth century, this area had been an important agricultural region of the Russian Empire with several industrial and merchant cities, the most important of which were Kazan, Samara, Nizhnii Novgorod, Ufa, and Orenburg. The region had an ethnically-mixed population, although most of the non-Slavic and non-Christian-Orthodox people at the beginning of the twentieth century lived in the countryside. Historically, attempts at Russification and

8 Commission for the Improvement of Work and Everyday Life of Women – GARF, fond 6983, 1926–1931.

9 '*Soveshenno sekretno*' *Lubianka Stalinu o polozhenii v strane* (2001–2008), Moskva, v. 1–8; *Islam i Sovetskoe gosudartstvo (1917–1936), Sbornik dokumentov,* sost. D. Yu.Arapov, red. V. O. Bobrovnikov (Moscow: Iazdatelskii dom Marzhani, 2010).

10 *Culturalization* [kulturnost] was used for defining a set of skills, knowledge, and values including those of literacy and hygiene, but also knowledge of Soviet ideology.

11 I am aware of the limitation of this approach – the Russian language publications could 'soften' conflict-provoking view points while describing Russian policies in the region differently from the documents written in the Tatar, Bashkir, or Mari languages. According to Faller, for example, only speakers of the Tatar language constitute the community that corresponds to the discourses of the Tatar nation – Faller, *Nation, Language, Islam.*

Christianization of the local population were combined with the continued recognition of the groups' differences, placing non-Slavic peoples into the category of '*inorodtsy*'[12] to indicate their otherness.[13]

The Muslim population of the region – namely the Tatars and Bashkirs – enjoyed certain autonomy with respect to the juridical and education systems.[14] The Russian imperial centre, some have argued, perceived the Muslims of central Russia as more integrated than their Jewish contemporaries.[15] Nonetheless, the perception of Islam as a danger to the Russian state and for Christian religion remained strong and persistent, and was usually connected to fears of pan-Turkism and pan-Islamism in the context of confrontation with the Ottoman Empire.[16] From the beginning of the twentieth century, the Russian imperial administration was particularly suspicious of the Muslim renovation movement, *Jadidism,* which became popular among Crimean Tatars and Muslims of Central Russia, which advocated the modernization of the education system through changes to the curriculum and gender-mixed education.[17] As a result of the radicalized context around the first Russian revolution (1905–1906), Muslim schools that taught according to jadidist programmes experienced much pressure; some of them, including jadidist schools for girls, were

12 Although not 'inorodtsy' in a strict sense (like the people of Central Asia who were governed through special institution on 'inorodtsy'), the non-Christian population of the region was seen as culturally different and suspicious and, according to Cadiot; were included in the category of 'inorodtsy' in its broad everyday meaning – Juliette Kadio (Cadiot), *Laboratoriia imperii, Rossiia/SSSR, 1960–1940* (Moscow: NLO, 2010).

13 While some researchers analysing the complexity of imperial politics towards non-Russian and non-Christian subjects of the empire focus more on the attempts of Russification of the inhabitants of the region, see, e.g. Robert Geraci, *Window to the East. National and Imperial Identities in the Late Imperial Russia* (Ithaca, NY: Cornell University Press, 2001), others explore more imperial strategies of population management that use assimilation strategies very selectively. See, e.g. Robert Crews on situation of Muslims in the Russian empire – Crews, *For Prophet and the Tsar: Islam and Empire in Russia and Central Asia* (Cambridge, MA: Harvard University Press, 2009); Vladimir Bobrovnikov, 'Chto vyshlo iz proektov sozdaniia v Rossii inorodtsev', in *Poniatiia o Rossii: K istoricheskoi semantike imperskogo perioda* vol. 2, edited by Alexei Miller, Denis Sdvizhkov and Ingrid Schierle (Moscow: NLO, 2012), 259–291.

14 Jane Burbank, 'An Imperial Rights Regime: Law and Citizenship in the Russian Empire', *Kritika: Explorations in Russian and Eurasian History* 7(3) (2006), 397–431.

15 Vladimir Levin, presentation on the Conference *Jews and Muslims in the Russian Empire and in the Soviet Union*, Munich, July 2013

16 Michael Reynolds, *Shattering Empires. The Clash and Collapse of the Ottoman and Russian Empires, 1908–1918*. (Cambridge: Cambridge University Press, 2012); Crews, *For Prophet and the Tsar*; Geraci, *Window to the East.*

17 Iskhakov, 'Jadism'; Hilary Pilkington and Galina Emelianova (eds), *Islam in Post-Soviet Russia. Public and Private Faces* (London and New York: Routledge Curzon, 2003); Vladimir Gankevich and S. P. Shendrikova, *Ismail Gasprinskii i vozniknoveniie liberalno-musulmanskogo politicheskogo dvizheniia* (Simferopol, 2008).

closed down by the Russian government. This, in turn, provoked anti-government and anti-Russian sentiment among the Muslim population.[18]

Population groups that preserved partly local, non-Christian religions – like Mari, Udmurts, or Chuvash – were seen as subjects for policies of Russification and assimilation. A notable example is the work of the Russian missionary, Nikolai Ilminski, who developed a system of Russian schools for *inorodsty* children.[19] However, in contrast to the Muslim population of the region, the 'animists'[20] were not looked upon as a threat to imperial security. In particular, Mari peoples' beliefs in nature did not have the status of a religion, but were mainly considered to be kind of 'backward tradition'.[21]

Scholarship demonstrates that the emancipation of women was an important part of the intellectual and public discussion about progress and development of the Tatar nation and the Muslim people of Russia in general.[22] Jadidists, mainly Tatar intellectuals who supported the Europeanization of Muslim education, often saw women as 'mothers of the nation'.[23] According to them, educating women would contribute to the modernization of the local economy and everyday life and thus secure more possibilities for the administrative and cultural autonomy of Muslim people and thus further the development of the Tatar language and culture.[24] The 'women's question' was pursued through several fora. The Muslim party in the first Duma had already raised the issue of a need for equality of men and women in 1906.[25] Several women's magazines for Muslim women were published in the territory of the Russian Empire; one of them was *Siyumbike*, published in Kazan from 1913. Furthermore, girls were accepted into jadidist schools, and special schools preparing female teachers were opened in different cities and villages where Tatar and Bashkir

18 Marsil Farkhshatov, *Samoderzhavie I traditsionnye shkoly Bashkir I tatar v nachale XX veka (1900–1917)* (Ufa: Gilem, 2000); Alta Makhmutova, 'Lish tebe, narod, sluzhenie!' *Istoriia tatarskogo prosveshcheniia v sudbakh dinastii Nigmatullinykh-Bubi* (Kazan: Magarif, 2003).
19 Lallukka, *From Fugitive Peasants to Diaspora*, 146–149.
20 Mari-people worshiped nature, their religion was not centred around one God.
21 Lallukka, *From Fugitive Peasants to Diaspora*, 140–141.
22 Alta Makhmutova, 'Lish tebe, narod, sluzhenie!'; Tamina Biktimirova, *Stupeni obrazovaniia do Sorbonny* (Kazan: Alma, -Lit, 2003); Rafilia Gimazova, *Prosvetitelskaia deiatelnost Nigmatullinykh-Bubi (konets 19- nachalo 20 veka)* (Kazan, 2004); Rorlich, 'The Challenge of Belonging'.
23 Bashkir intellectuals were using the term as well – Rabiga Kushaeva, a village teacher, spoke on the need for equality of women at the Bashkir congress in Orenburg in July 1917 because women were 'mothers of the nation' (Milletebez aselare) – R. N. Suleimanova, 'R. Ya. Kushaeva, Neutomimyi borets za ravnopravie bashkirskikh zhenshchin', *Bashkortostan v XX stoletii, istoricheskie portrety* Ufa: (Gilem, 2006), 26–41, p. 29.
24 Rorlich, 'The Challenge of Belonging'.
25 Diliara Usmanova, *Musulmanskie deputaty gosudarstvennoi Dumy. Sbornik dokumentov i materialov* (Kazan: Kitap, 1998).

populations lived.[26] Also, Muslim women, like their ethnic Russian counterparts,[27] became increasingly involved in public discussions about education, culture, and the future of the nation.[28]

The seizure of power by the Provisional government in February 1917 presented new opportunities. In April 1917, female activists from different parts of the former empire gathered in Kazan for the first All-Russian Muslim Women Congress. The Congress accepted the resolution supporting the enfranchisement of women, the right to divorce, and stated the need for creation of Muslim women's offices through the country.[29]

In other parts of the Volga-Ural region, and among representatives of other ethnic groups, the voices for women's emancipation were less radical, but demands for better education for girls and women were common. For example, the First Congress of Mari People took place in Birsk in July 1917, although among 178 delegates there were only 13 women. Notwithstanding, the Congress made a resolution on opening new schools for the preparation of teachers, both male and female,[30] and stated that kindergartens and children's open air playgrounds (for care and education – *ploshchadki*) should be provided 'everywhere where possible'.[31] The delegates also discussed educational activities for adults including 'evening classes, readings, lectures conversations, and village libraries (*izby-chitalni*).[32]

Bolshevik 'anti-colonialism', civilizing mission and 'the backward women of the orient' – problems and contradictions in the work of the VTsIK Commission

According to Communist theory, the dictatorship of the proletariat will end different kinds of inequalities and forms of oppression, including inequality between different ethnic groups and gender inequality. However, while declarations on equality of all the citizens of the new Soviet state followed the Bolshevik's seizure of power, the Bolshevik leaders were quite aware of the

26 Makhmutova, '*Pora i nam zazhech zariu svobody*'; Gimazova, *Prosvetitelskaia deiatelnost Nigmatullinykh-Bubi.*

27 The first All-Russian Women's Congress (1908) discussed ideas of franchise, work, education, prostitution, mothers' welfare, and abortion.

28 For more about national questions in the late Russian Empire see Theodore Weeks, *Nation and State in the Late Imperial Russia: Nationalism and Russification on the Western Frontier, 1863–1914* (DeKalb, IL: Northern Illinois University Press, 1996).

29 Makhmutova, '*Pora i nam zazhech zariu svobody*'; Sagit Faizov, *Dvizhenie musulmanok Rossii za prava zhenshchin v 1917 godu: stranitsy istorii* (Nizhnii Novgorod: Makhinur, 2005); Sengul Hablemitoglu and Necip Hablemitoglu, *Sefika Gaspirali ve Rusya'da Turk Kadin Hareketi (1893–1920)* (Ankara, 1998).

30 *Pervyi vserossiskii siezd Mari, Birsk, 15–25 iunia 1917*, Ksenofont Sanukov red. (Ioshkar-Ola: muzei im V.Kolumba, 2006), 43 and 48.

31 *Pervyi*, 41.

32 *Pervyi*, 6.

long road to real equality. The legacy of past regimes was considered to be the most important obstacle on the way to the new society. Therefore, formerly dominated people *(ugnetennye narody*) and dominated women (*ugnetennye zhenschiny*) had to learn about their new rights and start working in the new socialist economy. In order to do so, they had to become literate, learn Communist theory, acquire modern habits and working skills, and stop sharing 'backward' local beliefs and traditions.[33]

The Bolsheviks declared several important national organisations and publications (including *Siyumbike)* to be counter-revolutionary and nationalist and closed them down in the first post-revolutionary year. Furthermore, many activists emigrated under pressure, including several female Muslim activists like Shafika Gaspirali from Crimea, a participant of one of the women's offices created after the All-Russian Muslim Congress in Kazan in 1917.[34] Indeed, most of the pre-revolutionary women's organizations in the region, as with the central Russian women's organizations,[35] were closed down for distributing ideas of bourgeois feminism.

The Bolshevik mass campaign for the development of a new culture and 'new everyday life' *(byt)* in the former periphery and among former '*inorodtsy*-women', already declared in 1917, took its shape several years later in the mid-1920s. At that time, several autonomous Soviet republics and districts – including Bashkir Autonomous Republic (1919), Tatar Autonomous Republic (1920), Mari Autonomous District (1920) – had been created in the territory of the Volga-Ural region.[36] While the Bolshevik party's departments for work among women (*Zhenotdel*s) started working in 1919,[37] the massive campaign for emancipation of non-Russian women in the Volga-Ural region began only in the late 1920s and after VTsIK created the special Commission for the Improvement of Work and Everyday Life of Women in 1926.

The documents of the Commission show that, in spite of its generalised title, it was created specifically for accelerating the emancipation and culturalization of non-Russian (former *inorodtsy*) women and increasing their

33 See, for example, Catriona Kelly, *Refining Russia. Advice Literature, Polite Culture and Gender from Catherine to Eltsin* (Oxford: Oxford University Press, 2001), 230–311.

34 Safika Gaspirali (1886–1974), the daughter of a famous Crimean jaded Ismail-Bey Gaspirali, emigrated to Turkey in 1922. More about her – Hablemitoglu and Hablemitoglu, *Sefika Gaspirali ve Rusya'da Turk Kadin Hareketi.*

35 See Iukina, *Russkii feminism kak vyzov sovremennosti*,

36 According to Bobrovnikov, the creation of autonomies in those regions where former inorodtsy people were living, also followed some of the pre-1917 perception of the importance of not destroying 'natives'' way of life too fast – see Bobrovnikov, 'Chto vyshlo iz proektov sozdaniia v Rossii inorodtsev'. However, as quoted documents show, the establishment of autonomous republics and districts in Volga-Ural region were to a large extent the result of the struggle for independence, where women were taking important part.

37 On Zhenotdel see more Engel, *Women in Russia.*

involvement in the construction of socialism.[38] The draft of the new redaction of the aims of the Commission discussed in 1927–1928 proposed to name this organization the 'Commission for the Improvement of Work and Everyday Life of Women of the Culturally Backward People' [*Kommissiia po uluchsheniiu truda i byta zhenschin kulturno-otstalykh narodnostei*].[39] Although this title disappeared from use, the working documents of the Commission, including circular letters and reports from the regions, frequently addressed it as 'Commission for the Improvement of Work and Everyday Life of Women of the Orient' (*zhenschin Vostoka* or just *vostochnits*).[40] The Commission had a broad remit and focussed on issues of education, everyday cooperation (*bytovaia kooperatsiia)*, and health care and did not limit itself to political work, as was in the case with *Zhenotdel.*[41] It consisted of the representatives of most of the Soviet ministries and of *Zhenotdel* and had to be financed through these institutions. In order to organize work locally, the Bolsheviks created similar commissions consisting of the representatives of the local executive power institutions and local *Zhenotdel*s. Indeed, archival documents demonstrate that approximately 1927 such commissions were created in most of the 'national autonomies', including those in the Tatar, Bashkir, and Mari autonomous territories.

As the title of the Commission and its broad purview demonstrate, it preserved a lot of the civilizing rhetoric and goals that constituted the politics of culturalization of non-Russian women in the region under Russian imperial rule. While refusing the politics of Christianization and Russification, the Bolshevik centre maintained the notion of non-Russian people as backward and in need of assistance from the Russian centre to aid their development.[42] 'The women of the Orient' were presented as having difficulties in understanding their new rights and opportunities owing to their 'extreme backwardness'; it was necessary to educate them in the use of resources and their rights. The rhetoric of the 'hard situation' of local women[43] typical of pamphlets and films of the time,[44] could be found in most of the Commission's documents;

38 GARF, 6983, 1, delo 1, list 1–2.

39 For more on the Commission see Yulia Gradskova, 'Svoboda kak prinuzhdenie? Sovetskoe nastuplenie na "raskreposhchenie zhenshchiny" i "nasledie imperii"', *Ab Imperio* 4, 2013b.

40 GARF, 6983, 1, delo 17, list 10.

41 The Communist Party Department for work among women (*Zhenordel*) was created in the 1920 for organizing communist work among women. More on *Zhenotdel* see Engel, *Women in Russia.*

42 For more about it see Gradskova, 'Kuli semii kuli'.

43 Non-Russian women were usually presented as suffering from forced marriages, lack of rights in their families, hard work, and illiteracy.

44 See Yulia Gradskova, 'Speaking for Those "Backward": Gender and Ethnic Minorities in Soviet Silent Films', *Region: Regional Studies of Russia, Eastern Europe, and Central Asia* 2(2) (2013), 201–220; Antonina Nukhrat, *Bytovaia potrebitelskaia kooperatsiia v natsionalnykh raionakh* (Moscow: Tsentrizdat, 1930).

women were portrayed as having a tougher life than men. One such example presented the life of Mari women as 'absolutely unhappy' (*bezotradnaia*).[45]

At the same time, archival documents demonstrate that the Commission was very limited in its financial and organizational possibilities. Firstly, the documents state a lack of interest to work with women among those who were supposed to be part of the Commissions. For example, the Secretary of the Commission in Bashkortostan, Marina Maksimova, wrote in her personal letter to one of the functionaries of the central Commission, Liubimova,[46] that the Head of the Commission, Muchametkulov, 'starts to be bothered by his work there, the commission requires too much attention while one campaign is followed by another one.'[47] One of the first secretaries of the Commission in Tatarstan, member of Komsomol, Faizullina, in her letter to one of the members of the Central Commission, Comrade Akivis, expressed similar feelings: 'Here in our Commission everything is developing slowly. Yes, slowly, because the members of the Commission do not hurry to perform their duties.'[48]

Archival documents demonstrate that the members of the Commission in the region had difficulties in explaining new ideas to the local population, often due to a lack of literature published in the local languages. Indeed, after several years of the Commission's work in Bashkortostan, the report from 1930 stated that 'publication of books on Bashkir language does not go over the pure talk about it. The literature on work among women and women's movement on Bashkir language at the local offices is totally absent.'[49] However, communication with the local population was also hindered by the lack of clarity with respect to the complicated system of the division of labour in the new Soviet bureaucratic structures like the Commission. It was equally hindered by the lack of trust of the work of the Commission from other party and state structures. The Commission, alongside the clubs, houses of working women and other ventures created by this body, were under the strict control of the Bolshevik party, and the *Zhenotdel* acted as a means of executive oversight. For example, Faizullina complained that, 'for a long time I could not understand well the work and functions of the Commission. Indeed, I could not understand where *Zhenotdel* ends and where the work of the Commission starts.' Faizullina also highlighted the difficulty of separating party work from broader work with the population:

> Comrade Akivis, if you would find time, please, write to me, in which form the Commission should work with women-activists (*obshchestvennitsy*).

45 Otchet about the work of the commission of the Mari District, protocol from 26 April 1928, GARF, 6983, 1, p. 171.
46 Unfortunately, the archive file does not contain information about Liubimova, we can assume only that she was one of the secretaries of the Commission. In most of the documents she and other officers of the Commission usually are addressed only as 'Comrade' or 'Komsomol member'.
47 GARF, 6983, 1, delo 44, list 8–9 (letter by Maksimova from 9.04.1928).
48 GARF, 6983, 1, delo 3, list 6, (letter by Faizullina).
49 GARF, 6983, 1, delo 207, list 107.

> I think myself that it is the Commission that should lead this work, but our *Zhenotdel* wrote that I am wrong and this work corresponds only to the executive power.[50]

Maksimova, from the Commission in Bashkortostan, expressed similar concerns: 'We all are taught here to get approval for everything from *Zhenotdel*.'[51]

Amongst the archival documents, many detailed applications for financial support and reports on expenditure highlight that the Commission usually lacked sufficient finances for its activities. For example, a report dated 14 November 1929 concerning the use of money sent by the Commission from the Mari district stated that, of the 600 Rubles given by the Ministry of Agriculture (*Narkomsem*), 150 Rubles were spent in organizing courses on producing butter for Tatar women in a village, Paranga. The remaining 450 Rubles were spent on three-month long courses on milk production and two-week long courses on butter production. The document highlights that the financial report was delayed due to the long procedure of filling all the student places.[52] The archives reveal further examples. A letter to Tatarstan's Commission for the Improvement of Work and Everyday Life of women from 1928, signed by the canton's health officer, Paklin, stated that 80 per cent of the people being served by the maternity ward were of an ethnic minority and that the ward needed money for reparation and medical equipment. The applicant stressed that the creation of the delivery department in the district's hospital became possible thanks to a 'significant amount of money' already given by the local population.[53]

The pleas to the centre for support is an evident theme in the sources. The aforementioned Faizullina from Tatarstan's Commission, argued for funding from the centre: Faizullina contended that it would be very important to obtain funding to train nursery teachers for an upcoming campaign for summer nurseries. The personalised plea in this letter – 'Comrade Akivis, please, help us to get extra-money for the summer nursery, we sent already our application'[54] – suggests that privately lobbying a significant powerbroker was believed to be a promising way of securing funding for women's projects. Indeed, the Commission could receive many similar applications and the needs of a particular national territory could easily be ignored in the new centralized Soviet economy.

In facing financial restraints, the language of the 'deepest backwardness' (*krainiaa otstalost*) could also be useful in securing monetary support for particular projects. For example, one request from Bashkortostan to the central Commission stated that,

> The money we ask for – 44,564 Rubles – is for the activities that we describe in our application. It is the minimal sum that could satisfy at least the most

50 GARF, 6983, 1, delo 3, list 6.
51 GARF, 6983, 1, delo 44, list 8–9.
52 GARF, 6983, 1, delo 31, list 8.
53 NART, C67.
54 GARF, 6983, 1, delo 3, list 6.

> minimal needs of Bashkir women. That is why we ask you to take into account the backwardness of Bashkir women and fully satisfy our application.[55]

The frequent repetition of the tropes of 'subordination' and 'backwardness' highlights that this was perceived by applicants as an effective method of securing financial support.

The Soviet campaign of emancipation and culturalization of 'the women of the Orient', in spite of its apparently anti-colonial and emancipatory rhetoric, shared many similarities with the attempts of enlightenment of *inorodtsy* made by the Russian imperial state. The Soviet government perceived the local population to be backward and relied on the control and centralized distribution of money to achieve its aims, but it also faced problems communicating with the local populations. The documents demonstrate that the emancipation of women lagged far behind industrialization and collectivization of agriculture among the government's priorities. Thus, the Soviet policies of emancipation of 'women of the Orient' at the central and local level suffered from a lack of finances and bureaucratism.

Creating new opportunities for women – Soviet versus national interpretations

This section focuses on continuities and changes in the socio-political and cultural spheres where the status of women was, from the beginning of the twentieth century, at the centre of heated discussions: namely religion, popular enlightenment, work and cooperatives.

The religious sphere provided fertile ground for a discussion around the status of women. Women's magazines published in Baku, Bakhchisaray, and Kazan at the beginning of the twentieth century, as well as the jadidist magazines *Shura* and *Vaqt*, well known among Muslims in Russia, used different and sometimes conflicting arguments to defend ideas surrounding women's contribution to society that went 'beyond the confines of the private space, hearth, home and family'.[56] At the same time, as Asade Rorlich demonstrated, the social role of women was advocated through their special function as mothers and educators of the new generation, and thus responsible for the future of the nation; they were the mothers of the nation. The jadids insisted that ideas of women's education simultaneously did not contradict Sharia law, but also fully corresponded to the will of the Prophet.[57] Furthermore, the documents of the Muslim Women's Congress in Kazan and of the women's offices show that, while not questioning the legitimacy of the Islamic laws, some parts of society required very radical changes in the everyday life of Muslim communities, including the right of women to teach religion.[58]

55 GARF, 6983, 1, delo 120, list 13–14.

56 Rorlich, 'The Challenge of Belonging', 160–161.

57 Gankevich and Shendrikova, *Ismail Gasprinskii i vozniknoveniie liberalno-musulmanskogo politicheskogo dvizheniia*.

58 Hablemitoglu and Hablemitoglu, *Sefika Gaspirali ve Rusya'da Turk Kadin Hareketi*; Faizov. On the Central Asian context see Douglas Northrop, *The Veiled*

In contrast to the Orthodox Church, which the Bolsheviks viewed as part of the state machinery to exploit the people, minority religions could not be criticized so easily, at least, in the immediate aftermath of taking power. Indeed, freedom of language and religion was an important slogan of the liberal revolution in February 1917 and could not be ignored during the early post-revolutionary years. As for Islam, as shown by previous research, the Bolsheviks were particularly careful with its followers during the years immediately following the revolution, whilst hoping for a wider revolt of Muslim people in the British and French colonies in Asia.[59] Indeed, in 1926 the Soviet delegation, led by the head of the Muslim Spiritual Department, Rizaetdin Fakhreddin, took part in the World Muslim Congress in Mecca, where it was sent in order to present the Soviet Union as a country of progress and an example for other Muslim and colonized countries.[60] Thus, even if after October 1917 all religions found themselves to be under attack by the proletarian state, some of the pre-1917 discussions on religious aspects of life, and the role of Muslim women in the social transformation to a certain extent, continued for at least the first ten post-revolutionary years, when the Soviet government attempted to guarantee the loyalty of the Muslim population to the new regime.[61]

One of the important changes in the religious life of the Muslims of Central Russia that happened after the liberal revolution of February 1917, and continued to be important during the first ten post-revolutionary years, was the reorganization of the Muslim Spiritual Department in Ufa. This institution was established in the Volga region by the Russian administration in the late-eighteenth century with the aim of controlling the religious life of Muslims. The Department experienced a certain amount of democratization after the February Revolution of 1917 and, in 1922, Rizaetdin Fakhreddin, a famous jadid, researcher and writer, was elected as a mufti.[62] Further changes included the recognition of women's right to pray alongside men in mosques and the

Empire. Gender and Power in Stalinist Central Asia (Ithaca, NY: Cornell University Press, 2003).

59 Imanutddin Sulaev, 'Musulmanskie s'ezdy Povolzhia i Kavkaza v 1920e gody', *Voprosy istoryy* 9 (2007), 141–143.

60 'Vsemusulmanskii Kongress v Mekke (Interviu s glavoi delegatsii musulman SSSR – predsedatelem TsDUM muftiem Rizauddin Fakhretdinovym)', *Islam i Sovetskoe gosudartstvo (1917–1936), Sbornik dokumentov,* sost. D. Yu. Arapov, red. V. O. Bobrovnikov (Moscow: Iazdatelskii dom Marzhani, 2010), vol.1, 60–63.

61 As is known, the Soviet attack on Islam had several important faces: they started by closing important religious schools and organizations soon after the revolution as being nationalist, continued by the condemnation of the Muslim Communism of the Tatar leader Sultan-Galeev in 1923, and reaching the level of full-size repressions around 1928–29 when Muslim magazines were closed, Arabic scripture was replaced by Latin (Yanalif), and mosques were destroyed. See Hilary Pilkington and Galina Yemelianova, *Islam in Soviet and Post-Soviet Russia* (London and New York: Routledge Curzon, 2003), 36–46.

62 Aidar Useev, 'R.Fakhreddin v tatarskoi obshchestvenno-filosofskoi mysli 20 veka', *Gasyrlar Avazy/Ekho vekov* 2 (2007) – www.archive.gov.tatarstan.ru/magazine/go/anonymous/main/?path=mg:/numbers/2007_2/10/10_6/

election of the first woman, the well-known teacher, Mukhlisa Bubi (Bobinskaia, 1869–1937), former director of the school for girls in the Tatar village of Izh-Bobia, as a member of the Spiritual Department.[63] Mukhlisa Bubi became a woman-kadi and prior to her arrest and subsequent murder in 1937 she was active in defending, among other things, the rights of women to teach religion. For example, according to the documents preserved in the secret police archive, the head of the Department, Rizaetdin Fakhretdinov, supported Mukhlisa Bobinskaia when she requested the Bolshevik authorities' permission to open courses for women in the main mosque of Ufa; she received negative responses from the Bashkir Executive Committee and the Bashkir ministry of internal affairs.[64] A further document describes Bobinskaia claiming that women should be allowed to teach religion in religious schools.[65]

The Bolsheviks were suspicious of educated Muslims and those described as the 'Muslim clergy'; a comparison to the system of Orthodox priesthood. As abovementioned, Islam was also perceived as a threat to territorial integrity due to the dual menaces of pan-Turkism and pan-Islamism. Thus, in connection with the international Muslim Congress of 1926, the internal congress took place in Ufa in November 1926.[66] OGPU materials show that the Soviet authorities were particularly worried about multiple mandates claiming freedom of religious education, opening of new religious schools and courses, the creation of Muslim typography, and giving civil rights to mullahs.[67] The Soviet secret police reports from 1924 notice different opinions among Muslims on the status of women as well: some communities and groups of Volga-Ural Muslims argued against the equality of men and women[68] or against the possibility of women being present in mosques during worship.[69]

As the protocols of the First Congress of Mari People demonstrates, giving the functions of registration of marriages and childbirths to local religious communities and special 'priests' was seen as important step on the way to getting recognition not only for religion, but also for culture and language.

63 Makhmutova, 'Lish tebe, narod, sluzhenie!'.

64 'Pismo muftiia R. Fakhretdinova v Prezidium VtsIK, dekabr 1927', *Islam i Sovetskoe gosudartstvo*, vol. 1, 136.

65 Kadi of the Central Spiritual Office, Mukhlisa Bobibinskaia, in her letter to the TNKP asked from the name of CSO to take the decision about permission for women to teach spiritual knowledge (*verouchenie*) in the religious schools and mosques. She asked for such a permission already some time ago, during her visit to Kazan. (*Islam i Sovetskoe gosudartstvo (1917–1936), Sbornik dokumentov,* sost. D. Yu. Arapov, red. V. O. Bobrovnikov (Moscow: Iazdatelskii dom Marzhani, 2010), vol. 3, 35; 'Svodka faktov kharakterizuiushchikh deiatelnost dukhovenstva za vtoruiu polovinu 1926 goda', ibid., 34.

66 'Dokladnaia zapiska o siezde musdukhovenstva i predstavitelei veruiushchikh v Ufe', ibid., 77–85.

67 '*Sovershenno sekretno*' ..., t. 4 – 1926 god, Ch. 2, 794; t. 4 –1926 god, Ch. 1, p. 641, p. 548, p. 517, p. 303, p. 644.

68 '*Sovershenno sekretno*'..., t. 2 – 1924 god (2001), 159.

69 Ibid., 88.

However, as with the documents of the Muslim Women's Congress, the Congress of Mari People insisted on the recognition of religion as fully compatible with 'modern' views on the status of women. Indeed, it considered resolutions on: prohibiting bride money; the kidnapping of brides; on recognition of the right of men and women to divorce and remarry; polygamy; and the equality of men and women with respect to the use of land.[70] However, after the Bolshevik revolution the Mari religion, much like the pre-1917 period, started to be seen as not 'a proper' religion. For example, the reports of the secret police do not mention Mari 'clergy' or religious ceremonies. The reports describe worship in the forest and the tradition of making offers of animals again as a symbol of a 'lack of culture', which would disappear with further education.[71] The questionnaire written by the Mari Society for Regional Knowledge (*kraevedy*) distributed in 1930 indicated that traditional religions continued to be treated as an object of research.[72] Such an attitude to religions may have appeared to participants, both male and female, to be not only a matter of faith but also a symbol of national rebirth which were not incompatible with female emancipation.

The sphere of public enlightenment and education also provided a forum for the discussion of the status of women. The numerous attempts by the Russian imperial government to Russify the people of the region through missionary schools and the restriction of education in the national languages for pupils of the advanced level, contributed to the development of schools and publications in the local languages into one of the main hallmarks of the Bolshevik programmes for the progress and development of each nation.[73] Education and popular enlightenment was a complex task and included preparation of male and female teachers, creation of public libraries, and educational facilities for preschool children and adults.

Research has shown that, before the 1917 Bolshevik revolution, the Muslim population of the Volga-Ural region had created a broad, if uneven, network of schools, public libraries, periodical publications, professional schools, and different charitable societies and associations created with the aim of supporting national culture, language, and education. For example, according to Zavdat Minullin, social associations supported Muslim public libraries in Orenburg and Troitsk. Indeed, there were more than 10,000 such establishments which welcomed more than 19,000 visitors in 1911.[74] Different societies and individuals

70 *Pervyi*, pp. 21, 37–38.

71 Gradskova, 2013.

72 The questionnaire includes questions on special forests and the number of animals offered to gods – *Mariiskoe oblastnoe obshchestvo kraevedov, Programma opisaniia derevni MAO* (Ioshkar-Ola, 1930), 8, 32. These questions coexist with others, asking about abortion, cohabitation, and women-activists.

73 See Makhmutova, 'Lish tebe, narod, sluzhenie!'; Gimazova, 2007.

74 Zavdat Minnullin, 'Tatarskie blagotvoritelnye obschestva vo vtoroi polovine X1X–nachale XX veka', in *Blagotvoritelnost v Rossii*, edited by O. L. Leikind (St Petersburg: Liki Rossii, 2003), 219–223.

supported schools for girls, female students, and magazines for women.[75] One female charity association from Ufa, the Muslim Ladies Society, supported seven schools for Muslim girls in 1914.[76] According to the report of St Petersburg Muslim Charitable Society from 1908, it supported a co-educational Muslim boarding school in St Petersburg, and, from 1911, both male *and* female university students.[77] Finally, it is important to note that Muslim women who joined the teaching profession were widely recognized by Tatar society at the beginning of the twentieth century. Indeed, many of those famous women who were described by Fakhretddin as living their life according to the Prophet's will were teachers and were involved in great efforts for the education of girls.[78]

After the February Revolution of 1917, the documents concerning women's rights and changes in their social status, presented popular enlighenment as an important task for educated Muslims. For example, in the appeal to Muslim-sisters we can read that: young women should have the possibility to study in high schools; that courses for women as well as 'organizations for the improvement of practical and spiritual life of women' should be created; and Muslim clinics and kindergartens opened.[79] The documents also highlight the need for further cultural enlightenment through special institutions for the education of society's adult population, both male and female. For example, an article from the newspaper *Kaspii* from October 1917 advertises the opening of evening courses 'for adult Muslims (*musulman i musulmanok)*' following the model of both male and female Russian-Tatar high-schools in Kazan.[80]

The educational institutions of the Mari to a larger extent were Russified, primarily by training teachers in schools where the study of Christianity and Russian language were central. Nonetheless, *Marla calendar*, a yearly literary and advice magazine on Mari language, was founded in 1907, and the Mari People's Congress declared the need for the creation of a special foundation for the support of the cultural and educational efforts of the central organization of Mari.[81] In the Congress's documents it is also possible to find the description of a diverse and specified system of institutions of education and popular enlightenment that had to be created for different groups within the population for the cultural development of Mari. Herein are myriad educational activities: kindergartens, nurseries, playgrounds (*ploshchadki*) for preschool

75 Gelnar Galiullina, 'Zhenskii vopros v Rossii. Regionalnyi aspekt'. Dissertation in History, Kazan, 1995.

76 Minnullin, 'Tatarskie blagotvoritelnye obschestva vo vtoroi polovine X1X–nachale XX veka'.

77 *Otchet musulmanskogo blagotvoritelnogo obschestva v S.Peterburge* (St Petersburg, 1909), 9.

78 'Fakhreddin Ruzaeddin bin. Znamenitye zhenshchiny [Famous women]', *Belskie prostory*, January 2008, 128.

79 Translated by Faizov, www.gender-az.org/index.shtml?id_main=43&id_sub=120

80 'U povolzhskikh Musulman', *Kaspii*, 25 October 1917.

81 *Pervyi,* 28.

children, village libraries, excursions, courses for adults, schools for professional preschool and school teachers, museums, and public lectures.[82] In the *ploshchadki* children were taught not only the Mari language, but also national games, whilst parents could receive advice on their children's' education. The materials highlight the significant role of female teachers in national enlightenment.

Support and development of national languages was one of the central slogans of the Bolsheviks; it was an important way of getting support of the former *inorodtsy*-people. However, while declaring that schools, courts and state offices must work in the language that is spoken in one or another region, they simultaneously declared that most of the local programmes on national enlightenment were counter-revolutionary. And, at the same time, the Russian language preserved its dominant position, becoming 'the language of the revolution'. Also the new Bolshevik government prohibited religious schools, which further damaged education in local languages.

For the Volga-Ural region, new educational policies ushered in the end of the most famous Muslim high schools (*medrese*) in Kazan, Ufa, Orenburg, and other cities in 1918. In spite of the Bolsheviks declaration that education was a high priority, many schools for children whose mother tongue was Tatar and Bashkir continued to be financed and organized rather traditionally throughout the 1920s. According to Lena Suleimanova, in the mid-1920s about 11 per cent of all the schools in Bashkortostan functioned due to collections organised by parents; the salaries of the teachers and school costs were paid from this money.[83] Furthermore, it was not uncommon for pre-revolutionary teachers of non-religious subjects to remain in post after 1917.[84] Even if religious schools were prohibited, evidence from the secret police highlights that, in reality, schools continued to teach religion as well. For example, according to OGPU data, in 1927 some cantons in Tatarstan and Bashkortostan still had about 27–49 religious schools.[85]

According to the Bolshevik vision, institutions outside of formal schooling offered new opportunities for education and cultural enlightenment during the 1920s. National languages formed the working basis for courses, evening schools, village libraries and excursion, but the content was disconnected from religion and nationalism. As documents of the Commission show, with a lack of finances and limited knowledge of local languages and cultures it was a very difficult task. Indeed, the new Soviet institutions of education and culture, much like the 'women's corners' or village libraries (*izby-chitalni*),[86] were often maintained by the peasants themselves and thus they could occasionally escape strict central control. For example, a 1927 report of the

82 *Pervyi,* 41–45.

83 Lena Suleimanova, *Natsionalnye uchebnye zavedenia v Bashkortostane v pervoe sorokaletie XX veka* (Ufa: Bashkirskii gosudarstvennyi universitet, 2000), 175.

84 Ibid., 136.

85 '*Sovershenno sekretno',* t.5–1927 god (2003), 259.

86 Women's corners – spaces dedicated to cultural enlightenment activities for women.

Commission for the Improvement of Work and Everyday Life of Women in Tatarstan stated that village communities maintained 11 kindergartens, 9 playgrounds, 21 nurseries, 5 maternity clinics, 2 orphanages, 1 pioneer camp, and 3 peasant women's corners.[87] Other reports to the Commission highlight the difficulties that courses for nursery teachers and women-activists faced in involving local women. Concurrently, it was the method of the local financing of work for 'women's emancipation' that showed itself to be the most effective; while many of the Commission's documents indicate that work among women in 1920s was usually hindered by a lack of money, both from the central Commission in Moscow and from the local budgets, some Tatar activists from Kazan decided to organize a cafeteria for women. In the case of NEP, it was proposed as a reasonable way of financing different activities for the education of women and, at the same time, utlise the premises as a club.[88]

The conditions and status of women's work inside the household, as well as outside of it, was another important sphere in the period before 1917, particularly in the context of discussions surrounding modernization and national progress. The ideas of modernization of everyday life and production in connection to the 'women's question' were often evoked in public discussions in connection with issues of education for women, in particular, after the February Revolution of 1917. For example, the newspaper *Kaspii* highlights the opening of the professional school for Muslim women in Baku in October 1917 as an important event because,

> The cultural education of Muslim women will also have an economic impact. At present about half of the Muslim population remains outside the production of the national wealth. Thus, our spiritual poverty also becomes an economic poverty; it diminishes our chances in the fight for existence with other people, more advanced spiritually and economically.[89]

Similarly, the Congress of Mari People in July 1917 discussed the need for development of skills for improvement of household production in Mari villages and women's participation in the cooperatives.[90]

Even if the Bolsheviks aspired to include non-Russian women in the proletariat,[91] Soviet initiatives targeted at non-Russian women from the Volga-Ural region did not involve factory work. Rather, they were centred on improving the quality of production in the household and around the creation of cooperatives.[92] Courses for planting vegetables for Bashkir women organized by the

87 GARF, 6983, 1, delo 3, list 14.

88 GARF, 6983, 1, delo 3, list14.

89 Asad Mamedov-Akhliev, 'Blagoe nachinanie', *Kaspii*, 28 October 1917.

90 *Pervyi.*

91 Gregory Massel, *The Surrogate Proletariat. Moslem Women and Revolutionary Strategies in Soviet Central Asia, 1919–1929*, (Princeton, NJ: Princeton University Press, 1974).

92 GARF, 6983, 1, list 182

house of working Bashkir women,[93] as well as previously mentioned courses on making butter and milk production in Mari district, were aimed first of all at those women who were responsible for these duties in their households. The documents of the Commission imply that non-Russian women showed great interest in cooperatives and were interested in obtaining support for their endeavours. For example, the application from Bashkortostan to the Central Commission, signed by Maksimova, highlights the material needs of a working cooperative (*artel*) of 48 women involved in traditional knitting: '112kg of brown cotton threads, 48 of white cotton and 200kg of down'.[94]

In spite of mass campaigns for the improvement of conditions of women's work and everyday life, as well as the promotion (*vydvizhenie*) of women, and in particular women of national minorities, to higher positions and new work places, women met many obstacles in their attempts to work or improve their professional status. The examples given in a 1930 report of the regional meeting of the Commission for the Improvement Work and Everyday Life of Women of the *Zhenotdel* of Bashkortostan are rather striking: 'The comrades presented facts on bureaucratic attitudes. For example, a woman-worker from Beloretsk had to be promoted to be a machine operator, but the managers (*khoziaistvenniki*) said that even a drunkard (man) is better than a woman'. In one more case, the head of the school in Ufa made the new teacher sign a paper declaring that, over the next three years, she would not give birth to a child, otherwise she would be dismissed.[95]

The importance of women's rights in the sphere of religion and education was recognized by some of the local intellectual and women's activists from the region well before the Bolshevik programmes of women's emancipation. Also Muslim women supported, and after 1917, continued to support schools, libraries, and other educational institutions that could contribute to the development of the national culture and economic growth. Simultaneously, the prominent Bolshevik campaign for the education of women of national minorities and their emancipation from religious enslavement, to a large extent, proved rather vague during the 1920s, when a cautious attitude to Islam and a lack of finances prevented Moscow's active interference in the spheres that had historically been a target for Russification. However, slow changes in women's social roles during the 1920s were hindered not only by resistance from local nationalists and conservatives, but equally a general reluctance of the Soviet bureaucracy to involve women in traditionally 'male' spheres.

The 'new woman' between enthusiasm, surveillance and repression

Several women – Russian and non-Russian, local and delegated – were quite enthusiastic about their tasks. Faizullina, a Tatar who, according to data by

93 GARF, 6983, 1, 15, lists 3–8.

94 GARF, 6983, 1, delo 44, list 4.

95 In both cases we do not know about the women's ethnicity, rather these examples show obstacles that every woman could meet while participating in working or political life. GARF, 6983, 1, delo 207, list 80.

Rafilia Gimazova, graduated from the jadidist school for women organized by Mukhlisa Bubi,[96] was enthusiastic about several aspects of her work in the Commission, in particular, the work for the protection of maternity and childhood. Indeed, she was responsible for this work before beginning as secretary of the Commission in Tatarstan and maintained an active interest in these issues, later writing: 'If you meet Vera Pavlovna Lebedeva, give her my greetings and tell that I am still very interested in the problems of protection of motherhood and childhood'. She continued to engage with these subjects once her occupation changed:

> As for the congress of protection of motherhood and children (to Moscow) I will definitely come there: I am still an ardent supporter of these issues. I want so much to continue working in this sphere and, sometimes, I even believe that in my work I can create some special benefits for this direction of activities.[97]

Biographies of other women active during the 1920s and early 1930s affirm the notion of partial involvement of female pre-revolutionary activists in the transformation of everyday life after the Bolshevik revolution. Even if a lot of data is missing, published studies and biographical materials highlight the significance of activism, particularly among Tatar women after the February Revolution of 1917. In April 1917, the first All-Russian Muslim Congress took place in Kazan. It accepted the resolution demanding equality of civil rights, prohibition of child marriage, right of divorce, and the demand for a medical certificate confirming the 'absence of dangerous illness' from groom and bride.[98] The Congress also elected the Central Office of Muslim Women and wrote a Proclamation to All the Muslim Women in Russia. The proclamation called all 'Muslim sisters' to be active, to use the recently obtained right to vote, and not to leave all the tasks of national rebirth to men.[99]

Among women who continued their activities after the Bolshevik revolution was Zahida Burnasheva (1895–1977) a Tatar born in Riazan region, who finished school organized by Bubi.[100] Burnasheva started working as a teacher before 1917 and took part in the All-Muslim Congress of May 1917 as member of the Muslim women's bureau.[101] After the Bolshevik revolution,

96 Gimazova, *Prosvetitelskaia deiatelnost Nigmatullinykh-Bubi*, 214.
97 GARF, 6983, 1, delo 3, list 6.
98 Hablemitoglu and Hablemitoglu, *Sefika Gaspirali ve Rusya'da Turk Kadin Hareketi*; Faizov *Dvizhenie musulmanok Rossii za prava zhenshchin v 1917 godu: stranitsy istorii*, Nizhnii Novgorod: Makhinur, 2005; *Materialy i dokumenty po istorii obshchestvenno-politicheskikh dvizhenii sredi Tatar, 1905–1917* (Kazan: KGU, 1998).
99 Hablemitoglu and Hablemitoglu, *Sefika Gaspirali ve Rusya'da Turk Kadin Hareketi*, translation by Faizov www.gender-az.org/index.shtml?id_main=43&id_sub=120.
100 Gimazova, *Prosvetitelskaia deiatelnost Nigmatullinykh-Bubi*, 196.
101 Faizov, *Dvizhenie musulmanok Rossii za prava zhenshchin v 1917 godu*, 26; Marianne Kamp, *The New Woman in Uzbekistan. Islam, Modernity and Unveiling under Communism*, Seattle: University of Washington Press, 2006 Kamp, 48.

she became a Bolshevik party member and her poetry was translated into Russian in 1922.[102] In the 1920s, she worked as a head of one of the first teachers' school for women in Central Asia.[103] During the Civil War, Mariam Zainullina (1900–198?), another former pupil of Bubi's school,[104] joined the Red Army's cultural department, and for many years worked as a teacher, taking part in the campaign for the elimination of illiteracy alongside working as a leader of a popular theatre group.[105] Finally, Rabiga Kushaeva, a teacher in Bashkir village and participant of the Bashkir Congress in July 1917, worked as *Zhenotdel* instructor in Sterlitamak in the early 1920s.[106]

This data mainly coincides with the general assumption about Bolshevik supporters among local women, made by one of the most prominent Soviet activists of the work among women-*nationalki* in *Zhenotdel*: a Chuvash, Antonina Nukhrat (1900–1983). In her memoirs, she highlights women-teachers as important supporters of the cultural transformation.[107]

However, the period of enthusiastic work of women for the cultural transformation was rather short. The beginning of forced industrialization and collectivization changed the language of work among women while the 'women's question' was declared to be solved in 1931. At that time, the functioning of the Commission for the Improvement of Work and Everyday Life of Women of the Orient no longer seemed necessary. While many documents on the future life of many of the women from Volga-Ural region who were active in defining new freedoms for women in the 1920s are still lacking, and much biographical data needs to be verified, the existing evidence suggests that these activists suffered persecution and death in the late 1930s. For example, Amina Mukhitdinova, who was vice-minister of Justice in Tatarstan and Abrui Saifi in 1920–1921, and the editors of the Communist magazine in Tatar language *Azat Hatyn,* were arrested in the 1930s, as was Mukhlisa Bubi. Rabiga Kushaeva[108] was found dead in Moscow in 1937 in uncertain circumstances.[109]

Thus, many female activists were removed from social activism and their experiences were totally silenced. Nonetheless, they still remembered female participation in the national movements and recalled that the protection of women's rights could exist without conflicting with religious beliefs and the struggle against Russification.

102 Burnasheva's literary pseudonym was Hiffat Tutash, Her book 'Zora Yulduzh' was published in Moscow in 1922.
103 Kamp, *The New Woman in Uzbekistan*, 86–88.
104 Gimazova, *Prosvetitelskaia deiatelnost Nigmatullinykh-Bubi*, 201.
105 Damira Zainullina, Mariam – http://history-kazan.ru/2003/03/maryam/
106 Suleimanova, 'R.Ya.Kushaeva'.
107 Nukhrat, *Bytovaia potrebitelskaia kooperatsiia v natsionalnykh raionakh*, 259.
108 Kushaeva was sent to work in Moscow in early 1930s.
109 Suleimanova, 'R.Ya.Kushaeva', 39.

Conclusion

Early Bolshevik policies for the emancipation of non-Russian women were based on a mixture of proletarian slogans and old imperial ideas relating to the need to civilize and educate non-Christian people, who, theretofore, had preserved traditional occupations, hierarchies, and beliefs. At the same time, most of the 'new' institutions and forms of work that were developed under central Soviet pressure – mixed schools for boys and girls, village libraries (*izby-chitalni*), nurseries, and evening literacy classes for adults – were familiar to some educated parts of the local population. Furthermore, the new rights of women in the family, divorce, prohibition of bride money, and polygamy did not always have to be explained to local women. Indeed, jadidist intellectuals and female activists, like participants of the All-Muslim Congress in Kazan in April of 1917, demanded these rights long before the elaboration of the statute of the Commission for the Improvement of Work and Everyday Life of Women in 1926. As for the Commission, it seems it did not garner enough support within Soviet structures, lacked money, and was perceived as bureaucratic by part of the local population.

At the same time, the archival evidence suggests that, during the 1920s, the Soviet authorities were unable to guide and control all the aspects of life connected to the 'women's question'. Most of the Muslim population of the region continued to follow their religious traditions, including teaching religion and observing Sharia laws. Indeed, the secret police material suggests that even conservative ideas on religious practice, including ideas on prohibiting women from being present in mosques during worship, had a certain support among local village communities.

On the other hand, the Bolshevik project of wide involvement of non-Russian women into the cooperative movement and in factory production was successful due to a lack of interest in collective work, a lack of finances for professional education, as well as resistance to women's new roles on behalf of the new Soviet managers.

Still, documents and publications show that some local women, including those who became interested in female emancipation before the Bolshevik revolution, were actively participating in the campaign. But they were often disappointed that issues of culturalization and emancipation of women were seen as secondary by the party leaders.

The example of Volga-Ural region demonstrates that the early period of the Soviet 'emancipation of women of the Orient' was not particularly effective and relied on pre-revolutionary skills and methods. Starting in the late 1920s, the open repression of Muslim 'clergy', the closing of mosques, and forced involvement of women into *kolkhozes* and factory work led to a growing resistance from the side of the non-Russian people and, not least, resistance by women. The repression of female activists and intellectuals in the mid-1930s marked the end of earlier attempts to preserve the 'national' and 'anti-colonial' agenda alongside the solution of the 'women's question' in the region.

7 Devotion and revolution

Nursing values

*Susan Grant**

The 'across 1917' trajectory is by now a familiar one – for quite some time scholars have been arguing for more synchronic and diachronic approaches to assessments of Russian and Soviet history.[1] Metaphorical bridges have been built between the nineteenth and twentieth centuries, with modernity figuring as the key link. The 1905 and 1917 revolutions, as well as the First World War, have been reassessed under an overarching framework of continuity. This essay follows a similar vein of seeking continuities but posits the case for a *longue durée* assessment that connects the pre-revolutionary roots of the nursing profession to its Soviet incarnation. It explores 'across 1917' through an examination of nurse biographies that span the pre-revolutionary and post-Stalinist years. By taking my analysis into the 1950s and 1960s, the revolutionary divide fades considerably. Continuities between what might seem an obsolete imperial nursing past actually gained currency in the post-World War II Soviet Union. From this perspective the October Revolution, while naturally still considered the crucial watershed, was not the primary signifier for nurses in the 1940s and beyond. Professional roots in the imperial era eclipsed the Bolshevik revolution: rather than advance the professionalization of nursing, the revolution instead interrupted it. In the case of nursing, therefore, looking beyond the 1917 October Revolution is certainly appropriate. For Soviet nursing it was, in fact, war experience, whether in the Crimean War, First World War, Civil War, or Great Patriotic War, that became the determining factor in a nurse's social standing and endowed her with an air of professional gravitas.

* Acknowledgements: I thank Seth Bernstein, Judith Devlin, Yulia Gradskova, and Jonathan Waterlow for their comments on this paper, and also the editors for their suggestions and advise.

1 David Hoffmann's work in particular advances the case for such approaches, see especially *Russian Modernity: Politics, Knowledge, Practices* (London and New York: Palgrave Macmillan, 2000). See also Peter Holquist, '"Information is the Alpha and Omega of our Work": Bolshevik Surveillance in its Pan-European Context', *The Journal of Modern History* 69(3) (1997), 415–450; Michael David-Fox, *Crossing Borders: Modernity, Ideology, and Culture in Russia and the Soviet Union* (Pitt Series on Russian and Eastern European Studies) (Pittsburgh, PA: University of Pittsburgh Press, 2015).

It was not until the postwar period, the 1950s and 1960s in particular, that the true significance of war experience – imperial or Soviet – really manifested itself. The idealized image of the pre-revolutionary nurse in the post-World War II period speaks to the idea of a 'usable past' and the celebration of heroes from the late Tsarist period whose exploits served to inspire future generations. Nursing was very much part of a broader political postwar shift that created new narratives by drawing on the past.

The fact that the core nursing values of care and compassion remained stable is important to our understanding of the revolutionary divide, showing that while the October Revolution caused ruptures in the nursing profession it did not eliminate these values. Once the initial chaos of revolution, civil war, and famine passed, many nurses who remained in Soviet Russia appeared to adapt to the new conditions of life, or so their postwar biographies would suggest. Nurses trained prior to the Bolshevik revolution had valuable experience and postwar retrospectives indicate that they transmitted this experience to colleagues entering the profession. Many of the retrospectives analysed here were published in the 1950s and 1960s and are problematic. They might very well be genuine accounts but it is more likely that they were designed to fit constructed postwar narratives – part of the 'usable past' and 'invented tradition' discussed by David Brandenberger and Eric Hobsbawm.[2] Nurse participation in war was lauded in the medical press and they were presented as models for a younger generation of nurses. This narrative of war participation and professional experience painted a picture of nurses as true Soviet patriots.

This chapter is largely based on an analysis of the nursing periodical *Meditsinskaya sestra* from the 1940s to the 1960s. The first year of its publication, 1942, points to the strong connection between war and nursing, with the former becoming a driving force for developing the latter. A problem that arises from relying on this material is its centralized nature; *Meditsinskaya sestra* was Russian centric in its content. Many of those featured were Russian or worked in Russian cities. Leningrad features heavily, perhaps owing to the nursing profession's strong roots in in St. Petersburg/Petrograd and the strength of the Leningrad nurses in organizing themselves.[3] The journal's reach, however, was wide. Nurses across the Soviet Union would have read *Meditsinskaya sestra* and it was *the* key publication for Soviet nurses. Also drawn on here is material from the State Archive of the Russian Federation (GARF) which holds a number of collections on nurses (files pertaining to inter alia the medical trade union, Procuracy, and the All-Russian Union of the Sisters of Mercy). Not a great deal of work has been done on Soviet nursing, especially in the postwar era; this essay is therefore important in illuminating

2 David Brandenberger, *Propaganda State in Crisis: Soviet Ideology, Indoctrination, and Terror under Stalin, 1927–1941* (New Haven, CT: Yale University Press, 2012); Eric Hobsbawm, *The Invention of Tradition* (Cambridge: Cambridge University Press, 1983).

3 This tradition of a strong nursing organization continues in St Petersburg today, where the Russian Nurse's Association is based.

continuities in Soviet society across 1917 and also in connecting Soviet nursing history to current scholarly debate in the field.[4]

The impact of war and revolution on nursing

Before the Second World War, the history of Russian nursing received scant attention. This changed later when the pre-revolutionary past was harnessed and attention drawn to the values and principles espoused by nurses under late Tsarism. The eminent surgeon Nikolai Ivanovich Pirogov (1810–1881) and founder of the Sisters of Mercy, Grand Duchess Elena Pavlovna, were held up as beacons of propriety and models for Soviet nurses almost a century after they had come to prominence.[5] The valiant, self-sacrificing actions of nurse Dasha Sevastolpolskaya during the Crimean War were presented as heroic efforts worthy of emulation. Such models served an important purpose by connecting the heroism of prerevolutionary war and patriotism to the present. Drawing on, inter alia, the Crimean War, Civil War and Great Patriotic War, representative of the Moscow union of nurses, N. G. Lin'kova, wrote in 1951 that using 'outstanding examples from the past demonstrates the devotion and modesty of everyday, honorable work…reinforcing the defence of the motherland and construction of socialism, and these modest workers make a huge contribution to public health'. Sister of mercy involvement in the Crimean, Russo-Turkish and Russo-Japanese wars signaled crucial steps in the development of the nursing profession.[6] Other crises such as famine and epidemics were significant too, leading to the expansion of sister of mercy communities as well as increased Red Cross involvement in nursing. War and general disaster, it seemed, catapulted nurses and their work into the spotlight.

From 1844 nurses were organized into nursing communities (*obshchiny sester miloserdiya*) that oversaw living and working conditions. Sisters of mercy (as nurses were called until 1926) were composed of women from

4 Some of those who have written about Russian and Soviet nursing include Laurie S. Stoff, *Russia's Sisters of Mercy and the Great War: More than Binding Men's Wounds* (Lawrence, KS: Kansas University Press, 2015); Natalia Leonidovna Lopatkina, *Kul'turologicheskie aspekty v razvitii sestrinskogo dela* (Kemerovo: Izdatel'stvo Aksioma, 2009); A. V. Posternak, *Ocherki po istorii obshchin sester miloserdiia* (Moscow: Izdatel'stvo Sviato-Dmitrievskii uchilishche sester miloserdiia, 2001); V. P. Romaniuk, V. A. Lapotnikov, and Ia A. Nakatis, *Istoriia sestrinskogo dela v Rossii* (St Petersburg: SPbGMA, 1998); Elena Kozlovtseva, *Moskovskie obshchiny sester miloserdiya v XIX-nachale XX veka* (Moscow: Izdatel'stvo PSTGU, 2010).

5 See for example 'Vsesoiuznoe soveshchanie shkol medistinskikh sister', *Meditsinskaya sestra* 8 (1950), 28–32; Prof Z. Iu. Rol'e (Moscow), 'Molodym sestram, okonchivshim shkolu med-kh sester', 1 (1956), 24–28; Nurse N. I. Potovina, 'Povedenie meditsinskoi sestry u posteli bol'nogo', 4 (1954), 20; M. M. Chumak, V. P. Tarasiuk, 'Drug i sovetnik bol'nogo', *Meditsinskaya sestra* 2 (1966), 61–62; Z. F. Illarionova, 'Avtoritet medistinskoi sestry', *Meditsinskaya sestra* 6 (1969), 31–32.

6 N. G. Lin'kova, 'Moral'nyi oblik meditsinskoi sestry', *MS* 1 (1951), 2–25 (25).

aristocratic stock, those with religious inclinations, women with no means, or those seeking adventure. Women entering the nursing communities were aged between 18 and 40 years and their religious and moral character was expected to be of a high standard. Life for the Russian sister of mercy was generally hard, with long hours and arduous living and working conditions leaving many nurses physically exhausted. Although women were still drawn to the nursing communities, when war broke out in 1914 the 150 nursing communities in existence did not meet state needs and so short-term Red Cross courses were established.[7] During the war difficult conditions took an immense physical and psychological toll on nurses.[8] Meanwhile, the increase in the number of women with nurse training had an immediate impact on the profession, swelling the ranks of those calling themselves sisters of mercy. Both of these factors – conditions and expansion – necessitated urgent reform of the nursing communities.

The task of reforming the communities was taken up by a group of nurses from Petrograd who set up the All-Russian Union of the Sisters of Mercy (*Vserossisskii Soiuz Sester Miloserdiia*). The union leaders published a journal (*Pervyi vestnik sestry miloserdiya* – The First Herald of the Sisters of Mercy) and in its first issue the editors wrote that the union had been established to provide support and leadership to nurses. They also noted that the new union, formed in August 1917, would unite all nurses. The nursing union was one of many medical unions formed over the course of the tumultuous year 1917 and similar to other unions, nurses came under pressure from the new Bolshevik authorities to join a single medical union. Having never been in a particularly strong position, the All-Russian Union of the Sisters of Mercy leadership proved unable to resist this pressure and the union was eventually disbanded some 18 months after its formation.[9]

Although nurses worked within the newly emerging healthcare system, sisters of mercy, with their veils and crosses, did not fit the image of the dynamic revolutionary. During the years 1919 to 1920 nursing courses across the former Russian empire were closed and then reopened under the Bolshevik authorities (the Commissariat of Education and later the Commissariat of Public Health). Nurses were to come from the proletariat and religion was no longer tolerated.[10] Yet this did not mean that sister of mercy values of care and compassion were destroyed. In spite of the rupture induced by the

7 For more on the Union of Sisters of Mercy see my chapter, 'From War to Peace: The Fate of Nurses and Nursing under the Bolsheviks', in *Russia's Home Front 1917–1922: The Experience of War and Revolution*, edited by Adele Lindenmeyr, Christopher Read, and Peter Waldron (Bloomington, IN: Slavica, 2016).

8 For more on First World War nursing see Laurie Stoff, 'The "Myth of the War Experience" and Russian Wartime Nursing during World War One', *Aspasia: International Yearbook of Central, Eastern, and Southeastern European Women's and Gender History* 6 (2012), 96–116 and also Stoff, *Russia's Sisters of Mercy and the Great War*.

9 For more on the All-Russian Union of Sisters of Mercy, see Grant, 'War to Peace'.

10 Ibid.

October Revolution and the practical implementation of the revolutionary ideals of the Bolsheviks, the continued presence of pre-revolutionary nurses working in medical institutes, hospitals, and clinics across the Soviet Union helped maintain the core values of the sister of mercy tradition. In the unfolding public health crisis that was engulfing Russia, nurses were urgently needed because of their professional training. Care was fundamental to Bolshevik conceptions of nursing and the new nurse training schools were to produce 'caring personnel' who were 'skilled and conscientious'.[11]

In spite of Bolshevik commitments to providing care, a combination of the public health crisis and lack of resources meant that the quality of nurse training and care suffered in the early years of the Soviet state. Claims of callous, inconsiderate, even incompetent nurses and medical workers produced under the Soviet system show that values of care, morality, and compassion were in many ways compromised.[12] But by the mid-1930s and into the postwar period there was a move to reassess nursing standards. The first half of the 1930s saw continued changes in the function of the nurse and shortened courses in training and education. Nursing was not an attractive occupation, with lowly paid nurses failing to make the status of hero worker. The contribution of nurses was difficult to quantify in the labor productivity obsessed period of the late 1920s and 1930s. But there was a more certain place for Soviet nurses in the late 1930s. After the introduction of the Stalin Constitution in 1936, Soviet citizens were to expect a better quality of life. Only the highest standards of care and service would suffice for the new Soviet person. By 1938, articles appeared in praise of nurses with 20 and 40 years of nursing experience, their 'wrinkles' and 'lines' testifying to their hard work.[13] These nurses were modest and sympathetic, characteristics that would become hallmarks of later representations of the Soviet nurse.

The outbreak of the Second World War highlighted the significance of nursing work and the value of well-trained nurses. Now, it seemed, nurses had a place in the socialist world. They had proven their worth in the eyes of the state and no longer lingered in the shadow of their proletarian sister-heroes. In

11 *Plan obucheniya i programmy shkol sester miloserdiya* (Moscow, 1919), 1. This was a joint publication by the Red Cross and the Commissariat of Public Health, published 18 February 1919.

12 For specific examples of mistreatment see GARF, f. 4049, op. 1, d. 152, l. 52 (1918). To the senior doctor of the 4th Lazaret of the Red Cross, from the Guberniya Commissar for Military Affairs, 7 May 1918; GARF, f. 3341, op. 1, d. 103, l. 64. The letter to the Main Administration of the Red Cross was written by Aleksandr Ivanich [sic] Gorokhov and Maksim Donilovich [sic] Gorb. 1918/1919. For a general discussion of problems in the training, education, and practice of nursing in the 1920s, see F. Kogan, 'Srednee meditsinskoe obrazovanie i potrebnosti zdravookhraneniya',*Na fronte zdravookhraneniya* (later *Voprosy zdravookhraneniya*) 15 (1929), 31–36.

13 N. Evgen'eva, 'Sestra Ivanova' (Liudi sovetskoi meditsiny) *Meditsinskii rabotnik* 4 (1938), 3; Z. Medvedovskaya, 'Sorok let v selskoi bol'nitse', *Meditsinskii rabotnik* 6 (1938), 4

1942, nurses were finally rewarded with a professional journal, *Meditsinskaya sestra*. Through its discussions of 'excellent health workers' the journal represented an important forum for depicting the kind of nurse required in the Soviet Union. It became increasingly evident that the type of nurse the Soviet Union wanted was one with experience. Articles titled 'Forty years in the honourable post' confirmed the value placed on years of work.[14] This ties in with the broader historical narrative of the late 1930s, where, as David Brandenberger argues in the context of education 'the official historical narrative during the postwar years was virtually driven by pre-revolutionary Russian state heroes'.[15] The Soviet Union had its own pantheon of nursing heroes from which to draw on, and nursing heroes from the Great Patriotic War and pre-revolutionary wars featured in *Meditsinskaya sestra*. Amir Weiner has argued that the memory of the Great Patriotic War overtook the revolution as being most symbolic in post-World War II politics and society.[16] Nursing discourse develops this idea further and shows that the general experience of war and the imperial past replaced the October Revolution as most relevant in shaping both state and nurse perceptions of the past and present role of nurses in Soviet society.

Past meets present

In 1947 four Leningrad nurses who had worked through the First World War, the Civil War, Finnish War, and Great Patriotic War were singled out for praise. Seventy-two year old Matrena Ivanovna Prozorova had worked as a nurse in the 'In Memory of 25th October' hospital for 49 years and was 'sensitive' with patients, had immense experience, and was disciplined in carrying out her duties.[17] She was a model nurse for young colleagues to emulate. All four of the Leningrad nurses had trained in the pre-revolutionary nursing community 'Exaltation of the Cross' and were all commended for their commitment to providing excellent care. This piece in the '*meditsinskie sestry – otlichnitsy zdravookhraneniya*' ('nurses – excellent health workers') section of the journal set the tone for subsequent decades. The tropes employed here changed little over the next 20 years and established a definitive and formulaic narrative that diverged little as time passed. The best nurses in the Soviet Union were experienced medical workers who were middle-aged to elderly, committed to providing patients with high standards of care, and forthcoming in sharing their knowledge and skills with younger nurses. Any

14 I. A. Kliuev, 'Sorok let ne pochetnom postu', *MS* 7 (1952), 27–29. Nurses awarded the Order of Lenin usually received the prize for their length of service and commitment to the profession.

15 David Brandenberger, *National Bolshevism: Stalinist Mass Culture and the Formation of Modern Russian National Identity, 1931–1956*, (Cambridge, MA and London: Harvard University Press, 2002), 202.

16 Amir Weiner, *Making Sense of War: The Second World War and the Fate of the Revolution* (Princeton, NJ: Princeton University Press, 2000)

17 *Medistinskaya sestra* (hereafter *MS*) 3 (1947), 31.

political or public misgivings concerning sisters of mercy carried over from the revolution and civil war years into the 1920s had seemingly vanished.

Indeed, the 'sister of mercy' appeared to be enjoying a postwar renaissance courtesy of the war and the ideals that nurses personified. It was, effectively, the war that facilitated the virtual reinstatement of the pre-revolutionary nurse, thus creating the context for their changing representation during late Stalinism and the Thaw period. This suited the needs of the postwar Soviet state, which sought to modernize Soviet healthcare. The image of an experienced, caring, and professional nurse was the perfect antidote to the brutality of war as well as the ideal accompaniment to the projection of a softer side to socialism. The fact that these nurses had trained in a Tsarist nursing community did not negatively impact their career; if anything, they were valued more because of the training and discipline acquired prior to the Bolshevik revolution. This was far removed from the general attitude towards nursing in the 1920s, however, when some of those publishing on nursing criticized the pre-revolutionary system and its low standard of education and training.[18]

The convergence of past and present was made explicit at a conference in Moscow, in October 1954, where nurses from the 'older generation' met with the young, so that the former could pass on their 'immense years of experience in caring for the sick'.[19] Nurse Aleksandra Ardal'ovna Tomilina recalled that 40 years had passed since she 'first walked up to the bed of a patient'.[20] She had been working in Moscow's Botkin hospital for over 30 years. She began her career in 1914 as a young 18-year-old in the nursing community attached to the hospital, then known as the Bauman. She told those gathered in the conference hall that nurses then were 'accustomed to order: one was not allowed [*nel'zya*] ... to be dressed untidily, or have unclean hands or long fingernails. A love for the sick person and a love for work was instilled in us.' Then, she continued, 'after two years of study we went on to independent work but even here the senior nurse kept a very close eye on us'. She added that the words 'I do not want to' were not a part of their vocabulary; every task was carried out carefully. The years passed and she became a senior nurse. Many young people had 'passed through her hands', and she always taught them 'honesty, accuracy, and how to address patients and each other in a cultured way'. She was awarded the Order of Lenin.[21] Such postwar accounts demonstrate that

18 The change became apparent in the late 1930s and continued through the war and afterwards. Yet there was also some criticism of pre-revolutionary nursing. In an article in *Meditsinskaya sestra*, one nurse with some 42 years' experience portrayed her pre-revolutionary nursing experience as a negative one. She claimed that the strict discipline of the communities produced nurses who were not 'kind-hearted' but bitter and frightened. In spite of this she added that much 'could be learned from the good habits' of the pre-revolutionary nurse and communities, in particular discipline, cleanliness, tidiness, and 'respect for the elderly', 'Vospominaniya meditsinskoi sester', *MS* 11–12 (1942), 25; 27.

19 A. V. Ikonnikova, 'Konferentsiya Meditsinskikh sester', *MS* 6 (1955), 22.

20 Ikonnikova, 'Konferentsiya', 22.

21 Ikonnikova, 'Konferentsiya', 22.

pre-revolutionary trained nurses taught younger nurses in the 1920s and 1930s, transferring their values in the process.

At this conference younger nurses showed their appreciation. A student of A. A. Tomilina's, Mariya Federovna Gerasimova, noted that initially she found her new role as nurse difficult but she coped thanks to the support of older nurses such as Tomilina. The reciprocal relationship between young and old was a postwar construct designed to nurture cadres of nurses that were more similar to the image of the pre-revolutionary sisters of mercy than the interwar Soviet nurse. Sometimes an air of uncertainly still hung over the younger generation, in spite of the efforts of older nurses to train and educate them. A 1966 article lamented the passing of the older generation with the 'soft unhurried movements of their hands' and their 'quiet manner'.[22] The author wondered if the younger nurses would be able to emulate such outstanding examples of care and empathy. It was vital that the values passed on by the older generation would live on and not become history like their 'long old fashioned veils and red crosses'.[23] The self-image of the party-state was at stake. The nurse embodied the best intentions of the party-state and the nursing discourse reflected this through its 'excellent worker' section and the tropes it employed. By consciously drawing on nursing's pre-revolutionary heritage, the party-state anchored itself in a past that preceded and succeeded the October Revolution. This rooting in the past helped to legitimize not just the profession but the postwar state, which was now seen to be building and modernizing the existing system but without betraying the original ideals of the revolution. The integration of the pre- and post-revolutionary nursing heritage represented the state's intent to nurture a harmonious relationship among generations of nurses and, perhaps, an attempt to heal the rupture that had occurred in the immediate years after October 1917.

The depiction of what were essentially pensioner hero nurses also tells us a great deal about Soviet society in the 1940s, 1950s, and 1960s. Gone were the dynamic young charges of the interwar period. Now younger people were not to be inspired by their peers but by their elders. The Bolshevik revolution, while still important, was frequently overshadowed by the experience of war as one of forging identity and discipline. The roots of the nursing profession – traced back to the Crimean War and Pirogov, spoke to the values and principles of the imperial era where care and compassion were the defining characteristics of nursing. This was evidently valued in the post-World War II period. The figure of the nurse represents a valuable barometer of 'care' in postwar society. The Khrushchev period certainly placed an emphasis on family values (epitomized by the Moral Code of 1961), as did the Stalin Constitution of 1936. But the core values of nursing in the late 1940s–1960s had more in common with pre-revolutionary nursing than with the young, Red Cross hero nurses of the late 1930s.

Nurses in the postwar period are undoubtedly presented as professional career women, but there is also no mistaking that they are providers of care.

22 I. Borisov, 'Sestra miloserdiya', MS 6 (1966), 60.
23 Borisov, 'Sestra miloserdiya', 61.

Their character, conduct, and conscientiousness mattered and had, it seemed, a profound influence on the quality of care they provided to patients. After the Great Patriotic War, there was an overwhelming sense of respect for the past and the traditions of Russian nursing, which became deeply enmeshed in contemporaneous Soviet nursing values and concepts of professionalism. The 'ideal' professional nurses were those who combined the traditional Russian sister of mercy ethos with their new Soviet identity. In the 1950s alone there were 17 *Meditsinskaya sestra* biographies of nurses who achieved this and were awarded the Order of Lenin. Their contributions to Soviet society were in many cases based on the skills developed through their training in the imperial nursing communities. As recipients of state awards, the imperial and Soviet experience of these nurses was recognized.

The rise of the pre-revolutionary nurse

These hero nurses, even if trained in the pre-revolutionary system, were also products of the Soviet system. They were women who were shown to have negotiated the transition from sister of mercy to medical sister. This transition, after all, was more than a mere change of title – it was part of a major ideological shift that brought with it cultural, social, and political consequences. But the professional history of a number of nurses, as well as their recognition by the state, indicates that those educated before the October revolution adapted to the new system and worked within it. For example, Nurse M. V. Petropavlovskaya, who had worked in the Dzerzhinskogo district of Moscow for some 52 years, attended new Soviet training courses to improve her skills. She had finished a two-year midwifery course in Moscow, then a two-year *feldsher* course at Moscow's Mariinsky hospital (which had since been renamed the Dzerzhinsky hospital). The 76-year-old had displayed all the attributes of the ideal Soviet worker, carrying out the instructions of the hospital administration and the district *zdravotdel* (health section). After the October revolution she had been 'very active' in social work when the medical service was being organized. During the Civil War Petropavlovskaya endeavoured to establish sanitary conditions in the hospital and in the apartments of medical workers. As the author of her *Meditsinskaya sestra* mini-biography noted, Petropavlovskaya 'participated in different events to improve the health of the people'.[24] This included conducting classes with members of the Red Cross, participating in the 'cleanliness troika' (*troika po chistote*), and in village *shefstvo* campaigns. In the sphere of healthcare, it was not the young (or certainly not only the young) who led the way. Nurses of a pre-revolutionary vintage were frequently depicted as the leading lights of the Soviet path to communism.[25]

24 M. Karaulova, 'Meditsinskaya sestra M. V. Petropavlovskaya', *MS* 7 (1952), 28.
25 Karaulova, 'Meditsinskaya sestra', 28. Petropavlovskaya was one of those awarded an Order of Lenin.

O. A. Yakovleva similarly advanced through the Tsarist and Soviet medical systems.[26] The daughter of an army officer, Yakovleva was born in Smolensk in 1874. She overcame personal and social obstacles to attend a medical course in Perm in 1891 while also working as a *feldsheritsa*. She graduated with a *feldsher* diploma in 1895 and went on to work in hospitals in Perm, Ekaterinburg, and the Far East until 1914, spending the years of war and revolution in Perm with her young family. She eventually settled in Ivanovo in 1924 where she remained for 24 years working as a senior nurse. The professional biography of A. A. Surnina is another example of a nurse breaching the revolutionary divide.[27] During the time of the Russo-Japanese War she attended a nurse and *sanitar* course in a Ekaterinburg hospital, organized by surgeon N. A. Russkikh under the auspices of the Urals Medical Society and attached to the Red Cross community. She and 26 other nurses were sent to Harbin where they worked in a military hospital. Surnina, who was an 'energetic' 83-year-old in 1969, 'remembered everything very well and spoke very highly of her teacher, the famous Urals surgeon Aleksandr Andreevich Mislavskii'.[28] She went on to nurse during the First World War, where she was awarded a St George's Cross for her bravery at the front. At the time of the October Revolution she was working in Rovno. After the revolution she returned to Ekaterinburg (Sverdlovsk) where she continued to work in the eye clinic founded in 1906 by her former mentor Mislavskii. She remained working there for 44 years until it closed in 1950. She then moved to work in the eye (ophthalmology) department of the city clinical hospital No 1 and left in January 1964. As her biographer notes, Surnina was a 'simple worker, a nurse' who had come a long way. She was a public figure of the 'new form' and was awarded an Order of Lenin in 1951. Elderly nurses, even by the 1960s, still featured in *Meditsinskaya sestra*, valued for their 'simplicity'. The modesty and work ethic of the pre-revolutionary nurse were once again hallmarks of the ideal Soviet nurse, who continued to be represented by the older generation. These accounts formed part of the postwar narrative that framed nurses as Soviet patriots committed to building socialism through their medical work.

Such accounts show how the state related to its nurses and how nurses responded to state needs. Mariya Yakovlevna Rodionova (also awarded the Order of Lenin) finished the Iverskaya Sister of Mercy community school in 1913 and was afterwards sent as part of the Red Cross detachments to fight typhus in Serbia.[29] This is where she was at the outbreak of the First World War. Until 1918 she worked in military hospitals, first Tsarist ones and then after 1917, for the Red Army. The Civil War met with a huge demand for medical workers and Narkomzdrav started to use the former Red Cross nursing

26 Prof. P. M. Maksimov (Ivanovo), 'Vysokoe schastye', *MS* 1 (1966), 43–44. Yakovleva received an Order of Lenin.
27 Dr. Iu. E. Sorkin, 'Sestra miloserdiya A. A. Surnina', *MS* 2 (1969), 59–60.
28 Sorkin, 'Sestra miloserdiya', 60.
29 V. I. Bazdrev, 'Primer chestnogo sluzheniya narodu', *MS* 12 (1953), 27.

communities to train 'proletarian nurses'. Her experience meant that she was appointed course director of the nursing school of the Iverskaya community. She worked in this role for six years, 'contributing to the training of proletarian medical cadres'.[30] In 1924 she moved to work in a tuberculosis sanatorium for Moscow workers where she remained until the outbreak of the Second World War, at which point the sanatorium became an evacuation hospital for Soviet army officers and later a military hospital for invalids. She remained throughout the war years and was head of the nurse's council there. It is not possible to know how much Rodionova actively engaged in her professional promotion; these accounts are, after all, primarily about presenting nurses in a positive light. Readers are only provided with bare outlines of these women's movements, but enough to know the kind of nurse the state wanted and the values it espoused. But the accounts are also a sign of the porosity of the revolutionary period, when nurses from across the 1917 divide worked alongside one another.

Through their service to the state, nurses are shown to reap rewards and satisfaction by virtue of their upward professional mobility, but more importantly, by the gratitude they received from patients and colleagues. A nurse born in 1879, Mariya Mikhailovna Kotova, had worked as a nurse for 50 years and at age 76 continued to 'work tirelessly' – she was also a member of the Communist party, a 'model of honest and flawless fulfillment of her patriotic duty'.[31] She had trained over 100 surgical nurses and had earned the respect and trust of colleagues. (Kotova also received an Order of Lenin.) Aleksandra Ivanovna Popova, begun her medical career as a *sanitarka* in 1913 and eventually became head nurse of a women's psychiatric department. She is one of the ultimate examples of someone making their way up through the ranks. Born in 1897, she moved to Archangelsk at 16 where she worked as a nanny in the municipal hospital. She worked there for 11 years, during which time she 'continually worked on herself' to improve her level of education. As an 'honest, conscientious worker', she was promoted to a domestic nurse. In 1931 she was recommended to attend a nursing course. After the successful completion of this she was appointed nurse in the same section of the hospital where she had been working until 1936. From 1936 she remained as a nurse in the women's psychiatric department of the hospital. She was head nurse there for 15 years until failing health forced her to take the position of attending nurse in 1951.[32] These professional histories neatly fitted the narrative being constructed that downplayed revolutionary breaks and instead focused on nurses who remained in their careers and in fact managed to progress and flourish under Soviet power. The key message here was that the October Revolution was an opportunity, not an obstacle.

Nurses working in the 1920s but particularly in the 1930s – those lauded in *Meditsinskaya sestra* in the 1960s – advanced in their careers with considerable

30 Ibid., 27.
31 G. I. Klyagin (Tblisi), 'Mariya Mikhailovna Kotova', *MS* 9 (1955), 30.
32 V. V. Bataeva, 'Tat'yana Veniaminovna Pogrebnaya', *MS* 1 (1959), 45–46.

speed. These patriots and model workers were *vydvizhentsy* who took advantage of the Soviet system or benefitted from it. As soon as the Commissariat of Health was put in place medical workers could avail of the promotions available to them. Consequently *sanitarki* such as Popova were able to advance with relative ease through the ranks. Women who began their medical careers as nannies (*nyani*) could potentially end up working as senior nurses. Most important of all, however, was that the upward professional mobility of these nurses demonstrated their commitment to the state and the state's gratitude to its nurses. It showed nurses to be competent, modern, and willing to assume the responsibilities deemed necessary by the state.

The most striking example of this upward mobility is the career of Nadezhda Vasilievna Manannikova. She attended medical courses in Kiev in 1915 and in 1917 entered the medical faculty of Saratov University. While studying she also spent time working in Kiev medical institutes and worked as a nurse and *feldsheritsa* during the cholera and typhus epidemic. In 1922 she completed her medical education and went to Kazakhstan, where she became involved in medical work in Urdu. By 1925 she was working in the Kazakhstan Narkomzdrav and four years later was transferred to Narkomzdrav RSFSR to organize children's institutes in the major cities of the republic. This led to her taking work in the Institute for Motherhood and Maternity in 1932. Her meteoric rise through the Soviet healthcare system continued when in 1940 she was appointed Deputy People's Commissar of Health. During her time there she was engaged in training and development work for the protection of mother and child health. In 1951 she began work as a lecturer in the Central Institute for Physicians. She was also editor of *Meditsinskaya sestra* for 15 years and published several books on the protection of mother and child health.[33] As a qualified medical worker, her skills were in demand and her commitment to improving the health of women and children was valued by the new Soviet health authorities. She was another nurse who managed to breach the revolutionary divide and continue along her own professional path, eventually excelling in her chosen field. Her biography provided yet further evidence of nurses answering the state's call by dedicating their lives to helping others.

The revolution still featured in this discourse, albeit in an idealized way that celebrated the professionalism of nurses. For Mariya Ivanovna Mishina, who completed her training with the 'Soothe my Sorrows' community in 1917, the October Revolution was key. The revolution had awakened in all medical workers a 'selfless' desire to care for the sick.[34] But commitment and experience were more important. Mishina had since dedicated 24 years of her life to medical work, with

33 'Nadezhda Vasilievna Manannikova' (Towards her 70th Birthday), *MS* 5 (1966), 53–54. Manannikova with Evgenii Dmitrievich Ashurkov co-authored *Okhrana materinsntva i detstva v SSSR. Lektsii po organizatsii zdravookhraneniya dlya studentov meditsinskikh institutov* (1956) and wrote *Okhrana materinsntva i detstva v SSSR* (1959). She published widely in the 1950s on topics related to the health of mother and child.

34 'Mariya Ivanovna Mishina', *MS* 10 (1948), 32.

her 'gentle character' and 'conscientious attitude to her profession' earning her the 'love and trust of patients and authority amongst her colleagues'. Praskov'ya Aleksandrovna Reznichenko, a nurse trained in 1914 and who went on to nurse in the First World War, Civil War, and Great Patriotic War, always remembered that she was to 'serve her people, country (*rodina*) and the October Revolution'.[35] Her greatest rewards were words of thanks from patients. By now, these tropes dominated the 'excellent worker' section of *Meditsinskaya sestra*. The vast majority of nurses featured were in their fifties and sixties; the few young nurses singled out for praise were considered fortunate to have been the recipients of knowledge from their more senior colleagues. The short biographies suggest that their commitment to their profession and helping their patients was most important.

These cases, especially that of Manannikova, show that the pre-revolutionary training of nurses, though initially viewed with suspicion in the radicalism and experimentalism of the immediate post-revolutionary years, was soon overcome. Demonstrating commitment to the 'Soviet cause' was enough to catapult nurses into senior positions. Nursing values – care and compassion, duty and devotion – outlasted the early revolutionary fervour for imparting change and the restructuring of the profession. It is worth noting too that this rhetoric of devotion and care could be read as having religious overtones in light of the Cold War discourse of the day, part of what Victoria Smolkin-Rothrock has called the 'moral crusade of good against evil' during Nikita Khrushchev's anti-religious campaigns (1958–1964).[36] In medical discourse a strong case was being made to show that Soviet nurses were just as kind as the imperial sisters of mercy or their capitalist counterparts in the West. The Soviet Union might have been godless, but such narratives showed that humanity and compassion were important to the atheistic state. Student nurses of the 1940s–1950s knew no alternative to Soviet power but their parents and teachers carried their pre-revolutionary culture with them through the years, especially, according to Natalia Lopatkina, their Orthodox traditions. Lopatkina claims that parents could not fail to teach children and students 'compassion, human decency, and a sense of honour'.[37] However, by the start of the 1960s, she claims, this all changed and Soviet people began to 'forget about mercy and charity'.[38] Although Khrushchev's 1961 Moral Code went some way in addressing this, it generally bypassed their 'atheistic consciousness'.[39]

Hidden nurses

If the *Meditsinskaya sestra* accounts frame state need within the rhetoric of an idealized nurse, files from the Procuracy show a nurse experience that was

35 F. A. Korneliuk (Leningrad), 'Praskov'ya Aleksandrovna Reznichenko', *MS* 3 (1969), 58–59.

36 Victoria Smolkin-Rothrock, 'The Ticket to the Soviet Soul: Science, Religion, and the Spiritual Crisis of Late Soviet Atheism', *Russian Review* 23 (2014) 171–197 (178).

37 Lopatkina, *Kul'turologicheskie aspekty*, 116–117.

38 Ibid., 118.

39 Ibid., 118.

more variegated and reflective of the wider Soviet experience. This becomes clear when one looks at the case of a 62-year-old nurse who wrote to the Procurator in 1956 requesting to have her case re-examined.[40] Nurse Ponomareva, at the time in Kazakhstan, had worked as a nurse in Moscow's nervous-psychiatric dispensary No 12 from 1927 to 1944. She was from a working class background, originally from Sverdlovsk, but in March 1945 was arrested and sentenced to five years corrective labour in the gulag for her 'anti-Soviet mood'. She had become caught up, it seemed, in the 'guilt' of the director of the hospital where she worked (Professor N. P. Brukhanskii, who was also arrested). She had defended him, claiming that over the course of nine years she had not noticed him commit any anti-Soviet agitation. Ponomareva had been unlucky and was just one of the many who happened to be persecuted for 'guilt by association'. T. A. Kil'dyaeva, a senior nurse working in Rtish-chevskaya polyclinic (Saratov) was another who fell prey to the underbelly of Stalinism, arrested as part of a group accused of a 'mood of terror in relation to Stalin'. The group had gathered in an apartment and told anecdotes, during which time Kil'dyaeva allegedly claimed that in the Soviet Union 'democracy was for display only'.[41] Her case had come up for review in 1954. Petropavlovskaya's experience highlighted the stark contrast between state rhetoric and individual realities.

Similarly another nurse, Natal'ya Ivanova Uskova, an 88-year-old Kursk native working as a senior nurse in a Moscow children's infectious diseases hospital, was arrested in 1949 for her 'anti-Soviet mood' and her 'anti-Soviet' agitation amongst 'her circle'.[42] She was also accused of making 'vile, slanderous fabrications' against party leaders and the Soviet government, and 'spreading provocative rumours'. In her own defence, Uskova claimed to have little interest in politics. The 1956 'amnesty' resulted in the curtailment of her sentence on account of her 'low political education, old age, and poor state of health'.[43] The fact that she had spent 43 years working as a senior nurse in a surgical department – prized Soviet experience – did not help mitigate her case. She wanted full rehabilitation, as well as the return of her apartment in Moscow. Alone and in poor health, she still worked in the district hospital.[44] All she asked was to see out the rest of her days quietly 'in her own corner without the label of enemy'. Duration of service was, however, taken into consideration in the case of nurse Alla Aleksandrovna Burma who was eventually pardoned her ten-year sentence in a corrective labour camp because she had worked as a public transport *zdravpunkt* (health centre) nurse in the Caucasus for 20 years. Also considered was her 'low level of development', her 'present status as an invalid', and absence of any prior

40 GARF, f. R-8131, op. 31, d. 14302, ll. 178–179.
41 GARF, f. R-8131, op. 31, d. 30258, l. 19. 12/7/1954.
42 GARF, f. R-8131, op. 31, d. 18238, l. 1.
43 GARF, f. R-8131, op. 31, d. 18238, l. 28, l. 40.
44 GARF, f. R-8131, op. 31, d. 18238, l. 40.

convictions.[45] The vagaries of the Stalinist system ensured that nurses, like everyone else, could momentarily turn from hero to villain. But the experiences of nurses as a professional group, and as depicted in the pages of *Meditsinskaya sestra*, represent a fascinating process of rejection, tolerance, acceptance, promotion, and admiration – a process that formed a part of the postwar Soviet state's quest to place nurses within a discourse of modernization, evolution, and humanity.

Conclusions

Taking the nursing profession as a prism through which to view broader developments in Soviet society from the October Revolution until the 1960s presents us with a complex picture of nurse experiences but also, more to the point, how nurses were perceived and represented by the state. Because of the religious, aristocratic, and philanthropic nature of pre-revolutionary nursing, this particular profession affords a unique take on values across the 1917 divide. A *longue durée* approach allows us to see the changing representation of the nurse. The sister of mercy who came to prominence during the Crimean War and successive imperial wars embodied values of care and compassion. After the revolution, these values and the image of the Sister of Mercy had become associated with a bourgeois past that was incompatible with socialism. As a result, some nurses were persecuted and murdered, others fled. But the acute need for medical workers meant that there was a pre- and post-revolutionary continuum in medical personnel. During the interwar period the new Soviet state set about creating its own cadre of medical workers, to which the pre-revolutionary sister of mercy did not belong. The medical sister was initially just another 'technical' worker. But the reality was that sisters of mercy worked alongside younger medical sisters and helped train them. The values, discipline, and skills acquired in the sister of mercy communities outlasted the Bolshevik experimentalism of the 1920s. By the postwar period the pre-revolutionary trained nurse was held up as a model for all young nurses to follow. Her wealth of experience and knowledge was valued and she was considered an exemplar of the moral and professional needs of the modern, Soviet nurse. War experience, more than revolutionary credentials, ultimately validated the Soviet nurse and acted as a common thread linking the imperial past and the Soviet present.

45 GARF, f. R-8131, op. 31, d. 18238, ll. 20–21. General Maior Iustitsii N. Khokhlov (General Mayor of Justice Khokhlov).

8 What did historians do at the time of the great revolution?

*Vera Kaplan**

On 9 January 1917, on the 12th anniversary of Bloody Sunday, Vladimir Lenin, who was still in political exile in Zürich, delivered a lecture at a meeting of Swiss working youth. He concluded his analysis of the first Russian revolution with the remarkable sentence: 'We old men may not live to see the decisive battles of the future revolution'.[1] There were, however, people who assessed Russia's revolutionary prospects differently and, as it became clear in retrospect, more correctly. Some weeks earlier, on 12 December 1916, Nadezhda Platonova, wife of the eminent Petrograd historian, Sergei Platonov, and herself a kind of chronicler of the life of historians, wrote in her diary: 'The moods in Moscow are absolutely revolutionary' and described the terrible feeling (*zhutkoe chuvstvo*) with which her daughter, a secondary school history teacher, taught the subject of the French revolution in those winter days of 1916 in Petrograd.[2] A more detailed analysis of the situation can be found in a letter from the Moscow historian, Stepan Veselovskii, to Platonov in April 1917, in which he wrote:

> The inevitability and proximity of the revolution already became obvious in January and February. The numerous signs of extreme disorder in the entire administrative machinery made it possible to predict the imminent paralysis of the authorities. Meanwhile it continues and is deepening. The revival of authority and restoring it to health in such a huge and insufficiently cultured country as Russia is the 'music of the future'. From this perspective, the events of late February–early March are minor episodes. Undoubtedly, the war is slowing down the process of disintegration, which provides the last hope, but, at the same time, makes the tasks of the new regime more difficult.[3]

* This research was supported by the Israel Science Foundation (grant no 936/15).

1 V. I. Lenin, 'Doklad o revoliutsii 1905 goda', *Polnoe sobranie sochinenii*, vol. 30 (Moscow: Politizdat, 1969), 307–328, here 328.

2 Note of 12 December 1916, Otdel rukopisei Rossiiskoi natsional'noi biblioteki (OR RNB), f. 585 Platonov S. F., op. 1, d. 5696, Dnevnik N. N. Platonovoi, November 1916–December 1917, l. 22, 23.

3 S. B. Veselovskii to S. F. Platonov, 5 April 1917 in L. G. Dubinskaia and A. M. Dubrovskii (eds), *Perepiska S. B. Veselovskogo s otechestvennymi istorikami*

These and other diaries and letters of Russian historians enable us to examine how they experienced the revolution of 1917. Such prominent Petrograd historians as the above-mentioned Platonov, Alexander Lappo-Danilevskii and Alexander Presniakov, as well as their colleagues in the academic institutions, archives, scholarly archival commissions and historical societies, acted vigorously in order to preserve the existing archives and collect documents created in the course of the revolution. For this purpose they participated in various voluntary associations, supported the reorganization of the existing historical societies, collaborated with governmental bodies – first of the Provisional Government and later of the Soviets – and, in so doing, maintained both their professional status and cultural continuity in a time of profound social upheaval. Moreover, their professional networks proved to be effective in opening paths for integration into the new Soviet academic world where some of the 'old' historians made surprisingly successful careers. This was the result of more than the ability of individuals to adapt themselves to the new circumstances: historians acted as members of a community, which proved to be sufficiently resilient both during the revolutionary crisis and in the problematic post-revolutionary years. This chapter therefore seeks to go beyond the historians' personal biographies in order to explore the life of the historical community and its institutions across 1917. How did the community of historians function before and during the revolutionary years? What was the source of its resilience, or, in terms of social psychology, its ability 'to deal with a state of continuous, long term stress, to find unknown inner strengths and resources in order to cope effectively' with disturbing events, while manifesting the necessary 'measure of adaptation and flexibility'?[4] And last, but not least, what role did historians play in turning revolution into history, in other words, in monitoring, documenting and providing a preliminary description of the events of 1917 – activities that started in the very midst of the dramatic events themselves?

The community of historians on the eve of the great revolution

One of the main characteristics of the pre-revolutionary historical community was its heterogeneity. The documentary sources of the late nineteenth to early

(Moscow: Drevlekhranilishche, 2001), 188. For Veselovskii's biography see Dmitrii Sporov and Sergei Shokarev, 'Istorik Moskovskogo gosudarstva v stalinskoi Rossii: k biografii S. B. Veselovskogo (1876–1952)', *Novoe literaturnoe obozrenie* no 78 (2006), http://magazines.russ.ru/nlo/2006/78/spo6.html, accessed 27 October 2015.

4 I borrow the term 'community resilience' from a comparatively new branch of social psychology, known as community psychology. See Fran H. Norris, Susan P. Stevens, Betty Pfefferbaum, Karen F. Wyche, and Rose L. Pfefferbaum, 'Community Resilience as a Metaphor, Theory, Set of Capacities, and Strategy for Disaster Readiness', *American Journal of Community Psychology*, 41 (2008), 127–150, especially 129, from which the quotation is taken; and Judith C. Kulig, Dana S. Edge, Ivan Townshend, Nancy Lightfoot, and William Reimer, 'Community Resiliency: Emerging Theoretical Insights', *Journal of Community Psychology* 41(6) (July 2013), 758–775.

twentieth century portray lively interaction among university professors, employees of the state archives, amateur members of voluntary historical societies, and activists of the gubernia scholarly archival commissions, and reveal a complex web of professional connections, personal networks, and patronage relationships. These documents demonstrate that not only university departments but also historical societies and local archival commissions functioned as institutional centres for the community of historians. Interaction among these governmental and voluntary bodies reveals their surprising hybridity and provides impressive examples of successful cooperation between state and society. The dynamics of the historical community's pre-revolutionary life, norms and practices that were formed in the course of its diverse activities influenced the historians' responses to the revolutionary events. It is therefore important to understand the internal structure and inner workings of that community in order to decipher historians' behaviour during and after 1917.

Its most influential faction consisted of the professoriate at the universities and the historical-philological, pedagogical, and archaeological institutes. In the discourse of that time the term 'professoriate' referred not only to professors per se, but also to the entire corpus of those who were involved in scholarly research and teaching in institutions of higher education, including the large number of privat-docents (*privat-dotsent*).[5] It is hard to assess the proportion of historians among the Russian professoriate as a whole. According to A. E. Ivanov's calculation, by February 1917 there were 124 institutions of higher education in Russia (including 11 universities), and in the previous two decades there was a sharp rise in the overall number of those who taught in these institutions – from about 2,500 in 1899 to about 4,500 in 1914.[6] The University Statutes of 1884 allotted 12 ordinary (*ordinarnyi*) and five extraordinary (*ekstra-ordinarnyi*) professors to a historical-philological faculty.[7] In addition, each university could make its own decision regarding the number of privat-docents it required: in 1892 for example, 21 privat-docents

5 A. I. Ivanov and I. P. Kulakova, 'Russkaia professura na rubezhe XIX–XX vekov', *Rossiiskaia istoria*, no 2 (March–April 2013), 44–62, especially 44; V. I. Chesnokov and I. V. Chesnokov, 'K voprosu o podgotovke professorov istorii v universitetakh Rossii XIX–XX v'. in *Istoriia i teoriia istoricheskoi nauki i obrazovaniia: Khar'kovskii istoriograficheskii sbornik*, no 1 (1995), 73–85; L. A. Sidorova, 'Stil' zhizni i nauchnogo tvorchestva istorikov Rossii na rubezhe XIX–XX vekov', in *Istoriia i istoriki. 2007. Istoriograficheskii vestnik*, edited by A. N. Sakharov (Moscow: Nauka, 2009), 108–120; V. I. Chesnokov, 'Puti formirovaniia i kharakternye cherty systemy universitetskogo istoricheskogo obrazovaniia v dorevoliutsionnoi Rossii', in *Istoricheskaia kul'tura imperatorskoi Rossii: formirovanie predstavlenii o proshlom*, edited by A. N. Dmitriev (Moscow: Izdatel'skii dom Vysshei shkoly ekonomiki, 2012), 113–117, especially 120; A. V. Antoshchenko and A. V. Sveshnikov, 'Istoricheskii seminarii kak mesto znaniia', in ibid., 138–160.

6 A. E. Ivanov, *Vysshaia shkola Rossii v kontse XIX–nachale XX veka* (Moscow: Institut istorii SSSR, AN SSSR, 1991), 208.

7 Clause 460, 'Svod ustavov uchenykh uchrezhdenii i uchebnykh zavedenii vedomstva ministerstva narodnogo prosveshcheniia' in *Svod zakonov Rossiiskoi imperii*, vol. XI, part I (St Petersburg: Russkoe Knizhnoe Tovarishchestvo 'Deiatel', 1912), 53.

taught at the historical-philological faculty of St Petersburg University.[8] As the first rung on the academic ladder, the post of privat-docent was open to those who successfully defended the first, *magister*'s dissertation, but defence of the second, doctoral dissertation was necessary in order to be eligible for the position of professor.[9] However, according to a study by E. A. Rostovtsev and D. A. Barinov, only 54 of the 448 privat-docents at St Petersburg University in the period from 1884 to 1916 attained the post of professor (i.e. 12 per cent), while at the historical-philological faculty this percentage was even lower – only 8.2 per cent.[10]

Those who had no hope of attaining the rank of professor in one of the institutions for higher education had to seek alternative career opportunities. One attractive option was to work as an archivist; indeed, archivists, whom M. M. Bogoslovskii once defined as 'hunter' historians (*razyskateli*), constituted a numerous, albeit less visible faction of the historical community.[11] In the late nineteenth–early twentieth century archivists as a professional group underwent profound educational and generational changes. On the one hand, the central state archives were still populated by 'elderly keepers of archives', whom Aleksander Kizevetter in his well-known memoirs defined as 'the living debris of the patriarchal past'.[12] Recent university graduates constituted a new kind of archivist, who, according to Kizevetter, contributed a 'serious scholarly approach' to archival work.[13] However, an archivist's career was perceived as less prestigious for a historian than that of university

8 Chesnokov, 'Puti formirovaniia i kharakternye', 129.

9 On the praxis of dissertation defence see Thomas Sanders, 'The Third Opponent: Dissertation Defense and the Public Profile of Academic History in Late Imperial Russia', in *Historiography of Imperial Russia: The Profession and Writing of History in a Multinational State*, edited by Thomas Sanders (Armonk, NY: M. E. Sharp, 1999), 69–97. In addition, a three-year term as privat-docent was necessary for promotion to the level of professor – see clauses 499, 509–512 in 'Svod ustavov uchenykh uchrezhdenii i uchebnykh zavedenii', 56–58. In practice, those who had yet to receive their doctoral degree could be appointed acting professors – E. A. Rostovtsev and D. A. Barinov, 'Prepodavatel'skaia korporatsiia stolichnogo universiteta 1884–1916 gg.: Osnovnye cherty i problemy kollektivnoi biografii', in *Professorsko-prepodavatel'skii korpus rossiiskikh universitetov 1884–1917 gg.: Issledovaniia i dokumenty*, edited by M. V. Gribovskikh and S. F. Fominykh (Tomsk: Izdatel'stvo Tomskogo universiteta, 2012), 35–51, here 38.

10 Rostovtsev and Barinov, 'Prepodavatel'skaia korporatsiia stolichnogo universiteta', 47–48.

11 M. M. Bogoslovskii, 'O trudakh S. A. Belokurova po russkoi istorii', *Russkii istoricheskii zhurnal* 8 (1922), 230, quoted in Sidorova, 'Stil' zhizni i nauchnogo tvorchestva istorikov Rossii na rubezhe XIX–XX vekov', 109. On historian-archivists see also L. I. Shokhin, *Moskovskii arkhiv ministerstva iustitsii i istoricheskaia nauka/Les archives du Ministère de la Justice à Moscou et la science historique de la Russie: Arkhivisty i istoriki vo vtoroi polovine XIX–nachale XX veka* (Moscow: Pamiatniki istoricheskoi mysli, 1999).

12 A. A. Kizevetter, *Na rubezhe dvukh stoletii: Vospominaniia 1881–1914* (Prague: Orbis, 1929; republished, Cambridge: Oriental Research Partners, 1974), 271–272.

13 Ibid., 271.

professor, and the main advantage of an archival job – direct access to historical documents – was sometimes deceptive. Formally, an archivist was a state functionary, and despite their aspiration to scholarly research, they were expected to perform much more technical functions. Thus, Kizevetter noted that the 'young historians' who successfully combined their work in the Archive of the Ministry of Justice with their scholarly studies in the 1880s were pressed to stop their research activity when a new director, the historian of Russian law and archaeologist, Dmitrii Samokvasov, assumed this post in 1892:

> He decided to set everybody to work making inventories of the archival documents and demanded that the archive's employees would not be distracted from this work by writing any essay of a research character. This made the young archivists very annoyed. Essentially, Samokvasov was right, but it would have been possible to implement this reform in a more tactful way.[14]

Kizevetter's uneasy expression of support for Samokvasov's archival policy, as well as his use of the word 'reform', was related to the new developments taking place in the field of archives in the fin-de-siècle years. The same Samokvasov whom Kizevetter accused of preventing young archivists from fulfilling their scholarly aspirations conceived a major archival reform intended to create a network of empire-wide historical archives, which were to take the form of scholarly institutions. He proposed establishing a central archive administration and three types of state archives open to the public: the central archive, 12 district archives, and one archive in each gubernia.[15] A more detailed version of the plan was presented in Samokvasov's book *Archival Work in Russia* (*Arkhivnoe delo v Rossii*) issued in 1902, which proposed establishing a main archive administration, specialized institutes for training archivists and 90 gubernia archives.[16]

His plan to set up special institutions for training archivists was based on the existing examples of archaeological institutes that had been established in St Petersburg in 1877 and Moscow in 1907 with the aim of training specialists for 'posts (*dlia dolzhnostei*) in state, public and private archives, museums and

14 Ibid., 274–275.

15 'Otnoshenie Departamenta Ministerstva Narodnogo Prosveshcheniia ot 13 aprelia 1903 no 12033' in *Sbornik materialov otnosiashchikhsia do arkhivnoi chasti v Rossii,* vol. I (Petrograd: Russkoe Istoricheskoe Obshchestvo, 1916), 675.

16 D. Ia. Samokvasov, *Arkhivnoe delo v Rosiii v 2-kh knigakh* (Moscow: Tovarishestvo tip. A. I. Mamontova, 1902), 26. For Samokvasov's biography see S. P. Shchavelev, *Istorik russkoi zemli: Zhizn' i trudy D. Ia. Samokvasova* (Kursk, Izdatel'stvo KGMU: 1998) and idem (ed.), *Arkheologiia, istoriia i arkhivnoe delo Rossii v perepiske professora D. Ia. Samokvasova, 1843–1911* (Kursk: Izdatel'stvo KGMU, 2007); T. I. Khorkhordina, 'D. Ia. Samokvasov: konservator-reformator', *Otechestvennye arkhivy,* no 2 (2000), 26–41.

libraries'.[17] The Regulations of the St Petersburg Archaeological Institute even used the term 'specialists in *arkhivovedenie*', that is, 'the science of archives' or the scholarly supervision of archives.[18] According to Samokvasov's plan, the first stage in the archival reform would be the establishment of a temporary commission at the State Council, followed by the creation of the main archival administration, state archives in the gubernia towns and, finally, a professoriate in archival studies in the Schools of Archives (*shkoly arkhivovedeniia*) which would be modelled on the European (especially French) schools. While the actual idea of archival reform was enthusiastically supported by both academic institutions and governmental bodies, the scope and, especially, the huge funding demanded for its implementation (up to 1,130.000 rubles according to Samokvasov's calculation) led to fierce debates.[19] Eventually they focused on one particular aspect of the reform – its possible impact on the fate of the gubernia scholarly archival commissions. They thus brought yet another segment of the historical community into the limelight – the members of these commissions.

The gubernia scholarly archival commissions had been established from 1884 in order to locate materials of scholarly value among the documents destined for destruction by gubernia and uezd governmental, estate (*soslovnyi*), and public (*obshchestvennyi*) bodies, to deposit them in historical archives that were to be established at the commissions and, finally, to catalogue the documents in these archives in order to make them available for scholarly purposes. In addition, the local archival commissions were allowed to 'explore other relics (*pamiatniki stariny*) of the past'.[20] According to the original idea of the 'founding father' of the commissions, Nikolai Kalachov, a member of the Academy of Sciences and the founder of the St Petersburg Archaeological Institute, these commissions were to constitute the first level in the future structure of the country's scholarly studies. Significantly, the decree (*polozhenie*) of 1884 on the gubernia scholarly archival commissions conceived the latter as private (*chastnye*), not governmental bodies: each of them was to be established by agreement between the director of the St Petersburg Archaeological Institute (until 1885 this was Kalachov himself) and the local governor, who

17 'Polozhenie o Moskovskom Arkheologicheskom Institute', *Sobranie uzakonenii i rasporiazhenii pravitel'stva, izdavaemoe pri Pravitel'stvuiushchem Senate*, 20 February 1907 (St Petersburg, 1907), part 1, 414. See more on these institutions in M. F. Khartanovich, *Gumanitarnye nauchnye uchrezhdeniia Sankt-Peterburga XIX veka* (St Petersburg: Izdatel'stvo St. Peterburgskogo otdeleniia Instituta Istorii RAN 'Nestor-Istoriia', 2006), 188–200.

18 Tsentral'nyi Gosudarstvennyi istoricheskii arkhiv St. Petersburga (TsGIA Spb), f. 119, Arkheologicheskii Institut, op. 2, d. 48, O reorganizatsii instituta, l. 11.

19 'Otnoshenie Ministra Vnutrennikh Del ot 28 Iiunia 1903 za no 15.234 po voprosu ob arkhivnoi reforme v Rossii' in *Sbornik materialov otnosiashchikhsia do arkhivnoi chasti v Rossii*, vol. I, 675.

20 'Proekt polozheniia o gubernskikh istoricheskikh arkhivakh i uchenykh arkhivnykh komisiiakh [13 April 1884]' in *Sbornik materialov otnosiashchikhsia do arkhivnoi chasti v Rossii*, vol. I, 662–663.

was given the status of custodian (*popechitel'*) of the commission. The commission's chair, his deputy, and secretary (*pravitel' del*) were to be elected by the commission itself, while the commissions as a whole were subordinated to the Archaeological Institute and, via the latter, to the Academy of Sciences. Moreover, the Archaeological Institute was to subsidize the commissions from its own budget, with additional funding to be raised from 'local donations to the benefit of scholarship'.[21] The members of the commission were expected to be 'well educated' – a condition that the Ministry of the Interior's official documents interpreted as 'holding a university degree', but no particular historical education was required. However, these documents also made it clear that the members were not supposed to serve in the gubernia's administration, in other words, they were not expected to be *chinovniki*.[22] The gubernia scholarly archival commissions were originally envisioned, therefore, as voluntary learned societies under the auspices of the local governors. The commissions' essentially voluntary character enabled local lay 'enthusiasts for the past' (*liubitely stariny*) to join the community of historians.

At first, four gubernia scholarly archival commissions were established in Tambov, Riazan, Tver and Orel,[23] and subsequently in other, mainly central gubernias. As they increased in number and broadened the scope of their activity, the question of their status eventually arose, triggered by Samokvasov's project of archival reform. Samokvasov himself saw the growing number of commissions as rather alarming: from his point of view, their laymen members did not meet the expected criterion of education and were unable to fulfil the functions they were charged with. In his 1902 book he argued that 'it is not enough to have a general education in order to assess the historical value of an ancient act or file; a knowledge of archival science and its auxiliary disciplines is necessary for this purpose.' Noting that most members of the commissions were former students of ecclesiastical seminars or former gymnasia pupils, elementary school teachers, officers, landowners (*pomeshchiki*), merchants, booksellers, and local governmental officials without any university education, he warned that 'With such composition of the commissions, it is by no means certain that the relics of the Russian land's historical life are being more preserved than destroyed.' Archival work, he insisted, needed 'specially trained well-educated archivists', and suggested transferring such work from the voluntary scholarly archival commissions to such well-trained specialists in the government service.[24]

Surprisingly, an opposing point of view was expressed in 1903 by the conservative Minister of Interior Vyacheslav von Plehve, who asserted that:

21 Ibid., 663.

22 'Predstavlenie Ministra Vnutrennikh Del 17 marta 1884 g. no 7867', in *Sbornik materialov otnosiashchikhsia do arkhivnoi chasti v Rossii*, vol. I, 661.

23 'Proekt polozheniia o gubernskikh istoricheskikh arkhivakh i uchenykh arkhivnykh komisiiakh' and 'Vypiska iz zhurnala Komiteta Ministrov 3 Aprelia 1884 g', in *Sbornik materialov otnosiashchikhsia do arkhivnoi chasti v Rossii*, vol. I, 662–664.

24 Samokvasov, *Arkhivnoe delo v Rosiii*, 26.

> until that distant time when Professor Samokvasov's plan for establishing a main archival administration is realized and state archives with their special staff are created in every gubernia city, the gubernia scholarly archival commissions are destined for many years to come to be the only local scholarly institution that can be entrusted with managing archival work in the gubernias.[25]

He regarded the gubernia scholarly archival commissions as 'governmental bodies' (*pravitel'stvennoe uchrezhdenie*), thus ascribing the role of state institution to what had originally been conceived as voluntary associations. This new approach led to proposals to grant the archival commissions governmental financial support. At the same time, however, the Minister of Interior proposed that the reform plan should be placed under the scholarly supervision of a commission of experts from the Imperial Academy of Sciences and 'other learned societies'.[26] He thus drew attention to the historical societies, which were another kind of voluntary institution that, irrespective of their particular goals and location, served as flexible frameworks in which academic historians, archivists, history teachers, publishers of historical journals and erudite amateurs could meet and cooperate. The members of such societies constituted yet another segment of the historical community.

It is difficult to establish how many historical societies existed in Russia in the early twentieth century. According to the reliable *Encyclopedic Dictionary* by Brokgauz and Efron, there were 11 historical societies in 1894, when the volume containing the relevant entry was published.[27] A later list of learned societies compiled by the Ministry of Education in the early 1900s and kept in Platonov's personal archive, included 27 historical and archaeological societies.[28] Although they all had the same juridical status of voluntary or private

25 'Otnoshenie Ministra Vnutrennikh Del ot 28 Iiunia 1903 za no 15.234 po voprosu ob arkhivnoi reforme v Rossii', in *Sbornik materialov otnosiashchikhsia do arkhivnoi chasti v Rossii*, vol. I, 678.

26 Ibid.

27 V. Rudakov, 'Istoricheskie obshchestva', in *Entsyklopedicheskii slovar'*, vol. XIIIa, edited by F. A. Brokgauz and I. A. Efron (St Petersburg: Tipo-Litografiia I. A. Efrona, 1894), 483–488.

28 OR RNB, f. 585, op. 1, d. 526, Spisok Uchenykh Obshchestv Vedomstva Ministerstva Narodnogo prosveshcheniia, l. 1–2ob. The list included 134 learned societies concerned with a variety of scholarly disciplines. See also A. D. Stepanskii, 'K istorii nauchno-istoricheskikh obshchestv v dorevoliutsionnoi Rossii', in S. O. Shmidt (ed.), *Arkheograficheskii ezhegodnik za 1974 g.*, (Moscow: Nauka, 1975), 38–54; idem, *Istoriia nauchnykh uchrezhdenii i organizatsii dorevoliutsionnoi Rossii* (Moscow: MGIAI, 1987); Wladimir Bérélowitch, 'History in Russia Comes of Age: Institution-Building, Cosmopolitanism, and Theoretical Debates among Historians in Late Imperial Russia', *Kritika: Explorations in Russian and Eurasian History* 9(1) (Winter 2008), 113–134; V. V. Boiarchenkov, 'Obshchestvo istorii i drevnostei rossiiskikh v seredine 1840-kh gg', *Voprosy istorii*, 4 (2008), 114–121; idem, '"Sekretar' antikvarnogo sosloviia": O. M. Bodianskii v Obshchestve istorii i drevnostei rossiiskikh', *Slavianovedenie* no 2 (2009), 91–102; Vera Kaplan, 'From Soslovie to Voluntary

societies (*chastnye obshchestva)*, there were certain hierarchical differences among them, which were reflected, in particular, in Plehve's letter of 1903. His list of the societies that, he believed, could participate in the commission of experts for the archival reform was headed by those designated as Imperial – the Moscow and the Russian Archaeological Societies, the Russian Historical Society (*Russkoe istoricheskoe obshchestvo* [RIO]), the Society of Lovers of Ancient Russian Literature (*Obshchestvo liubitelei drevnei pis'mennosti*), and the Society for Russian History and Antiquities at Moscow University (*Obshchestvo istorii i drevnostei rossiiskikh*). Next came the Society of Zealots of Russian Historical Education in Memory of Alexander III (*Obshchestvo revnitelei russkogo istoricheskogo prosveshcheniia v pamiat' imperatora Aleksandra III*), the Historical-Philological Society at Khar'kov University and the Odessa Society for Russian History and Antiquities.[29] The list included both the oldest societies (the Society for Russian History and Antiquities at Moscow University established in 1804 and a similar Odessa society founded in 1839) and the relatively new Society of Zealots of Russian Historical Education launched only in 1895, but did not contain the societies at the leading St Petersburg and Moscow universities.

The common denominator among the societies chosen by Plehve was not only their scholarly reputation, but also the leading role played by historians from among the dignitary (*sanovnye istoriki*). The highest-ranking among them were Grand Duke Nikolai Mikhailovich, who headed the Imperial Russian Historical Society, Count Sergei Sheremetev, who chaired the Society of Lovers of Ancient Russian Literature and the Society of Zealots of Russian Historical Education, and Countess Praskovia Uvarova, who was chair of the Moscow Archaeological Society. In 1911, Emperor Nicholas II, acting in his capacity of honorary chair of the Russian Historical Society, suggested that the society take upon itself the task of supervising the gubernia commissions in developing a network of local archives.[30] The Emperor's intervention in the long-standing discussions on the status of the gubernia scholarly archival commissions led to paradoxical results: while increasing their importance as state agents, it also accentuated their non-governmental character by subordinating them to a voluntary historical society. From 1912 the Russian Historical Society served as a channel through which information about the preservation of documents by local

Associations: New Patterns of Collective Identities in Late Imperial Russia', *Cahiers du Monde Russe* 51, 2–3 (April–September 2010), 369–396; idem, 'Istoricheskie obshchestva i ideia istoricheskogo prosveshcheniia', in *Istoricheskaia kul'tura imperatorskoi Rossii: Formirovanie predstávlenii o proshlom*, edited by A. N. Dmitriev (Moscow: Vysshaia Shkola Ekonomiki, 2012), 355–380.

29 'Otnoshenie Ministra Vnutrennikh Del ot 28 Iiunia 1903 za no 15.234 po voprosu ob arkhivnoi reforme v Rossii', 678.

30 'Protokol zasedaniia Imperatorskogo Russkogo Istoricheskogo Obshchestva 3 Maia 1911', in *Sbornik materialov otnosiashchikhsia do arkhivnoi chasti v Rossii*, vol. I, 680–681.

bodies was conveyed by gubernia scholarly archival commissions to the centre, and governmental financial support was transferred from the Council of Ministers to the gubernia commissions.[31]

In addition to these main sectors of the historical community, there were other groups such as members of the governmental Archaeographic and Archaeological Commissions and employees of gubernia statistical committees.[32] All these various groups and factions were closely interconnected through multiple formal and informal links and networks of professional and personal relations, while archaeological congresses and conferences constituted an important channel of communication among different segments of the historical community. The first of such congresses, initiated by the Moscow Archaeological Society, took place in Moscow in 1869, after which they were held every three years in various localities throughout the Russian Empire until the beginning of the First World War – the last archaeological congress (the 16th) was scheduled to be held in Pskov in 1914 but never took place. These events stimulated public interest in local history and generated the formation of local archaeological expeditions, new scholarly gubernia archival commissions and local historical societies.

As a result, the State Duma's report of 1908 mentioned 'the hundreds of members in each of the local archival commissions', and claimed that, taken together, the members of all the 25 commissions (that existed at that time) constituted 'an archival and archaeological force (*druzhina*) of some thousands of activists'.[33] By 1914 a report of the Russian Historical Society already noted 27 commissions, including that of Irkutsk, opened in 1911, and provided information on the state of archives in western and eastern Siberia, Sakhalin, Kamchatka and Manchuria.[34] The growing 'density' of the archival commissions made it possible to organize regional activity. In 1903 the gubernia archival commission of Iaroslavl' initiated the first local archaeological conference, followed by those of Tver (1904), Vladimir (1906), and Kostorma (1909).[35]

31 'Izvlechenie iz godovogo otcheta Imperatorskogo Russkogo Istoricheskogo Obshchestva, 13 Marta 1914', in *Sbornik materialov otnosiashchikhsia do arkhivnoi chasti v Rossii*, vol. I, 688.

32 On the Imperial Archeographic and Archeological Commissions see Khartanovich, *Gumanitarnye nauchnye uchrezhdeniia Sankt-Peterburga XIX veka*, 72–127; for the involvement of gubernia statistical committees in regional historical studies, see the comprehensive research by Viktor Berdinskikh, *Uezdnye istoriki: Russkaia provintsial'naia istoriografiia* (Moscow: Novoe literaturnoe obozrenie, 2003).

33 'Doklad Komissii po napravleniiu zakonodatel'nykh predpolozhenii Gosudarstvennoi Dumy po vnesennomu Ministrom Vnutrennikh Del zakonoproektu ob assignovanii iz kazny denezhnykh sredstv na vydachu gubernskim uchenym arkhivnym komissiiam ezhegodnykh posobii (predstavlenie ot 23 Oktiabria 1908 goda za no 19868), 12 Dekabria 1908 g', in *Sbornik materialov otnosiashchikhsia do arkhivnoi chasti v Rossii*, vol. I, 669.

34 'Izvlechenie iz otcheta godovogo sobraniia Imperatorskogo Russkogo Istoricheskogo Obshchestva, 13 Marta 1914', in ibid., vol. I, 688.

35 'Doklad Komissii po napravleniiu zakonodatel'nykh predpolozhenii Gosudarstvennoi Dumy', 670.

Addressing the Iaroslavl' conference, Platonov (already a distinguished professor at St Petersburg University) outlined the desirable pattern of cooperation between scholars from leading universities and local amateur historians. According to him, 'the more broadly and actively the local past is studied, the more national history as a whole benefits from this'. But he insisted that 'local studies will be useful only if they are conducted in full accordance with scholarly standards and deliberately apply the methods of historical scholarship'.[36]

The notion of expertise, regarded as a kind of absolute yardstick, played a significant role in 'gluing together' the various segments of the historical community: University historians, in accordance with the Russian intelligentsia's ideals and norms of behaviour, saw their mission as imparting scholarly knowledge to provincial *kraevedy*.[37] This attitude to their professional and public duty may explain the willingness with which Platonov and his colleagues participated in the various projects launched by the archival commissions – from organizing special courses for local history enthusiasts to time-consuming editing of the commissions' publications. Yet the cooperation between historians in the capital and the provinces was beneficial not only to the latter. Local and all-Russian archaeological conferences and congresses were a tribune where young university scholars could obtain their first lecturing experience. Involvement in the activity of the local archival commissions also had an impact on the status of the historical societies. In May 1914 the Russian Historical Society organized the first all-Russian congress of the scholarly gubernia archival commissions which took place in the palace of the society's head, Grand Duke Nikolai Mikhailovich, in St Petersburg. The decisions of this conference, which asked to increase the number of commissions and provide each of them with an annual grant of 3,000 rubles, concluded, in a sense, the previous discussions on the archival commissions. The conference supported the affiliation of the gubernia commissions' members with the special archival committee of the Russian Historical Society, which meant, *inter alia*, placing the commissions under the Emperor's auspices.[38] These decisions could have 'upgraded' the institutional

36 S. F. Platonov's address to Iaroslavl's regional archeological conference (a conference of researchers of history and antiquities of Rostov-Suzdal region), 12 August 1901, supplement to Smirnov, Ia. E. Smirnov, 'S. F. Platonov i iaroslavskoe kraevedenie', in *Arkheograficheskii ezhegodnik za 2009–2010 gg.*, edited by S. O. Shmidt (Moscow: Nauka, 2012), 227–286: here 282.

37 V. P. Makarikhin, *Gubernskie uchenye arkhivnye komissii Rossii* (Nizhnii Nogorod, 1991); V. V. Mitrofanov, 'Sotrudnichestvo S. F. Platonova s gubernskimi uchenymi arkhivnymi komissiiami', *Novyi istoricheskii vestnik* 17(1) (2008), 76–83; E. N. Gruzdeva, 'S. F. Platonov and S. V. Rozhdestvenskii', in *Pamiati akademika Sergeia Fedorovicha Platonova: Issledovaniia i materialy*, edited by A. Iu. Dvornichenko and S. O. Shmidt (St Petersburg: St Petersburg State University and OIFN RAN, 2011), 362–374, here 365.

38 'Izvlechenie iz otcheta godovogo sobraniia Imperatorskogo Russkogo Istoricheskogo Obshestva 12 Marta 1915', in *Sbornik materialov otnosiashchikhsia do arkhivnoi chasti v Rossii,* vol. I, 691.

standing of both the commissions and the Russian Historical Society, but the outbreak of the First World War postponed their implementation.

Another proposed project whose realization would have had a significant impact on the Russian historical community in general if it had not been thwarted by the war, was the Fourth International Historical Congress scheduled to be held in St Petersburg in 1918. Preparations for this congress started in 1913; the committees and commissions engaged in preparing the congress became the new centre of the historical community's life, but their activity was curtailed when it became clear that there was no chance of holding the congress at the scheduled time.[39] Yet, while the war disturbed the realization of some major projects, it also stimulated the activity of the historical community. Thus, in March 1915, a conference of Russian history professors that took place at Moscow university decided to organize congresses of Russian historians every five years, under the title of Russian Historical Congresses in the Name of Emperor Nicholas II; these congresses were defined as a 'new institution, extremely important for the development of Russian historical scholarship'. They were planned to be held in one of the university cities; the corresponding university would be responsible for the preparations. The first of such congresses was scheduled for December 1919 in Moscow, when the 25th anniversary of Nicholas II's reign was expected to be celebrated.[40] In the course of preparation for this congress, the Historical Society at Moscow University launched its journal, *Historical News* (*Istoricheskie izvestiia*): the Society's members, claimed the rector of Moscow University, Matvei Liubavskii, refused to contemplate the idea that the future congress would take place without Russian historians having their own 'scholarly and informative organ'.[41] A year later, in 1916, a group of Petrograd historians associated with the Historical Society at Petrograd University, including Lappo-Danilevskii and Presniakov, launched their own *Russian Historical*

39 Arkhiv Sankt-Peterburgskogo Otdeleniia Instituta Istorii Rossiikoi Akademii Nauk (ASpbOII RAN), f. 193 Presniakov A. E., op. 3, d. 2 Protokoly zasedanii predvaritel'nogo Soveshchaniia po voprosu ob ustroistve Mezhdunarodnogo istoricheskogo s'ezda v Sankt-Peterburge v 1918 g., l. 21–26. The fourth international historical congress was finally held in 1923 in Brussels. For a history of the international historical congresses see Karl Dietrich Erdmann, *Toward a Global Community of Historians: The International Historical Congresses and the International Committee of Historical Sciences, 1898–2000* (New York and Oxford: Berghahn Books, 2005); for the participation of Russian historians in such congresses, see N. S. Zonova, 'Rossiiskie istoriki na mezhdunarodnykh kongressakh istoricheskikh nauk nachala XX veka', PhD dissertation (Nizhnii Novgorod: Nizhegorodskii Gosudarstvennyi Arkhitekturno-Stroitel'nyi Institut, 2004).

40 V. G. Bukhert, 'Soveshchanie professorov russkoi istorii i istorii russkogo prava Rossiiskikh universitetov (Moscow, 26–28 marta 1915 g.)' in *Arkheograficheskii ezhegodnik za 2009–2010 gg.*, edited by S. O. Shmidt (Moscow: Nauka, 2012), 179–194, here 184–189.

41 Ibid., 189; Obrashchenie Redaktsionnogo komiteta, *Istoricheskie izvestiia izdavaemye istoricheskim obshchestvom pri Imperatorskom moskovskom universitete*, no 1 (1916), 3–4.

Journal (*Russkii istoricheskii zhurnal*) with the similar aim of informing all 'workers in Russian history' about recent developments in the field.[42]

The first volumes of the journals, issued in 1916 and early 1917 in Moscow and Petrograd respectively, contained information about lively activity in both the centre and the provinces and revealed new trends in the life of the historical community, in particular a growing tendency for closer cooperation.[43] This was strikingly manifested by a project to 'unify' the activity of historical, archival and archaeological societies in order to enhance their 'greater productivity' without limiting the societies' independent status. This suggestion was made in October 1915 by the Society of Zealots of History, which had been founded only in 1911 and whose name emulated that of the already existing Society of Zealots of Russian Historical Education. Although the more established societies regarded this proposal as the insolent initiative of a novice body and furiously rejected it, the very idea of unification became part of the contemporary discourse.[44] Another new trend was to collect materials connected with the great contemporary event, the First World War. This shift in emphasis from the study of the past to creating a documentary database on the ongoing events led to the appearance of new modes of historical work. The governmental 'commissions of captured materials' (the Commission on Cataloguing the Russian Army's Military Trophies and the Old Banners and the Commission on the Collection and Preservation of Trophies of the Current War), created in 1911 and 1916, were to record the heroic deeds of both combat units and individual soldiers and officers, and to gather information about all holders of the St George Cross.[45] Historical societies and local historical, archival and archaeological commissions opened special departments for studying 'the great war'. Thus, the Voronezh historical and archaeological church committee collected information about clerics' participation in the war,[46] while the Society of Zealots of History started to accumulate documents and visual materials for founding a Museum of the Great War.[47]

All in all, the Russian historical community lived an intense and rich life on the eve of the revolution. In the autumn and winter of 1916–early 1917

42 'Ot redaktsii', *Russkii istoricheskii zhurnal* 1(1–2) (1917), 3–7.

43 'Khronika', *Russkii istoricheskii zhurnal* 1(1–2) (1917), 143. Issues 1–4 of *Istoricheskie izvestiia* appeared in 1916; the first issue of *Russkii istoricheskii zhurnal* was published in early 1917.

44 Rossiiskii gosudarstvennyi istoricheskii arkhiv (RGIA), f. 746 Russkoe istoricheskoe obshchestvo, op. 1, d. 195 Ob organizatsii Vserossiiskogo soiuza istoricheskikh obshchestv, ll. 1–5ob.

45 A. A. Vasil'ev, 'Deiatel'nost' russkikh trofeinykh komissii v period Pervoi mirovoi voiny 1914–1018 (po materialam RGVIA)' in *Pervaia mirovaia voina: Prolog XX veka,* V. L. Mal'kov (Moscow: Nauka, 1998), 657–665.

46 'Khronika', *Russkii istoricheskii zhurnal* 1(1–2) (1917), 168.

47 TsGIA Spb, f. 2168 Obshchestvo revnitelei istorii, op. 1, d. 16 'Otchety, postanovleniia, vozzvaniia, stikhi, ob'iavleniia, prislannye gorodskimi i zemskimi uchrezhdeniiami, uchebnymi zavedeniiami, voennymi shtabami v sviazi so sborom obshestvom materialov dlia muzeia velikoi voiny'.

Russian historians, although closely following political, war, and court events (especially those connected with Rasputin and his murder), had their own agenda as well. In August 1916 the historical and archaeological societies undertook a joint attempt to prevent the construction of a railway line between Petrograd and Orel which would lie too close to the famous Spasa-Nereditsy Church and thus threaten to cause irreparable damage to its precious frescoes.[48] From October 1916 the capital's historians were involved in the establishment of the new University of Perm as a branch of Petrograd University.[49] In November 1915 the Kazan' gubernia scholarly archival commission was solemnly opened, which brought the number of commissions to a total of 40.[50] In the same month, the commission on the scholarly cataloguing of the Archive of the Ministry of Education, which was established on November 1915 on Platonov's initiative and under his chairmanship, announced the appearance of the first volume of its proceedings.[51] In December 1916 the Ministry of Education reminded the *popechitel'* of the Moscow educational district of the necessity to solicit from the rector of Moscow University a draft of the Statutes of the historical congress in order to publicize it well in advance.[52] In January–February 1917 historians talked about the unforeseen blossoming of the book market and discussed the resignation of the popular Minister of Education Ignatiev.[53] All these topics, however, lost their relevance from late February 1917 – along with the historians' previous plans and schedules. Nadezhda Platonova wrote in her diary:

> And now revolution has broken out! On the 25th of February we still thought that Sergei Fedorovich would go to Perm [where he was supposed to lecture from 27 February to 30 March], but by the evening of the 26th it became clear that it was impossible.[54]

The new situation raised the question formulated by Platonov in his letter to Veselovskii in the most straightforward way: 'What can we, armchair people,

48 'Khronika', *Russkii istoricheskii zhurnal* 1(1–2) (1917), 174.
49 Note of 8 December 1916, OR RNB, f. 585, op. 1, d. 5696, Dnevnik N. N. Platonovoi, November 1916–December 1917, ll. 17–18; 18–18ob.
50 'Khronika', *Russkii istoricheskii zhurnal* 1(1–2) (1917), 168. I have based the number of gubernia scholarly archival commissions on N. V. Brzhostovskaia, 'Gubernskie uchenye arkhivnye komissii', in *Sovetskaia istoricheskaia entsiklopediia*, vol. 4, edited by E. M. Zhukov (Moscow: 'Sovetskaia entsiklopediia', 1963), 871–873.
51 'Khronika', *Russkii istoricheskii zhurnal* 1(1–2) (1917), 143.
52 Bukhert, 'Soveshchanie professorov russkoi instorii i istorii russkogo prava Rossiiskikh universitetov (Moscow, 26–28 marta 1915 g.)', 189.
53 Notes of 11 and 29 December 1916, OR RNB, f. 585, op. 1, d. 5696, ll. 20–21, 23–24, 29ob.–32.
54 Note of 6 April 1917, OR RNB, f. 585, op. 1, d. 5696, l. 43. 'I was sent by the Minister of Education to lecture in the Perm branch of Petrograd University from 27 February to 30 March', Platonov informed Grand Duchess Elizaveta Mavrikievna, see OR RNB, f. 585 d. 1772, Pis'ma v. kn. Elizavete Mavrikievne, l. 23.

do in the current circumstances?'[55] His own answer was 'just wait', but it soon became clear that some of the revolutionary developments would not allow him and his colleagues to remain aloof.

What caused the 'armchair people' to get up and take action?

On the last day of February and the very first days of March 1917, when the Provisional Government had just been established, a huge bonfire was already blazing near the police headquarters. Crowds of unknown people burned piles of documents, and as witnesses to such a conflagration recalled later, former policemen frequently participated in these spontaneous pogroms.[56] No less alarming than the mob's behaviour was the lenient tone in the revolutionary press: thus, the most influential of the newly established organs, the *News of the Soviet of the Workers Deputies* (*Izvestiia Soveta Rabochikh Deputatov*), wrote in its very first issue:

> The district court and *Okhranka* [secret political police department] are burning down, some police stations are on fire, the papers of *okhranniks* and provocateurs have been burned. The people have made short work of the papers of these scum who are corroding the country and dealing painful blows to the revolutionary people. It is necessary to destroy everything that could help the minions of the old regime, but it is essential to avoid conflagrations and acts of arson that threaten the safety and property of peaceful citizens.[57]

Furthermore, even the organized process of replacing the old offices with new ones frequently led to a massive loss of documents: the new staff usually had neither the time nor the desire to think about preserving their predecessors' papers. Yet, the same papers that the revolutionaries perceived as the unnecessary remains of the old regime were regarded as valuable documents by members of the historical community. The debates on preserving the archives, which had taken place in the previous years, had made them especially sensitive to the issue and can explain the historians' quick response to this emergency situation.

As early as 3 March 1917 the Academy of Sciences obtained Minister of Law A. F. Kerenskii's permission to remove from the Department of Police all papers and documents that the Academy's representative, Nestor Kotliarevskii, would deem necessary and to house them in the Academy of Sciences.[58] In the following days Alexander Lebedev, the supervisor of the Navy Ministry's

55 S. F. Platonov to S. B. Veselovskii, 12 April 1917, in *Perepiska S. B. Veselovskogo s otechestvennymi istorikami*, 189.

56 T. I. Khorkhordina, *Istoriia i arkhivy* (Moscow: RGGU, 1994), 11.

57 'Ne dopuskaite grabezhei', *Izvestiia Soveta Rabochikh Deputatov*, 28 February 1917. From 2 March 1917 the newspaper was called *Izvestiia Soveta Rabochikh i Soldatskikh Deputatov*.

58 Ministr Iustitsii, ch. G[osudarstvennoi] D[umy] Kerenskii, 'Prikaz o vyvoze bumag iz Departamenta Politsii', *Izvestiia Soveta Rabochikh i Soldatskikh Deputatov*, 3 March 1917.

archive, a Navy officer and a graduate of the St Petersburg Archaeological institute, sent a letter to the capital's archivists and historians suggesting that they should create their own organization to protect historical documents from the danger of destruction.[59] The first meeting of the proposed association took place on 18 March 1917; on 8 April the Statutes of the Union of Archive *Deiateli* (*Soiuz Rossiiskikh Arkhivnykh Deiatelei* [Soiuz RAD]) were confirmed by its general meeting and on 16 June they were approved by the Minister of Education, A. A. Manuilov.[60] The word *deiateli* in the title of the association implied a strong element of activism and a broad interpretation of eligibility for membership. Indeed, it embraced both archive employees and university professors; Lappo-Danilevskii was elected chairman of the Union, while its Council comprised representatives of the capital's governmental, court and academic archives. All in all, 'more than 30 bodies from the capital and provinces participated in the Union', Presniakov noted a year later.[61]

Although the establishment of the union was primarily the result of the widely recognized urgent necessity to preserve archival documents due to the critical circumstances, its bylaws included the protection of archive employees' professional interests. The appearance of this new theme in the historians' discourse was closely connected with the tendency to professional self-organization characteristic of this period of revolutionary development: on 9 March 1917 *Izvestiia* was already issuing a call to 'Become organized (*Organizuites'*)!'; in early May 1917 Nadezhda Platonova wrote about 'the epidemic aspiration to become organized (*sorganizovat'sia*)', which reminded her of 1905.[62] Professional organizations were seen as an essential element of the new revolutionary *obshchestvennost'* which was now expected to demonstrate not only the virtues of activism and social engagement, but also a readiness to cooperate with the new revolutionary power.[63] For the community of

59 Khorkhordina, *Istoriia i arkhivy*, 15–16. For A. I. Lebedev's biography see V. S. Sobolev, 'Aleksandr Ivanovich Lebedev, kratkii biograficheskii ocherk', in *Port-Artur: Deistviia flota v 1904 g.*, edited by K. P. Guber (St Petersburg: Rosarkhiv/RGAVMF, 2003).

60 'Ustav soiuza Rossiiskikh arkhivnykh deiatelei', Tsentral'nyi moskovskii muzei-arkhiv lichnykh sobranii (TsMAM LS), f. 110, I. L. Maiakovskii, op. 1, d. 226, l. 6.

61 A. E. Presniakov, 'Reforma arkhivnogo dela', *Russkii istoricheskii zhurnal* 5 (1918), 205–222, here 209.

62 'Organizuites'!', *Izvestiia Soveta Rabochikh i Soldatskikh Deputatov,* 9 March 1917; Note of 8 May 1917, OR RNB, f. 585, d. 5696, l. 56ob.

63 For the concept of *obshchestvennost'* see Catriona Kelly and Vadim Volkov, 'Obshchestvennost', Sobornost': Collective Identities', in *Constructing Russian Culture in the Age of Revolution, 1881–1940*, edited by Catriona Kelly and David Shepherd (Oxford: Oxford University Press, 1998); Abbot Gleason, 'The Terms of Russian Social History', in *Between Tsar and People: Educated Society and the Quest for Public Identity in Late Imperial Russia*, edited by Edith W. Clowes, Samuel D. Kassow, and James L. West (Princeton, NJ: Princeton University Press, 1991), 15–27; Joseph Bradley, 'Voluntary Associations, Civic Culture and *Obshchestvennost'* in Moscow', in ibid., 131–148; Christine Ruane and Ben Eklof, 'Cultural Pioneers and Professionals: The Teachers in Society', in ibid., 199–211;

historians, however, this call for unification reverberated with the already existing trend towards closer cooperation among its various segments. The dynamics of the revolutionary process apparently intensified this tendency. Furthermore, the appearance of a new institution such as a professional union made it possible to at least attempt to resolve the old problem of the status of the gubernia scholarly archival commissions.

Indeed, in the very first month of its existence the Union was approached by gubernia commissions, whose members felt lost in the revolutionary festival of reorganization. In response, on 11 July 1917, the Union convened an 'inter-departmental meeting' (*mezhduvedomstvennoe soveshchanie*) in the Academy of Sciences, which brought together representatives of bodies involved in the establishment, maintenance, and control of the local archival commissions in the past, along with the Union of the Archive *Deiateli* which was supposed to protect them in the unstable present, in order to discuss the situation of the local archival commissions and make plans for the future.[64] Consequently, the representatives of two Ministries (Education and the Interior), two academic institutions (the Academy of Sciences and Petrograd Archaeological Institute), two 'old' historical societies (the Moscow Archaeological Society and the Russian Historical Society), and of the Union of Archive *Deiately*, which constituted a new type of voluntary association, participated in that *ad hoc* initiative on an apparently equal footing. However, the identity of the participants complicated this seemingly clear-cut division. While each of the invited institutions sent two persons to this meeting, its chair, Lappo-Danilevskii, as well as the representatives of the Ministry of Education, the Moscow Archaeological Society and the Russian Historical Society, were also active in the new Union. They, therefore, represented both the state and *obshchestvennost'*, and both old and new types of voluntary historical societies. As a result of this peculiar duality the Union of Archive *Deiateli* apparently prevailed over other participants of the meeting.

Alice K. Pate, 'Workers and *Obshchestvnnost'*: St Petersburg, 1906–14', *Revolutionary Russia* 15(2) (December 2002), 53–71; Tsuyoshi Hasegawa, 'Gosudarstvennost', Obshchestvennost', and Klassovost': Crime, the Police, and the State in Russian Revolution in Petrograd', *Canadian-American Slavic Studies* 35 (2–3) (Summer-Fall 2001), 157–188; Karl Loewenstein, 'Obshchestvennost' as Key to Understanding Soviet Writers of the 1950s: "Moskovskii Literator", October 1956–March 1957', *Journal of Contemporary History* 44(3) (July 2009), 473–492. Michael David-Fox's review of I. N. Il'ina, 'Obshchestvennye organizatsii Rossii v 1920-e gody', published in *Kritika: Explorations in Russian and Eurasian History* 3(1) (2002), 173–181, is especially useful for analysing the question of *obshchestvennost's* translation and conceptualization. For the process of transformation from the pre-revolutionary to the post-revolutionary perception of *obshchestvennost'*, see Andy Willimott, 'The Kommuna Impulse: Collective Mechanisms and Commune-ists in the Early Soviet State', *Revolutionary Russia* 24(1) (June 2011), 59–78 as well as Matthias Neumann's chapter in this volume.

64 TsGIASpb., f. 119, op. 2, d. 55, Obrashchenie istoriko-arkheologicheskikh obshchestv ob okazanii im pomoshchi, ll. 9–10.

In the course of discussions its participants depicted an impressive and alarming picture. On the one hand, they talked about the new tasks of the archival commissions, which were now seen as bodies intended not only to save from destruction governmental, public, and private materials from the past, but also to collect what was called 'documents of the revolution'. On the other hand, it was unclear how to support the commissions in a situation where old mechanisms had stopped functioning and new ones had yet to be created. The Russian Historical Society, which had lost not only its designation as 'Imperial' but also its sources of funding, willingly relinquished its responsibility for local commissions in favour of the Union, while representatives of the Ministry of Interior expressed a similar readiness to transfer the commissions to the Ministry of Education. This created a situation equivalent to the pre-revolutionary practice of divided subordination, but provided no real solution for the archival commissions. In view of the circumstances, the meeting charged the Union with the tasks of summoning an All-Russian Congress of Archive *Deiateli* in fall 1917 and of preparing a draft Law on Archives which was to reconsider the status of all archival institutions.

Yet, while entrusting the solution of the problem to a voluntary association – the Union of Archive *Deiateli* – the meeting also proposed the establishment of a central governmental body intended to supervise all archival institutions.[65] In accordance with this proposal, Konstantin Zdravomyslov, who was a member of the Union and, simultaneously, the head of the Synod's archive, wrote a memorandum (*Zapiska*) which became the basis for a draft law produced by the deputy head of the Union, Count Nikolai Golitsyn, who was director of the State and Petrograd Main Archives of the Ministry of Foreign Affairs. Therefore, the proposed law was written by public activists who were at the same time senior civil servants; not surprisingly, they produced a document of an essentially etatist character. While declaring the task to be the 'proper organization of archival work in Russia', it actually suggested implementing the archival reform that had been discussed in previous years on the basis of Samokvasov's project, which involved, first and foremost, the centralization and rationalization of the archives' administration. Yet the painful experience of the first days of the revolution led to the principle of centralization being translated into the idea of nationalizing the archival documents of all governmental bodies, including the abolished ministries and departments: archival materials were now defined as 'the scholarly property of the whole state'. Accordingly, the proposed law demanded a complete prohibition on the destruction of documents on the part of any governmental body and stipulated the indivisibility of archival collections, insisting on the necessity, from the scientific point of view, of preserving them as a whole. This attitude to archives as state scholarly institutions led logically to the proposal to subordinate them to the Ministry of Education in whose framework a special

65 Ibid., l. 10ob.

archival department would be established.[66] Nonetheless, while suggesting such a state-oriented model of the archival system, the Union did not address the new kind of archives that started to emerge on a voluntary basis in spring–summer 1917 with the specific aim of preserving the historical materials created by the revolution.

How to preserve history – and to survive it

The attempt to create a new type of archive challenged the existing perception both of historical documents and of the historian's work. The view of contemporary events as a worthy subject of historical studies, which had been developing since the beginning of the First World War, assumed the radically new idea of the necessity to create historical sources that would reflect the momentous changes that Russia was experiencing. Thus, Moscow historian Iurii Got'e, while describing the fall of the monarchy and the subsequent events of the spring and summer of 1917 as a national catastrophe, also noted that it was 'an episode that has few analogues in world history'. He therefore saw his duty as an 'educated man who had the misfortune to choose the history of his own country as his academic profession' to record his personal impressions in order to produce 'a very incomplete, very subjective, but still a historical source which may be of use to somebody in the future'.[67] In July 1917 Got'e started to write a diary, which he kept until July 1922, thereby choosing a rather traditional format for the source he wished to generate.

His Petrograd colleague, Presniakov, on the contrary, welcomed the February Revolution ('my heart is growling with joy'), he wrote to an actor of the Moscow *Khudozhestvennyi* theatre, Vasilii Luzhskii in March 1917, and saw it as the beginning of a new historical epoch.[68] In order to document this historical moment he took part in an innovative attempt to create sources for future historians, as he explained in an article of 1918:

> From the very first days of the February Revolution various groups of society, swept up by the huge significance of the events being experienced, became filled with the aspiration to collect and preserve materials that could serve as a means for studying these events in future, when the time will come to look back on the path of struggle, revolutions and experiences of new political and social creativity. This tendency was particularly salient in some army units and military circles. In several regiments of the Petrograd garrison 'historical commissions' were formed by soldiers and

66 Khorkhordina, *Istoriia i arkhivy*, 27–29.

67 Iu. V. Got'e, 'Moi zametki', *Voprosy istorii* 6 (1991), 155–175, here 155. On the fate of Got'e's diary see Terence Emmons and S. V. Utechin, 'Iu.V. Got'e i ego dnevnik', ibid., 150–154.

68 E. A. Shingareva, 'Pis'ma A. E. Presniakova k V. V. Luzhskomu, khraniashchiesia v muzee MKhAT', in *Arkheograficheskii ezhegodnik za 2000*, edited by O. Iu. Shmidt (Moscow: Nauka, 2001), 263–270, here 259.

> young officers in order to preserve the memory of the actions of military units and their role in the [revolutionary] movement. The short-lived Union of Republican Soldiers attempted to organize this matter systematically and asked for the help of the intelligentsia – the young forces from the universities. In that way, on the initiative of the Union of Republican Soldiers, the Society for the Study of the Revolution of 1917 was formed. This society undertook not only to collect various printed materials, of a fluctuating and ephemeral nature (*tekuchii i letuchii*), which reflected the rapidly changing events, but also to create sources for the future study of the Russian revolution by interviewing its prominent activists and rank-and-file participants in order to preserve the factual traces of the events while they are still fresh in memory.[69]

As Presniakov's article shows, the distinctiveness of this project lay not only in the idea to produce a collection of documents, but also in the very fact of cooperation between university historians and new actors in the field – officers and soldiers who wanted to commemorate their own participation in the revolutionary event. However, this form of cooperation accorded with the practices and hierarchies of the pre-revolutionary voluntary historical societies and scholarly archival commissions. Presniakov, himself an academic historian, became the head of the project. According to his notebook of 1917, the commission for collecting materials for the study of the revolution was established as early as April 1917. The commission's chair and bureau were elected on 16 April 1917 and included representatives of the unions of republican soldiers and officers, the Soviet of Soldiers Deputies and historical commissions at military units (the Volynskii and Finliandskii regiments were referred to in particular).[70] At the same meeting, Presniakov noted, the society discussed its 'relation to the Museum'. Since Gor'kii's address and telephone number appeared together with that note, it is reasonable to infer that Presniakov meant the Museum in Memory of Freedom Fighters (*Dom-muzei pamiati bortsov za svobodu*), which was founded on Gor'kii's initiative in April 1917. The actual relations between the society and the museum at that time remain unclear: the latter, according to an article by Gor'kii in June 1917, was conceived as an 'institute of social sciences and civic education',[71] which would thus pursue both educational and research goals, while the Society for Study of the Revolution of 1917 focused on collecting documentary materials. The society aimed to establish a network of sub-commissions among students and in military units, factories, trade unions, political parties, and administrative bodies (*uchrezhdeniia*) – the Tauride Palace, which in the first months of the

69 Presniakov, 'Reforma arkhivnogo dela', 205.
70 ASpbOII RAN, f. 193, op. 1, d. 159, *Zapisnaia knizhka*, l. 4–4ob., 8.
71 Maxim Gor'kii, 'Na slovakh vse soglasny ...', [29 June 1917] in *Revoliutsiia i kul'tura: Stat'i za 1917 g*. (Berlin: Tovarishchestvo I. P. Ladyzhnikova, 1918), 43–47, here 45.

revolution hosted both the Provisional Government and the Petrograd Soviet, was specially mentioned.[72] In addition, it was planned to found branches of the commission in other towns, from Petrograd's closest suburbs such as Tsarskoe Selo and Kronshtadt to university towns such as Moscow, Perm, Khar'kov, and Tomsk. The heads of the branches were supposed to be mainly fellow-historians: Presniakov noted the names of Grekov and Ottokar for Perm's branch, Kizevetter and Mel'gunov for Moscow, and Klochkov for Khar'kov.[73] As Semion Lyandres has shown in his pioneering study based on the documents of the Society for Study of the Revolution of 1917, one of the commission's first practical steps was a call to the citizens of the new Russia 'to collect any materials pertaining to the history of the February Revolution – from official documents, memoirs, notes, diaries, and personal accounts to books, leaflets, songs and verses, drawings and photographs, advertisements, and records of meetings by political and social organizations – and send them to the Society for the Study of the Revolution's temporary depository in the Manuscript Division of the Academy of Sciences Library in Petrograd'.[74] Disseminating this call through gubernia scholarly archival commissions, and assigning the key role in the Moscow branch to Sergei Mel'gunov, who on 8 March 1917 had already been made responsible for inspecting and receiving the archives of the secret police (*okhrana*), gendarmerie, and the Ministry of Interior in Moscow, the new society sought to position itself within the expanding network of official and voluntary historical bodies.[75]

The society also suggested a new and rather unusual form of activity – interviewing the participants in the revolutionary events. The novelty of the enterprise might explain the special attention Presniakov paid to work procedures: in his notes he mentioned 'the method of interview', 'registration of interviewees', 'the fate of the records', and 'the place and procedure of their conservation'.[76] Presniakov's notebook also contained a list of names, telephone numbers, and details of the society's agents in the military units – including,

72 ASpbOII RAN, f. 193, op. 1, d. 159, l. 4ob.: 'the Tauride Palace and other offices'. The Provisional Government moved to the Winter Palace in the second half of July 1917; the Petrograd Soviet was transferred to Smol'nyi in early August 1917 – see V. T. Sushko, 'Zimnii dvorets do i posle 25 oktiabria 1917', *Voprosy istorii* 8–9 (1992), 151–155, here 151; P. V. Volobuev (ed.), *Petrogradskii Sovet Rabochikh i Soldatskikh Deputatov v 1917 godu: Protokoly, stenogrammy, rezoliutsii, postanovleniia obshchikh sobranii, sobranii sektsii, zasedaniia ispolnitel'nogo komiteta i fraktsii 27 fevralia – 25 oktiabria 1917 goda*, vol. 1 (Leningrad: Nauka, Leningradskoe otdelenie, 1991), 8.

73 ASpbOII RAN, f. 193, op. 1, d. 159, l. 5ob.

74 Semion Lyandres, *The Fall of Tsarism: Untold Stories of the February Revolution* (Oxford: Oxford University Press, 2013), 38–39.

75 On 22 March Mel'gunov's post was upgraded to head of the commission responsible for the reorganization of the former archive of the Okhrana department and publication of its documents – see Iu. N. Emel'ianov, *S. P. Mel'gunov: v Rossii i Emigratsii* (Moscow: Editorial URSS, 1998), 44–45.

76 ASpbOII RAN, f. 193, op. 1, d. 159, l. 8ob.

for example, ensign (*praporshchik*) Kirpichnikov, who played a key role in the Volynskii regiment's decision to join workers' demonstrations on 27 February.[77] It also gave the initials of the person in charge of 'the Tauride Palace' – 'M. A. P-v',[78] which, as Lyandres has revealed, referred to Presniakov's friend and close collaborator, Mikhail Aleksandrovich Polievktov, who in May–June 1917 conducted interviews with such leading contemporary political figures as B. A. Engel'gardt, A. A. Chikolini, P. V. Gerasimov, M. V. Rodzianko, L. S. Tugan-Baranovskii, N. V. Nekrasov, N. S. Chkheidze, M. I. Skobelev, A. F. Kerenskii, and M. I. Tereshchenko. As Lyandres observes, it was no easy task to solicit such interviews from people who were still playing an active role in the ongoing events.[79] Moreover, while embarking on the venture, the Society for the Study of the Revolution had to take into consideration the existence of another, overwhelmingly political 'interviews' project – that of the Provisional Government's Extraordinary Commission of Inquiry into the malfeasance of former ministers, chief administrators, and other persons of high office.[80]

Established on 11 March 1917, this commission gradually changed the nature of its activity from a strictly judicial to a more historical investigation. As its chair, the Moscow barrister (*prisiazhnyi poverennyi*) N. K. Murav'ev, claimed in his statement to the First All-Russia Congress of Soviets of Workers' and Soldiers' Deputies in late June 1917, the materials of the investigation not only revealed the crimes of the old regime, but above all depicted 'a historical picture of the life of the ruling class and ruling power in the last period of their existence'.[81] The commission summoned for questioning not only officials of the first three ranks who were suspected of political crimes, but also leading public figures – from Rodzianko and Guchkov to Miliukov and Chkheidze. Their answers were supposed to prove both the criminal behaviour of individual Tsarist servitors and the inevitability of the fall of the old regime as such. This was especially noticeable in the testimony of the historian and leader of the Kadet party, Pavel Miliukov. His evidence, defined by the session's chair as an 'explanation', provided a general description of the political situation since 1905.[82] All 88 sessions at which 59 persons were questioned were carefully recorded in shorthand and checked by an editorial

77 'Geroi revoliutsii', *Iskry: Prilozhenie k gazete Russkoe Slovo*, 30 April 1917.
78 ASpbOII RAN, f. 193, op. 1, d. 159, l. 8ob.
79 Lyandres, *The Fall of Tsarism*, xiii, 42–44.
80 Robert Paul Browder and Aleksandr F. Kerensky (eds), *The Russian Provisional Government, 1917: Documents*, vol. 1 (Stanford, CA: Stanford University Press, 1961), 193–194.
81 Isvestiia Petrogradskogo Soveta Rabochikh i Soldatskikh Deputatov', 28 June 1917; P. E. Shchegolev, 'Chrezvychainaia gosudarstvennaia komissiia Vremennogo Pravitel'stva', in *Padenie tsarskogo rezhima: Stenograficheskie otchety doprosov i pokazanii, dannykh v 1917 g. v Chrezvychainoi Sledstvennoi Komissii Vremennogo Pravitel'stva*, vol. 1, edited by P. E. Shchegolev (Leningrad: Gosudarstvennoe izdatel'stvo, 1924), xi,
82 'Pokazaniia P.N. Miliukova, 4 August 1917', Shchegolev, ed., *Padenie tsarskogo rezhima*, vol. 6 (Leningrad: Gosudarstvennoe izdatel'stvo, 1926), 295–319.

commission headed by the famous poet Alexander Blok; these materials were subsequently to be included in an expanded report to the Provisional government. The preparation of the report (which was never finalized) was assigned to Evgenii Tarle, at that time a privat-docent at St Petersburg University and professor of history at Dorpat University.[83]

Yet, despite the serious attention paid to the historical potential of the extraordinary commission's findings, they were intended first and foremost for immediate political goals. This can probably explain the wording of Presniakov's letter to potential interviewees by the Society for the Study of the Revolution, some of whom were also being summoned to appear before the extraordinary commission, and sometimes at approximately the same time. For example, the chairman of the Soviet of Workers' and Soldiers' Deputies, Nikolai Chkheidze, was interviewed by the society on 27 May and two days later was summoned to the extraordinary commission.[84] In this context Presniakov's letter might be seen as an attempt to emphasize the distinctive scholarly character of their project. Noting that the society consisted mainly of professors teaching at Petrograd University and other institutions of higher education, he explained that its aim was to collect both written and oral materials that would shed light on the history of the great upheaval. While briefly outlining the structure of the society, he focused specifically on the 'section of the study of the Tauride Palace', which was charged with conducting interviews with participants in the revolution whose activity was mainly concentrated in the Tauride Palace and linked to the revolutionary institutions there. However, the most significant message was Presniakov's promise that the society would regard these interviews as scholarly materials only and had no intention of publishing them immediately. He even stated that the information they conveyed could be kept secret for a certain period of time if they so desired.[85] Indeed, these interviews remained in Polievktov's safekeeping during the turmoil of the following months of 1917 and subsequently vanished almost without trace. It was only in 2006 that Lyandres discovered these interviews and published them some years later, thus realizing Presniakov's dream.[86] For the purpose of this chapter, however, the story of the interviews is interesting because it demonstrates the new practice of historians' public activism, which was closely connected to the new vision of their obligations as professionals and representatives of *obshchestvennost'*.

83 Ibid., vol. 1, xxiii. Blok partly summarized the results of the commission's activity in his book *Poslednie dni imperatorskoi vlasti* (Petrograd: Alkonost, 1921)
84 Lyandres, *The Fall of Tsarism*, 159–165; 'Pokazaniia N. S. Chkheidze' in *Padenie tsarskogo rezhima*, vol. 3 (Leningrad: Gosudarstvennoe izdatel'stvo, 1925), 484–506.
85 Letter of Introduction by A. E. Presniakov, 1917, Department of Rare Books and Special Collection, University of Notre Dame Libraries, available at http://rarebooks.library.nd.edu/exhibits/polievktov/ssrr.shtml, accessed 30 October 2015.
86 Lyandres, *The Fall of Tsarism*, 3–14.

Indeed, the appearance of this and other historical-revolutionary societies – according to Presniakov, there were some additional similar 'circles and bodies' in the capital cities and the provinces[87] – reflected the increased role of voluntary public initiatives in the sphere of culture and education. This tendency accorded with the democratic ideals of the February Revolution, but contradicted the state-oriented and more practical approach of the Union of Archive *Deiateli*. The Ministers of Education of the Provisional Government, each of whom was a distinguished professor in his particular field of expertise and a part and parcel of the liberal intelligentsia, recognized the necessity to find a balance between the two tendencies – inevitable centralization and the desirability of strengthening the role of *obshchestvennost'*.[88] One possible solution was to re-define the institutional status of voluntary historical societies vis-à-vis the new governmental bodies, in order to secure their autonomy, to provide them with sufficient state support, and at the same time, to create a mechanism of cooperation with the Ministry of Education. As early as in May 1917 the observant Platonov wrote about the tendency to replace 'officials' with representatives of the learned societies in the committees of the Ministry of Education.[89] The proposals for educational reform which were elaborated in May–November 1917 by the State Committee on Education emphasized the need to secure the participation of voluntary associations (*obshchestvennye organizatsii*) in the administration of new autonomous educational institutions.[90] Furthermore, historians participated in the governmental bodies dealing with the preservation of the cultural heritage: Lappo-Danilevskii and Mikhail Rostovtsev, for example, represented the Academy of Sciences in the Arts and History Commission responsible for receiving the Winter Palace's properties from the Palace's administration in August 1917.[91]

87 Presniakov, 'Reforma arkhivnogo dela', 205.

88 The Provisional Government's Ministers of Education were the former rector of Moscow University, A. A. Manuilov (2 March–4 June 1917), the permanent secretary of the Academy of Sciences, S. F. Oldenburg (25 July–31 August 1917) and the former director of the St Petersburg Women Medical Institute, S. S. Salazkin (8 September–25 October 1917). For the Provisional Government's ministers, see V. S. Izmozik, 'Vremennoe Pravitel'stvo: Liudi i sud'by', *Voprosy istorii* 6 (1994), 163–169.

89 S. F. Platonov to S. D. Sheremetev, 19 May 1917, in *Akademik S. F. Platonov: perepiska s istorikami*, vol. 1, edited by S. O. Shmidt and V. G. Bukhert (Moscow: Nauka, 2003), 229.

90 'Rukovodiashchie polozheniia, priniatye Gosudarstvennym komitetom po narodnomu obrazovaniiu pri razrabotke voprosov o reforme narodnogo obrazovaniia, 6 June 1917', http://biblio.narod.ru/gyrnal/publicat/komitet-2.htm; accessed 30 October 2015. For the activity and structure of the State Committee of Education, see RGIA, f. 733, op. 228, d. 108, ll. 112–120; Nauchnyi arkhiv Rossiskoi Akademii Obrazovaniia (NA RAO), f. 19, op. 1, d. 265, l. 39. In 2000 the Ushinsky State Pedagogical Library placed a significant portion of the Committee's documents online – available at http://biblio.narod.ru/gyrnal/publicat/oglavlen.htm.

91 Sushko, 'Zimnii dvorets do i posle 25 oktiabria 1917', 151. For Rostovtsev's biography see Marinus A. Wes, 'The Russian Background of the Young Michael

The mode of collaboration between the state and the historical community that evolved in the time of the Provisional Government was adversely affected by the political developments of fall 1917, but nonetheless had an impact on historians' relations with the early Soviet state. The new regime, which ostensibly rejected the Provisional Government's plans for reform, in practice appropriated a significant part of them: the main notions of the Law on Archives proposed by the Union of Archive *Deiateli* were included in the Soviet decree 'On the Reorganization and Centralization of the Archives' of 1 June 1918.[92] This decree, therefore, laid the legislative basis for realizing the ideas that had been initially formulated by Samokvasov in the late nineteenth century and had constituted the main axis of historians' discussions for almost two decades. This appropriation of ideas that were acceptable to the historians enabled their cooperation with the Soviet government despite the historical community's overwhelmingly negative response to the Bolsheviks' seizure of power in October 1917.

A striking example of historians' attitude to the new Soviet authorities can be found in Platonov's letter of 21 February 1918 to I. V. Egorov, a commissar of the Department of Institutions of Higher Education in the newly created People's Commissariat of Education. Addressing the representative of the new Soviet power in a perfectly old-fashioned way, 'Dear Sir (*Milostivyi Gosudar'*) Ivan Vasil'evich', Platonov informed him about the activity of the commission on the scholarly cataloguing of the Archive of the Ministry of Education which he had chaired since its establishment in November 1915. He updated Egorov about the commission's draft budget for 1918, which had been submitted to the Ministry of Education in May 1917, and informed him that the Ministry (that of the Provisional Government) had intended 'to comply with his request in full'. Platonov insisted also that it was time to pay 'for the ongoing work of the Archive's cataloguing', reminding the commissar that while he himself and other members of the commission worked 'gratis', the commission employees' labour had to be paid since it was their only source of income.[93]

Rostovtzeff', *Historia* 37 (1988), 207–221; idem, *Michael Rostovtzeff, Historian in Exile: Russian Roots in an American Context: Historia-Einzelschriften,* 65 (Stuttgart: Franz Steiner Verlag, 1990); G. M. Bongard-Levin, *The Great Russian Historian M. Rostovtsev in the USA: The Years of Exile* (Lewiston, NY: Edwin Mellen Press, 1999); Caspar Meyer, 'Rostovtzeff and the Classical Origins of Eurasianism', *Anabases* 9 (2009), 185–197; and a brief but very interesting article by Sergei Krikh, 'M. I. Rostovtsev: byt' v obraze i byt' obrazom', *Novoe literaturnoe obozrenie*, no 95 (2009), available at http://magazines.russ.ru/nlo/2009/95/kr11-pr.html, accessed 30 October 2014.

92 E. V. Starostin and T. I. Khorkhordina, 'Dekret ob arkhivnom dele 1918 goda', *Voprosy istorii* 7 (1991), 41–52.

93 S. F. Platonov to I. V. Egorov, 21 February (6 March) 1918, OR RNB, f. 273 (Egorov I. V.), op. 1, d. 116, Platonov S. F. Pis'mo Ivanu Vasil'evichu Egorovu, l. 1–1ob.

Platonov's demand that the Soviet commissar carry out promises made by the Provisional Government in order to continue a project launched by the Tsarist Ministry of Education was far from naïve. By inserting the *Narkompros* into a kind of unbroken chain of officialdom, Platonov demonstrated his commission's acceptance of the new authorities that until recently had been boycotted by civil servants, including archivists and librarians. Moreover, according to Kharkhordina, there had been no contacts between the Union of the Archive *Deiateli* and the *Narkompros* until 28 January 1918.[94] From this perspective, Platonov's reference to his commission's 'ongoing work' had an important legitimizing effect. Yet there was also an undertone of challenge in his letter: in effect, it implied that the commission was willing to cooperate with the new power on condition that the latter took upon itself the state's responsibilities, including the commitments of its predecessor. This attitude may have been strengthened by the belief that the Soviet power was a merely temporary phenomenon which would soon disappear under the threat of the approaching German army. Only a day later, on 22 February 1918, Platonov advised Druzhinin not to go to Egorov's office: 'they are in panic: fleeing from Petrograd' and added: 'They urgently demanded my opinion on whether to evacuate the archive. Tomorrow I will give a negative answer', thus emphasizing his independent professional position vis-à-vis the panicking regime.[95]

On these very same days Platonov's wife recorded in her diary widespread rumours linking the approaching Germans to anticipations that 'things are quickly coming to a head, in other words to restoration', and that 'an entire cabinet of ministers has been already composed'. In her opinion, all these rumours were 'nonsense', but she still confessed: 'how agonizingly we long for order!'[96] This view of the Soviet power as a temporary phenomenon and the hopes for its inevitable fall influenced the position adopted by the Union of Archives *Deiateli* in its contacts with the *Narkom* of Education, Lunacharskii, in March 1918.[97] Yet at that time a new motif appeared in the writing of Nadezhda Platonova, who devotedly recorded every nuance in the moods and feelings of her husband and his professional milieu. On 15 March she wrote that

> S. F. talked twice with the governmental commissar Griunberg about the Archive of the Ministry of Education and found that Griunberg is exceptionally smart, grasps the essence of the problem very fast and is willing to consider all scholarly and educational initiatives.[98]

Her comment echoed Got'e's impression from his first encounter with P. P. Malinovskii, the Bolshevik Commissar of the 'Properties of the Republic' a

94 Khorkhordina, *Istoriia i arkhivy*, 41–42.
95 Shmidt and Bukhert (eds), *Akademik S. F. Platonov: perepiska s istorikami*, vol. 1, 232.
96 Note of 21 February 1918, OR RNB, f. 585, op. 1, d. 5697, l. 12.
97 Khorkhordina, *Istoriia i arkhivy*, 42–43.
98 Note of 15 March 1918, OR RNB, f. 585, op. 1, d. 5697, l. 25–25ob.

month earlier. Acting in the capacity of the deputy director and main librarian of the Ruminatsev museum (the future Russian State Library), Got'e discussed with Malinovskii the question of the museum's budget for 1918 and was favourably impressed by the latter's behaviour: 'The new chief (*nachal'nik*) was exceptionally obliging: we inflated the budget proposal to around a million rubles, and he knocked much less off this sum, and far more politely, than the former imperial Petersburg officials.'[99]

In both cases the historians were willing to have contacts with representatives of the new regime only because they were obliged to, and on a limited basis. Platonov was annoyed by what he saw as Griunberg's 'Jewish' behaviour as manifested in the latter's attempt to call himself Platonov's student.[100] Got'e perceived the whole situation as completely fake, noting that they seemed to be regarded as 'the Roman augurs who should laugh if they speak the truth', and concluded: 'all this is just a vain enterprise, and, from our side, the only reason for conducting such talks is the aim of protecting our Museum.'[101] Still, the discovery of some positive qualities in certain agents of the new regime enabled historians' steadily increasing collaboration with the Soviet authorities. The appointment of the intellectual David Riazanov to head of the Main Archive Administration undoubtedly contributed to Platonov's and Presniakov's willingness to join the Soviet archive apparatus as its high-ranking employees.[102] As suggested by a letter of July 1918 from Platonov to Ivan A. Ivanov, an old friend and head of the Tver scholarly gubernia archival commission, this step became possible both because Riazanov's figure was 'acceptable' to historians and because it provided an opportunity to fulfil tasks that the historical community regarded as having top priority:

> I have been elected deputy chair of the Main Archive Administration and I stand side by side (and in accord) with the 'left social-democrat' and 'revolutionary-Marxist' Riazanov-Goldendakh who leads this Administration. He is an *educated, decent* (*poriadochnyi*) and kind Jew, a revolutionary theoretician, who is acknowledged and favourably regarded by *all* members of the Administration. After two months of persistent work in P[eters]b[urg] and Moscow we have organized 'the main' and two 'regional' archival administrations; I am head of the Petersburg administration ….

99 Note of 19 January 1918, Got'e, 'Moi zametki', *Voprosy istorii* 9–10 (1991), 160–185, here 163.
100 OR RNB, f. 585, op. 1, d. 5697, l. 25ob.
101 Got'e, 'Moi zametki', *Voprosy istorii* 9–10 (1991), 163.
102 The first Soviet administrative body for archives, the Central Committee for Archival Administration (*Tsentral'nyi komitet po upravleniiu arkhivami [Tsentrarkhiv]*) was established on 2 April 1918 in Petrograd; on 1 June 1918 it was reorganized into the Main Archive Administration (*Glavarchiv*) which was located in Moscow. See A. V. Dobrovskaia, I. Iu. Gorbunov and S. V. Mironenko, 'Gosudarstvennyi Arkhiv Rossiiskoi Federatsii: Istoriia formirovaniia i komplektovaniia (1920–1995)', in *Arkheograficheskii ezhegodnik za 1995 god*, edited by S. O. Shmidt (Moscow: Nauka, 1997), 3–28.

> Due to Riazanov's wisdom and tact everything has been placed in the hands of scholars, is led by collegiums (*rukovoditsia kollegiiami*) and guided only by the archives' interests, without any politics. Many archives have been rescued and preserved; many archivists have been returned to their work and provided for (*obespecheny*). One feels satisfied after all the pains of organizing everything (*posle suety ustroitel'stva*) and does not fear the future difficulties, which are of course inevitable. However, the historians were not afraid of them and, thank God, they all got down to work (*stali k delu*).[103]

The complex mixture of sentiments revealed in this letter – the recognition of opportunities to protect the archives and to provide fellow historians with work and a safe haven; satisfaction with the possibility of realizing long-standing professional projects; and the joy of returning to the normality of routine work amidst the chaos and uncertainty of war and revolution – gives us an insight into the dynamics within the historical community that eventually enabled the historians' integration into the Soviet system. Nonetheless, even though they became Soviet *sluzhashchie*, historians retained their professional and personal networks and brought their norms, values, and codes of behaviour into the Soviet institutions. In so doing, they made a deep impact on the latter's mode of operation – at least until the first wave of repression of the late 1920s heralded the fateful changes in the nature of the Soviet system and dealt a harsh blow to the historical community.

Conclusion

On 1 July 1919 Got'e wrote in his diary:

> I am 46 years old today, five years of which should be erased from my life. I have always said, and I am now even more convinced than ever before, that it is much better to live in times of quiet and stagnation than in such an 'interesting' time as the one we are now living through.[104]

He, however, chose not to try to forget these agonizing years but to cope with their traumatic effect by recording them in detail in his diary, which he gave in 1922 to an American acquaintance who was collecting materials for the library of the recently (1919) established Hoover Institution.[105] Got'e thus took a step that was of great risk to him personally but was intended to preserve his diary as a document for future historians.

Indeed, his writings – together with the diaries of Platonova and letters of Platonov, Veselovskii, and Presniakov – serve as an indispensable source not

103 S. F. Platonov to I. A. Ivanov, 7 (20) July 1918 in Shmidt and Bukhert (eds), *Akademik S. F. Platonov*, vol. 1, 235 (emphasis in original).

104 Got'e, 'Moi zametki', *Voprosy istorii* 4–5 (1992), 107–118, 107.

105 Emmons and Utechin, 'Iu.V. Got'e i ego dnevnik', 150.

only for the history of the revolution, but also for the study of the history of Russian historians, who endeavoured to connect the threads of time and to bridge the revolutionary divide in their own living experience. These sources suggest that the historical community's resilience in the situation of political and social crisis derived from the supportive interaction among historians of various standing, combined with cooperation among formal and informal centres of their professional life. Responding to the political developments by establishing new institutions such as the Union of the Archive *Deiateli* and participating in the new public and governmental bodies, historians as a community managed to use these new structures for advancing and realizing those ideas and projects that had been defined as the most important in their professional discussions in the pre-revolutionary years. Moreover, while integrating into new academic institutions, historians maintained and even expanded their personal and professional connections by including in these networks those figures of the new regime who were both powerful and acceptable from the perspective of the community's value system. Yet, this protective strategy had its price. Although this policy made it possible for historians to cooperate with the Soviet government and enabled them to influence the Soviet archival and academic system from inside, in the long term it led to the steady erosion of the historical community's autonomy and its increasing etatization: historians were enforced to become a kind of cog in the Soviet apparatus. It also meant losing those colleagues who were unwilling to cooperate with the new regime or were rejected by the latter: a considerable number of historians emigrated from Russia in the early 1920s. Their fates constitute another meaningful chapter in the history of Russian historical scholarship and its historical community.

9 Speaking more than Bolshevik

Humour, subjectivity, and crosshatching in Stalin's 1930s

Jonathan Waterlow

Stephen Kotkin's idea of 'Speaking Bolshevik' has been a mainstay or touchstone of early Soviet historiography for two decades. The idea that Soviet citizens could learn to speak the language of the regime to get by and get ahead, whether they believed what they said or not, seemed to explain so much in its elegant simplicity. Stalinism changed from being a somewhat external, repressive force, into a civilization in which ordinary people participated (because they had to), and thereby stabilized and substantiated it.[1] The concept of 'speaking Bolshevik' would go on to inspire many scholars to investigate what it meant to write, read, or even to think Bolshevik, moving our focus away from traditional 'totalitarian' binaries of support and resistance and into more complex grey areas.

Kotkin's approach was directly and personally influenced by Michel Foucault's theories of Power, but it was two other scholars who would propose a more deeply Foucauldian reading of Stalinism – an approach that became known as the 'Soviet subjectivity school'. Jochen Hellbeck and Igal Halfin critiqued Kotkin, arguing that citizens might *willingly* inscribe themselves – their identities and autobiographies – into official ideology, particularly within the personal setting of their diaries.[2] In Hellbeck and Halfin's reading, acts of speaking Bolshevik represented going well beyond using regime ideology as a tool, and into playing it like a role you hoped to actually *become*, either by immediate near-spiritual conversion, or, like the diarists Hellbeck studied, faking it till they made it.[3]

1 My thanks to the editors for inviting me to be part of this project, and to my fellow contributors to this volume for their stimulating criticisms and advice on this chapter from its inception. Thanks to Brendan McGeever in particular for his feedback and for sending me an invaluable book; and to Daniel Beer, David Priestland and Steve Smith for criticism, advice and support. Research for this chapter was supported by an Arts and Humanities Research Council doctoral award and latterly by the British Academy. Stephen Kotkin, *Magnetic Mountain: Stalinism as a Civilization* (Berkeley, CA: University of California Press, 1995), especially Ch. 5.

2 Igal Halfin and Jochen Hellbeck, 'Rethinking the Stalinist Subject: Stephen Kotkin's "Magnetic Mountain" and the State of Soviet Historical Studies', *Jahrbücher für Geschichte Osteuropas* 44(3) (1996), 456–463.

3 See in particular, Jochen Hellbeck, 'Fashioning the Stalinist Soul: The Diary of Stepan Podlubnyi (1931–9)', *Jahrbücher für Geschichte Osteuropas* 44(3) (1996),

For subscribers to the Soviet subjectivity approach, learning to speak Bolshevik seemed to necessitate forgetting or at least disowning any other language you might have known. If Bolshevik language did not come to think for contemporaries, they nevertheless tried their hardest to think within it. All of which seemed to imply a marked disconnection with the pre-revolutionary period – mirroring a more general tendency to consider the Soviet Union's 1930s in some fundamental way to be cut off from the past: Stalin's 'Great Break' finding ironic reflection in the historiography.

However, in characteristically direct fashion, Sheila Fitzpatrick criticized this position, pointing out that 'everyone over 30 in 1937 could perfectly well remember a pre-Soviet world'.[4] Even if they did not consider themselves opponents of the new regime, their memories could not simply be disregarded or wiped clean; and unless they never spoke to their parents or grandparents, they were not 'isolated from alternative information' or lacking all 'exposure to an alternative set of references (the past)', as a recent study claims.[5]

As an undergraduate, I found Hellbeck and Halfin's work fascinating – in many ways, it propelled me towards my PhD – but that line from Fitzpatrick continued to resonate in the back of my mind. When I decided to explore ordinary people's political humour as a means to answer questions about how contemporaries made sense of life under Stalinism, I began to see Fitzpatrick was more right than perhaps even she knew. Not only did contemporary jokes constantly compare the present to the past, but the language they used, the stock-characters and traditional concepts within them all pointed to a cultural and personal dialogue with a pre-revolutionary period that not only survived but was vibrantly alive and growing more than a decade after the Revolution. And, as we'll see, one did not need to be over the age of 30 to be involved.

During conversations with the present volume's editors, I realized that despite my own research focusing on the 1930s, the rich unofficial world of joke-telling under Stalin could tell us a lot about continuity and change in everyday life and what we can loosely term popular culture across the revolutionary divide. After all, in the words of Lawrence Levine, 'Culture is a

344–373; idem, 'Working, Struggling, Becoming: Stalin-Era Autobiographical Texts', *Russian Review* 60(3) (2001), 340–359; idem, *Revolution on My Mind: Writing a Diary Under Stalin* (Cambridge, MA: Harvard University Press, 2006); Igal Halfin, *From Darkness to Light: Class, Consciousness, and Salvation in Revolutionary Russia* (Pittsburgh, PA: University of Pittburgh Press, 2000); idem, *Terror in My Soul: Communist Autobiographies on Trial* (Cambridge, MA: Harvard University Press, 2003). Further analysis and critique of these approaches is provided by Andy Willimott, 'Everyday Revolution: The Making of the Soviet Urban Communes', in C. Read, A. Lindenmeyr and P. Waldron (eds), *Russia's Great War and Revolution, 1914–1922: The Home Front* (Bloomington, IN: Slavica Publishers, 2015), 431–454.

4 Sheila Fitzpatrick, *Everyday Stalinism: Ordinary Life in Extraordinary Times. Soviet Russia in the 1930s* (New York: Oxford University Press, 2000), 225.

5 Olga Velikanova, *Popular Perceptions of Soviet Politics in the 1920s: Disenchantment of the Dreamers* (Houndmills: Palgrave, 2013), 189.

process, not a fixed condition; it is the product of unremitting interaction between the past and the present'.[6] We can certainly accept that, as Hellbeck and Halfin argued, many contemporaries were not simply mouthing the words of ideological Bolshevism while inwardly rejecting the regime, but these were not the only words they used. In the sources I discovered, many people were demonstrably and often gleefully speaking more than Bolshevik, even though they seemed a far cry from being dissidents or self-conscious opponents of the regime. How might we make sense of this?

In Hellbeck's view, 'Stalin-era contemporaries were constantly asked to rationalize, to make their daily observations fit ideological mandates. The more their observations parted from the required viewpoint, the more they were expected to struggle to reinhabit the grid'.[7] This was certainly the case, but citizens were nevertheless simultaneously driven by the basic human desire to have the world around them make sense: this was not merely an ideological or state imperative, and it was not shaped solely by official expectations and values. If there was a conceptual 'grid', reference to which enabled contemporaries both to understand the Soviet world and their place and meaning in society, it was not a grid composed solely of regime ideology inside which citizens had to manoeuvre. Instead, this was a grid formed of two sets of hatching – the vertical lines of official ideology *and*, intersecting them, their horizontal counterparts, representing alternative popular values, experiences, priorities, and memories. Each moment of intersection was a fleeting but repeated encounter of ideology and lived reality which, through their interaction – their crosshatching – began to form a map by which citizens could navigate.

Hellbeck quite rightly argues that ideology was altered when it interacted with the individual and their subjective perspectives, their experiences and sense of self, but he (and the Soviet subjectivity approach more generally) severely restricts the extent and nature of that alteration. While he extols the virtue of restoring agency to the Soviet citizen, his interpretation still only allows for a given individual to be 'an ideological agent' – meaning an agent of regime ideology – *even if* the ideology was in fact adulterated by the uniquely subjective, personal, biographical, and emotional life of its carrier.[8] Soviet citizens in truth had more agency than this – agency to deploy, entwine, and overwrite Soviet ideology with ideas, values, and other discourses drawn from pre-revolutionary paradigms and which, together, became *neither* the regime's values, *nor* simply the purely individual, biographical inflections of the citizen-agent. The agency of the citizen lay in the when and in what manner they crosshatched their personal and cultural material with official

6 Lawrence W. Levine, 'William Shakespeare and the American People: A Study in Cultural Transformation', *American Historical Review* 89(1) (1984), 48.

7 Jochen Hellbeck, 'Liberation from Autonomy: Mapping Self-Understandings in Stalin's Time', in *Popular Opinion in Totalitarian Regimes: Fascism, Nazism, Communism*, edited by Paul Corner, (Oxford: Oxford University Press, 2009), 56.

8 Hellbeck, 'Liberation from Autonomy', 56.

ideology; they orientated themselves with reference to this confluence, seeking meaningful patterns in the crosshatching, rather than simply attempting to find the most comforting or comfortable perspective to place themselves within a 'grid' of regime ideology alone. It is these interactions and patterns which I will explore in this chapter.

Why humour?

Humour can show us how significant yet deeply entwined and changing these pre-revolutionary discourses, values, and ideas were with the new Soviet world. It is a particularly useful entry-point because it was shared socially: it was part of a living everyday culture and can therefore tell us more about that culture than the more introspective and personal writings of diarists. Humour is intrinsically a product of a particular context, but it is also dynamic: it is a genre of judgement and comparison and therefore does not straightforwardly portray a given sociocultural, political, or economic reality but simultaneously challenges the assumptions, contradictions, and difficulties of those norms.

It is also not to be understood as unqualified 'resistance'. As Gábor Rittersporn neatly puts it, 'People can take their world quite seriously while simultaneously poking fun at it.'[9] But more than this, by poking fun at it, they also test it, grapple with it, and in the process come to create personal and shared ways of relating to and understanding it. Indeed, as the writer and critic Viktor Shklovskii noted as early as 1922, 'the abundance of Soviet *anekdoty* in Russia is explained not by a particularly hostile attitude to [Soviet] power, but by the new phenomena of life and the contradictions of daily living (*byt*) that are perceived as comic'.[10] Humour, in other words, is a way of dealing with the unfamiliar and, as countless psychological and sociological studies have shown, also with the disturbing yet inescapable.[11]

Although unofficial critical humour was often dangerous to exchange in the 1930s, many people did so all the same. The Soviet regime found this humour disproportionately threatening, meaning that regardless of the usually limited nature of criticism they contained, *anekdoty* (jokes), *chastushki* (humorous ditties) and other witticisms about the regime were often recorded and hence remain available to us now. Numerous anthologies of *anekdoty, chastushki*, and ironic comments, printed contemporaneously and later, attest to the breadth of this oral culture; Mikhail Mel'nichenko's remarkably extensive research documents, critiques and cross-references these and other source-bases.[12] While Mel'nichenko's work considers *anekdoty* as a folkloric or quasi-literary

9 Gábor T. Rittersporn, *Anguish, Anger, and Folkways in Soviet Russia* (Pittsburgh, PA: University of Pittsburgh Press, 2014), 189.

10 Viktor Shklovskii, 'K teorii komicheskogo', *Epopeia* 3 (1922), 63.

11 For a helpful overview, see Alessandra Lemma, *Humour on the Couch: Exploring Humour in Psychotherapy and Everyday Life* (London: Whurr Publishers, 2000), 34–43.

12 M. Mel'nichenko, *Sovetskii anekdot. Ukazatel' siuzhetov* (Moscow, 2014), 7–76.

discourse, my interest is to use joke-telling as a source both embedded in and richly illustrative of its historical context. That being said, this chapter is not concerned to reconstruct how joke-telling was transacted or the social bonds it forged, broke, or strengthened; here, my focus is on the content of this humour and what it reveals about people's palettes of judgement, value systems, knowledge, and critical mores. I make use of diaries, near-contemporary interviews, secret police reports on 'the mood of the people', and the criminal case files of those arrested and sentenced for sharing or collecting humour deemed unacceptable and hence punishable under the infamous Article 58–10 of the RSFSR Criminal Code ('antisoviet agitation').[13] As such, we are able to identify with far greater reliability those jokes which actually circulated during the 1930s, rather than being invented by anthology-compilers, or dimly recalled by memoirists decades later.

The chapter is organized into two main sections. The first examines the survival of pre-Soviet paradigms, or what we might call 'cultural registers', evident in citizens' critical humour, focusing specifically on the awareness of pre-1917 times and the persistence of religious discourse. The second studies from several perspectives the manner in which ordinary citizens related to Power, drawing parallels with practices under tsarism but also criticizing such comparisons when they focus more on form than upon content, contemporary meaning, and perception. I conclude by reflecting on what the 'crosshatching' approach can add to our understanding of change and continuity in these tumultuous times.

1 Pre-Soviet cultural registers

That 1930s citizens could perfectly well remember a pre-revolutionary world is immediately evident in their joke-telling. Deciphering the myriad official acronyms of state institutions was a key element of critical humour, with contemporaries dreaming up numerous mocking alternatives.[14] Consider, for example, decipherments of the Party's own acronym. Officially, this was VKP(b), standing, in Russian, for 'All-Union Communist Party (Bolsheviks)'. But this was also decoded as 'All-Union Serfdom of the Bolsheviks' (*Vsesoiuznoe krepostnoe pravo Bol'shevikov*),[15] and, with more precision, 'Second Serfdom

13 Equivalent articles applied in the Soviet republics.

14 cf. Aleksandra Arkhipova and Mikhail Mel'nichenko, *Anekdoty o Staline: Teksty, kommentarii, issledovaniia* (Moscow: OGI, 2010), 341–351; see also Jonathan Waterlow, 'Intimating Trust: Popular Humour in Stalin's 1930s', *Cultural and Social History* 10(2) (2013), 221–226.

15 *Gosudarstvennyi arkhiv Rossiiskoi Federatsii* (hereafter GARF), f. 8131, op. 31, d. 9963, l. 26 (May 1940). See also, omitting 'Bolsheviks', *Rossiiskii gosudarstvennyi arkhiv sotsial'no-politicheskoi istorii* (hereafter RGASPI), f. M-1, op. 23, d. 1128, l. 64 (January 1935). Dates in parentheses following archival references refer to the date when a given joke was told, according to that document, where available. Translations are my own; I provide transliteration only when some aspect of it is useful to readers who do not speak Russian.

of the Bolsheviks' (*Vtoroe krepostnoe pravo Bol'shevikov*).[16] Similarly, an *anekdot* ran:

> Stalin asks an old man how old he is. The latter answers, 'I don't know,' and asks Stalin in turn, 'How many years were there between the first serfdom and the second? That'll be how old I am'.[17]

These and countless other examples suggest how readily citizens would directly compare the Soviet regime to tsarism and find it to be either just the same or considerably worse. This was a dual criticism, for to name the new regime 'the Second Serfdom of the Bolsheviks' was both to compare it to serfdom, but simultaneously to accuse the Bolsheviks of fundamentally reneging on their revolutionary promises.

Such comparisons were often underlain by a nostalgic, generalized equation of the tsarist regime with 'good times'. A short rhyming couplet, which Komsomol students pointedly wrote in their textbooks beneath a passage on building 'the foundation of socialist economics', is a prime example:

Byl tsar' i tsaritsa,	[When] there was the tsar and tsarina,
Byl khleb i pshenitsa.	There was bread and wheat.[18]

Historical comparisons were not always overtly negative, however, as an *anekdot* in which an old woman simply makes Stalin admit that he is now 'in [tsar] Nikolai's place' suggests.[19] Nevertheless, even in instances of comic yet not explicitly negative comparison between the present and the previous regime, the very hint that the two were similar – the source of their humour – meant that the claim of the Bolshevik Party to be creating an entirely new life and political system was still being explicitly repudiated.

An underlying awareness of older socio-political structures and standards in this way repeatedly provided a benchmark against which the Soviet regime was judged, and found wanting, by the populace. Although citizens would often call the regime out for various reasons by citing its own claims, language, and ideology, they were just as ready to turn to personal or historical memory, too. This proposition moves us immediately beyond the more limited range of interpretative faculties which the Soviet subjectivity approach allows Soviet citizens, yet doing so clearly requires little stretch of the

16 RGASPI, f. M-1, op. 23, d. 1106, l. 86 (November 1935); ibid., d. 1102, l. 130 (May 1935); *Galuzevyi derzhavnyi arkhiv sluzhby bezpeky Ukrainy* (hereafter HDA SBU), f. 6, d. 18170, l. 25 (1934). Also noted in the entry for 22 October 1929 in I. I. Shitts, *Dnevnik 'Velikogo pereloma' (mart 1928–avgust 1931)* (Paris, 1991), 149. See also Arkhipova and Mel'nichenko, *Anekdoty o Staline*, 345–346.

17 GARF, f. 8131, op. 31, d. 88411, l. 9 (1938).

18 RGASPI, f. M-1, op. 23, d. 1106, l. 21 (December 1934).

19 GARF, f. 8131, op. 31, d. 82045, l. 9 (1936–7).

imagination – by either the historian or the 1930s Soviet citizen, who was in many ways also a student of history.

A second, more specific cultural register to inform interpretations of the 1930s was one of religious values and discourse. Karen Petrone has, in relation to memory of the First World War, emphasized the 'continuities in religious discourse across the revolutionary divide. Despite the radical break between tsarist and Soviet religious policy, there were strong currents of religious thinking that traversed the revolution to make their appearance in Soviet culture'.[20] Such currents were not limited to engagements with the First World War: with over half the population registering themselves as 'believers' in the 1937 census,[21] it is little surprise that we find further evidence of religious discourse within contemporaries' humour.

Occasionally, the appearance of religion in critical humour took the form of mockery directed at leading Bolsheviks. For example, in response to his wages being delayed, a worker in tannery number 2 in Odesa loudly declared that, 'Jesus Christ rode on one donkey, but Stalin [rides] on 150 million donkeys'.[22] In other words, Christ's demands were dramatically fewer than Stalin's; on the journey to Communism, Stalin alone rode in comfort, while everyone else was, in this telling, reduced to pack animals. Such direct attacks involving religious references or assumptions seem to have been rare, however. More commonly, religion remained in the background of 1930s humour, but was no less significant as a result.

For example, some *anekdoty* featured God or St Peter in positions of power over Bolsheviks' lives and afterlives. A widespread joke involved the ghost of a Bolshevik (the identity of whom varies) attempting to enter Heaven, but he is denied entry. A passing stranger volunteers to help the despondent Bolshevik, shoving him into a sack and marching back up to the pearly gates: 'Do you have Marx [or Lenin] in there?'. 'Yes,' comes the reply. 'Well, here's his trash,' the helpful stranger answers, tossing the sack over.[23] The idea of Marx, Lenin, Stalin, or other Bolsheviks (i.e. atheists) entering Heaven is of course absurd, but the focus of this joke is actually centred upon the denigration of a current Soviet leader as the 'trash' or leftovers of his predecessors. Religion thus defines the world of the *anekdot*, even if this is not the *anekdot*'s central purpose. This is echoed in a *chastushka* that a worker sang in Odesa's Petrovskii factory:

20 Karen Petrone, *The Great War in Russian Memory* (Bloomington, IN: Indiana University Press, 2011), 74.

21 V. B. Zhiromskaia, I. N. Kiselev and Iu. A. Poliakov (eds), *Polveka pod grifom "sekretno": vsesoiuznaia perepis' naseleniia 1937 goda* (Moscow, 1996), 98, Table 17.

22 *Tsentral'nyi derzhavnyi arkhiv gromads'kykh ob"ednan' Ukrainy* (hereafter TsDAHOU), f. 1, op. 20, d. 3548, l. 33 (October 1930).

23 e.g. GARF, f. 8131, op. 31, d. 70803, ll. 23–24 (December 1934) and d. 83654, l. 10 (1936).

Ленин, Ленин	Lenin, Lenin
Ты на небе	You're in Heaven
Тут твои детки	Here your bairns
Умирают от пятилетки.	Are dying from the Plan.[24]

Lenin himself is again, in complete contradiction of his atheism, placed in Heaven. But even though the proposition clearly implies that this area of Bolshevik ideology is trumped by traditional religious belief, again the motivation behind this expression of opinion appears to be the suffering of the people under the Five-Year Plan, rather than a desire to actively push a religious agenda.

More inconspicuous still, religious language continued to colour emotional outbursts, with expressions like 'To hell with you!' (чёрт с тобой), or 'Devil take you!' remaining common currency.[25] Ways of discussing certain topics – particularly death – were still significantly shaped by pre-revolutionary, religious categories and terminology. If 'speaking Bolshevik', with its learned phrases, slogans, and values, was as important in everyday life as some historians have implied, then the survival of these overtly religious elements in open popular speech should not be overlooked in their significance.

The new Soviet world was not a blank sheet of paper on which culture could be written afresh; at both the conscious and unconscious levels, the past continued to echo across and embed itself into the present. And not just at the popular level, either. The picture is still more complex when we consider that, according to Molotov,

> One day Stalin told an *anekdot* popular in Georgia, about how God created the nations out of different materials, but for the Russians nothing remained, so he had to make them out of dirt (грязь). Which is why we're so swinish.[26]

Similarly, in a 1938 speech, Stalin recited a wry Russian proverb for its relevance to the unstable international situation: 'God save us from "friends"; we'll rid ourselves of enemies'.[27] That Stalin might repeat such religiously-infused jokes or aphorisms hints at the contradictions surrounding this issue. Indeed, he also continued, like countless others, to use expressions such as 'My god!',[28] or 'God forbid!', even in print.[29]

24 TsDAHOU, f. 1, op. 20, d. 3548, l. 33 (*c.* October 1930).

25 e.g. *Tsentral'nyi gosudarstvennyi arkhiv istoriko-politicheskikh dokumentov Sankt-Peterburga* (hereafter TsGAIPD), f. 25, op. 5, d. 54, ll. 65 and 70 (December 1934); RGASPI, f. M-1, op. 23, d. 1102, l. 115 (May 1935); TsDAHOU, f. 1, op. 20, d. 2987, l. 49 (May 1929); GARF, f. 5451, op. 43, d. 13, l. 16 (February 1932); HDA SBU, f. 6, d. 35889FP, l. 10 (1934).

26 Feliks Chuev, *Molotov: Poluderzhavnyi vlastelin* (Moscow, 2002), 329–330.

27 Speech at reception of deputies of the Supreme Soviet, 20 January 1938: RGASPI, f. 558, op. 11, d. 1121, l. 13.

28 According to his daughter: Svetlana Allilueva, *Tol'ko odin god* (London: Harper & Row 1969), 341.

29 I. V. Stalin, 'Blok oborontsev', *Sochineniia*, tom 3 (Moscow, 1954), 73 (although this piece came from 1917, that it was republished in the official collected works is

Many historians have suggested that the Bolsheviks' (and in particular Stalin's) years of working in the shadow-world of the revolutionary underground was a formative experience which instilled in them a paranoia of hidden enemies and traitors which they would never shed. There is doubtless some truth in this, but what is less often recognized is that this was just one formative context among many, as the (implicit) persistence of religious discourse suggests. In such respects, the Bolshevik leaders were no more capable than ordinary citizens of shedding their pasts; they, too, were not untainted vessels for ideology. People cannot break entirely cleanly with their pasts, and those pasts involve more than specific, individual experiences; they also include the far more expansive and less quantifiable cultural environments, linguistic practices, and value systems with which they grew up.[30]

This highlights the central tension both in terms of analysing change versus continuity in general, and for the Soviet project specifically. The Bolsheviks sought to create New Soviet People who would both generate and then live in the ideal communist society; they were to craft themselves and the world around them. On the other hand, physical environments were consciously designed to promote a new, communalist consciousness; environment was to craft the citizens. These tendencies essentially approached the same issues from opposite directions, and the tension between the assumptions underlying each sums up the fundamental chicken-and-egg problem of the Soviet Union: which comes first, the new world or the new person?

The concept of 'utopia' as discussed by Eric Naiman offers both an apposite and enlightening way to think about the problem: 'Utopias are contaminated not only by linguistic but also by historical transmission. The question of how one gets from here to there requires the establishment of a link between the flawed present and the unflawed future (or past).' Therefore, 'the process of transition is fraught with danger'.[31] He continues:

> since the ideal often springs from passionate rejection of the Real, it is not surprising that the utopian text tends to reinscribe that which it attempts to purge. The detested object may disappear, but its indented characteristics leave a visible and ineffaceable mark on the world that has defined itself by that object's banishment.[32]

significant); idem, 'Zakliuchitel'noe slovo', *Sochineniia* tom 9 (Moscow, 1948 [1926]). As did Molotov, for example: cf. Chuev, *Molotov*, 48, 122, 128, 521, 557, 564, 640.

30 Ronald Grigor Suny's biography of Stalin argues explicitly (and convincingly) that the man can 'be better understood in the spatial and temporal contexts and influences that he experienced'. Suny, *Stalin and the Russian Revolutionary Movement: From Koba to Commissar*, manuscript, Introduction. My thanks to Ron for allowing me to read the unpublished manuscript.

31 Eric Naiman, *Sex in Public: The Incarnation of Early Soviet Ideology* (Princeton, NJ: Princeton University Press, 1997), 13, 14.

32 Naiman, *Sex in Public*, 17.

The new Soviet world was significantly defined in opposition to the past and, on their way to that promised new world, neither ordinary people nor the Party faithful dumped their personal and cultural baggage at the border of 1917, nor of 1929 when forced industrialization began. In the case of religion, this does not imply, let alone prove, a continuity of religious belief amongst citizenry or leadership; what it does show, however, is that the premium scholars have placed on instances of citizens 'speaking Bolshevik' has been at the cost of attending to when they (and even the leaders themselves) spoke within and across other, non-Bolshevik discourses. There were no clean or sharp divisions between these discourses, even in public fora; even as beliefs or values were officially excised from Soviet life, they left their indented traces behind, blemishing the utopia which the regime was attempting to construct.[33]

But what of the new generation, who had not directly experienced the world before the Revolution? In fact, when clandestine decipherments of official acronyms were revealed to the authorities, it was almost always schoolchildren who were to blame. This raises an intriguing question as to whether we should consider this a 'continuity' of critical outlook drawing upon pre-revolutionary knowledge, because these children were too young to have first-hand knowledge of the world before 1917. Indeed, younger children would have had very limited understanding of the political significance of these 'codes' – hence they brazenly copied them out in classrooms, while adults seem largely to have kept them safe. We can certainly speculate that teenagers would have had a greater understanding of the political charge these 'codes' held, but the pre-1917 world to which they and other comparative *anekdoty* referred was still unknown to them personally.

It must therefore have been adults – most likely the respective children's parents or grandparents – who passed on, inadvertently or otherwise, comparison-based criticisms of the Soviet Union. This represents a different but no less important continuity – that of handing knowledge or 'know-how' down the generations, reminding us that we must avoid the assumption that the younger generation in the USSR was straightforwardly brainwashed by official ideology for lack of alternative sources of information about the past. The only way to cut off the past from the present, as well as burning all the history books, would have been – in Robert Thurston's words – for the state 'to liquidate the grandmothers'.[34] While it was certainly wary of the older generation, the regime did not go quite this far, so whether or not this alternative source of knowledge made a lasting impact on the younger generation, it is important to recognize that it was potentially available to them (and, indeed, potentially attractive to an age-group given to rebellion against state authority).

33 On the complexity, ambivalence and adaptational strategies which characterized the assault on religion and its reception, see the insightful work of William B. Husband, *'Godless Communists': Atheism and Society in Soviet Russia, 1917–1932* (DeKalb, IL: Northern Illinois University Press, 2000).

34 Robert W. Thurston, 'The Soviet Family During the Great Terror, 1935–1941', *Soviet Studies* 43(3) (1991), 563.

2 Continuities in relating to power

For all the changes that 1917 ushered in, historians have in various ways argued that the relationship between people and ruler remained much the same under Stalin as it had been under the tsars. It has, for example, been argued countless times that it was a 'tsarist carryover' that facilitated the rule of Stalin as a direct substitute for the tsar, because the inhabitants of the former Russian Empire were well used to (and hence simply continued to practise) obedience to a single, all-powerful figure seated in the distant capital.[35] Late-Soviet scholars critical of Stalin's cult of personality also perceived this 'carry-over', though they characterized it in suitably Marxist-Leninist terms, calling it, for instance, 'an attempt to build socialism using petit-bourgeois means, [thereby pursuing] petit-bourgeois interests, ideals ... [and] morals'.[36] Some Russian scholars even today continue to essentialize this as a peculiarly 'Asiatic despotism'[37] – a claim which serves as an explanation only if one holds certain xenophobic (if not outright racist) views. In this section, I examine several aspects of how tsarist subject and then Soviet citizen related to Power and question how far these different yet related claims of continuity can be substantiated.

Pictures of abuse

That portraits of Stalin and other leaders were hung in the same places (and many more besides) where those of the tsar used to be inevitably implies a continuity in the symbology of power – an observation that has become a truism in the historiography. However, we should not simply equate this with a continuity in the *meaning* of that power, the regime it represented, or the bases of authority upon which it rested. These were all significantly different under the Soviet Union. Moreover, while the portraits might be hung with the intent to project power, in practice they often became targets for verbal abuse and vandalism, reports of which litter the archives. As well as disfiguring portraits – from gouging out the eyes to extinguishing cigarettes on them[38] – when citizens sought to vent their anger against particular leaders, they could also make use of these portraits with (a little) more subtlety.

35 Quoting Jan Plamper, himself adapting Matthew Truesdell's 'royal carryover', used to describe Louis-Napoleon Bonaparte; 'Introduction: Modern Personality Cults', in *Personality Cults in Stalinism/Personenkulte im Stalinismus*, edited by Jan Plamper and Klaus Heller (Göttingen: Vandenhoeck and Ruprecht, 2004), 20.

36 Z. I. Fainburg, *Ne sotvori sebe kumira ... Sotsializm i 'kul't lichnosti' (Ocherki teorii)* (Moscow, 1991), 306.

37 Recent examples include V. V. Viktorov, *Kul't lichnosti v Rossii: Popytka osmyslenniia* (Moscow, 2012), 7–8; V. V. Cherepanov, *Vlast' i voina: Stalinskii mekhanizm gosudarstvennogo upravleniia v Velikoi Otechestvennoi Voine* (Moscow, 2006), 491.

38 e.g. HDA SBU, f. 16, op. 31, d. 77, l. 400 (1938); RGASPI, f. M-1, op. 23, d. 1106, l. 21 (January 1935); TsGAIPD, f. 24, op. 5, d. 2685, l. 8 (March 1935).

At an Urazovskii military training post on the Moscow–Donbas railway line, a portrait of Lenin was discovered to have been hung beneath a coat-rack, meaning that everyone's coats and hats were unceremoniously draped over the great leader's image. Given that the portrait was hung so low, and the enormous official prestige of Lenin at this time (1935), it was evidently no accident or misunderstanding.[39] Similarly, in 1936 a portrait of Stalin was discovered 'nailed to an old wheelbarrow' in a garage; several Komsomol members found themselves in trouble for not reporting this outrage.[40] In addition to ironic juxtapositions like these, written commentaries were also used. It was not uncommon to decipher the acronym 'MTS' (Machine-Tractor Station) as *Mogila Tovarishcha Stalina* (Comrade Stalin's Grave), and it was a natural extension to append this to portraits of the man himself, as did an 11-year-old at a school in Zhitomir.[41] Similarly a 15-year-old peasant's son in Tiraspol'skii raion, a certain Stepanov, sneaked into the kolkhoz administration office and defaced the nameplate beneath a portrait of Voroshilov, deleting all bar the first three letters – 'VOR' – the Russian word for 'thief'.[42] In each case, this was to write an explicatory commentary – to seize control of the meaning of an official image. Captions can wield great power, as they did daily in the pages of *Pravda* and the wider Soviet press, with their ability to shape and define the meaning of an image; if the symbology of power might here remain the same under the Bolsheviks, they did not possess a monopoly over its interpretation.

Crosshatching of past, present, religious, and secular also arose in this context. In response to Leningrad Party Boss S. M. Kirov's assassination, S. P. Logachev, a 50-year-old machinist at a textile *artel'* in Leningrad, grumbled to his colleagues that

> There's no difference between the old times and now. Then, Alexander II was killed and the murderer was shot; now Kirov's been killed, and the murderer will also be shot; and just look at the portrait of Kirov, it's just the same, like on an iconostasis.[43]

The abuse of images of the country's leaders was certainly not new: Boris Kolonitskii has demonstrated how official portraits of the tsar were also not one-way, top-down conduits of power: while they represented the monarch both visually and legally (swearing in front of a portrait constituted almost as much of a crime as doing so before the tsar himself), the same image often provided a ready target, functioning as a lightning rod for popular anger or frustration.[44] Mocking the country's leader via his image in portraits does not

39 RGASPI, f. 17, op. 120, d. 176, l. 135 (February 1935).
40 RGASPI, f. M-1, op. 23, d. 1184, l. 57 (August 1936).
41 HDA SBU, f. 16, op. 28, d. 12, l. 33 (1935).
42 TsDAHOU, f. 1, op. 20, d. 6642, l. 27 (April 1935).
43 TsGAIPD, f. 24, op. 5, d. 2288, l. 67 (3 December 1934).
44 B. I. Kolonitskii, *'Tragicheskaia erotika': obrazy imperatorskoi sem'i v gody pervoi mirovoi voiny* (Moscow, 2010), Ch. 3; in rough English translation: Boris

represent a continuity of that power, but rather a continuity in popular practices of engaging with it: the Soviet regime was in a sense setting itself up for this abuse by appropriating the symbolic practices of tsarism. The abuse also suggests that the elevated and less critical devotion to Stalin so often said to characterize popular opinion during his rule – due to his cult of personality – is rather misleading. This, then, is a further continuity: the absolute ruler was certainly not loved absolutely, and the prevalence of his image was also an invitation to his becoming the primary target for anti-regime anger.

Nevertheless, this continuity in relating to power was not purely negative: some citizens placed images of *vozhdi* in ikon frames, and even crossed themselves and prayed in front of them, thus bringing a religious devotion to bear on a regime which officially rejected it. That such actions represented a continuity of practice was apparent to contemporaries, as, for example, the diary of Andrei Arzhilovskii attests.[45] Reports noting such actions were, however, strongly disapproving; as Sarah Davies has argued, this was clearly a practice which grew from below, rather than one implemented from above.[46]

In each case, then, whether hurling abuse at or saying their prayers before the painted images of the Soviet leaders, we can see continuities in popular relations to power and authority. But in neither case was this a simple transfer of obedience from old regime to new: in the former, this was a continuity of critical engagement and assertiveness; in the latter, direct substitution of new for old was undertaken in a form that was anathema to Soviet ideology, thereby implicitly undermining a key tenet of its rationale for holding power at all.

Traditional forms

The *anekdot* and *chastushka* forms themselves have a rich history in Russian oral culture as a means by which to criticize power and authority, and thereby to share interpretative judgements of contemporary social and political life.[47] Indeed, many of the central premises and tropes which characterized popular *anekdoty* in the 1930s owed a clear debt to pre-revolutionary popular culture, as Aleksandra Arkhipova, Mikhail Mel'nichenko, and Seth Graham have demonstrated.[48] Certain scholars suggest that the *anekdot* only solidified into its modern, recognizable form in the 1920s–30s, at which time, they claim, the

Kolonitsky, 'Insulting the Russian Royal Family: Crime, Blame and its Sources', in *Shame, Blame and Culpability: Crime and Violence in the Modern State*, edited by Marianna Muravyeva and David Nash (Abingdon: Routledge, 2013).

45 Diary of Andrei Arzhilovskii, in *Intimacy and Terror: Soviet Diaries of the 1930s*, edited by Véronique Garros, Natalia Korenevskaya and Thomas Lahusen, trans. Carol A. Flath (New York: The New Press, 1995), 118.

46 Sarah Davies, *Popular Opinion in Stalin's Russia: Terror, Propaganda and Dissent, 1934–1941* (Cambridge: Cambridge University Press, 1997), 163.

47 Rittersporn, *Anguish, Anger, and Folkways*, 207–208.

48 Arkhipova and Mel'nichenko, *Anekdoty o Staline*, 36–63; Seth Graham, *Resonant Dissonance: The Russian Joke in Cultural Context* (Evanston, IL: Northwestern University Press, 2009), especially Chs 1 and 2.

word *anekdotchik* (*anekdot*–teller) also appeared. If true, this would make a case for the *anekdot* being a natively Soviet form of expression, but in truth it would take an extraordinarily narrow definition of the *anekdot* to substantiate such a claim, and even these particular authors note that this was still a form which developed from longer-standing, traditional speech genres.[49] Moreover, that a 1904 study considered the genre significant enough to conduct a survey of its local specificities, even claiming that '*Anekdoty* about Viatka residents are already of venerable antiquity',[50] strongly suggests that a distinct form both called and recognizable to us as the *anekdot* predated the Revolution and was developed and varied enough to justify study even on the local level.[51]

In any case, as Graham puts it, 'Although the *anekdot* rapidly acquired new, historically specific features in the transformed sociopolitical atmosphere following the October Revolution, it is a mistake simply to draw a thick red boundary at 1917 on the time line of its generic evolution'.[52] Even as it developed to engage with Soviet realities, the *anekdot* was both furnished and given actual meaning by a 'language of traditional subjects and motifs';[53] as such, it, like its close relative the *chastushka*, was a form that could feel genuinely pre-Soviet, familiar and unofficial to contemporaries. It was a language that seemed more their own, even as it increasingly interacted and became coloured by Soviet discourse.

The Party did not approve of this adulteration and was deeply concerned about the power of popular speech genres to spread ideas and sentiments not to its liking. It was not that the forms themselves were considered counter-revolutionary, however, and a solution proposed at the first Soviet Writers' Congress in 1934 was effectively to colonize these folkloric forms in order to bring them under state control. Thus a Mordovian delegate noted that a recent expedition to collect both Mordovian and Russian *chastushki* from the countryside had revealed 'a very bad situation'. 'Of the thousands of *chastushki* we collected,' he explained, 'a substantial part were anti-kolkhoz, counter-revolutionary, or just indecent. The percentage of Soviet *chastushki* was not high'.[54] He blamed this shortcoming on Soviet poets at large ignoring the form; too concerned with *belles lettres* which neither reached nor were intelligible to the peasant masses, they had allowed kulaks and other class enemies

49 E. Ia. Shmeleva and A. D. Shmelev, *Russkii anekdot: Tekst i rechevoi zhanr* (Moscow, 2002), 20.

50 D. Zelenin, *Narodnaia prislov'ia i anekdoty o russkikh zhitel'iakh viatskoi gubernii (etnograficheskii i istoriko-literaturnyi ocherk)* (Viatka, 1904), 37.

51 We should also note in passing that this was not a specifically Russian heritage, either, even though studies of Soviet *anekdoty* almost exclusively trace the Russian roots. Even if the complexities of establishing truly discrete 'national' folklores are significant, there have been attempts to do just that. e.g. V. K. Bandarchyk et al (eds), *Zharty, anekdoty, humareski. Belaruskaiia narodnaia tvorchasts'* (Minsk, 1984).

52 Graham, *Resonant Dissonance*, 18.

53 Arkhipova and Mel'nichenko, *Anekdoty o Staline*, 28.

54 Speech of F. M. Chesnokov, 9th Session, *Pervyi vsesoiuznyi s"ezd sovetskikh pisatelei, 1934: Stenograficheskii otchet* (Moscow, 1934), 257.

to take over the *chastushka*, and it had therefore become a 'weapon' aimed against Soviet power. This interpretation obviously ignores the agency of the non-kulak speakers of these *chastushki*, let alone the potential ambivalence of their performance but, on this superficial basis, Soviet poets were simply to seize control of the genre, and to 'quickly produce several collections of *chastushki* and distribute them in large numbers …'.[55] This proposal for cultural colonization was never taken up, but it illustrates the degree of official anxiety that certain traditional genres of expression could become a foaming channel of critical opinion. Indeed, immediately after the end of the Second World War, the political police destroyed all the examples of *chastushki* they could find in the holdings of Leningrad's Pushkin House.[56] Such concerns were not without foundation, but criticism was frequently more oblique and less wilfully destructive than feared.

Anekdoty could often function like parables (and as a literary form shared common roots with them),[57] summing up truths about life as contemporaries experienced it, in an adroit, memorable form.[58] A closely related genre – a brand of moral fable known as 'animal folktales' (сказки о животных) – performed a similar function in the 1930s. Akin to Aesop's Fables, these, too, had a venerable, printed heritage in pre-revolutionary Russia, with journals such as *Otechestvennye zapiski* under the editorship of Nikolai Nekrasov using Aesopian language to mask the critical positions which had caused Nekrasov's previous publication, *Sovremennik*, to be shut down in 1866;[59] journals such as *Zritel'* took up this model after another relaxation of censorship in 1905.[60]

In the 1930s, numerous examples of this sub-genre appeared. For example, A. F. Klevakin, a village schoolteacher in Ol'khovskii raion, told the following joke while at work:

> At the border with Germany a louse met a pig. The pig asked the louse, 'How's life in Germany?' The louse answered, 'I'm suffocating! I don't know what to do; the linen is all new and clean, and they iron it every day!' The pig replied, 'Come to the USSR, life is better with us. You'll live like you're in heaven: we have sheets in every hut and kolkhoz house

55 Ibid.

56 Rittersporn, *Anguish, Anger, and Folkways*, 208.

57 cf. E. K. Nikanorova, *Istoricheskii anekdot v russkoi literature XVIII veka: Anekdoty o Petre Velikom* (Novosibirsk, 2001), 313–322; Mel'nichenko, *Sovetskii anekdot*, 7–8.

58 On which, cf. Waterlow, 'Intimating Trust', 221–222; idem, 'More than Resistance: Political Humour under Stalin in the 1930s', in *Humour and Laughter in History: Transcultural Perspectives*, edited by Elisabeth Cheauré and Regine Nohejl (Bielefeld: Transcript-Verlag, 2014).

59 Geoffrey Hosking, *Russia and the Russians: From Earliest Times to the Present* (2nd edn, London: Penguin, 2012), 298. *Otechestvennye zapiski* was itself shut down in 1884 (ibid., 298–299).

60 Mel'nichenko, *Sovetskii anekdot*, 8, n. 9.

> which aren't washed for months!' Then the louse asked the pig how his life was, to which the pig answered, 'I've been left barely alive. You can't find a bite [to eat] in a single slop pit; all the starving *kolkhozniki* have taken them'.[61]

The joke functions by taking Soviet ideological claims to have created the greatest state in the world to their logical conclusion: for *whom* (or what) was the filth and deprivation of the USSR attractive?

G. F. Narozhnyi, a doctor, told the following *anekdot* to his colleagues as they travelled by car to the town of Kuba, Azerbaijani SSR:

> Durov gathered all the animals together but [then] explained that the meeting was for Party members only and asked all the non-Party animals to leave. Only the donkey remained, flapping its ears.[62]

Here, non-Party people are dismissed, in both senses, as biddable animals, but the minority Party 'person' is still more ridiculous: an ass, dumbly and comically flapping its ears.

Animal folktales could arise in response to specific events, too. After the Kirov murder on 1 December 1934, the head of Leningrad's NKVD, F.D. Medved', was arrested by his superior, Iagoda, and sentenced to three years imprisonment. Shortly thereafter, this was reimagined in a popular *anekdot* via wordplay on the literal meanings of the two men's names: *medved'* means 'bear', and *iagoda* means 'berry'.

> What's the difference between the forest and Leningrad?
>
> In the forest, the bear eats the berries. But in Leningrad the berry has eaten the bear.[63]

Novel examples like this highlight the continued creativity of popular, political humour: citizens were not simply repeating pre-revolutionary jokes in the 1930s, but were using established forms (or genres) inventively to deal with new issues. This was, therefore, to mix together the old and the new – enabling citizens to indulge in a critique of the new regime in a language which they could feel was their own, or at least was *not* the regime's. Furthermore, using the Aesopian mode was to induce the sense of a 'moral' judgement, giving further weight to the critique they offered.

61 GARF, f. 8131, op. 31, d. 6410, l. 4 (1936).

62 GARF, f. 8131, op. 31, d. 88415, l. 11 (1937). Also recounted in the Harvard Interview Project on the Soviet Social System (hereafter HPSSS), 24/A/3, 24. Another *anekdot* casts all Party members as cattle: HPSSS 54/A/5, 28.

63 TsGAIPD, f. 25, op. 5, d. 50, l. 25 (December 1934); with slight variations (e.g. replacing 'Leningrad' with 'the NKVD') see also: f. 25, op. 5, d. 47, l. 18 (December 1934); d. 54, l. 79 (December 1934); GARF, f. 8131, op. 31, d. 69568, l. 9 (*c*. 1936).

Anekdoty could be used within another related sub-genre – that of vulgar, demeaning, and even pornographic abuse of the powerful. Jokes about Stalin getting pubic lice or being sodomized by Kalinin circulated in these years, for instance.[64] This was a tradition in itself; the crude jokes made at the expense of the last Romanovs, especially the tsarina,[65] survived as a genre or practice to attack the *vozhdi* of the Soviet Union. Subverting hierarchies in exuberantly vulgar ways was also to continue the spirit of the carnivalesque – age-old inversions performed in the face of Power by ordinary people with ambivalent results, as Gábor Rittersporn has explored in depth.[66]

Overall, it is perhaps unsurprising that citizens used traditional forms and language to criticize the leadership and the world around them; nevertheless, the historiography of the past 15–20 years has so often dwelt on the principle of contemporaries' confinement – willingly or otherwise – within the language and conceptual categories of the Bolshevik regime, that it is now rather unorthodox to emphasize their access to and use of pre-revolutionary knowledge, language, and interpretative frameworks. In fact – and as the Soviet regime itself remained cautiously aware – traditional forms like *chastushki, anekdoty*, and versions of animal folktales continued to be used and to evolve in order to critique Soviet realities: citizens could and many did make use of these forms in order to speak in a language which lay outside regime control. Form does not dictate content, but the two inevitably influence and shape each other. If there was such a thing as Soviet folklore, it was arguably what we find in the crosshatching of these old and new values and practices.

Avatars

Within the imagined scenarios of popular humour, aside from the targets of the jokes, we also find certain protagonists or avatars chosen to be the mouthpieces for Soviet citizens' discontent and criticisms. Frequently, these were either a peasant or an old *babushka* (or her male counterpart, the *starik*), as in this example: Kontsov, a Komsomol member and metalworker, told the following *anekdot* at a factory in Leningrad:

> A peasant came to Stalin and asked: 'When will socialism be built?' Stalin replied that it will be soon, after a year or two. 'But will the GPU and the other security forces still exist then?' Comrade Stalin answers that they won't. In response, the peasant declares: 'Then we will shoot you all!'[67]

64 See Jonathan Waterlow, 'Popular Humour in Stalin's 1930s: A Study of Popular Opinion and Adaptation', D.Phil. Thesis, University of Oxford, 2012, 118–120.

65 cf. B. I. Kolonitskii, 'K izucheniiu mekhanizmov desakralizatsiia monarkhii (slukhi i "politicheskaia pornografiia" v gody pervoi mirovoi voiny)', in *Istorik i revoliutsiia. Sbornik statei k 70-letiiu so dnia rozhdeniia Olega Nikolaevicha Znamenskogo*, edited by N. N. Smirnov et al (St Petersburg, 1999), 72–86.

66 Rittersporn, *Anger, Anguish, and Folkways*, Ch. 7.

67 TsGAIPD, f. 25, op. 5, d. 47, ll 8 (December 1934).

As soon as the apparatus of repression is removed, this peasant makes clear, the population will violently overthrow the Bolsheviks – a fantasy no doubt indulged to some extent by many Soviet citizens. The peasant character here allows this sentiment to be expressed with an uncomplicated directness which increases both the humorous effect, via the incongruity of Stalin being spoken to this way, but also the sense of certainty that this will indeed come to pass.

This instinctively accurate and uncomplicated peasant 'wisdom' is likewise evoked even when the avatar technically misunderstands Bolshevik policies: for example, a joke made about the Bolsheviks' obsessive use of the word 'tempo'. Bolshevik propaganda was strewn with this term as part of the general emphasis on rapid, mass-scale industrialization. In this joke, a *kolkhoznik* visits Kalinin in order to ask what the word 'tempo' means, for he and his fellow farmers can't understand its significance. Kalinin escorts him to the window and points at a passing tram: 'You see, if we have a dozen trams at the moment, after five years there will be hundreds'. Armed with this knowledge, the *kolkhoznik* returns home, where he is immediately surrounded by his comrades who demand to know the meaning of 'tempo' for themselves. Looking around for inspiration, the peasant points at the cemetery, declaring 'You see those dozen graves? After five years, there will be thousands!'[68] The peasant's 'misunderstanding' (and bold inflation of the quantity) in fact reveals the truth of Bolshevik forced industrialization policies: suffering and death on a mass scale. The uncomplicated, canny peasant simply cuts through the deceptions of ideology and immediately identifies the reality behind it.

A final example sees Stalin try to use an old saying to deny a *babushka*'s request:

> An old woman went to ask Stalin for permission to leave the country, because elsewhere life is better. Stalin said: '*Babushka*, it always seems better where we are not'. She answered: 'Ah, but I want to live where *you*, you devils, are not'.[69]

The *babushka*'s authority to speak the truth – to voice folk wisdom – trumps Stalin's efforts to draw on that same shared cultural store. She uses a shard of reality as it was experienced by the Soviet population to slice through his obfuscation and thereby outwits him.

68 GARF, f. 8131, op. 31, d. 99140, l. 3 (1935); d. 16230, l. 36 (1935). The archival recordings are a shortened summary of the joke's content. I have reconstructed it with reference to Dora Shturman and Sergei Tiktin, *Sovetskii Soiuz v zerkale politicheskogo anekdota* (London, 1985), 133. A related witticism was made by a worker in a Leningrad factory, who noted simply that 'Lenin led us to death by a gentle route, but Stalin does so with a faster tempo!' (GARF, f. 5 451, op. 43, d. 13, l. 101 [October 1932]).

69 GARF, f. 8131, op. 31, d. 41217; version in which the *babushka* goes to see the People's Commissar of foreign affairs: d. 21326, l. 6 (1941).

These folkloric avatars – or even, indeed, the 'moral fable' genre itself – could be usefully interpreted as the literary equivalents of the iconic figure of the Holy Fool (*iurodivyi*) who, by virtue of both tradition and his[70] perceived dislocation from the hierarchies and strictures of the material world, may with impunity speak truth to Power.[71] Predominantly, this takes the form of inversions which highlight the oddities or shortcomings of the present; the Holy Fool is a one-man Carnival who throws rules into absurd relief by acting according to their direct opposite.[72] Maureen Perrie observed this in Russian folktales more generally, noting that in 'tales about "master and man"' the desire of the latter, the powerless ordinary person, is frequently played out in folktales, and that 'these tales therefore involve a utopian element of psychological wish fulfillment for the performer and his audience, in which the tables are turned, often with a disproportionate degree of cruelty and violence, on the exploiter'.[73] Perhaps, though, when traditional authority figures were used to critique the Soviet world, there was as much a sense of restoring order to a world turned upside-down by revolution, as there was one of inverting the status quo.

The peasant, *babushka*, and *starik* figures were obvious avatars for Soviet citizens; they could personify traditional, *popular* authority, and represented earthy, traditional peasant life and values. Much of this lay in a fundamental common sense and ability to state the bald facts of life, an attribute augmented by the moral authority or wisdom associated with old age or simply with the perceived moral 'purity' of working the land. They represented a distinct source of non-Bolshevik, pre-revolutionary authority, the knowledge and acumen of whom was turned to in order to attack the failings of the new order and its rulers. In these imagined confrontations, the old could, for a moment, triumph over the new.

Crosshatching: integrating change and continuity

Triumphs of this kind were imagined and short-lived, however, and to think in terms of the struggle between the old and new as a zero-sum game is misleading. When examining periods of significant change and transition, we must try to

70 They were always male.

71 On the character type of the 'Holy Fool', cf. Lesley Milne, 'Introduction', *Reflective Laughter: Aspects of Humour in Russian Culture,* edited by idem (London: Anthem Press, 2004), 2, 8; Ivan Esaulov, 'Two Facets of Comedic Space in Russian Literature of the Modern Period: Holy Foolishness and Buffoonery', in ibid., 73–77. Consider also the character of Ikonnikov in Vasilii Grossman's masterpiece, *Life and Fate*, trans. Robert Chandler (London: Vintage, 2006).

72 cf. a brief consideration of the didactic function of Holy Fools' inversions in B. A. Uspenskii, 'Antipovedenie v kul'ture drevnei Rusi', *Izbrannye trudy,* Tom 1: *Semiotika istorii, semiotika kul'tury* (Moscow, 1994), 326–327.

73 Maureen Perrie, 'Folklore as Evidence of Peasant *Mentalité*: Social Attitudes and Values in Russian Popular Culture', *Russian Review* 48 (1989), 126.

escape our training as historians and not attempt only – as exam questions usually go – to identify 'the extent to which' a particular issue or phenomenon was 'most important' in a given context. When studying a society in flux, there are always many elements involved, both old and new, but which were experienced by contemporaries synchronically and hence were *mixed*. This is easy enough to state – to declare that we are dealing with a 'hybrid' of some kind – but alone it is insufficient.[74] We must go a step further and explore the nature and effects of that mixing, which is where I think the crosshatching metaphor is particularly useful.

The continuities across 1917 we've discussed do not represent a fortress of pre-revolutionary values attempting to hold out against a besieging Soviet regime. Although critical humour might be caustic, it was almost never an outright rejection of the regime at large. Indeed, reading the *svodki* on 'unhealthy attitudes' suggests time and again that the people reported for telling critical jokes were not the same individuals who called for the downfall of the Soviet system *tout court*; reading hundreds of criminal records for *anekdot*-telling confirms this picture.[75] A disgruntled citizen summed this up when defacing his ballot paper for the 1938 Supreme Soviet elections. As he put it, '[I'm] for the dictatorship of the proletariat *without* the party'.[76] Sentiments of this kind, favouring a kind of halfway-house between change and continuity, of accepting the Revolution but not its leaders, was itself far from new: it had been expressed (and recorded) during the First World War in calls for a republic, but one over which Grand Duke Nikolai Nikolaevich (who had commanded the Russian forces until Nicholas II disastrously took control) would rule as tsar.[77] Half joke, half serious, it is within this crosshatching of change and continuity, of acceptance and rejection, that contemporaries struggled to make sense of the molten world of the early USSR.

Within the crosshatching, the old and new were being integrated – even if this was frequently a tense and contradictory integration. This is why even in letters written to Power, many barely literate citizens attempted to bolster their various pleas for redress with a mixture of *both* clichés drawn from the Soviet newspapers *and* proverbs and folk wisdom.[78] And hence Soviet citizens might hang portraits of Soviet leaders in ikon frames and treat them (in formal terms) like saints, but they might also use such portraits as imagined channels by which to communicate their displeasure. Form, again, does not simply determine meaning. Similarly, the evocation of religious categories and language when dealing with the failures and frustrations of Soviet life does not straightforwardly indicate the survival of a religious belief positioned in

74 cf. *Ab Imperio* 4 (2013), which considers some of the theoretical and conceptual implications of hybridity theories for the study of post-Soviet spaces.
75 cf. Waterlow, *Popular Humour*, Introduction and Ch. 1.
76 HDA SBU, f. 16, op. 31, d. 77, l. 519. Emphasis added.
77 Kolonitskii, *'Tragicheskaia erotika'*, 456.
78 Aleksandr Livshin and Igor' Orlov, *Vlast' i obshchestvo: dialog v pis'makh* (Moscow: ROSSPEN, 2002), 19.

direct opposition to Soviet power. Instead, as a team of sociologists writing in the 1950s perceptively noted: 'much of the religious sentiment that remains [in the Soviet Union] has become more secularized and is expressed in the form of social ethics.'[79] Religious values had become crosshatched with new, overtly secular times and were thereby reconfigured and neither simply wiped out, nor left unchanged (a conceptualization we might likewise apply to religious values in modern Europe).

Although the world before 1917 was often evoked to criticize the Soviet present, both regimes could just as easily be criticized side-by-side by citizens who held little regard for either. For example, when Kirov was murdered, the Leningrad worker Vatulkin responded with wordplay: '*Odnim tsar'kom stalo men'she*', meaning literally 'One princeling fewer'.[80] This was mocking in itself, but the grammatical form of 'princeling' – '*tsar'kom*' – also echoes Bolshevik nomenclature, which shortened the title 'People's Commissar' to 'Narkom'. Here, Vatulkin seemed to merge local elites old and new, simultaneously treating both of them derisively.

But crosshatching was not, as I have tried to suggest, only or predominantly a cynical or negative affair. Both Karen Petrone's and Malte Rolf's studies of Soviet mass festivals highlight how, regardless of the state's intentions and careful planning, when ideology met the people, the people transformed it to suit not only their experience and perceptions, but also just to have as much fun as they could. Festivals and holidays were particularly fertile ground for the creative mixing of traditional and Soviet rituals and practices: while the state tried to wipe religious holidays off the calendar by creating their own, many (probably most) people simply took the opportunity to celebrate both. Many continued to celebrate Easter, but were just as happy to raise a glass and snack on a *kulich* (the traditional pastry blessed at the Easter service) on an otherwise Red 1 May.[81] And even if you chose only to mark the new Soviet holidays, you might still use the Orthodox calendar to give temporal shape to the year, not from religious conviction, but because the seasonal rhythms were engrained to the point they simply felt 'natural'.[82] And just as people sought to find meaningful patterns in the year, they continually sought to find or create such patterns in the crosshatching of the rest of their lives.

Even if using traditional folkloric genres to criticize the regime suggests a distinct, non-Bolshevik discourse available to contemporaries, Kolonitskii's

79 Alex Inkeles and Raymond A. Bauer, *The Soviet Citizen: Daily Life in a Totalitarian Society* (Cambridge, MA: Harvard University Press 1959), 380–381. Their comment related to the postwar USSR, but it seems to me to fit the prewar context, too.

80 TsGAIPD, f. 24, op. 5, d. 2288, l. 11 (December 1934).

81 Malte Rolf, *Soviet Mass Festivals, 1917–1991*, trans. Cynthia Klohr (Pittsburgh, PA: University of Pittsburgh Press, 2013), 132–134; Karen Petrone, *Life has Become More Joyous, Comrades: Celebrations in the Time of Stalin* (Bloomington, IN: Indiana University Press, 2000), 19.

82 Rolf, *Soviet Mass Festivals*, 133.

work highlights the important point that in nature and function, even the act of 'speaking Bolshevik' was not a straightforwardly new phenomenon. For a variety of reasons, and whether voluntary or not, 'inhabitants of the Russian Empire had for centuries studied how to "speak monarchist"' (говорить 'по-монархически') – that is, to use the appropriate words and phrases in relation to the monarchy and monarchical system, including with regards to their own self-representation.[83] As such, the practice of speaking the regime's 'language' should neither be seen as unique to the Soviet period, nor as solely the preserve of the modernizing 'total' state. 'Speaking Bolshevik' is therefore itself more accurately understood as an act of crosshatching: it was not to enwrap oneself in a web of purely Soviet discourse, for it could be in its very nature an admixture: like the *anekdot* itself, it was a popular speech practice which, though its content changed with the times, actually predated the Soviet regime as a way to speak to, about, and by which to relate oneself to Power.

Contemporaries were blending criticism and acceptance in the attempt to make sense of the confusing, disruptive world around them; they did not need to be over 30 to do this, but nor did they 'perfectly well remember a pre-Soviet world': memory and practices do not pass through time perfectly unchanged, but they do continue to resonate and affect how people understand and engage with the present (and the future). Many learnt to 'speak Bolshevik' – just as we all take on some of the culturally-sanctioned language and values of the times – but this neither meant they forgot older 'languages', let alone that they became trapped in the Soviet one. Continuity and change are not opposites: they are both processes which in the realm of culture interact and are inescapably shaped by each other. The banks shape the river, just as the river shapes the banks.

83 Kolonitskii, *'Tragicheskaia erotika'*, 12.

Epilogue

The Russian tradition? Discourses of tradition and modernity

Peter Waldron

In 1974, with the dead hand of the Brezhnev regime exerting a stifling grip on Soviet society and politics, two books were published in the West that sought to show that the Soviet system was a profoundly Russian phenomenon. The Cold War appeared to have settled into a stalemate, and Western critics of the USSR sought to explain the Soviet system not just as a product of the 1917 revolution, but as an inevitable evolution of traditional Russian structures and values. Tibor Szamuely's *The Russian Tradition* argued that the twin Russian traditions of an oppressive state and of a destructive intelligentsia had produced the Bolshevik revolution and the Soviet regime that followed it.[1] For Richard Pipes, whose *Russia under the Old Regime* appeared in the same year, the Soviet regime was the consequence of immutable environmental and social forces that had given rise to a police state before 1917 and that continued to determine the shape of the post-revolutionary world.[2]

For both Szamuely and Pipes, the nature of the Russian state had been shaped by its geographical position. The poor soils and harsh climate of much of northern Russia made farming a largely unprofitable endeavour, and this was one of the central motors for Russian territorial expansion as new land was needed to grow crops to feed an expanding population. Pipes quoted Kliuchevskii's analysis that 'The history of Russia is the history of a country which colonises itself' approvingly,[3] and he argued that this imperial expansion was an integral part of the way in which the Russian state developed its coercive and centralist character. For Pipes, Russian society did not exist independently of the state, as a patrimonial regime took shape that did not recognize that its subjects held individual or property rights. The Russian nobility was bound to the state by the requirement that they provide service to the monarch, while the peasantry was enfeebled and impoverished by serfdom. Russia failed to develop a thriving middle class, and it was foreign investment and enterprise that were responsible for much of Russian

1 Tibor Szamuely, *The Russian Tradition* (London: Secker and Warburg, 1974).
2 Richard Pipes, *Russia under the Old Regime* (London: Weidenfeld and Nicolson, 1974).
3 Ibid., 14.

economic development, especially in the 1880s and 1890s when the Ministry of Finance aggressively promoted economic growth. The power of the state was intensified as it institutionalized its powers over politics itself, prohibiting the existence of political parties and refusing to accept that Russia's population should play any part in the political process. The 1881 emergency legislation that was enacted after the assassination of Tsar Alexander II placed Russia firmly on the road to becoming a police state, even if the system of repression in the last decades of the Tsarist state was ineffective.

The nature of the Russian state, both Szamuely and Pipes argue, was instrumental in creating a revolutionary movement that was intent on bringing about the downfall of the Romanov state. 'Revolution was the intelligentsia's *raison d'être*', wrote Szamuely,[4] and he argued that the Russian intelligentsia was alienated from Russian society, since the weakness of the bourgeoisie meant that there was no proper conduit by which the concerns of Russia's intellectuals could be transmitted to the regime. The intelligentsia, Szamuely argues, 'proved to be singularly uncreative. It produced only one thing: the Russian revolutionary movement'.[5] For both Pipes and Szamuely, the Russian intelligentsia performed a wholly destructive role in Russian social and political development, culminating in the Bolsheviks 'depriving Russian culture of that freedom of expression which it had managed to win for itself under the imperial regime'.[6]

The 'Russian tradition' as it was conceived by Cold War historians provided a mirror to the Soviet approach to the history of Russia. The Bolshevik victors of 1917 – Lenin and his successors – argued that their triumph was inevitable and that the history of Russia was a single process leading in a straight line to their seizure of power in the October revolution. The Soviet interpretation of Russian history concentrated on identifying every component cause of revolution and subjecting it to intense and detailed analysis. Soviet historians minutely dissected every hint of revolt in the Russian past, alert to the slightest expressions of discontent that could demonstrate the deep roots of the October revolution. Russia's social structures were analysed in great detail to provide evidence of the long-held commitment of peasants and working people to the overthrow of the Tsarist state. The Soviet explanation of revolutionary change was thus as one-dimensional as that of western Cold War historians: for the Soviet Union's rulers, the inevitability of the collapse of Tsarism was mirrored by the certainty of proletarian victory. Both sides writing history during the Cold War had at their heart simplistic narratives that were essentially products of their political opinions and, in some ways, showed remarkable similarities. Both conservative Western writers and the Soviet Union's own historians argued that there was a clear line of development in the history of Russia that stretched back long before 1917 and that the

4 Szamuely, *Russian Tradition*, 189.
5 Ibid., 239.
6 Pipes, *Russia*, 280.

emergence of the Bolshevik regime was no quirk of history, but rather the culmination of long processes of historical evolution.

As the chapters in this book show, however, the character of the Russian and Soviet states was not so straightforward. Indeed, starting with Imperial Russia, the empire's political system was rooted in autocracy, but it was not simply based on coercion and during the nineteenth century the Romanov regime developed a clear intellectual justification for the nature of its political authority. Articulated in 1831 by Count Sergei Uvarov, Minister of Education between 1833 and 1849, the trinity of Orthodoxy, autocracy, and nationality became the lodestone for Russian conservatism until the demise of Tsarism. Uvarov viewed his theory not just as a means of legitimizing autocracy, but also as a means of enhancing the cohesiveness of Russian society and strengthening the cement that bound an increasingly diverse society to the ruling regime. He stressed that it was vital to identify Russia's distinctive elements and thus to establish a Russian identity that set the country apart from western Europe. In particular, he argued that Russia must not follow a path that led towards any weakening of monarchical authority. For Uvarov, the French Revolution had shown very clearly that republicanism was wholly inappropriate and he believed that autocracy was the only viable form of government for Russia. 'Autocracy' he wrote, 'constitutes the main condition of the political existence of Russia. The Russian giant stands on it as the cornerstone of his greatness', but Uvarov was insistent in drawing a distinction between autocracy and despotism. He described Russia's autocracy as 'strong, humane and enlightened' and placed Russia in an overall tradition of monarchical development, far removed from tyranny.[7]

The Orthodox religion was an essential concomitant of Russian autocracy: Russia's monarchs drew their authority from God and since Peter the Great's reign, the Orthodox Church had been tightly bound to the apparatus of the secular state with a lay official, the Procurator of the Holy Synod, acting as its most senior official.[8] The regime utilized the church as a means of disseminating important messages to the population so that, for example, the manifesto proclaiming the emancipation of the serfs was read from the pulpit in Orthodox churches across Russia in February 1861. Nationality, the third element of Uvarov's trinity, was a more nebulous concept. It represented both the popular application of Orthodoxy and autocracy, as well as encapsulating the historic mission that Uvarov and like-minded thinkers believed to be Russia's destiny. He defined Russia's identity as unique and insisted that Russia should find its own solutions to the issues that confronted it in the mid-nineteenth century. The ideas of Romantic nationalism helped to reinforce this approach and it found expression in both the state's policies towards

7 S. S. Uvarov, *Desiatiletie ministerstva narodnogo prosveshchenia 1833–1843* (St Petersburg: Gos. tipografia, 1864), 2–3.

8 Gregory L. Freeze, *The Parish Clergy in Nineteenth-Century Russia: Crisis, Reform, Counter-Reform* (Princeton, NJ: Princeton University Press, 1983), 11–42.

its non-Russian national groups and in the ways in which the state projected itself to its people. The visits of Nicholas I to Moscow in 1848 and 1849 showed how closely the emperor wished to identify himself with Russia's history and national identity. Nationalists saw the appearance of Nicholas I in the Kremlin as representing 'the union of Tsar and people' and viewed the monarch as the embodiment of Russia's national character.[9] Each of the three parts of Uvarov's concept of Official Nationality was intimately linked with the others and, taken together, they provided a definition of the Russian state that justified its position and activities as an autocratic and imperial power.

While the principles that Uvarov had developed during the 1830s remained constant, the way in which the Tsarist regime applied his ideas changed as the empire expanded, so that conservatism became more entrenched in the governing elite after the assassination of Alexander II in 1881. By the last decades of the nineteenth century, Official Nationality came to be interpreted as radical nationalism, driving Russia towards conceiving of its national characteristics and identity as superior to those of both its subject peoples and its European neighbours. In the final decades of its existence, the state acted with great vigour to buttress Russian identity and promoted Orthodoxy amongst the non-Russian peoples of the empire by encouraging conversion to Orthodoxy and ostentatiously building Orthodox churches, such as the Alexander Nevsky cathedral in the Estonian city of Tallinn. Russian conservative nationalism became a central feature of the late nineteenth-century Tsarist state, as the regime and its closest supporters sought to resist the effects of economic and social modernization.

However, pressures to modernize Russia that ran counter to this 'Russian tradition' persisted right through Romanov rule. Peter the Great had taken the first sustained steps towards transforming Russia into a recognizably modern society and economy, and his legacy continued to reverberate through the Tsarist state until its very end. The Petrine tradition was not just focused on practical steps that Russia could take to ensure its parity with other European powers, but it also introduced a new component into conceptions of Russian identity. By the nineteenth century, there were clear perceptions among sections of the Russian elite that Russia was backward by comparison to its European neighbours to the west, and that Russia could only catch up and keep pace with them by pursuing the path of modernization that western states had followed. The continuing existence of serfdom in Russia symbolized the gulf that existed between Russia and the West and, Russia's 'westernizers' argued that real social change had to take place before Russia could advance. Peter the Great's legacy was, however, deeply controversial and his approach to the modernization of Russia was contested by much of Russia's conservative elite. For Russia's Slavophiles, espousal of European models of development represented a betrayal of Russia's own heritage. They conceived

9 See Richard Wortman, *Scenarios of Power. Myth and Ceremony in Russian Monarchy*, vol. I (Princeton, NJ: Princeton University Press, 1995), 396–398.

of Russia as unique and wholly distinctive from western Europe, and believed that any attempt to reshape Russia on European lines would be fatal. Drawing on Russia's heritage of Orthodox Christianity and on its autocratic form of government, Slavophiles such as Konstantin Aksakov argued that Russia must remain true to its own traditions and that it could prosper by relying on its peasant agriculture.[10] These ideas were not in themselves reactionary: in the 1870s, elements of the radical Russian intelligentsia argued that Russia need not experience an industrial revolution – with all its attendant problems – along western lines, but could instead achieve prosperity through some form of peasant socialism. These Populists had little time for the political institutions of the Russian state, but they shared conservative mistrust of industrial development and believed too that Russia should adhere to its own traditions.[11] Both Slavophiles and westernizers saw Russia as possessing national characteristics that set it apart from Europe, but they disagreed over the extent of Russian exceptionalism.

As the Russian social and political elite argued about the broad conceptual issues of Russia's development, Russian society was changing quickly and radically, and challenging the established ethos and structures of the Tsarist state. The emancipation of the serfs in 1861 represented a fundamental shift in the balance of power in the countryside. In the 40 years following Emancipation noble land-holding fell by more than 40 per cent. Many nobles decided that farming no longer represented an attractive option and found other ways of earning a living, whether in the new professions or else by developing new businesses. Some, however, sank into the gloom and ennui depicted in Chekhov's plays, barely able to cope with the changing rural world. As many of the nobility disengaged from their traditional roles in the countryside, the regime's hold on the peasant population became less sure. At the same time, Russia's social structures were becoming more fluid as migration from countryside to city increased. Emancipation had resulted in some peasants receiving inadequate allocations of land and, together with the rapid increase in Russia's population in the second half of the nineteenth century, this meant that increasing numbers of young Russian peasant men needed to look for work away from their own villages. Spurred on by the examples of working people in western Europe, Russia's workers began to form clandestine organizations. Trade unions and embryonic political parties started to come into existence from the late 1880s, and the Russian Social Democratic Workers Party – eventually to seize power in October 1917 as the Bolsheviks – was founded in

10 K. S. Aksakov, 'Memorandum to Alexander II on the Internal Sate of Russia', in *A Documentary History of Russian Thought from the Enlightenment to Marxism*, edited by W. J. Leatherbarrow and D. C. Offord (Ann Arbor, MI: Ardis, 1987), 95–107.

11 Franco Venturi, *Roots of Revolution: A History of the Populist and Socialist Movements in Nineteenth-Century Russia* (Chicago, IL and London: University of Chicago Press, 1960), 316–330.

1898.[12] Formal political activity was the preserve of only a minority of Russia's workers, but the extraordinary growth of Russia's largest cities meant that when discontent spread beyond the politically active, the potential for major and subversive unrest was very significant. As Russian industry and business developed during the second half of the nineteenth century, other social groups experienced change. The Russian middle class developed slowly, but demand for new professions, the decline of the rural nobility, and increased access to education for Russia's social elites combined to increase its numbers. By the 1890s there were 60,000 rural teachers and 4,000 engineering students in the empire, and professional and business people were to be found right across the Russian Empire.[13]

Both Szamuely and Pipes are dismissive of the potential of Russian society to develop in a way that could provide a counterbalance to the power of the state, and they also underestimate the capacity of the state to reform itself. The Tsarist state was not the monolithic regime that would inevitably lead to Bolshevism. In the febrile atmosphere of St Petersburg at the end of the 1870s, as officials were assassinated month after month and the Tsar himself narrowly escaped death in the Winter Palace bombing of February 1880, the issue of democracy came to the forefront of the government's thinking. A week after the palace bomb explosion, Alexander appointed General M. T. Loris-Melikov to head a Supreme Executive Commission devoted to the suppression of sedition and the restoration of order. Improving policing was a crucial part of Loris-Melikov's plans, but he also wanted to address the root causes of radical discontent. There was a recognition at the highest levels of the Tsarist government that the established model of governing Imperial Russia had failed and that the apparatus of the state required fundamental change. Loris-Melikov initially rejected the idea of extending representation into national government, arguing that such reforms 'could be harmful [as] the people do not think of them and would not understand them, and the government is not yet ready to answer the criticisms that representation would express'.[14] But, as Loris-Melikov's experience of government deepened and he prepared more far-reaching plans for the reform of the Ministry of Internal Affairs, intending to turn it into the heart of the empire's government, he came to believe that the introduction of a limited form of representation could help to revitalize the autocracy. Loris-Melikov recognized that the existing method of legislating was inadequate since it was not based on any sound institutional framework. Introducing a limited degree of popular

12 See Robert Service, *Lenin: A Political Life*, vol. 1, *The Strengths of Contradiction* (Basingstoke: Macmillan, 1985), 65–84.

13 V. R. Leikina-Svirskaya, *Intelligentsiia v Rossii vo vtoroi polovine XIX veka* (Moscow: Nauka, 1971), 167; Harley D. Balzer, 'The Engineering Profession in Tsarist Russia', in *Russia's Missing Middle Class: the Professions in Russian History*, edited by Harley D. Balzer (Armonk, NY: M. E. Sharpe, 1996), 59.

14 B. S. Itenberg and V. A Tvardovskaia, *Graf M.T. Loris-Melikov i ego sovremenniki* (Moscow: Tsentropoligraf, 2004), 438.

participation into the legislative process would help to provide an outlet for the increasingly vociferous calls by social groups to play a part in the political process.

For Loris-Melikov the proposals that he put forward in January 1881 were deliberately presented as being firmly in the Russian tradition and owing nothing to European concepts of government. The first level would comprise commissions made up essentially of bureaucrats, but they could also include 'experts' appointed by the tsar. It was the second stage that would include elected representatives: a General Commission would consider all legislative proposals. This commission would include members of the preparatory commissions, along with two representatives from each of the provinces with *zemstva* and two representatives from each of the major cities of the empire. The final stage of the legislative process was to be the State Council, and Loris-Melikov proposed that its membership should be augmented by 10 to 15 representatives of the *zemstva* and cities. Discussions with the tsar and his senior advisers eliminated popular representation from this final stage of the legislative process, but the emperor was prepared to sanction the other parts of the reform and 4 March 1881 was set as the date for the formal enactment of Loris-Melikov's proposals. But on 1 March, Alexander II was blown to pieces.

Less than a week later, the new Tsar, the deeply conservative Alexander III, summoned his ministers to meet to discuss the proposals to introduce a very limited form of democracy into Russia. For three hours on the afternoon of 8 March 1881, 25 men decided the fate of the empire in a meeting that was as remarkable for the frankness of the opinions expressed as for the power with which the arguments were made. The central contribution – and the speech that doomed the fate of democracy in Russia – came from Konstantin Pobedonostsev, the lay head of the Orthodox Church and the man who had been Alexander III's tutor. A man dyed deep in the ethos of the conservative Russian state, Pobedonostsev described Loris-Melikov's plan as deceitful and declared that it meant the introduction of a western European constitution into Russia and 'the constitutions which exist there give rise to every sort of injustice and intrigue'. Russia, Pobedonostsev declared 'was strong because it was an autocracy, because of the unlimited mutual trust and the close ties between the people and their Tsar'. He launched a ferocious attack on the Great Reforms of the 1860s, asking what had been the result of the 'great and sacred ideal' of emancipating the peasantry? The outcome, Pobedonostsev, suggested was that 'the peasants had been given freedom, but without proper authority being established over them'. The 'dark masses', as he disparagingly referred to the peasantry, had simply taken to drink and led lives of idleness, easy prey to every sort of exploitation. The zemstvo – the elected local councils established in the 1860s and the new courts set up at the same time – Pobedonostsev dismissed as 'talking-shops' full of worthless, immoral men.[15] This broadside against the greatest achievements of the murdered Alexander II

15 Ibid., 573–576.

shocked the men of the 1860s – Dmitrii Miliutin and Petr Valuev in particular – who sat around the table and made it very clear to them that conservatism had returned with a vengeance. Pobedonostsev was only able to deliver such an attack on the recently-assassinated Alexander II because he knew his ideas were in tune with the new Tsar's beliefs. Two days before the 8 March meeting, he had written to Alexander III telling him that 'the mindless evildoers who killed your father will not be satisfied by any concessions … one cannot destroy this evil except by blood and iron'.[16] Dmitrii Miliutin, one of the architects of the Great Reforms of the 1860s, wrote in his diary that 'many of us could only shudder nervously at some of the phrases of this fanatical reactionary'.[17] But, even though the great majority of the men round the table spoke in support of Loris-Melikov's proposals to allow Russia to take its first steps towards democratic participation in government, the new Tsar postponed making any decision. It was obvious to the proponents of reform that their cause was doomed: within weeks Loris-Melikov and Miliutin had both resigned and Alexander III had approved a manifesto that declared that the government would 'have faith in the truth of autocratic power which we affirm and preserve in the national interest'.[18]

But hopes of reform were only subdued in 1881, rather than being extinguished completely and the tensions inside the Tsarist polity persisted. During 1905 the Romanov regime was assailed from all sides. Its army and navy were humiliated by the Japanese, while working people took to the streets of Russia's cities to protest about living conditions. In the countryside, peasant farmers erupted into inchoate revolt, burning landowners' houses. The Poles and Finns saw an opportunity to assert their own autonomy from their Russian rulers, and rebellion erupted on the streets of Warsaw and Helsinki. The scale of popular discontent made the foreign bankers on whom Russia depended for finance very cautious about making further loans to the Russian government so that, by the autumn of 1905, Russia faced both political and economic crises.[19] Sergei Witte, the architect of Russia's economic renaissance during the 1890s, returned to negotiate a peace treaty with Japan and he then seized the moment to extract political concessions from a reluctant Nicholas II. The October manifesto promised a national elected parliament – a Duma – for the first time in Russia and, at the same time, it granted Russians a range of fundamental civil rights. At the end of 1905, it appeared as if Russia had chosen the path of political modernization and that it was becoming a constitutional monarchy, alongside its west European neighbours. Newly legalized radical political parties dominated the First Duma that met

16 Petr A. Zaionchkovsky, *The Russian Autocracy in Crisis, 1878–1882* (Gulf Breeze, FL: Academic International Press, 1979), 205.

17 Ibid., 208.

18 Ibid., 237.

19 Peter Waldron, 'Russia's Finances and 1905', in *The Russian Revolution of 1905 in Transcultural Perspective. Identities, Peripheries and the Flow of Ideas*, edited by Felicitas Fischer von Weikersthal et al. (Bloomington, IN: Slavica, 2013), 311–324.

in spring 1906 and a new Prime Minister, Peter Stolypin, declared that he was committed to making reform across many areas of Russian life. The portents for Russia looked favourable to the liberal and centrist men who had found a voice in the new political landscape. Russian civil society appeared to be gaining the cohesion to act as a counterweight to the Tsarist regime.

The Tsarist regime, however, did not give up its power so easily. Stolypin was as committed to putting down revolt as he was to making reform and by the end of 1907, most traces of unrest had been dealt with. As rebellion subsided, the regime saw less reason to make political concessions to its opponents. During 1906 and 1907, the changes brought about by the October manifesto were hedged about with restrictions that constrained the power of the Duma. Most dramatically, in June 1907 the franchise was restricted with the aim of reducing the representation of radical political parties in the Duma. Reform slipped off Stolypin's agenda so that only a land reform was actually implemented. The conservative men who dominated Russian ruling elite believed in the main that they had successfully seen off the threat that had been posed to the regime's power in 1905 and that there was no need for them to make concessions to an opposition that was now cowed and largely impotent. By 1914 the Russian imperial state appeared to have regained its authority and its position as a Great Power bestriding Europe and Asia was secure. Signs of stress were, however, not far below the surface. The discontent that had flared into life during 1905 had only been pushed back below the surface, and its root causes remained unresolved. The tensions between an authoritarian political regime and the processes of modernization that were gradually taking place in Russian society were still present. A frustrated working class concentrated in Russia's great cities, an increasingly fractious peasantry no longer held in check by the noble elite and the rise of nationalism among Russia's subject peoples presented immense challenges to a political regime that was attempting to rule in the same style as its ancestors. The tercentenary of the Romanov dynasty in 1913 was celebrated by the imperial regime as showing that the bond between Tsar and people was as close as it had ever been. The Russian empire was presented as a united society, devoted to its monarch. The outbreak of war in 1914, however, was to show that this was merely a façade and the fissures inherent in the Russian polity were to be laid bare. The failure of the Tsarist regime to sustain its power at times of crisis suggests that the power of the state was far from unchallengeable and that countervailing pressures from a developing civil society were becoming more intense as modernization took hold across Russia's cities and villages. The 'Russian tradition' that Pipes and Szamuely posited significantly over-simplified the political culture and development of Tsarist Russia. The Romanov state was at times convulsed by debate over what was the most appropriate form of government for Russia and monarchs could be forced into making concessions to dilute the autocratic regime.

The experience of Russia after 1917 demonstrated a similar pattern of challenges to Bolshevik rule and intense debate about the direction that the

Soviet regime should follow. Civil war was an almost immediate consequence of the October revolution as anti-Bolshevik forces sought to dislodge Lenin and his comrades from power. Even during the tense period of civil war, when Bolshevik survival was very uncertain, the new regime was keen to put its principles into practice and to transform Russia into a socialist economy. It took the initial steps in this direction on its first day in power, issuing a Land Decree that abolished private landed property and nationalized land. This measure recognized the realities of the situation in the countryside where the peasantry had taken advantage of the disintegration of authority during 1917 to seize as much land as they could. But the peasants' liking for the communists swiftly dissipated as inflation continued to roar ahead and output of manufactured goods declined. The peasantry thus had no incentive to produce agricultural surpluses and the communists rapidly resorted to the forcible seizure of grain and livestock in order to be able to feed the urban population and the Red Army. The Bolshevik policy of War Communism was implemented right across the economy as industry was nationalized and private trade prohibited. This attempt at central control of the economy failed dismally, as industrial production continued to decline and the urban population deserted Russia's towns and cities in search of a reliable supply of food. Economic collapse was accompanied by popular discontent: a major peasant uprising in Tambov in 1920 could only be put down by the use of the Red Army. Most worrying for the communists, however, was the March 1921 rebellion by the sailors of the Baltic fleet at Kronstadt, the great naval base close to Petrograd itself. This showed the depths of disillusionment with the communist regime and prompted a fundamental change in economic policy. War Communism was abandoned and replaced by the New Economic Policy: most of Russian industry was returned to its former owners, with the state retaining control of only the 'commanding heights' of Russian industry. The peasantry were to receive a proper price for their produce and private trade was legalized.[20]

The nature of the discourse on modernization changed with the October revolution, but the nature of the issues facing the new Soviet regime remained familiar. As the Soviet economy stagnated during the 1920s and it became clear to the Bolshevik leadership that the process of achieving revolution was far from straightforward, fierce and prolonged debate took place about the way in which successful economic and social change could be brought about. Before 1917, this had been the staple of revolutionary discourse, but the experience of government and dealing with the real problems of a diverse society and economy meant that theoretical discussion was now transformed into real politics. The Bolsheviks had to address the same issue that their Tsarist predecessors had done – how to modernize Russia – but their particular ideological imperative meant that they took very different approaches to

20 See Lewis H. Siegelbaum, *Soviet State and Society between Revolutions, 1918–1929* (Cambridge: Cambridge University Press, 1992).

questions of economic and social change. The substance of post-1917 politics was hardly on the agenda after the first years of the Soviet regime, with the highly centralized and domineering regime established by Lenin acting as the foundation both for the Stalinist dictatorship of the 1930s and 1940s and for the stifling post-Stalin authoritarian regimes of Khrushchev and Brezhnev. The Soviet state conducted its discussion about the ways in which socialism and true communism could be achieved – in other words, how the Soviet Union could effectively modernize – within an unbending political framework that placed huge constraints on the ways in which economic development could take place.

The struggle for political succession that followed Lenin's death in 1924 was intimately bound up with arguments about how to achieve socialism and modernize the USSR. Industrialization demanded investment capital and the only realistic source for this was the Soviet peasantry. Agricultural output had to be increased to provide enhanced income that could then be invested in industry. For Bukharin and his allies on the right of the Bolshevik party, the New Economic Policy provided the model through which socialism could be reached. The enrichment of the peasantry would generate resources that would help to fund the development of Soviet industrial power, although this would be a slow process and socialism would evolve only gradually. For Stalin, however, NEP had to be abandoned. Stalin was intent on making an economic and social revolution in the USSR that would match the political revolution of October 1917. Motivated by a fear of attack from outside on a still isolated Soviet state, Stalin was determined to push for very rapid industrialization. Rapid industrialization was therefore essential, and it would also advance socialism by increasing the strength of the proletariat. Stalin intended that his industrial revolution would transform Soviet society by changing the outlook of the population and inculcating them with communist ideals and values. He wanted to create 'new Soviet man' and finally to destroy the remnants of Tsarist society. In 1928, the first Five Year Plan was promulgated, setting what appeared to be impossibly high targets for industrial output. Coal production, for example, was planned to increase by 115 per cent and steel output by 250 per cent. Even though these targets were not met, the progress of Soviet industry was startling: by 1937 gross industrial production had increased more than five-fold, electricity output had grown by more than 700 per cent and oil production had doubled.[21] This huge growth in Russia's industrial output was accompanied by an equivalent expansion in the industrial labour force and in the urban population. New cities sprang up: the city of Magnitogorsk was founded on virgin territory in 1929, but had more than 200,000 inhabitants by 1932.[22]

21 Alexander Nove, *An Economic History of the USSR* (London: Allen Lane, 1969) 191 and 225.

22 Stephen Kotkin, *Magnetic Mountain: Stalinism as a Civilization* (Berkeley, CA: University of California Press, 1995) 37–71.

Stalin was all too aware of the reaction of the peasantry to the intervention of the state during War Communism and was determined that his industrial revolution would not be frustrated by peasant resistance. He therefore set in train the greatest transformation ever experienced by the Russian countryside: the collectivization of agriculture. The process began in 1928 and within 12 months, more than 55 per cent of peasant households had been collectivized. The peasantry opposed collectivization with great vigour and their resistance posed severe problems for the regime. The disruption being caused to Soviet agriculture worried Stalin so much that he called a temporary halt to the process in March 1930, fearful lest the spring sowing be thrown into chaos. By the autumn of 1930, collectivization was under way again and by 1936 some 90 per cent of Russian peasant households and cultivated land had been collectivized. Great brutality was used in the countryside to subdue the peasantry. Peasants who opposed the process were condemned as kulaks – wealthy peasants – and deported, sent to labour camps or else simply killed.[23] 'Dekulakization' was intended both to remove opposition from the countryside and also to destroy an influential segment of rural society that could encourage resistance to Stalin's plans. The peasants who remained in the countryside did not give up their independence willingly: rather than see their produce and livestock seized by the new collectives, many embarked on an orgy of destruction, slaughtering their animals and devouring as much produce as they could.[24] This had drastic consequences in 1932 and 1933 when poor harvests combined with the state taking produce from collective farms to feed the urban workforce and for export. Famine struck the Soviet countryside as the peasantry were left with insufficient to eat. Between 4 and 5 million people perished in the countryside as a result of collectivization, but for Stalin the policy had proved its worth. He had broken the power of the peasantry once and for all and, even though the rural population still dominated the Soviet Union numerically, the centre of power had shifted irreversibly to the Soviet Union's cities.

The political dictatorship that Stalin established during the 1930s met with little real opposition inside the Soviet Union. Using a level of brutality unimaginable to the Tsarist state, he used great force to deal with any source of opposition – whether real or imagined – and to protect his own position and that of the communist regime. Terror had been a part of communist policy since the first weeks of the revolution as the instinct for survival pushed the new regime into taking drastic measures. Stalin, however, took the use of terror to new heights. He used it as a deliberate element of policy to impose the social ideals of the communist party on the Soviet people and to deter them from opposing his regime. The great industrial revolution of the

23 Lynne Viola, *Peasant Rebels under Stalin: Collectivization and the Culture of Peasant Resistance* (New York: Oxford University Press, 1996), 67–99.

24 Sheila Fitzpatrick, *Stalin's Peasants: Resistance and Survival in the Russian Village after Collectivization* (New York: Oxford University Press, 1994) 48–79.

early 1930s brought with it many examples of machine failures; the regime labelled this as deliberate sabotage and those held to be responsible were sent to labour camps. The communist party itself was purged of members judged to be unreliable, and Stalin also used this process to rid the party of most of its veteran members. More than half of the delegates to the party's 1934 congress were purged in the following five years. The assassination of Kirov, the Leningrad party chief, in December 1934 sparked off a wave of arrests: Kamenev and Zinoviev were put on trial in 1935 and executed the following year. During 1937 and 1938 terror ruled over Soviet society: central and local government were particularly ravaged as their members were arrested and shot. The military was not immune from terror, as more than 10,000 Red Army officers were arrested and eight of its most senior generals shot. The secret police itself was not immune from the process and Ezhov, its head between 1936 and 1938, was himself executed in 1940. Nearly 700,000 people were shot in the Great Terror of 1937–8 and over a million sent to labour camps.[25]

The experience of mass terror during the 1930s had a profound impact on Soviet society. Open discussion of the regime's policies became very risky, even after Khrushchev's speech at the 20th Communist Party Congress in 1956 when he denounced the excesses of Stalinism and appeared to be opening the way to a 'thaw' in the way in which Soviet life was lived. The political foundations of the USSR could not be challenged by its population, unless they wanted to run the risk of investigation by the political police – the NKVD and its successor the KGB – and Soviet politics became frozen after Stalin's death. The problem of how to modernize the Soviet economy could not be so easily ignored, however, since every Soviet citizen was aware of the fluctuations in their standards of living and were increasingly exposed to evidence of the performance of the economies of the USA and western Europe. The four years of war between 1941 and 1945 had ravaged the USSR. Almost 15 per cent of the population had perished during the conflict and the most productive areas of the country – both industrially and agriculturally – had been fought over as armies moved across them. The process of reconstruction was skewed by the continuing emphasis on military expenditure after 1945: although Soviet industrial production had returned to its pre-war level by 1949, the proportion of output devoted to consumer goods remained low. Agricultural output was much slower to recover, and it took a full decade before grain production returned to its pre-1941 level, with livestock production needing more than 15 years to recover. Housing remained a particular problem as the urban population continued to grow, but without a corresponding increase in the provision of living space.

25 The best history of the terror is J. Arch Getty and O. V. Naumov, *The Road to Terror: Stalin and the Self-Destruction of the Bolsheviks, 1932–1939* (New Haven, CT: Yale University Press, 1999).

The USSR thus encountered a much more difficult set of problems in the 1960s and 1970s than Stalin had faced at the end of the 1920s. The perennial issue of how to drag the Soviet economy away from its reliance on inefficient agriculture and unproductive industry continued to dog Soviet leaders. The Soviet economy stagnated in the decades after Stalin's death. The system of collective farming produced low yields, and the peasants' private plots that had been permitted since the early 1950s produced an ever-increasing proportion of the USSR's agricultural output. The state-controlled system of agriculture became steadily less efficient during the 1960s and 1970s: by 1977 the 3 per cent of farmland that was occupied by private plots produced more than a quarter of the USSR's entire agricultural output. Grain production was under particular pressure, but private plots could make little contribution towards Soviet grain output: by the end of the Brezhnev era, the USSR had to import more than 35 million tonnes of grain annually to feed its population.[26] Khrushchev was unable to formulate a consistent agricultural policy and failed to recognize the need for farming production to keep pace with the growing urbanization of the Soviet Union.[27] The Soviet population grew increasingly frustrated with food shortages and could only be kept placated by low prices in the shops. Industrial performance was equally disappointing, as the needs of the military took an increasing priority. The maintenance of the Soviet Union's superpower status demanded significant expenditure on sophisticated technological equipment, while the system of central economic planning grew evermore cumbersome and inefficient. The availability of consumer goods was a particular problem, as heavy industry and the military dominated Soviet industry and the USSR's scarce foreign currency resources were used to import grain and other basic materials. The rate of Soviet industrial growth steadily reduced from the 1950s, and by the time of Brezhnev's death in 1982, it had halted completely. Economic decline had a serious impact on living standards, and housing, food supply, and consumer goods were all deteriorating during the 1970s. Even though everyday existence was difficult for the Soviet people, there were very few overt demonstrations of discontent.[28] A type of social contract existed between state and society, by which the state provided social benefits and the population did not mount any challenge to the party's authority. The apparatus of coercion was powerful enough to act as a deterrent, while the Soviet people resorted to an enormous black market to try to obtain goods and services that were in short supply. In the same way as the Tsarist state had failed to confront the political consequences of economic change, so the Soviet leadership was not prepared to make economic reforms that would address the structural problems that lay at the heart of

26 See John Keep, *Last of the Empires: A History of the Soviet Union 1945–1991* (Oxford: Oxford University Press, 1996), 244–262.

27 Martin McCauley, *Khrushchev and the Development of Soviet Agriculture* (London: Macmillan, 1976).

28 Vladimir Andrle, *A Social History of Twentieth Century Russia* (London: Edward Arnold, 1994), 253–268.

declining output. The system of central planning and the dominance of the military sector were integral elements of the overall policy of the Soviet state and any attempt to reform them would, as Gorbachev discovered in the late 1980s, have dramatic implications for the stability of the USSR.

The final years of the Soviet Union, with Gorbachev's political liberalization, opened the way to a level of open debate in the USSR that had not been seen since the 1920s. Gorbachev understood that the Soviet economy needed radical reform to restore its efficiency and productiveness, but he was less sure at actually implementing effective change. Central control of the economy was reduced by allowing farm and factory managers much greater autonomy and by permitting the establishment of small business co-operatives that were entirely independent of the state. These measures had only limited impact, since local party authorities were jealous of their own power and were extremely reluctant to relax their control over economic affairs. Agricultural reform posed a particular difficulty, since Gorbachev could not risk selling off land to farmers for fear of conservative reaction and the most he could propose was to lease land. But this too ran into difficulties, with local communist party officials seeing the prospect of their influence declining, while farmers were mistrustful of the state's intentions and were reluctant to take the risk of moving from their secure, albeit unrewarding, collective farms. Gorbachev believed that one of the main brakes on Soviet economic performance was the population's dependence on alcohol. Vodka was easily and cheaply available and one of Gorbachev's first actions was to restrict its availability. But his approach failed completely: people turned to distilling their own vodka which both caused severe shortages of sugar in the shops but, more significantly for the state, resulted in a dramatic drop in revenue from taxes on alcohol. The relaxation of central control over the Soviet economy contributed to price rises, but the state was still subsidizing the costs of basic goods. Gorbachev's economic reforms were the worst of all worlds: he was constrained by the traditional conservatism that had been institutionalized under Brezhnev, but the problems that faced the Soviet economy were so substantial that small-scale change was inadequate to deal with them. Radical reform was needed, but the vested interests of the political establishment obstructed change, with the end result being a series of events that destroyed the Soviet Union by the end of 1991.

As the Cold War froze relations between the USSR and the West, writers on both sides of the ideological divide concentrated their attentions on the outward political differences that distinguished East from West. The 'Russian tradition' that Szamuely and Pipes discussed in their books of the 1970s was focused on the way in which the communist regime had achieved power and it saw every other aspect of Russian and Soviet life as subordinate to the political structures and ideologies of both the Tsars and the Bolsheviks. This was, however, a superficial approach to the history of Russia. The Cold War historians of both the West and the USSR would have learnt much from reflection on Marx's theories of social and political change and his insistence that political regimes were merely the product of wider economic and social issues. Both the Tsarist and communist rulers of Russia and the Soviet Union were faced with the same fundamental problems: how to modernize an economy that remained resolutely unproductive and uncompetitive. A great variety of solutions to the economic weakness of Russia and the Soviet Union have been tried since 1700. Foreign models of economic development and foreign investment formed the heart of Peter the Great's programme and of Sergei Witte's policies during his tenure of the Ministry of Finance at the end of the nineteenth century. Autarky – 'socialism in one country' – and industrial and agrarian revolution imposed from above was Stalin's solution to the Soviet Union's economic difficulties. But for much of the history of Russia and the Soviet Union, economic stagnation was the consequence of government policy. Szamuely and Pipes asked the wrong questions in their works of the 1970s: they concentrated on identifying political continuity across 1917, rather than seeing the real Russian tradition as being an inability to reform a stagnant economy. Dmitrii Medvedev, then President of the Russian Federation, asked in 2009:

> Should a primitive economy based on raw materials and endemic corruption accompany us into the future? And should the inveterate habit of relying on the government, foreign countries, on some kind of comprehensive doctrine, on anything or anyone – as long as it's not ourselves – to solve our problems do so as well? And if Russia can not relieve itself from these burdens, can it really find its own path for the future?[29]

He was echoing the words of Sergei Witte, Tsarist Russia's most successful economic reformer, from 1898:

> The French state budget is 1,260 million rubles for a population of 38 million; the Austrian budget is 1,100 million rubles for a population of 43 million. If our taxpayers were as prosperous as the French, our budget would be 4,200 million rubles instead of its current 1,400 million, and if we matched the Austrians, our budget would be 3,300 million rubles. Why can we not achieve this? The main reason is the poor condition of our peasantry.[30]

Post-Soviet Russia has again shown that radical political change has been unable to resolve Russia's persistent economic difficulties. The Russian revolution of 1917 did little to provide lasting economic prosperity and contemporary Russian rulers are grappling with the same issues that faced the Tsars before 1917. This Russian tradition still holds true. The point, as the chapters in this volume argue, is that by accounting for the social, cultural, and economic context in which modern plans were embraced we can better understand the way those these plans unravelled.

29 http://en.kremlin.ru/events/president/news/5413
30 Sergei Iu. Witte, *Vospominaniia. Memuary* (Moscow: AST, 2002), vol. 1, 724.

Bibliography

Adams'kyi, V. R. and B. S. Krushchuk (eds). *'Prosvity' Podillia v dobu Ukraïns'koï revoliutsiï* (Kamianets'-Podils'kyi: Medobory, 2014)

Andriichuk, Natalia. *Pidhotovka vchyteliv narodnoï shkoly v uchytel'skykh seminariakh Ukraïny, 1860–1917 rr.* (Zhytomyr: Vyd-vo ZHDU im. I. Franka, 2010)

Arendt, Hannah. *On Revolution* (London: Penguin Books, 1990)

Arnason, Johann P. 'Entangled Communisms: Imperial Revolutions in Russia and China', *European Journal of Social Theory* 6(3) (2003), 307–325

Baker, Keith Michael and Dan Edelstein (eds). *Scripting Revolution: A Historical Approach to the Comparative Study of Revolutions* (Stanford, CA: Stanford University Press, 2015)

Balashov, E. M. *Shkola v rossiiskom obshchestve 1917–1927 rr.: stanovlenie 'novoho cheloveka'* (St Petersburg: Rossiiskaia akademiia nauk, Sankt-Peterburgskii institut istorii, 2003)

Bauman, Zygmunt. *Modernity and the Holocaust* (Ithaca, NY: Cornell University Press, 1989)

Beer, Daniel. *Renovating Russia: The Human Sciences and the Fate of Liberal Modernity, 1880–1930* (Ithaca, NY: Cornell University Press, 2008)

Berdinskikh, Viktor, *Uezdnye istoriki: Russkaia provintsial'naia istoriografiia* (Moscow: Novoe literaturnoe obozrenie, 2003)

Bérélowitch, Wladimir, 'History in Russia Comes of Age: Institution-Building, Cosmopolitanism, and Theoretical Debates among Historians in Late Imperial Russia', *Kritika: Explorations in Russian and Eurasian History* 9(1) (Winter 2008), 113–134

Beria, Sergo. *Beria, My Father: Inside Stalin's Kremlin* (London: Duckworth, 2001)

Berman, Harold. *Justice in the USSR* (Cambridge, MA: Harvard University Press, 1963)

Boiarchenkov, V. V. 'Obshchestvo istorii i drevnostei rossiiskikh v seredine 1840-kh gg', *Voprosy istorii* 4 (2008), 114–121

Borovyk, Anatolii. *Ukraïnizatsiia zahal'noosvitnikh shkil za chasiv vyboriuvannia derzhavnosti, 1917–1920 rr.* (Chernihiv: KP Vydavnytstvo 'Chernihivs'ki oberehy', 2008)

Borys, Jurij. *The Sovietization of Ukraine, 1917–1923: The Communist Doctrine and Practice of National Self-Determination* (Edmonton: Canadian Institute of Ukrainian Studies, 1980)

Bourdieu, Pierre. *Outline of a Theory of Practice* (Cambridge: Cambridge University Press, 1977)

Bradley, Joseph. 'Voluntary Associations, Civic Culture, and *Obshchestvennost'* in Moscow', in Edith W. Clowes, Samuel D. Kassow, and James L. West (eds), *Between Tsar and People: Educated Society and the Quest for Public Identity in Late Imperial Russia* (Princeton, NJ, Princeton University Press, 1991), 131–148

Bradley, Joseph. *Voluntary Associations in Tsarist Russia: Science, Patriotism and Civil Society* (Cambridge, MA: Harvard University Press, 2009)

Brandenberger, David. *National Bolshevism. Stalinist Mass Culture and the Formation of Modern Russian National Identity, 1931–1956* (Cambridge, MA and London: Harvard University Press, 2002)

Brandenberger, David. *Propaganda State in Crisis: Soviet Ideology, Indoctrination, and Terror under Stalin, 1927–1941* (New Haven, CT: Yale University Press, 2011)

Brandenberger, David. '"Simplistic, Pseudo-Socialist Racism": Ideological Debates within Stalin's Creative Intelligentsia, 1936–39', *Kritika: Explorations in Russian and Eurasian History* 13(2) (2012), 365–393

Brovkin, Vladimir. *Russia after Lenin: Politics, Culture and Society, 1921–1929* (London: Routledge, 1998)

Browder, Robert Paul and Aleksandr F. Kerensky (eds). *The Russian Provisional Government, 1917: Documents*, Vol. 1 (Stanford, CA: Stanford University Press, 1961)

Bukhert, V. G. 'Soveshchanie professorov russkoi istorii i istorii russkogo prava Rossiiskikh universitetov (Moscow, 26–28 marta 1915 g.)', in S. O. Shmidt (ed.), *Arkheograficheskii ezhegodnik za 2009–2010 gg.* (Moscow: Nauka, 2012), 179–194

Bukov, V. *Ot Rossiiskogo suda prisiazhnykh k proletarskomu pravosudiiu: U istokov totalitarizma* (Moscow: Arkheograficheskii tsentr, 1997)

Bulgakov, Mikhail. *White Guard* (translated by Marian Schwartz) (New Haven, CT: Yale University Press, 2008)

Burbank, Jane. *Russian Peasants Go To Court: Legal Culture in the Countryside, 1905–1917* (Bloomington and Indianapolis, IN: Indiana University Press, 2004)

Bushkovitch, Paul. *Peter the Great: the Struggle for Power, 1671–1725* (Cambridge: Cambridge University Press, 2001)

Clowes, Edith W., Samuel D. Kassow, and James L. West (eds). *Between Tsar and People: Educated Society and the Quest for Public Identity in Late Imperial Russia* (Princeton, NJ: Princeton University Press, 1991)

Crummey, R. O. *Aristocrats and Servitors: the Boyar Elite in Russia, 1613–1689* (Princeton, NJ: Princeton University Press, 1983)

Dahlke, Sandra. 'Kampagne für Gottlosigkeit: Zum Zusammenhang zwischen Legitimation, Mobilisierung und Partizipation in der Sowjetunion der zwanziger Jahre', *Jahrbücher für Geschichte Osteuropas* 50 (2002), 172–185

David-Fox, Michael. *Revolution of the Mind: Higher Learning among the Bolsheviks, 1918–1929* (Ithaca, NY and London: Cornell University Press, 1997)

David-Fox, Michael. 'Review of Il'ina, *Obshchestvennye organizatsii Rossii*', *Kritika: Explorations in Russian and Eurasian History* 3(1) (2002), 173–181

David-Fox, Michael. *Crossing Borders: Modernity, Ideology, and Culture in Russia and the Soviet Union* (Pittsburgh, PA: University of Pittsburgh Press, 2015)

Dixon, Simon. *The Modernisation of Russia, 1676–1825* (Cambridge: Cambridge University Press, 1999)

Dmitriev, A. N. (ed.). *Istoricheskaia kul'tura imperatorskoi Rossii: formirovanie predstavlenii o proshlom* (Moscow: Izdatel'skii dom Vysshei shkoly ekonomiki, 2012).

Dornik, Wolfram (ed.). *Die Ukraine: zwischen Selbstbestimmung und Fremdherrschaft, 1917–1922* (Graz: Leykam, 2011)

Drob'iazko, P. I. *Ukraïns'ka natsional'na shkola: vytoky i suchasnist'* (Kyiv: Akademiia, 1997)

Dubinskaia, L. G. and A. M. Dubrovskii (eds). *Perepiska S.B. Veselovskogo s otechestvennymi istorikami* (Moscow: Drevlekhranilishche, 2001)

Dvornichenko, A. Iu. and S. O. Shmidt (eds). *Pamiati akademika Sergeia Fedorovicha Platonova: Issledovaniia i materialy* (St Petersburg: St Petersburg State University and OIFN RAN, 2011)

Dzhus, Oksana and Zinoviia Nahachevs'ka (eds). *Sofiia Rusova: z malovidomoho i nevidomoho*, 3 vols, Vol. 1 (Ivano-Frankivs'k: Hostynets', 2006)

Easter, Gerald. *Reconstructing the State: Personal Networks and Elite Identity in Soviet Russia* (Cambridge and New York: Cambridge University Press, 2000)

Eisenstadt, Shmuel Noah. 'Multiple Modernities', *Daedalus* 129(1) (2000), 1–29

Eklof, Ben. *Russian Peasant Schools: Officialdom, Village Culture, and Popular Pedagogy, 1861–1917* (Berkeley, CA: University of California Press, 1986)

Eklof, Ben. 'Russia and the Soviet Union: Schooling, Citizenship, and the Reach of the State, 1870–1945', in *Mass Education and the Limits of State Building, c. 1870–1930* (New York: Palgrave Macmillan, 2012), 140–166

Emel'ianov, Iu. N. *SP Mel'gunov v Rossii i Emigratsii* (Moscow: Editorial URSS, 1998)

Evans, Alfred B., Jr. 'Civil Society in the Soviet Union?', in Alfred B. Evans, Jr, Laura A. Henry, and Lisa McIntosh Sundstrom (eds), *Russian Civil Society: A Critical Assessment* (Armonk, NY: M. E. Sharpe, 2006), 28–54

Faber, Richard von. *Totale Institutionen?: Kadettenanstalten, Klosterschulen und Landerziehungsheime in Schöner Literatur* (Würzburg: Königshausen & Neumann, 2013)

Fainsod, Merle. *Smolensk Under Soviet Rule* (Cambridge, MA: Harvard University Press, 1958)

Fainsod, Merle. *How Russia is Ruled* (Russian Research Center Studies 11) (Cambridge, MA: Harvard University Press, 1967)

Finkel, Stuart. *On the Ideological Front: The Russian Intelligentsia and the Making of the Soviet Public Sphere* (New Haven, CT: Yale University Press, 2007)

Fisher, Ralph T. *Pattern for Soviet Youth: A Study of the Congresses of the Komsomol, 1918–1954* (New York: Columbia University Press, 1959)

Fitzpatrick, Sheila. *The Commissariat of Englightenment: Soviet Organization of Education and the Arts under Lunacharsky, October 1917–1921* (New York: Cambridge University Press, 1970)

Fitzpatrick, Sheila. *Stalin's Peasants: Resistance and Survival in the Russian Village after Collectivization*, (New York: Oxford University Press, 1994)

Frank, Stephen. *Crime, Cultural Conflict, and Justice in Rural Russia, 1856–1914* (Berkeley, CA: University of California Press, 1999)

Frierson, Cathy. 'Crime and Punishment in the Russian Village: Rural Concepts of Criminality at the End of the Nineteenth Century', *Slavic Review* 46(1) (1987), 55–69.

Gaudin, Corinne. *Ruling Peasants: Village and State in Late Imperial Russia* (DeKalb, IL: Northern Illinois University Press, 2007)

Getty, J. Arch. *Origins of the Great Purges: the Soviet Communist Party Reconsidered, 1933–1938* (Cambridge and New York: Cambridge University Press, 1985)

Getty, J. Arch. *Practicing Stalinism: Bolsheviks, Boyars, and the Persistence of Tradition* (New Haven, CT: Yale University Press, 2013)

Gorsuch, Anne E. *Youth in Revolutionary Russia: Enthusiasts, Bohemians, Delinquents* (Bloomington, IN: Indiana University Press, 2000)

Grant, Susan. 'From War to Peace: The Fate of Nurses and Nursing under the Bolsheviks', in Adele Lindenmeyr, Christopher Read, and Peter Waldron (eds), *Russia's Home Front 1917–1922: The Experience of War and Revolution* (Bloomington, IN: Slavica, 2016), 251–270

Gribovskikh, M. V. and S. F. Fominykh (eds). *Professorsko-prepodavatel'skii korpus rossiiskikh universitetov 1884–1917 gg.: Issledovaniia i dokumenty* (Tomsk: Izdatel'stvo Tomskogo universiteta, 2012)

Halfin, Igal. *From Darkness to Light. Class, Consciousness and Salvation in Revolutionary Russia* (Pittsburgh, PA: University of Pittsburgh Press, 2000)

Halfin, Igal. *Terror in my Soul: Communist Autobiographies on Trial* (Cambridge, MA: Harvard University Press, 2003)

Halfin, Igal. *Intimate Enemies. Demonizing the Bolshevik Opposition, 1918–1928* (Pittsburgh, PA: University of Pittsburgh Press, 2007)

Halfin, Igal. *Stalinist Confessions. Messianism and Terror at the Leningrad Communist University* (Pittsburgh, PA: University of Pittsburgh Press, 2009)

Harris, James R. *The Great Urals: Regionalism and the Evolution of the Soviet System* (Ithaca, NY: Cornell University Press, 1999)

Harris, Jonathan. *The Split in Stalin's Secretariat, 1939–1948* (New York: Lexington Books, 2008)

Hazard, John. 'Law and Tradition in the New Russia', *Oxford Slavonic Papers* 4 (1953), 132–150

Hazard, John. *Settling Disputes in Soviet Society* (New York: Columbia University Press, 1960)

Havryliuk, Iarasolav (ed.). *Kruty: sichen' 1918 roku: dokumenty, materialy, doslidzhennia, kinostsenarii*, 2nd edn (Kyiv: Vydavnychnyi tsentr 'Prosvita', 2010)

Havryliv, Myroslav. *Zhovtneva revoliutsiia i vchytel'stvo* (Kharkiv: Chervonyi shliakh, 1924)

Hellbeck, Jochen. *Revolution on My Mind: Writing a Diary Under Stalin* (Cambridge, MA: Harvard University Press, 2006)

Hillis, Faith. *Children of Rus': Right-Bank Ukraine and the Invention of a Russian Nation* (Ithaca, NY: Cornell University Press, 2013)

Hobsbawm, Eric and Terence Ranger (eds). *The Invention of Tradition* (Cambridge: Cambridge University Press, 1983)

Hoffmann, David. *Russian Modernity: Politics, Knowledge, Practices* (London and New York: Palgrave Macmillan, 2000)

Hoffmann, David. *Stalinist Values: The Cultural Norms of Soviet Modernity, 1917–1941* (Ithaca, NY: Cornell University Press, 2003)

Hoffmann, David. *Cultivating the Masses: Modern State Practices and Soviet Socialism, 1914–1939* (Ithaca, NY: Cornell University Press, 2011)

Holmes, Larry E. *The Kremlin and the Schoolhouse: Reforming Education in Soviet Russia, 1917–1931* (Bloomington, IN: Indiana University Press, 1991)

Holquist, Peter. '"Information is the Alpha and Omega of our Work": Bolshevik Surveillance in its Pan-European Context', *The Journal of Modern History* 69(3) (1997), 415–450

Holquist, Peter. *Making War, Forging Revolution: Russia's Continuum of Crisis, 1914–1921* (Cambridge, MA: Harvard University Press, 2002)

Holquist, Peter. 'New Terrains and New Chronologies: The Interwar Period through the Lens of Population Politics', *Kritika: Explorations in Russian and Eurasian History* 4(1) (2003), 163–175

Il'ina, I. N. *Obshchestvennye organizatsii Rossii v 1920-e gody* (Moscow: Institut rossiiskoi istorii RAN, 2000)

Ivanov, A. E. *Vysshaia shkola Rossii v kontse XIX–nachale XX veka* (Moscow: Institut istorii SSSR, AN SSSR, 1991)

Ivanov, A. I. and I. P. Kulakova, 'Russkaia professura na rubezhe XIX–XX vekov', *Rossiiskaia istoriia* 2 (March–April 2013), 44–62

Kappeler, Andreas. *Great Russians and Little Russians: Russian-Ukrainian Relations and Perceptions in Historical Perpsective* (Seattle, WA: Henry M. Jackson School of International Studies, University of Washington, 2003)

Kassow, Samuel D. *Students, Professors, and the State in Tsarist Russia* (Berkeley, CA: University of California Press, 1989)

Keenan, Edward L. 'Muscovite Political Folkways', *Russian Review* 45(2) (1986), 115–181

Kelly, Catriona and David Shepherd (eds). *Constructing Russian Culture in the Age of Revolution: 1881–1940* (Oxford: Oxford University Press, 1998)

Kenez, Peter. *The Birth of the Propaganda State: Soviet Methods of Mass Mobilization, 1917–1929* (Cambridge: Cambridge University Press, 1985)

Kharkhordin, Oleg. 'What is the State? The Russian Concept of Gosudarstvo in the European Context', *History and Theory* 40 (2001), 206–240

Khartanovich, M. F. *Gumanitarnye nauchnye uchrezhdeniia Sankt-Peterburga XIX veka* (St Petersburg: Izdatel'stvo St Peterburgskogo otdeleniia Instituta Istorii RAN 'Nestor-Istoriia', 2006)

Khorkhordina, T. I. *Istoriia i arkhivy* (Moscow: RGGU, 1994)

Kizevetter, A. A. *Na rubezhe dvukh stoletii: Vospominaniia 1881–1914* (Prague: Orbis, 1929; republished, Cambridge: Oriental Research Partners, 1974)

Koenker, Diane P. 'Urban Families, Working-Class Youth Groups, and the 1917 Revolution in Moscow', in David L. Ransel (ed.), *The Family in Imperial Russia* (Urbana, IL: University of Illinois Press, 1978), 280–304

Koenker, Diane P. *Republic of Labor: Russian Printers and Soviet Socialism, 1918–1930* (Ithaca, NY: Cornell University Press, 2005)

Kollmann, Nancy Shields. *Kinship and Politics: the Making of the Muscovite Political System, 1345–1547* (Stanford, CA: Stanford University Press, 1987)

Kollmann, Nancy Shields. *By Honor Bound: State and Society in Early Modern Russia* (Ithaca, NY: Cornell University Press, 1999)

Kollonitskii, Boris. *Simvoly vlasti i bor'ba za vlast': k izucheniju politicheskoj kultury Rossijskoj revoluzii 1917 goda* (St Petersburg: Dmitry Bulanin, 2001)

Kollonitskii, Boris. *Pogony i bor'ba za vlast v 1917 g.* (St Petersburg: Ostrov, 2001)

Kotkin, Stephen. *Magnetic Mountain: Stalinism as a Civilization* (Berkeley, CA: University of California Press, 1997)

Kotsonis, Yanni. *States of Obligation: Taxes and Citizenship in the Russian Empire and Early Soviet Republic* (Toronto: University of Toronto Press, 2014)

Kotsonis, Yanni and David L. Hoffmann (eds). *Russian Modernity: Politics, Knowledge, Practices* (New York: Macmillan Press, 1999)

Kowalsky, Sharon. *Deviant Women: Female Crime and Criminality in Revolutionary Russia, 1880–1930* (DeKalb, IL: Northern Illinois University Press, 2009)

Kozhevnikov, M. *Istoriia sovetskogo suda 1917–1956 gody* (Moscow: Gosudarstvennoe izdatel'stvo iuridicheskoi literatury, 1957)

Kozlovtseva, Elena. *Moskovskie obshchiny sester miloserdiya v XIX–nachale XX veka* (Moscow: Izdatel'stvo PSTGU, 2010)

KPSS o komsomole i molodezhi: sbornik rezoliutsii i reshenii sedov. konferentsii i postanovlenii TsK 1917–1956 (Moscow: Molodaia gvardiia, 1957)

Krasovitskaia, T. Iu. *Rosiiskoe obrazovanie mezhdu reformatorstvom i revoliutionarizmom, Fevral' 1917–1920 god* (Moscow: Institut rosiiskoi istorii RAN, 2002)

Krylenko, N. *Sudoustroistvo RSFSR (lektsii po teorii i istorii sudoustroistvo)* (Moscow: Iuridicheskoe izdatel'stva NKIU, 1923)

Kucherov, Samuel. *The Organs of Soviet Administration of Justice* (Leiden: E. J. Brill, 1970)

Kuhr-Korolev, Corinna. *Gezähmte Helden. Die Formierung der Sowjetjugend 1917–1932* (Essen: Klartext Verlag, 2005)

Lebina, N. B. *Povsednevnaia zhizn' sovetskogo goroda: normy i anomalii 1920/1930 gody* (St Petersburg: Zhurnal 'Neva', Letnii sad, 1999)

Lenin, V. I. *Polnoe sobranie sochinenii*, 5th edn, 55 volumes, (Moscow: Politizdat, 1971–75)

Lenoe, Matthew. *Closer to the Masses: Stalinist Culture, Social Revolution, and Soviet Newspapers* (Cambridge, MA: Harvard University Press, 2004)

Lewin, Moshe. *The Making of the Soviet System: Essays in the Social History of Interwar Russia* (New York: New Press, 1994)

Liber, George. *Soviet Nationality Policy, Urban Growth, and Identity Change in the Ukrainian SSR, 1923–1934* (New York: Cambridge University Press, 1992)

Liber, George. *Total Wars and the Making of Modern Ukraine, 1914–1954* (Toronto: University of Toronto Press, 2016)

Lindenmeyr, Adele. *Poverty Is Not a Vice: Charity, Society, and the State in Imperial Russia* (Princeton, NJ: Princeton University Press, 1996)

Lopatkina, Natalia Leonidovna. *Kul'turologicheskie aspekty v razvitii sestrinskogo dela* (Kemerovo: Istoriia zakonodatel'stva SSSR i RSFSR po ugolovnom protsessu i organizatsii suda i prokuratury) (Moscow, 1955)

Lopatkina, Natalia Leonidovna. *Kul'turologicheskie aspekty v razvitii sestrinskogo dela* (Kemerovo: Izdatel'stvo Aksioma, 2009)

Lyandres, Semion, *The Fall of Tsarism: Untold Stories of the February Revolution* (Oxford: Oxford University Press, 2013)

McDonald, Tracy. *Face to the Village: The Riazan Countryside under Soviet Rule, 1921–1930* (Toronto: University of Toronto Press, 2011)

McReynolds, Louise. *Murder Most Russian: True Crime and Punishment in Late Imperial Russia* (Ithaca, NY: Cornell University Press, 2013)

Mace, James E. *Communism and the Dilemmas of National Liberation: National Communism in Soviet Ukraine, 1918–1933* (Cambridge, MA: Harvard Ukrainian Research Institute, 1983)

Majstrenko, Iwan. *Borot'bism: A Chapter in the History of Ukrainian Communism* (New York: Research Program on the USSR, 1954)

Makarikhin, V. P. *Gubernskie uchenye arkhivnye komissii Rossii* (Nizhnii Nogorod: Volgo-Viatskoe kn. izd-vo, 1991)

Marochko, Vasyl', and Khillih H'ots. *Represovani pedahohy Ukraïny: zhertvy polichnoho teroru* (Kyiv: Naukovyi svit, 2003)

Martin, Terry. *The Affirmative Action Empire: Nations and Nationalism in the Soviet Union, 1923–39* (Ithaca, NY: Cornell University Press, 2001)

Materialy Narodnogo Komissariata Iustitsii [1918–22]

Mazower, Mark. *Dark Continent: Europe's Twentieth Century* (London: Penguin Books, 1998)

Morrissey, Susan. *Herald of Revolution: Russian Students and the Mythologies of Radicalism* (Oxford: Oxford University Press, 1998)

Morrissey, Susan. 'From Radicalism to Patriotism? Petersburg Students Between Two Revolutions, 1905 and 1917', *Revolutionary Russia* 13(2) (2000), 20–44

Neumann, Matthias. 'Revolutionizing Mind and Soul? Soviet Youth and Cultural Campaigns during the New Economic Policy (1921–8)'. *Social History* 33(3) (August 2008), 243–267

Neumann, Matthias. *The Communist Youth League and the Transformation of the Soviet Union, 1917–1932* (Abingdon: Routledge, 2011)

Neumann, Matthias. '"Youth, It's Your Turn!": Generations and the Fate of the Russian Revolution (1917–1932)', *Journal of Social History* 46(2) (2012), 279–287

Orlovsky, Daniel T. *The Limits of Reform: The Ministry of Internal Affairs in Imperial Russia, 1802–1881* (Cambridge, MA: Harvard University Press, 1981)

Pate, Alice. 'Workers and *Obshchestvennost'* St. Petersburg, 1906–14', *Revolutionary Russia* 15(2) (2002), 53–71

Pauly, Matthew D. *Breaking the Tongue: Language, Education, and Power in Soviet Ukraine, 1923–34* (Toronto: University of Toronto Press, 2014)

Peris, Daniel. *Storming the Heavens. The Soviet League of Militant Godless* (Ithaca, NY: Cornell University Press, 1998)

Pershyi Vseukraïns'skyi uchytel'skyi z'ïzd v Kharkovi vid 5 do 11 sichnia 1925 (zi znimkamy uchasnykiv z'ïzdu) (Kharkiv: Derzhavne vydavnytstvo Ukraïny, 1925)

Pipes, Richard. *Russia under the Old Regime* (London: Weidenfeld and Nicolson, 1974)

Plokhy, Serhii. *Ukraine and Russia: Representations of the Past* (Toronto: University of Toronto Press, 2008)

Plokhy, Serhii. *The Gates of Europe: A History of Ukraine* (New York: Basic Books, 2015)

Portnov, V. and Slavin, M. *Stanovlenie pravosudiia Sovetskoi Rossii (1917–1922 gg.)* (Moscow: "Nauka", 1990)

Posternak, A. V. *Ocherki po istorii obshchin sester miloserdiia* (Moscow: Izdatel'stvo Sviato-Dimitrievskoe Uchilishche sestry miloserdiia, 2001)

Presniakov, A. E., 'Reforma arkhivnogo dela', *Russkii istoricheskii zhurnal* 5 (1918), 205–222

Priestland, David. *Stalinism and the Politics of Mobilization: Ideas, Power, and Terror in Inter-war Russia* (Oxford: Oxford University Press, 2007)

Reshetar, John. *The Ukrainian Revolution, 1917–1920* (New York: Arno Press, 1972)

Rigby, T. H. 'Was Stalin a Disloyal Patron?', *Soviet Studies* 38 (1986), 311–324

Romaniuk, V. P., Lapotnikov, V. A. and Ia. A. Nakatis, *Istoriia sestrinskogo dela v Rossii* (St Petersburg: SPbGMA, 1998)

Ruane, Christine. *Gender, Class, and the Professionalization of Russian City Teachers, 1860–1914* (Pittsburgh, PA: University of Pittsburgh Press, 1994)

Rubl'ov, Oleksandr. *Zakhidnoukraïns'ka intelihentsiia u zahal'nonatsional'nykh politychnykh ta kul'turnykh protsesakh, 1914–1939* (Kyiv: Instytut istoriï Ukraïny, 2004)

Rusova, S. F. *Iedyna diial'na (trudova) shkola: vstupna lektsiia na katedru pedahohiky* (Leipzig: Ukraïns'ke vyd-vo v Katerynoslavi, 1923)

Rusova, S. F. *Nova shkola sotsiial'noho vykhovannia* (Leipzig: Ukraïns'ke vyd-vo v Katerynoslavi, 1924)

Rusova, S. F. *Moï spomyny* (L'viv: Khortytsia, 1937)

Rusova, S. F. *Vybrani pedohihichni tvory* (Kyiv: Osvita, 1996)

Russkoe i sovetskoe molodezhnoe dvizhenie v dokumentakh 1905–1937. (Moscow: OMP-Press, 2002)

Sahlins, Marshall. *Culture and Practical Reason* (Chicago, IL and London: University of Chicago Press, 1967)

Sahlins, Marshall. *Islands of History* (Chicago, IL: University of Chicago Press, 1985)

Sanborn, Joshua A. *Drafting the Russian Nation: Military Conscription, Total War, and Mass Politics, 1905–1925* (DeKalb, IL: Northern Illinois University Press, 2003)

Sanborn, Joshua A. 'The Zenith of Russian Progressivism: The Home Front during World War I and the Revolution', in Adele Lindenmeyr, Christopher Read, and Peter Waldron (eds), *Russia's Home Front in War and Revolution, 1914–22. Book 2: The Experience of War and Revolution* (Bloomington, IN: Slavica, 2016), 497–507

Sanders, Thomas (ed.). *Historiography of Imperial Russia: The Profession and Writing of History in a Multinational State* (Armonk, NY: M. E. Sharp, 1999)

Sbornik materialov otnosiashchikhsia do arkhivnoi chasti v Rossii, Vol. I (Petrograd: Russkoe Istoricheskoe Obshchestvo, 1916)

Schnell, Felix. '"Tear Them Apart… And Be Done With It!" The Ataman Leadership of Nestor Makhno as a Culture of Violence', *Ab Imperio* 3 (2008), 195–221

Scott, James. *Seeing Like a State: How Certain Schemes to Improve the Human Condition Have Failed* (New Haven, CT: Yale University Press, 1998)

Seregny, Scott. *Russian Teachers and Peasant Revolution: The Politics of Education in 1905* (Bloomington, IN: Indiana University Press, 1989)

Sewell Jr, William H. *Logics of History: Social Theory and Social Transformation* (Chicago, IL: University of Chicago Press, 2005)

Sharlet, R., P. Maggs, and P. Beirne (eds). *P. I. Stuchka: Selected Writings on Soviet Law and Marxism* (Armonk, NY: M. E. Sharpe, 1988)

Shchegolev, P. E. (ed.). *Padenie tsarskogo rezhima: Stenograficheskie otchety doprosov i pokazanii, dannykh v 1917 g. v Chrezvychainoi Sledstvennoi Komissii Vremennogo Pravitel'stva*, Vol. 1 (Leningrad: Gosudarstvennoe izdatel'stvo, 1924)

Shmidt, S. O. and V. G. Bukhert (eds). *Akademik S. F. Platonov: perepiska s istorikami*, Vol. 1 (Moscow: Nauka, 2003)

Shums'kyi, O. 'Na tret'omu fronti: do uchytel's'koho z'izdu', *Shliakh osvity* 11–12 (1924), v–xiv

Siegelbaum. Lewis H. *Soviet State and Society between Revolutions, 1918–1929* (Cambridge: Cambridge University Press, 1992)

Siegelbaum. Lewis H. 'Whither Soviet History? Some Reflections on Recent Anglophone Historiography', *Region: Regional Studies of Russia, Eastern Europe, and Central Asia* 1(2) (2012), 213–230

Skirda, Alexandre. *Nestor Makhno – Anarchy's Cossack: The Struggle for Free Soviets in the Ukraine 1917–1921* (Oakland, CA: AK Press, 2004)

Skorovoda, Hryhorii (ed.). *Vydatni ukraïns'ki pedahohy: informatsiinii dovidnyk* (Ternopil': Mandrivets', 2010)

Slavnyi put' leninskogo komsomola, Tom 1 (Moscow: Molodaia gvardiia, 1974)

Slezin, A. A. *Molodezh' i vlast. Iz istorii molodeznogo dvizhenia v Tsentral'nom Chernozem'e, 1921–1929* (Tambov: Izdatel'stvo TGGU, 2002)

Smirnov, N. N. *Na perelome: rossiiskoe uchytel'stvo nakanule i v dni revoliutsii 1917 goda* (St Petersburg: Nauka, 1994)

Smith, Stephen A. *Revolution and the People in Russian and China: A Comparative History* (Cambridge: Cambridge University Press, 2008)

Smolii, V. A. (ed.). *Narysy istoriï ukraïns'koï revoliutsiï, 1917–1921 rokiv*, 2 vols, Vol. 1. (Kyiv: Naukova dumka, 2011)

Smolkin-Rothrock, Victoria. 'The Ticket to the Soviet Soul: Science, Religion, and the Spiritual Crisis of Late Soviet Atheism', *Russian Review* 23 (2014), 171–197

Solomon, Peter. *Soviet Criminal Justice under Stalin* (Cambridge: Cambridge University Press, 1996)

Starostin, E. V. and T .I. Khorkhordina, 'Dekret ob arkhivnom dele 1918 goda', *Voprosy istorii* 7 (1991), 41–52

Stites, Richard. *Revolutionary Dreams: Utopian Vision and Experimental Life in the Russian Revolution* (New York: Oxford University Press, 1989)

Steinberg, Mark D. *Moral Communities: The Culture of Class Relations in the Russian Printing Industry, 1867–1907* (Berkeley, CA: University of California Press, 1992)

Steinberg, Mark D. *Proletarian Imagination: Self, Modernity, and the Sacred in Russia, 1910–1925* (Ithaca, NY: Cornell University Press, 2002)

Stoff, Laurie 'The "Myth of the War Experience" and Russian Wartime Nursing during World War One', *Aspasia: International Yearbook of Central, Eastern, and Southeastern European Women's and Gender History* 6 (2012), 96–116

Stoff, Laurie S. *Russia's Sisters of Mercy and the Great War: More than Binding Men's Wounds* (Lawrence, KS: Kansas University Press, 2015)

Svod zakonov Rossiiskoi imperii, Vol. XI, part I (St Petersburg: Russkoe Knizhnoe Tovarishchestvo 'Deiatel', 1912)

Suny, Ronald Grigor. 'Reading Russia and the Soviet Union in the Twentieth Century: How the "West" Wrote Its History of the USSR', in *Cambridge History of Russia* Vol. 3: *The Twentieth Century* (Cambridge: Cambridge University Press, 2006)

Suny, Ronald Grigor. 'On Ideology, Subjectivity, and Modernity: Disparate Thoughts about Doing Soviet History', *Russian History/Histoire Russe* 33(1–4) (2007), 1–9

Szamuely, Tibor. *The Russian Tradition* (London: Secker and Warburg, 1974)

Therborn, Göran. 'Entangled Modernities', *European Journal of Social Theory* 6(3) (2003), 293–305

Timasheff, Nicholas. *The Great Retreat: The Growth and Decline of Communism in Russia* (New York: E. P. Dutton & Company, 1946)

Timasheff, Nicholas. 'The Impact of the Penal Law of Imperial Russia on Soviet Penal Law', *American Slavic and East European Review* 12(4) (1953), 441–462

Triado, Isabel. *Young Guard! The Communist Youth League, Petrograd 1917–1920* (Westport, CT: Greenwood Press, 1988)

Triado, Isabel. 'The Komsomol and the Krest'ianka: The Political Mobilization of Young Women in the Russian Village, 1921–1926', *Russian History/Histoire Russe* 23(1–4) (1996), 345–366

Tsentr Khraneniia Dokumentov Molodezhnykh Organizatsiia (TsKhDMO). *Molodezhnoe dvizhenie v Rossii (1917–28 gg.). Dokumenty i materialy. Chast' I. i II.* (Moscow, 1993)

Tucker, Robert C. *Stalin in Power: the Revolution from Above, 1928–1941* (New York: Norton, 1990)

Tumarkin, Nina. *Lenin Lives! The Lenin Cult in Soviet Russia* (Cambridge, MA: Harvard University Press, 1983)

van den Berg, G. 'Elements of Continuity in Soviet Constitutional Law', in William E. Butler (ed.), *Russian Law: Historical and Political Perspectives* (Leyden: A. W. Sijthoff, 1977), 215–234

Velikanova, Olga. *Making of an Idol: on Uses of Lenin* (Gottingen: Muster-Schmidt Verlag, 1996)

Velychenko, Stephen. *Painting Imperialism and Nationalism Red: The Ukrainian Marxist Critique of Russian Communist Rule in Ukraine, 1918–1925* (Toronto: University of Toronto Press, 2015)

Venturi, Franco. *Roots of Revolution: A History of the Populist and Socialist Movements in Nineteenth-Century Russia* (Chicago, IL and London: University of Chicago Press, 1960)

Viola, Lynne. *Peasant Rebels under Stalin: Collectivization and the Culture of Peasant Resistance* (New York: Oxford University Press, 1996)

Viola, Lynne. 'The Aesthetic of Stalinist Planning and the World of the Special Villages', *Kritika: Explorations in Russian and Eurasian History* 4(1) (2003), 101–128

Vyhovs'kyi, M. Iu. *Nomenklatura systemy osvity v USRR 1920–1930-x rokiv: sotsial'ne pokhodzhennia personal'nyi sklad ta funktsiï* (Kyiv: Heneza, 2006)

Waldron, Peter. 'Russia's Finances and 1905', in Felicitas Fischer von Weikersthal et al. (eds), *The Russian Revolution of 1905 in Transcultural Perspective. Identities, Peripheries and the Flow of Ideas* (Bloomington, IN: Slavica, 2013), 311–324

Weiner, Amir. *Making Sense of War: The Second World War and the Fate of the Revolution* (Princeton, NJ: Princeton University Press, 2000)

Willimott, Andy. *Living the Revolution: Urban Communes & Soviet Socialism, 1917–1932* (Oxford: Oxford University Press, 2017)

Wortman, Richard. *Scenarios of Power: Myth and Ceremony in Russian Monarchy from Peter the Great to the Abdication of Nicholas II* (Princeton, NJ: Princeton University Press, 2006)

Yekelchyk, Serhy. *Ukraine: Birth of a Modern Nation* (New York: Oxford University Press, 2007)

Index